Ancient Whispers from Chaldea is one of those rare books that lets you glimpse into the mores and history of ancient cultures and their ways of looking at Astrology. Author Arthyr Chadbourne knows how to bring this "ancient" method into the 21st Century and lures you into trying it. I found it fascinating.
Marion March, Author: *The Only Way to Learn Astrology*

Arthyr Chadbourne is an astrologer's astrologer. *Ancient Whispers from Chaldea* represents a colossal effort in research and insight. What he has assembled is nothing short of the careful examination of astrology's ancient roots and fundamentals. From beginner to expert, there is much to learn in this book as Chadbourne communicates his ideas with a clarity not found in most astrological works. Through this amazing volume, old Chaldean gods and mythology are portrayed in a milieu still relevant to modern man. And we the readers experience anew an astrology exciting and meaningful to the source and flow of life. Arthyr Chadbourne has taken us back to old new ground, Chaldea. Look upon this book as a great path to deeper meaning. It has enriched astrology and I, for one, am grateful that Arthyr Chadbourne has crafted such a wonderful book that will, no doubt, turn the astrological world on its roots.
Spencer Grendahl, Author: *Astrology and the Games People Play*

As an astrologer for 26 years, I have found Arthyr's sunset techniques enlightening, quite unique and highly effective. I am looking forward for more revelations from his future lectures, workshops and books.
Laura DesJardins, *President and founder of SCAN*

I think this is an excellent piece of work; brilliant and self contained. I've been studying this method for some time and as a result have grown tremendously as an astrologer. Furthermore, I don't feel I've understood what makes a person or who they are until I have used Arthyr's Sunset Chart method; now all other methods are incomplete. The perfect astrology book for the new millennium.
Karen M. Magley, *West Coast Astrologer.*

ANCIENT
WHISPERS
FROM
Chaldea

Making *Babylonian* Work for You
Astrology

Arthyr W. Chadbourne

First Edition

INTELLI *GENESIS*
PUBLICATIONS
P.O. BOX 545 SEAL BEACH, CA 97040

ANCIENT WHISPERS ғʀᴏᴍ CHALDEA ©

Making Babylonian Astrology Work for You

Published by:

INTELLI *GENESIS* PUBLICATIONS
P.O. Box 545, Seal Beach, Ca 90740

FIRST EDITION First Printing, 1999

Library of Congress Catalog Card Number: **98-94250**

ISBN NUMBER: **0 - 9668966 - 3 - 7**

Printed in Canada

Cover Art and design: Arthyr W. Chadbourne and Eddie Young

The author gratefully acknowledges W.H. Kennedy for permission to repreduce the cylinder seals in this work.

TABLE OF CONTENTS

Introduction Discourse on the possibility that Babylonian astrology and/or Egyptian principles may have not been taught to the Greek scholars. Views of today's problems with current day astrological thought processes.

PART ONE

Description of early basic ideas about the cosmos. The conflation of Egypt and Babylonian principles. The emergence of astrology through Berosus and Sumerian myths. Brief outline about the Babylonian and Egyptian chapters in part II.

General information about this work. Opening statement with simple story lines to familiarize the reader with astrological symbology, planetary meaning and aspects.

The significance of the Sun as an indicator of time in the sunset chart. Clear instructions on setting up the sunset chart with explanations on the origins of the house meanings. Sunset chart compared with the birth chart and their aspects to each other. Instructions on the process of "rogression" for timing major events in the life.

The Moon's influence in the chart. Importance of tertiary and minor lunar progressions and lunar returns. A **neo-astrological** approach using new concepts about the lunar mansions with clear concise instructions

> Appearances and disappearances. Planetary meanings as they pertain to this system. Retrograde motion. The importance of the planets by their placement in the 30° wheel. Discussion on the trans-saturnian planets with regard to their effect on generations and indirect effect on individuals.

> Long considered outdated by many astrologers, the graph on exalted strength clearly shows and explains planetary positions as increasing or weakening in strength. A quick study on esoteric information giving the planets and houses various definition by their placement in the chart. The comparison to the sunset chart.

> Long considered as the "hidden one" in many ancient celestial lore, the Nodes are considered and explored as a pre-existing archetype for the "soul" and its reason for incarnation and fulfillment. The Node is further reviewed on the basis that it represents the personal attractions we seek for our learning experiences.

> The importance of sunset charts and how they are derived. The eight steps to chart construction: an overview with rules. The foundation matrix for registering personal planetary meaning and purpose based on sunset. Further instructions on "rogressing" the chart to identify important periods. The basic concept of interpreting the timing of events in a natal chart. The 30° wheel and its value in chart interpretation. A look at compatibility using different charts as examples.

New planetary reference and rogression as deduced from the foregoing chapters. In this discussion we will review the charts of John Lennon, Adolf Hitler and Mohondas Gandhi with full chart interpretation and illustration.

Chapter 10: The **Solar Return** 330

This unique Vedic system shows the reader how to divide the year based on the solar return into planetary periods. The sunset method of solar return as compared with the Vedic system.

Chapter 11: **The Horary Chart** 349

The single most powerful tool ever devised was the Ascendant for the horary chart developed by Ptolemy. The mathematical calculation of the Ascendant became so powerful that it has endured through the centuries to become the chief means of charting for genethliacal astrology today. The chart "for the chart of the moment" is compared to the sunset method.

Chapter 12: **Harmonics** 372

The Vedic system of house division harmonics covering the first twelve divisions and their interpretation. The Western view on harmonics based on John Addey's research and its uses. The sunset use of the harmonics and how it compares with the first two systems.

PART II: HISTORY

Overview 404

Philosophical discussion on the author's research material as he explores the possibility of Babylonian and Egyptian philosophical views. Astrology was based on principle laws that may have permeated each culture and why these principles are important to astrologers today.

About The Author

Arthyr W. Chadbourne is a third generation astrologer who has long been an advocate for exploring new dimensions of awareness in the astrological field. As a practicing astrologer and researcher, his open acknowledgment of individual spirituality as the core of the astrological chart has put him on the cutting edge of those in astrology who are creating the metaphysical arts of the future.

His client list reads like a who's who in the entertainment field and he is an astrological consultant for many captains of industry. The successful changes he has made in his own astrological practice prove he is a man not only of vision and deeds, but an author whose beliefs spring from the truths and experience of daily living.

Arthyr Chadbourne was astrological director as well as the star in the motion picture, *The Astrologer*. He has also worked as an executive producer for the independent television series *Meet The Astrologer*.

Chadbourne has also been an artist since childhood. As such, he worked in early *Star Trek* productions. He is a part-time commercial artist specializing in portraits. His artistic talents include designing watch faces for Paramount's Dark Shadows, magazine covers, CD covers and banners for various artists and production companies.

He was co-founder, artist and art director in developing Perceptions magazine in which he wrote many articles and reviews.

Mr. Chadbourne has also written, *YOUR Truth Will Set You Free*, a self-help book emphasizing the responsibility toward success is upon oneself (1975).

ACKNOWLEDGMENT

Since the time of about B.C. 3366, when the Egyptian Ptah - Hotep, wrote the first book, the written word has become paramount as a source of knowledge. The International Dictionary lists 107 entries for the word, "book" along with 101 sub-headings and many more secondary subdivisions. This plethora of entries clearly describes the creation of any book.

For each entry there is a person and for each subheading there is yet another who, each in his own way, made a contribution to this work. It is impossible to acknowledge all the teachers, clients, friends, relatives and acquaintances who are very important to me. However, there are those who I do wish to thank personally: Victoria Chadbourne, my mother, for bringing me up in a family of astrologers; Marion March for her wise astrological counsel, guidance and advice; Spencer Grendahl for his encouragement, friendship and advice on writing this book; Harriett Thompson who, in the early years of this work, supplied wonderful insights to the written word; Tom Withey who took the time to furnish much needed charts for this project; Karen Magley , the student every teacher wished they had; Pat Wright who spent many nights tirelessly reading and editing this work; Richard King for his efforts and keen editorial eye; Tasha Armstrong for helping me assess and compile this research; Sue Hansen who spent many hours in libraries with me researching files and all the while contributing her valuable insights and editorial views. And, to my guardian angel, Susan Chadbourne.

Editing: Sue Hansen, personal assistant; Pat Wright; Harriett Thompson; Karen Lushbaugh and Richard King.

A very special thanks to Kimberly P. Hardaker without whose help this project may have never reached the final stage.

Warning – Disclaimer

INTRODUCTION

Faith alone,
seeks understanding.
Understanding
is to act on faith.

    Ancient Whispers from Chaldea is at once a philosophy, a reference book on historical facts, a textbook for various astrological precepts and an introduction to a new concept within the field of astrology.

    The primary purpose of this work is to present a model of astrology that may correspond to the thinking of the Chaldean culture during the pre-Seleucid period and provide you with the basic concepts of which the ancient astrologers were probably aware.

    The most curious observation about the Chaldeans, based on their style of writing, is their implied lack of understanding of the laws of cause and effect. This one single element is the most likely basis concerning the extensive writings about omens. It also states another valuable insight; the Chaldean scribes did *not* recognize their astrological sightings as causal but synchronistic with events here on Earth.

    The study of Babylonian texts, which consist mostly of literary works, ancient myths, omens, epic tales and hymns, has presented characteristic features about their cultural pattern, and from this can be proposed a hypothesis about their historical background. My work is derived from this hypothesis. To be sure, the proof is by no means obvious and direct; there is no explicit statement in the ancient texts that points to astrological phenomena as we know it until after Hellenistic influence.

With no more than their fingers held at arms length to judge distance and possibly a water clock to designate time, ancient astrologers simply watched a succession of planets and star patterns and noted their activities as they appeared each night in the skies. Their primary concern was to determine the distance and relative timing between synodic arcs which, for them, was a given constant. Simply put, their ephemerides consisted of listing a phenomena (Sun trine Saturn for example) and then determining the number of rotations the Sun made around the zodiac (1 year) until the same phenomena occurred again. The early Babylonian standard procedure was to observe, calculate and journalize events, then draw analogous parallels for references at a later time. Their journals indicate celestial phenomena not only expressed in shorter periods of time but true synodic returns (each planet located in the same constellation and degree) decades and centuries later! The Babylonian methodology lacks sophistication by today's standards, sophistication, yet review of their records reveal not an indiscriminate collection of meaningless magic rituals, but the compilation of accurate and true observation–the reduction of periodic phenomena to a near precise mathematical description.

The hour of sunset served two purposes: it supported their religious view that creation began out of darkness, and it marked a starting point from which observations could be made to collect data from the heavens. This act in itself affirms that sunset and sunrise were the most important times of the day. Over a long period of time these observations took on embellishments that later developed into the famed omina of the Babylonians. The advent of the Chaldean culture further refined

b

omina into the much revered art known as the oracle of the heavens, and later still, astrology.

Because of their warring nature and poor weather, Babylonian astrologers appear to have interpreted heavenly observations as *negative* circumstances that had to be avoided. These observations were based mostly on the Moon and its eclipse patterns (although the ephemerides were not always accurate). Over a period of time, rituals to ward off the evil planetary influences evolved, and the "men of letters" became priests associated with astronomy and astrology.

Babylon's mathematical skills developed from Sumerian influence which later produced profound astronomical calculations. Often, because of rain or clouds, direct observation was impossible and we read of "calculating" the heavenly bodies—the positions of the Moon or planets were presumed with the aid of an ephemeris.

Observations were made without the aid of our modern astrological trappings or such references as Sidereal time or Greenwich Mean Time. Their initial starting time was Local Solar Time, from sunset to sunset. During the 24-hour time-frame, all star and planetary patterns, in reference to timing synodic arcs, were observed and *could* mark a point of departure. My proposal is that the time of sunset *marked a neutral matrix* where planetary positions created the standard for the next 24-hour period (sunset to sunset), monthly period (lunar return) or "goal" year (relationships between the planets and the Sun). In this book sunset is the context for birth charts. The time of sunset marks a neutral matrix or starting point for planetary positions. The charts are erected in a biWheel fashion thereby giving us two charts to compare. Most importantly, the time a baby chooses to be born presents a clear picture of his lifestyle found by the birth chart compared to the

c

sunset chart positioned angle to angle; a type of synastry chart between the baby at birth and the world at sunset.

My sunset chart hypothesis presents a unique and bold idea of astrology. The sunset chart is the foundation by which all charts are considered, especially the birth chart because the time-of-birth chart lies *within* the scope of the 24-hour sunset chart. Sunset marks the beginning of all events, and during the following 24 hour period, an individual's time of birth allows astrologers to distinguish between the character traits of the native and all the other individuals born on the same day. It is much the same as the rising sign fine tunes the nuances of the Sun sign. In short, the birth chart is to the sunset chart what the Ascendant is to the Sun sign in today's astrology.

Each chart at birth makes aspects to the sunset chart and those aspects create a standard and quality of life. In a biWheel fashion, we rotate the inner chart, as the chart rotates, all planets will aspect their own sunset position as well as the other planets during the following 24-hour period. Consequently, during a lifetime, the timing, quality and influence of major events are based on the planets' (its synodic) distance described by the Sun in the sunset chart. By adjusting ancient ideas to today's concepts, we can compare a birth chart to its local sunset position and in *this fashion* find that our entire life is encapsulated within the 24-hour period in which we were born!

Unfortunately, Greek misinterpretation of Babylonian clay tablets determines the basis for today's accepted (Tropical) astrological practices. One missing element is the lack of precession. This is not said out of any ill will toward the genius of the Greek scholars or today's astrologers, it's just a statement of the obvious. The ancient Greek

d

scholars, although aware of the Chaldean's knowledge of the stars, either ignored or never fully discovered what the Chaldeans had developed and used for centuries. The main reason for this is that Greek astronomers were more interested in finding a celestial location *for a given time* whereas the Babylonians were interested in finding the date and time *for any given phenomena.* The reason the Greeks found fault with the Babylonian lunar astrological system was that the Babylonians had no reliable method of finding longitude more precisely than by close association to zodiacal signs or stars. Subsequently, Grecian scholars developed their own invention of its replacement; Sun sign astrology based on geometric calculations of mathematical astronomy. However, it was not until some 500 years after the conquest of Babylon and Egypt that the ancient Greeks developed their astrological system–planetary elongation based on the position of the mean Sun using the Earth as the center of the planetary system.

During that 500-year period, many Grecian ideas about Babylonian astrology were very desultory and purely hypothetical. Early Greek writings out of that period indicate that their transcriptions of cuneiform tablets were mostly guesswork and compilations of inductive logic. By 200 A.D., Claudius Ptolemy compiled earlier works of Greek scholars, especially those of Hipparchus, and developed the concept of noting the rising constellation or Ascendant through his mathematical ideas of geometry.

Today, astrological theories vary in scope and importance, and though some describe part of our experience correctly, none has been singled out as the best. *Ancient Whispers from Chaldea* personalizes the horoscope chart in a way that has never been approached in the modern world. This concept of the birth chart is so powerful that it may be considered a cosmic DNA program that determines our circumstances much the same way sub-molecular DNA determines our physical makeup.

Self-understanding is what sets the human race apart from the animal kingdom. Our most significant journey on this planet is to become self-aware and understand the meaning of our own existence. It is not only to become involved with the trappings of wealth, eating well, sleeping well, finding lost articles or any other various and sundry items many clients ask about–that all comes to those who work for it. It is simply to understand what *we* are all about as human beings. Our individual nature is as diverse as humanity itself and astrology allows us to categorize its characteristics.

The way I see it, both the ancient Chaldean and Egyptian cultures adhered to spiritual laws which they believed enhanced their quality of life. The first fundamental law about ourselves begins with the triad: our three-fold emotional, mental and physical states. My proposal is the Egyptians used this law to learn the art of self-observation by observing: (1) one's inner being via reaction to the emotional states brought on from the external world, (2) obsession to the physical sensations and (3) the desire for intellectualism. Their quest in the development of spiritual understanding was gained through observing what they were doing, what they were becoming and how they were preparing for the final outcome. All of this was of great importance as indicated by the *Egyptian Book of the Dead*.

Although my book is designed to teach astrologers a simple and successful approach to astrological understanding, it is not my intention to offer a complete course in beginning astrology. If one is beginning the study of basic astrological tenets, I recommend that he read the six-volume series, *The*

f

Only Way to Learn Astrology by Marion March and Joan McEvers. Their work is a well-rounded standard for the basics and covers a broad base. Once the basics have been mastered, remember to keep an open mind, look for various patterns in charts, and be willing to combine different astrology systems.

Ancient Whispers from Chaldea will allow readers to experience a new/old form of astrology. Primarily intended to add insight, this work does not replace existing theories although it may rewrite and restructure some of the old horoscope and progression systems now in vogue. In addition, some pertinent Hindu methodology and an overview of the Egyptian culture is included which enhances the information in this work. My research was originally based on the idea that astrology was used without the house system but, in practice, the house system has proven to be extremely valuable in connection with this work. It is my intention to demonstrate for the reader a simplistic approach that will give astrologers a viable, although different, matrix from which to begin their delineation of charts and prognostication of probable future events.

We will initially use the circular diagram only as a foundation for timing sequences and to convert it into different graphs to form our own basis of examination, thus allowing us to begin research immediately. The following points are the six key factors or circumstances by which this work was examined and written.

1. <u>Sunset</u> works extremely well as a *neutral base matrix* for each chart, regardless of the type of chart desired.
2. <u>Sunset</u> was definitely the foundation of the lunar mansion.
3. The timing of events is easily seen and calculated at a glance.

4. The *time of birth* viewed *within the neutral matrix of sunset* gives a clear picture as to why we chose our particular time to be born; it is a clear picture of our destiny.

5. Events considered in the sunset fashion reveal, most concisely through the houses, the timing of major events during a lifetime.

6. The 30° wheel divided by ten-degree segments (referred to as "the stack") and its planetary relationships shows a remarkable insight into the quality and style of an individual's life.

This research is different from most astrological premises, and, as new ideas go, may take a little getting used to, but the effort is well worth the time spent to validate it.

In any profession, it becomes difficult to move away from lifelong beliefs, especially when educators invest considerable time writing about the current vogue. No one wants to appear foolish or demonstrate that he supported something proven later to be incorrect. Any discipline firmly entrenched with its own vested interest will shun any new or seemingly radical approach. This is why any new research or idea in most fields is simply "interesting" because, to save face, that is as far as the incumbent leaders *can* commit themselves.

Today, we can be thankful that the old archaic way of "doing things, the way they've always been done", is over. The new breed of researcher is more accepted in his/her views than ever before. The advent of the computer has shortened the time it takes to erect charts and, consequently, astrologers can now do complete research projects in the time that was formerly required just to set up the charts for such work. For the past thirty years or so astrological research has become "fertile ground." The computer has given us faster access to astrological

h

methods which have magnified existing loopholes previously ignored due to the lack of independent research. What has been long held in the astrological field as "indisputable" has started to crumble, leaving more room for astrologers to develop independently. The computer has given researchers not only a vast resource but a broader audience as well.

Still, even with all the modern trappings, finding inner direction is still one of our most basic drives as we search for meaning, purpose and probable outcome in our lives. Louis Pasteur once said, "Chance favors the prepared mind." Astrology has persisted through the ages because it is a tool that helps prepare our minds for greater self-understanding, thereby eliminating or reducing stress. Good astrologers know this, and practice their craft to help allay their clients' worries. Because of this need, over many years, different methods of progression have been introduced to indicate the possible changes one may experience throughout his life. They all contribute to the mix, but there still seems to be something missing. The purpose of this work is to start a bridge into the "something missing mist" and search for information to further our ability in prognostication.

The astrology chart is very much like a house. There are many rooms which have different characteristics and functions, none of which can completely take the place of the other without confusion. It is important for the astrologer to remember which level (or room) he is in when reading the chart. Understanding the "big picture," or one's ideal, gives direction and serves as the beacon; it clears away the cobwebs in those darkened rooms. The purpose of this work is to give the astrologer a systematic view of the astrology chart without getting lost in the maze.

To indicate the age of a person during an event, I have a coined a phrase for the sunset form of progression. It's called *rogression*. This is achieved by rotating the chart in a clockwise manner starting from the seventh house. Chart rogression clearly shows that the influence of the chart's motion initiates powerful responses *when planets pass* the Ascendant/Descendant or Meridian/Nadir axes *into* the so called "*cadent house*" placements. The sunset chart further emphasizes that planetary positions at sunset, *before* the day of birth, play a significant role in the *timing* of the birth. By comparing the sunset and time-of-birth charts, this can be seen.

This form of casting a chart creates a double-chart process that, when combined with the Gauquelin's research, produces dramatic mutual support. Additionally, when planets at sunset are placed in the Gauquelin sectors and combined with planets in the birth chart, this becomes an extraordinarily predictive tool for the native's success in a specified field!

For some reason, astute astronomical and astrological development declined for many centuries when Ptolemy compiled his essays. It was not until Kepler came on the scene that any changes in western astronomy or astrology started to take place. Since then, Sun sign astrology has evolved throughout the world into myriad forms of tables, methods and systems. This is beginning to change even though many astrologers today still study, learn and write the same rhetoric that supports the existing program, loopholes and all.

Why are there so many different forms of astrology? I think it is because astrology is in the same position as mathematics was before the concept of zero was discovered. In counting from the number nine to the number one, how does one formulate the mathematical vacant step after the

j

number one? With no zero to mark an absence it becomes quite a complex problem. Even though enumeration could still be worked out, it would be done so in a very clumsy manner (this is most obvious in Egyptian mathematics). The zero is not recognized as missing until after a vacant place is discovered or until it is needed as part of the bridge into the next decade of numbers (such as 20, 30, 40...). My understanding is that, in an astrological sense, the zero is missing and the purpose of this book is to take the next evolutionary step.

Section I covers the planets and their meanings, the calculation of the sunset chart, and how to evaluate the lunar mansion. The second section is an overview of the historical evaluation of the Chaldean omina stargazing, the Egyptian cosmos and the summation thereof. Each chapter will explore a different astrological approach with example charts. This method is easy but requires some time to grasp the fundamentals. However, once this method is understood, you will be able to read a life or event pattern the way the early astrologers did.

The Babylonians were interested in the timing of events. *Ancient Whispers from Chaldea* is written with the idea of identifying early Chaldean concepts and readjusting them to fit the various forms of astrological concepts used today. The reader may identify many of these concepts as the origin of contemporary astrology.

This book explores the value of *time* in the timing of events in the chart. Another item: since we are interested in the Chaldean aspect of astrology, the reader will notice that the planets take on a slightly different coloration or connotation than we are familiar with. However, planets in transit remain, for the most part, in agreement with contemporary understanding. Although the Chaldeans did not use the house system, I have found

k

that the house system works very well when marking the age of the native for rogression.

Another re-discovery is the concept of the lunar mansions. Long used as a rigid system with fixed positions assigned to various portions of the zodiac, it held no real connection to the living, breathing essence of a human being. The Chaldean lunar mansion, however, refers directly to the uniqueness of the individual as it is described in the sunset position before his birth hour.

Although I have found many profound revelations through Egyptian resources that are possibly related to astrology, research into the Babylonian culture has produced the most wonderful and exciting results. I am convinced that the Chaldean's developed the foundation of astrological premises, not necessarily in the form we are currently using, but close enough to make some good judgment calls.

In accordance to the sunset chart and its deduced premise, I have constructed many charts for different clients and celebrities and have discovered that the sunset chart system produces a *very dependable* source of information.

This method explores many of the permutations of the birth chart:

(1) The birth chart.
(2) The progressed chart.
(3) The lunar return.
(4) The real solar return based on the time of birth from sunset.
(5) Compatibility with a significant other.
(6) Predictive method.
(7) The daily quotidian or diurnal chart for events.
(8) Horary analysis.
(9) Most importantly, the re-discovery of the *lunar mansions*. The Chaldean lunar mansion concept

1

places the lunar mansion as a *personal reference*, giving a fuller meaning to the astrological scope of the entire lifetime.

Furthermore, the term "Sidereal astrology" or the observable zodiac, is a misnomer. The actual Sidereal zodiac has constellations that range in unequal arcs and sizes. Some constellations (based on Powell) are as small as 9° 23' in longitude (Cancer) and as long as 43° 00' in longitude (Virgo). As Sidereal astrologers, we do not use the constellations as they are placed in the heavens. We only use the mathematics based on the Vernal Point of (approximately) 5° Pisces 18' as fiducial instead of zero degrees of Aries. Its fiduciary is based on the Fagan/Bradley position for the Sidereal Vernal Point. This difference of 24° 42' between the two zodiacs is what all the fuss is about.

Today, most Sidereal astrologers in the United States and Europe use the Tropical astrologer's form of horoscope through the use of the 30° equal arc house system (aside from the European form of wheel). Other Sidereal astrologers use only the four major angles. The reason for this is that there is not a true Sidereal program or ephemeris available to the public that fulfills this need. Most of the real work must be done the old-fashioned way, we use our heads, figure it out for ourselves and write it down on paper.

I have noticed that the results are far more satisfactory using the *mathematics* of the Sidereal or observable zodiac in favor of the Tropical system. This is especially true, as the reader will find out for himself, when arranging the stack by planetary longitude. The highest planet noted by its degree of longitude in each decanate simply does not work using the Tropical system.

Most importantly: The use of the 30° equal house system is not to be confused with the Tropical form of the astrological wheel. Its use is to easily divide the house divisions as six-year periods of time.

This method will give the astrologer insights into a solid basis of Sidereal astrology: an astrology that clearly defines the relationship of the planets to the person in the horoscope and how the client personally relates to those planets. The sunset chart is a bold step away from the conventions of modern day astrology but one that will reveal a greater depth of understanding of the world around us and within us.

A last note: Often the reader will see references inserted at the end of a comment or paragraph, for example: (see 23). These are numbered paragraph sections located in part II for the convenience of locating references found throughout chapters thirteen and fourteen of this book. They are not page numbers. Page numbers and chapter references will be specifically noted, (see page so and so) as such.

This book has been written with the idea that the reader will not read it cover to cover but by the sections he is interested in learning about. In this manner, the book will be eventually read in full but at the reader's pace and understanding. Very often, portions of earlier chapters are repeated and integrated in the chapter you may be currently reading. I used this license of writing to reinforce various points and to prevent you from having to break your train of thought by looking up references. It is only when these references are too long to repeat that I asked the reader to read pages or sections elsewhere in the book.

CHAPTER 1
INTELLIGENESIS

The real voyage of discovery
lies not in finding new lands
but seeing with new eyes.

Marcel Proust

The most significant tool of intelligenesis is self-observation, which is the correct form of meditation, wherein we are re-birthed and able to draw from our own innate knowledge. The coined phase, intelligenesis, is an intelligent approach to old patterns of thought, using a different / objective outlook to reconstruct and evaluate hidden agendas resulting in fresh new concepts. Applied correctly we can thereby create a better understanding of ourselves and the world about us. Those of us who are willing to learn from our triumphs and past foibles bring about the genesis of Self-awareness.

Reconstructing History

In every pro-literate culture, the style of writing has its own idiomatic syntax — a specialized regional dialect and vocabulary. Later in history, idiomatic syntax created problems for those who attempted to interpret earlier forms of texts. Compounded by the problem of piecemeal artifacts and misinterpretation of earlier records, scholars were limited and could only partially deduce from such data their evaluations about early cultural life styles, methods and philosophies. Even with minimal data, once such judgments are accepted by the majority of peers in any field, the lack of clear information creates awkward situations when new discoveries dispute what has long been accepted, thereby making it difficult for the old school to accede to the new.

1

Having said that, I want to begin with a overview of the last two chapters in part two of this book. The following is a brief outline of the Babylonian and Egyptian calendar, planet and star systems. Looking at Egyptian hieroglyphs, we find that they *suggest* a culture aware of its subjectivity and mortality. The Egyptians had an understanding of the constant state of flux, coalescence and disintegration of life itself. To them the universe was one of cause and effect .

The Babylonian culture looked to the universe for events of repetition, synchronicity and supplication. It had a more negative view of the cosmos. The Babylonian texts about omens, poems, stories and epochs all confirm this.

The diversity between Egypt's artistic concepts and the Babylonian posture of defense are revealed by their respective architecture and written records. Also, the texts written by early scribes give us descriptions of gods, wars and natural phenomena that indirectly reveal their values and agendas.

The basis of communication in any culture contains ingrained fundamental principles of elementary assumptions. Because of this we can evaluate, at some level, the mental outlook of any culture in which we are interested. This is suggested by the focus of their general written subject matter regarding its needs as a society in terms of philosophical hypotheses, religious views, life directives, goals, cultural attitudes, state and local government, and personal relationships. By studying the nature of a culture's reality, we can gather bits and pieces of information that further develop our understanding of even earlier cultures.

For our purpose, one such principle is the naming of the constellations in the ancient skies. Each culture viewed the heavens in an entirely different fashion but with intrinsic assumptions that reveal hidden criteria. The people of ancient Egypt developed their perceptual abilities by attuning mostly to the worlds of thought, emotion and spirit. Egyptians saw all of life as an interplay of artistic, harmonious and interdependent energy fields and viewed the heavens and all natural forces as a consequence or an outcome in itself.

The Egyptians repeatedly related to the heavens with the belief that life here on earth was reflected in the stars and planets. Egyptian texts that date from earlier pre-dynastic periods speak of Egypt's simplistic and poetic reference to the planets as *the stars which knew no rest* or the star-fields as *flowers of the night*. The songs of Nephthys and Isis speak of the intercourse between the Sun and the moon during eclipses. Popular Egyptian pictographs of the Sun and stars show rays of energy emanating from heavenly bodies to the consciousness of human beings. These references dramatically speak of their observations of the heavens and indicate that the Egyptians were associating the heavens with mundane life on earth, correlating to a gnostic point of view.

Egyptian writings, discovered to date, show that the Egyptians made no contingency plans for mundane circumstances based on their knowledge of the heavenly movements except for those which occurred simultaneously with natural events. An excellent example is the star Sirius' heliacal rising before the rising of the Nile.

To the ancients, stars and planets were hidden in the Sun's radiance and their first view of a planet or a star seemed to come from "out of the Sun" hence, (from the Greek *helios* for Sun) heliacal rising. The planets and constellations were primarily named (mythical associations excepted) by their synchronous activities in the heavens with events on Earth. Consequently, if Venus set in the evening, it was an evening star. If Venus rose in the morning, it was a morning star. To the Egyptian, life was lived in a Zen-like manner. Theirs were the lives of harmonious accord where one simply accepted nature's ways and followed its dictates.

The pragmatic Babylonians, who were not as poetic as the Egyptians, were more interested in observing the mundane phenomena of nature as an *outside force* with which they had to deal with. Circumstances in connection

3

with planetary activity were observed, calculated and written down as they occurred. In this manner they were empiric. The probable reason for classification and indexing of their experiences in association with the planets and constellations was to be able to make decisions effecting mundane life. It would be much later in the development of the culture that the stars were associated with the physical deeds performed by the mythological gods of their culture.

Later, the Babylonians reduced their empirical evidence to mathematical schemata. With this corpus of information, they believed their conclusions enabled them to formulate parallels for later reference to ensure survival. These ideas became the fundamental premise behind Babylonian omina and although most scientists of today scoff at such notions, the fact is that both cultures were truly scientific in every sense of the word.

Although both cultures lived with completely different stellar concepts, they did have one thing in common. Weather permitting, observations by sight would take place each night, otherwise the planetary positions were faithfully "calculated" from pre-existing configurations in the form of an ephemeris which was developed by earlier generations of scribes.

Both Egypt and Babylon based their religious views on the idea that creation began out of darkness before there was light. In following this idea, each *sunset* started the day anew. The notation and timing of different phenomena appearing on the horizon were obviously seen in succession from dusk until dawn.

Star patterns were mentioned by their assigned names but an anomaly of Babylonian astronomers was the arbitrary use of partial star patterns, and yet at other times they used the full constellation. This practice indicates that some portions of the constellations were either not very important to them or, depending on the time of observation, there may have been observations of a partial constellation on the horizon at the time of sunset or when a planet appeared. Often the whole constellation of

Taurus is mentioned, and sometimes just the Pleiades (a portion of Taurus). Other times, just singular stars were mentioned: Aldebaran at 15° Taurus, Regulus at 5° Leo, Antares at 15° Scorpio. These particular positions, coupled with the proper planetary arrangement, were regarded as war omens. Other constellations, such as Cancer or Virgo, indicated prosperity for the king and the country.

Another curious practice by the Babylonians and one that caused problems with later translators–they assigned different names to the same planet in different constellations to reflect the planet's movement and position. This practice of assigning different planetary names to the same planet later confounded, not only Greek scholars, but many contemporary translators and produced considerable confusion. It appears that this practice was simply their way of noting different locations of the planets. The different name inferred the planet by its location. We could do that today by referring to Mars in Sagittarius as "the arrow," or in Scorpio as "the stinger" and so on.

The Sun was difficult to observe directly, so its position was generally described by constellational association as seen at dusk or dawn or, during the daytime hours, by shadows and seasonal changes. Taking this one step further, at the time of the spring equinox, the Chaldeans would have seen the constellation of Aries setting, thereby placing the constellation of Libra on the Ascendant.

Throughout history, the first full Moon of spring has remained one of the most cherished, if not the most important, indicator of religious holidays. The Chaldeans were no exception, and their full Moon, which was extremely important to them, would rise the constellation of Libra. Instead of Aries ruling the head, maybe we should look to the constellation of Libra to rule the head and face, after all it has been recognized for centuries that one born with the Sun or Venus in Libra, regardless of the sex, is considered a cutie who has a "sweet looking face."

Skymaps

The Babylonians divided the elliptic belt into three 30° bands called Anu, Enlil and Ea with 12 monthly segments of 30 days each, primarily for their lunar calendar [see 435]. The *idea* of the zodiac signs (lu-mash), called the 12 X 30 (lu-mash-mesh), was already in place, located in the central band of Anu (15° north and south of the ecliptic) but only as a model for mathematical usage. No evidence has been found to show elliptical coordinates of house systems using longitude and latitude. Calculations for positions of longitude and latitude were generally determined with fingers to measure the distance of nearby constellations and, when applicable, from positions of the Moon.

One degree of celestial arc (called "an") is equivalent to about the distance of two full Moons placed side by side (approximately 347 full Moons span the arc of 180 degrees) or two fingers extended by two cubits. A cubit is equal to 24 fingers or the length from the tip of the middle finger to the elbow (about 22 inches). The equation relates to two fingers held at arm's length. The transiting Moon was mostly observed, again with fingers, by its *latitude* which is based on the Sun's ecliptic throughout the zodiac.

All heavenly bodies transiting these stars and constellations were addressed as in *front* or *behind* the stars and constellations. It is clear from the usage of these terms that stars and constellations, not zodiacal signs, were the points of interest. This indicates that constellations were nothing more than celestial identity markers much like an *address* for lunar or planetary placement[17]. By this, we can recognize that their observations of heavenly phenomena was neither Tropical nor Sidereal.

By B.C. 419, the 12 constellation signs were introduced in Greece by Euctemon. He devised a calendar of 12 equal solar months relating to the equinoxes and solstices (something Sumer had done 3,000 years earlier).

Each month evolved out of the same names of asterisms from Babylonian (not Egyptian) months which were then changed into equivalent Greek names. Each month was named for a zodiacal sign starting with the month of Aries for April.

By the time of Aristotle (B.C. 350), the Chaldeans had long held the reputation as astrologers. Proclus (5th century A.D.) quoted Theophrastus as saying, "Chaldeans were able to predict in their time not only the weather but the life and death of all persons." However, Herodotus claimed that the Egyptians, "assign each month and each day to a god" and that "they can tell what fortune, what end, and what disposition a man shall have according to his birth."

It is not until after Alexander the Great conquered Egypt and Chaldea (332 B.C.) that pre-astrology began to shape itself into a form which we could easily recognize today. Shortly after Alexander's death, Seleucus, one of Alexander's commanders, proclaimed the Persian territories for himself and he as its ruler. The reign of Seleucus and his successors lasted 248 years from B.C. 312 to 64, this is known as the Seleucid period.

At first, the Babylonian mathematical prowess and interest in time was probably based on Sumerian ephemeride tables, but eventually the Babylonians developed their own system based on their observations of stellar and lunar positions and its motion. The accuracy of such tables later helped the Greeks develop and further their mathematical knowledge of the heavens. These mathematical tables were so well developed that even today we use the Babylonian methodology to describe periods of time and compass direction.

Over the centuries, celestial observation by the Babylonians developed into the science of mathematical astronomy. Their rigid sense of discipline did not allow them to waver off accepted protocol and procedure. By contrast, the Greeks were free thinkers—a trait that allowed them to question authority, even though they abided by it. Through the course of time, the highly inquisitive Greeks studied Egyptian sources on magic and sacred geometry as well as Babylonian mathematica and omens.

The mental climate and discipline of the Grecian culture was quite removed from that of the Egyptian. The Babylonian mind-set, on the other hand, because of its pragmatic and scientific views, was a little more compatible with that of Greek mental characteristics. The Greeks had an easier time with learning Babylonian concepts concerning mathematical measurements rather than the Egyptian artistic and spatial concepts. Grecian scholars needed to understand, by reason and classification, how to mechanically catalog celestial phenomena upon which the Babylonians already had a handle.

Although enthralled by the highly developed mathematical skills of the Chaldeans and their revelations of heavenly omina; the Greek scholars were more concerned with *why* (mathematically) the planets traveled the way they did in contrast to the Babylonians who simply wanted to know *when* the configurations would recur. Grecian scholars wanted rational explanations for cosmic events such as planetary courses, retrograde motions, the mystery of eclipses and the mathematical variables of conjunctions.

With Alexander's conquest, the Greek language and political influence became dominant throughout Persia and Egypt. All in all, this period is considered the most important to the Greeks. It was during this time that concise mathematical procedures of astronomy were being developed. It was for this purpose that Greek scholars ventured into Babylon to visit, study or live. Many of these scholars studied astronomy at the schools that flourished during this time. However, things were different in Egypt during the Ptolemaic dynasty (B.C. 323 to 30 A.D.). Only *the finest and preferred* Grecian scholars, who were well versed in Greek philosophy, were granted admittance to the library in Alexandria. And those in attendance constantly praised the Egyptian mind and its methodology.

Egyptian beliefs held the number 12 to be sacred; it dictated all things religious. There were 12 major gods, and 12 celestial divisions with 12 celestial bodies to govern each one. Day and night were each divided into 12 hours with 12 gods accompanying each hour. Egyptian texts do list lucky and unlucky days which contain the predicted fate of a person born on certain days and hours. But, these texts are not directly related to celestial phenomena but to the gods that governed hourly, daily and monthly periods. These "god appointed" periods of time strongly relate to today's form of astrology because of the 12 celestial divisions and their rulers (our monthly Sun sign) along with the 12 different daily gods who ruled every two hours (our houses). This concept has led some Egyptologists to postulate that this may have been the beginning of horoscopic astrology as we know it. More research is needed.

Figure 1.1 - The gnomon.
Today, on the walls and ceilings of Egyptian tombs, we can still see diagrams depicting the gnomon-like thrones on which the pharaohs or gods sit.

One of "the finest Grecian scholars" in legend is Pythagorus. Although it has been suggested that some of the teachings of Pythagorus were Babylonian in origin, he was also an honored scholar who lived in Egypt for more than 20 years. As legend has it, he was well acquainted with Egypt's esoteric traditions, especially that of universal divine harmony. Pythagorus taught that the Egyptians were an esthetic culture who had blended their artistic concepts with science.

We cannot help but notice how their work exhibits profound mathematical formulations as well as an artistic layout. An example of mathematical formulation that underlies the construction, placement, sizing and location of their designs is the gnomon, (Figure 1.1) which pictorially reflects a dynamic knowledge of geometric and numerical relationships. Pythagorus must have been exposed to numerous examples of symbolic wall paintings, hieroglyphic features and diagrams.

Most Egyptian knowledge of reincarnation, harmony of the spheres, mathematics, astronomy, and so on was the basis for Grecian philosophical development. It would be many years later, during the Hellenistic period, (Alexander commenced this period) that Hellenistic sciences would eventually lead to the emergence of their own understanding of such principles. But history demonstrates that although Greece benefited from the knowledge gained from both cultures, the Greeks later forbade both cultures to practice ancient rituals.

Principle Origins

Throughout the known world most cultures had difficulty aligning the solar year of 365.6 days to the lunar year of 354 days and early Grecian culture was certainly no exception. As early as the Mycenaean period (B.C. 1400-1200), the Greeks had chosen the Moon as the basis for their civil calendar. Heavy emphasis on the Moon figured prominently in all their festivals but, they too, found it difficult to align the new Moon with the first of the month and have the months coincide with the seasons.

Additionally, the early Grecian calendar did not divide the month into weeks but into ten-day periods. The first ten-day period was referred to as the *beginning month*; the last ten-day period was the *waning month* and the middle section had no name. It is reasonable to assume that the all initial concepts of astrology may have been lunar, as Cyril Fagan postulated.

Following the concept that lunar astrology *did* exist in ancient history, then the transition from lunar astrology to solar astrology did not fully develop until a much later period. Claudius Ptolemy re-introduced the concept of the circular zodiac with the addition of his contribution of the Ascendant as late as 200 A.D. His ideas came from earlier formulations and were based on Eudoxus (B.C. 370), Euclid (B.C. 300), Apollonius (B.C. 200) and then again from Menelaos (B.C. 100). Also, Ptolemy's calculations of spherical trigonometry were primarily based on Hipparchus' partial translations of Babylonian texts. The idea of the circular zodiac and the use of the Ascendant helped to postulate more precisely the timing of stellar and planetary activity. This was astrology's finest hour. An interesting side note relates that Ptolemy was given much of the credit. He did not, however, initiate zodiacal boundaries or the zero point of Aries on the ecliptic.

During this time of transition, much of the Babylonian omina appeared to have found its way to India by way of Greece. It is not until later (around 550 A.D.) that mathematical rules for lunar computation found their way into Hindu astronomical and astrological methodology. According to David Pingree, whose study of the principal offshoot of Hindu astrology, the *Yavanajataka*; Hellenistic astrology can be traced to this transitional period through the similarity of Grecian planetary names, constellations and mathematical procedures (this is not to imply that the Hindi did not have some form of heavenly oracle of their own).

Although the Chaldeans have been given great credit and were lauded by the Greek scholars for their astrological abilities, there is very little physical evidence supporting the claims that Chaldean concepts correspond to contemporary astrology. Chaldean astrologers must have had a completely different system than that with which we are currently accustomed. The lack of physical evidence may be due to the fact that Chaldean teachings were transmitted orally.

In B.C. 270, 40 years after Seleucus, (one of Alexander's military generals who became ruler of the conquered Persian empire) a Chaldean priests believed to be Bel-Usur, traveled to the island of Cos and began to teach Chaldean history and astronomy lore to the Greeks. He was known to the Greeks as Berossus. Three books are attributed to Berossus, one of which details the *Epic of Creation* [4] and its origin by sea monsters and deities. It is in his creation book that we find a detailed account of Chaldean astrology. At first, most of Berossus' teachings were questioned by modern scholars. His writings do, however, bear a hint of truth as early Greek and modern scholars have found cuneiform tablets that support his account of the early Chaldean myths and legends. However, his other books regarding history and chronological events, such as his king list, have not been supported by earlier texts.

It is difficult to determine when astrology first came into Greek hands, but the general consensus is that Berossus is responsible for introducing the Greeks to astronomical and astrological knowledge. In praise of Berossus, the Greek philosopher Pliny, was quoted as saying, "The Athenians raised a statue in his (Berossus) honor".

Other books that Berossus quoted were from earlier Babylonian texts that explained mathematical formulations of the heavens. His teachings state that these formulas were supposedly given earlier to the Sumerians, and were to be followed without deviation. The catch-word here is *given*. Given by whom? It has been suggested by a small group of researchers that early man witnessed ancient astronauts observing skymaps for information that was purely astronomical.

Consider this: Legends indicate that a Sumerian high priest whose name was Enmeduranki, (En-[lord]Me-[laws]Dur-[bond]An-[heaven]Ki-[earth]) or *The Lord of Laws that Bond Heaven and Earth,* was given instructions by the gods on how to observe oil and water, the secrets of An, Enlil and Enki (Ea). He was also given the Divine Tablet, (on which were) the engraved secrets of heaven and Earth. Additionally, successive generations of priests were taught how to use numbers to produce accurate calculations. Along with the knowledge of mathematics, they learned about astronomy and the art of measurement, including that of time. As with Moses, it seems that great leaders are always "given" these principles to extend to mankind. The question, albeit an interesting one, is not *who* taught all this to the ancient observers but *what* was taught and where are those teachings?

The Bible hints at such knowledge when God asks Job, "Knowest thou the ordinances of heaven? Canst thou set the dominion thereof in the earth?" (Chap. 38 V.33) Here we are reading a directive from God questioning Job about the celestial laws and how they regulate laws of the Earth. Although farfetched, if this were true, it is reasonable to assume that early man, given their limited mental capacity, could not have completely understood how the astronauts were using the heavens.

If this is the case, ancient mankind probably adopted the belief that the skies had a kind of magical influence which could help guide *them* in their quest for survival, as it did for the ancient astronauts. This view presents a problem. If the above scenario were true, today's astrology should employ a different approach. For one thing, the naming of constellations and planets relating to ancient Sumerian mythological characters sets a background other than that with which we are familiar.

Getting back to Berossus, he must have conveyed the idea that there were more than just three central figures in the historical mythological background of Sumer. A hierarchy of lesser god figures also existed under the guise of planetary association, called "the seven luminary gods of the night."

As a teacher, Berossus would impart his knowledge of the *Epic of Creation,* which centers around three main characters known as Anu, Enlil and Ea. They were, after all, the basis for the three broad bands of constellations that divided the ancient skies of Sumer, Babylon and Chaldea [15-16].

The Sumerian epics were the foundation of Babylon religion and the Babylonians were not the type of people to venture beyond set parameters. By the time of the emergence of Kaldu or Chaldea, much of the Babylonian famed omina and heavenly observations became empirically organized into a standard form of prediction. Later, the Babylonian approach would be set in stone, literally, by those who followed their teachings; a predicated astronomical and astrological terminology that would last for centuries to come, just as their ideas of time and compass directions did. Somehow, over time, the origin of these teachings were lost and/or forgotten.

Sumerian Creation Myth

This item is placed in this section because it is pertinent for our conclusion. However, it must be said that the Sumerian myths and poems are confusing because different texts explain creation under different circumstances and with different gods. In one poem, An's first consort is with Antu who helped him produce the Anunnaki. Yet, in another text, Enki is the first born by An's consort with Anshar making him the half brother of Enlil, the storm god. But it was Enlil who was first born in the beginning of all creation with An's union with Ki. In yet another myth it is Ishtar who is not only An's daughter but also Anu's second consort.

This confusion may be due to different scholars' interpretations or the different scribes' agenda on furthering an explanation on cosmogony. However, regardless of this confusion, the Sumerian thinkers evolved theological doctrines that became the basic fundamental creed in most of the Near East. What we do have as one source of evidence for the Sumerian conception of creation comes from the poem titled: *Gilgamesh, Enkidu, and the Nether World.* In the introductory passage of the epic poem, five lines describe the creation myth:

> After heaven had been moved away from earth,
> After earth had been separated from heaven,
> After the name of man had been fixed,
> After An carried off heaven.
> After Enlil carried off the earth

In another tablet there is mention of the ever-present primal sea, Nammu, from which heaven and Earth were conceived. In another tablet titled, *Cattle and Grain*, there is reference to the creation of the universe:

> After on the mountain of heaven and earth,
> An had caused the Anunnaki to be born...

The Anunnaki in this case are lesser gods who are followers of An, the god of heaven. From the above two partial passages, we can conclude that heaven and Earth were at one time joined together in a universal sea and through their union Enlil (air) was born. After his birth, he and An separated heaven from earth. Once this feat was accomplished, the heaven god An created his godlike followers to help build the rest of the universe.

The Three Chief Gods

Anu (Sumerian, An), the chief deity-king, whose title was *He of the Heavens,* did not live upon the Earth but in the sky. He visited Earth in times of great crises or for ceremonial reasons. One of the few times he came to Earth was to settle the disputes between his blood-line son Enlil and his half blood-line son, Ea. Although there are no direct depiction's by statue of this great god, his influence abounds throughout ancient Sumer. Anu possessed the highest power and could bestow kingship upon mortals by offering them *food and water of everlasting life*.

Enlil, The *Lord of Command* (Lord of Air), the first born offspring between An and Ki (heaven and Earth) who was second in command. In many Sumerian epics and poems, Enlil became the chief god of Earth, for it was he who "called forth the grain to rise from the earth." It was also Enlil who was given credit for creating the mountains, rivers, plains and forests, the building of cities, settlements and their trappings, clouds and moisture, but most importantly, he introduced farming implements to humans so they could work the fields. Enlil was well versed in labor "knowing the pick-ax, plow and farming." At some point Enlil sent his half brother Ea to Earth to be "responsible for the development of all things of the Earth," and to carry out Enlil's plans for creation.

After the world was nearly complete in its creation, Enlil came down to Earth and replaced his half brother Ea who was king of the world at that time. When pleased, Enlil was friendly, generous and bestowed favors. However, when angry, he was responsible for missions carried out against mankind. The two half-brothers became bitter and jealous of one another. Enlil eventually set out on a mission to destroy all of his brother's creations, one of which was humanity.

The third most important god was **Enki** (Lord of Earth) or **Ea**, *He Whose House is Water*, who was depicted as a scientist and engineer who loved to sail the seas and fish. The Sumerian name of En-Ki was later changed to the Babylonian counterpart, Ea (house of water). It was said that En-Ki was resourceful, skillful, hardy and wise, and that it was he who actually organized the world in accordance to Enlil's general plans and ideas. The actual details were left to En-Ki who devised the creative activities of instituting the natural and cultural phenomena necessary for civilization. His work, by legend, influenced all parts of civilization, including its laws. He was mostly responsible for the sea, marshes, and "clean streams." His love of the waterways is expressed by his boating and fishing, his home located underwater, was called the *Abzu* or the abyss, the ocean that supports the Earth.

En-Ki (Ea) also engineered the mines in the area now known as Africa and dug for gold. En-Ki was given domain over the Earth by Enlil, and En-Ki, in experimenting like a child working with clay, created all things in existence. Ea's interests lay in unraveling the secrets of life, reproduction and death. When his brethren, the Anunnaki, became rebellious in the gold mines and asked for slaves to take their place, it was Ea who helped create, (by genetic manipulation of DNA?), human workers for the mines. He was the all powerful god of wisdom, intelligence and incantations who ruled the Earth until his brother Enlil usurped the throne. Ea's reluctance to leave his kingship on Earth developed into bitterness and contention with his brother. In the ensuing disputes, they both attempted to disrupt plans and frustrate each other. The epic ends with Ea and Enlil recognizing the futility of their aggressive behavior and a truce was observed allowing Ea to continue his work.

The Myth as a Basis of Astrology

The following discussion *is* hypothetical but the above scenario does suggest many possibilities. Let's explore, for our own purposes, what we can conclude from this summary and see where it may lead.

Anu's attributes were power and wisdom; it was he who settled disputes. He was the god of heaven who was the father and king of all gods. Anu poses the idea of attaining power by having acquired knowledge, wisdom and a deeper understanding of life through experience. Anu epitomizes the idea that the attainment of goals and ideals begets its offspring, broadens horizons and even activates higher goals.

Enlil, the eldest half-brother of Ea, is antagonistic and opposed his brother's experiments suggesting that Ea/Enki, as a youngster, must later put away his childish ideas so he may enter adulthood. Enlil's title, Lord of Command, coupled with his knowledge of labor and driving sense of mission, bring us to the idea that Enlil had initiated mankind into hard labor in the fields. The whole act of farming suggests constant changes from the first tilling of the land to its final harvest. Enlil then, epitomizes the act of working and overcoming obstacles for attainment.

Ea is childlike in his love of humanity, the sea and his quest for knowledge. He satisfies his curiosity as an explorer in an unbridled, childlike manner as he learns about creation and life. His title, *His House is Water*, can be associated with our physical bodies which are about 72 percent water, or it could represent the "dwelling place" of the unconscious mind. Ea is representative of one's creative pursuits in preparation for attaining higher ideals in life. Ea epitomizes our natural inquisitive, creative selves which are most flexible when we are young and eager to learn about new things.

There were four main gods in the early pantheon: Nammu, the eternal sea–*water*; An of heaven–*fire*; Ki the *Earth*; and Enlil, the *air*. They alone were responsible for all creation. The entire sky was divided into three distinct sections or "roads" for the planets to travel and were associated with Anu, Enlil and Ea.

By projecting and building upon these myths, it is possible to imagine that Greek astrologers could have changed the three divisions of the celestial vault into the three qualities of cardinal, fixed and mutable. Ea, becoming the cardinal quality, was willing to move himself forward and learn new ideas. Enlil, becoming the fixed quality, recognized the promise of power through hard work and how it could be used to overcome obstacles and difficulties. Anu personifies the mutable quality of change and adjustment; his power is the wisdom of knowing the overall objective or goal and through détente he produced beneficial results, both for himself and his subjects.

Combined Worlds

The Chaldeans have been given credit and lauded by the Greek scholars for their astrological expertise, but there is very little physical evidence supporting these claims that Chaldean concepts correspond to contemporary astrology. Chaldean astrologers had a completely different system than that to which we are currently accustomed.

The books that Berossus quoted from were earlier Babylonian texts which explain the mathematical formulations of Astronomy. Later discoveries from the texts revealed that the Babylonians did not use methods of circular motion but used numerical linear methods that consisted only of zig-zag and step functions. The Egyptians, in the early Middle Kingdom (about B.C. 2000), began to outline their yearly star system by a division of ten-day periods. These were known as the step or diagonal calendar columns. However, in less than a century, the Egyptian ten-day method soon became outdated by precession.

During the Persian Seleucid period, Greek scholars were aware that both the Babylonians and Egyptians knew about calculating the motions of the planets and stars. Judging from the different quotes from many Grecian scholars, the Greeks suspected that both cultures knew how stellar energies reflected the destinies of mankind. However, the Greeks did not fully understand the inner workings of calculating or interpreting stargazing. All the fine points seem to have been missed by early interpreters of cuneiform and hieroglyphic texts. This is clearly reflected by the many different theories in the early Grecian corpus of astrological literature.

Having limited access to this information, the Greek scholars eventually devised their own astrological system by borrowing different interpretive schemes from each culture. In all probability, this was accomplished in part by reconstructing, combining and adapting the early Babylonian mathematical time tables and Egyptian philosophical texts.

Overall, both the Babylonian and Egyptian cultures made contributions which resulted in an interesting blend of philosophical as well as practical ideas. The Egyptian calendar gained popularity, but Greek scholars still divided the zodiacal signs as they did earlier (by 30-day periods) using outdated ten-day periods or decanates. The decans later found their way into the Hindu/Vedic philosophy system of astrology which underwent an incredibly complex metamorphosis before reaching the West.

My conclusion is this: Grecian scholars used Egyptian philosophies to develop the notion that the planets were, in effect, the *cause* of human experience. The Babylonian mathematical tables and omina gave birth to the idea that experiences occurred in repetitive cycles. To this the Greeks added their own cultural myths and stories to the mix. The Grecian mythological gods were associated with the planets; with zodiacal star patterns as their domain; planetary motions correlated with the synchronicity of events here on Earth. When all of this was combined, they formed their own deduced astrological hypotheses known today as Sun sign astrology.

In The Beginning...

The process of philosophy is *like a blind man searching for a black cat in a darkened room at midnight.* Through the ages, many such black cats explaining creation have been invented and then later examined by future generations. The greatest enigma of creation is defining its purpose. To what purpose does life exist? To what end is it directed?

Let's take a look at an early historical perspective. All early cultures observed the heavens in some fashion to gather knowledge by inspiration, intuition or reflection. It was believed that the heavens contained wisdom. The trick for early man was to convince his kinsmen that he could interpret this heavenly wisdom, bring it to Earth and use it to make life easier. Most likely, new ideas were met with open minds. New possibilities could lead to more secure forms of survival. But as time and circumstance set the mold, those in lesser positions were admonished not to stray from the beaten path. The old adage, "But that's the way its always been done," was familiar, even in the Babylonian courts over 5,000 years ago.

Some scholars suggest that early inhabitants of various cultures throughout the world would retreat into caves during severe winter storms. To ease the boredom and wile away the long empty hours, they would tell each other stories about their narrow escapes from death and discuss successful techniques for staying alive. At times, their discussions would turn to the likelihood that the extreme winter was the result of an angry spirit. Unable to come to any clear conclusion, early man fashioned various philosophies, told bigger and better stories and created different mysteries that distracted them from their harsh and subsistent lives. With a need to define life in a larger sense, the stories grew into myths, the myths into epics and these myths and epics culminated with the idea of all-powerful superhuman gods. Eventually, myths and epics began to describe the beginnings of humankind. Humans saw their gods as being helpful but who only occasionally stopped by every now and then to see how things were going here on Earth.

The early gods were said to have rule over every form of existence from the creation itself to the pickax. They were considered capricious, sometimes cruel, but always responsible for major events. The many gods were conceived as a pantheon headed by one who was recognized by the others as their chief. Eventually, the chief god appointed humans to be kings to watch over and rule the rest of the tribe and to act as emissaries between the people and their own god.

As civilization developed, different conqueror-kings came into power and, as a show of power, they would remove the chief god of the conquered city, depose him and replace him with the new king's god. During this time, kings claimed to receive godly instructions to wage war on the new king to reinstate the original god. The defenders would retaliate and the war would escalate until each killed the other tribes' male population. Each member of any individual tribe or community knew that the wars could have been avoided if only the enemy believed in *their* god. Some of the tribal members began to keep records of these deeds of gods and man; they became mythical stories. A black cat scenario was created, a cry we have heard for centuries: my needs are bigger and my beliefs are better than yours.

The idea of creating a god in man's own physical image emerged as a leadership tool. To some, life's purpose was to control others. The people who developed this tool were the leaders.

Throughout time humankind has continually persisted in believing the stories; the black cats they themselves originally fabricated. To others, life was a maze created by chance. These people were the followers.

Then there were also those who were seeking real knowledge by searching for wisdom, making pragmatic observations of the universe and their relationship to it. These are the preceptors whom we should emulate by studying their teachings. To the very few, life was a search for deeper meaning, understanding and preparation. They were the visionaries.

Early Observers

The measuring devices for time on which early man could always depend were celestial phenomena: the recurring events of sunset, the phases of the Moon, sunrise and the length of shadows throughout the day. The first sky-watching techniques were used to time mundane events. The heavens were watched with reverence and, as many cultures became more sophisticated, specific periods of celestial events were associated with their cycles. The more observant sky watchers noticed that seasonal periods could be predicted by association with certain recurring star groupings. One such notable occurrence was in early Egypt—by mid-July of each year, the star Sirius would rise just moments before sunrise, thereby "predicting" the flooding of the Nile.

There is further suggestion that early man may have had the gift of subconscious navigation, an internal planispheric clock or geomagnetic sense that aided his sense of direction to navigate during storms, fog or simply through the darkness of night.

Contemporary Developments

Perhaps astronomy began by noting simple observations of the Moon's quarters with markings on sticks or bones. The earliest form of star-knowledge, not necessarily for divination but in the form of astronomy, star-gazing, observing heavenly phenomena, etc., had to begin at sunset and end by sunrise—simply because the stars cannot be seen during the day. Through the centuries celestial observation became the science of its time.

In a much later period of time, the idea of circular celestial motion was developed by Menelaos (100 A.D.) who was one of the first "modern" scholars. His studies, along with many others, led to the discovery of "celestial mechanics." Not until shortly after the time of Claudius Ptolemy (200 A.D.) did the definition of astrology, *as we know it*, become the study of the positions and aspects of heavenly bodies by using the Ascendant for the purpose of divination. This marked the beginning of Sun sign astrology.

Through the dark ages and renaissance period, astrology flourished more in the Eastern part of the world such as China, Persia and India than it did in Europe. As we emerged from the dark ages, Johannes Kepler (1571-1630) proposed a new set of aspects: the "Quintile" group known as inconjunct, decile, semi-decile, quindecile and quintile–all of which were based on mathematical and numerological grounds. By 1619, Kepler developed his theories on celestial harmonics based on the Heliocentric celestial motions of the solar system and musical intervals. By the late 20th century many inroads into astrological thought had come into focus by serious astrologers; of which there are too many to mention by name.

The Observable Zodiac or Sidereal Astrology

In 1948, astrologers Cyril Fagan and Donald Bradley, using their combined knowledge of Egyptology and astronomy, devised a form of astrology known today as Sidereal or the observable zodiac. Cyril Fagan believed that the Egyptians were the probable originators of horoscopic astrology.

Hieroglyphs reveal that the Egyptians had three daily routines in which they used three types of mathematical procedures. The general populace began their day at sunrise and used the decimal system for business records. The temple priests observed their religious practices with sunset as the start of the new day and used the sexigesimal system. The third was to keep watch in the heavens using mathematics for celestial observations based on the sacred number 12. There were 12 parts to the heavens accompanied by 12 gods; 12 parts to the underworld accompanied by 12 gods. In following the Egyptian tradition we find that each month, week, and each two hour interval throughout the day, had a ruling deity."

Mr. Fagan's idea that the Egyptians originated horoscopic astrology, stems from the fact that the Egyptians divided day and night into 12-hour periods and believed that good and bad deities came into power every two hours during the day. They were considered good or bad depending whether or not they were friendly or antagonistic to the daily, weekly or monthly deity.

However, there is one other view that Mr. Fagan postulated—his ideas on the Egyptian pentades. Many celestial diagrams accompanied burial procedures and these diagrams often depicted the sky as the "happy hunting grounds" or the "Field of Reeds" as the home of the departed spirit. One such diagram has been discussed on page 476 where Mr. Fagan brilliantly concluded that each "decan" was actually a pentade consisting of five degrees rather than ten, as had been previously believed by modern scholars. Although there is little conventional agreement with his theory, it certainly correlates with the Babylonian concept of 5 times 72. Both concepts describe, by five-degree increments, the "aging process" of progression which I re-named rogression and introduced in this book.

Two Schools of Thought: Tropical or Sidereal?

Fagan and Bradley's research has resulted into two schools of astrological thought. One school prefers that all calculations be based on the *sign* of Aries beginning on the first day of spring as the fiducial or initial starting point. Using this method, each planet is associated with the different signs and houses thereby projecting an affinity each to the other, i.e., the planet Mars with the sign of Aries and the first house. Astrologers who support this form of astrology work with the *Tropical* zodiac. Tropical astrologers assign each 30-day segment of the zodiac to the sign that precedes the actual visible constellation. For example, when the Sun is actually seen in the *constellation* Pisces, it is referred to as being in the *sign* of Aries.

Due to the Earth's rotation, the time it takes for a 30° segment of a constellation to travel across the horizon is two hours. This two-hour segment, as it relates to the Tropical sign, is called a house. As there are 24 hours in a day, there are 12 such house divisions. Tropical astrology supports the view that the symbolic meaning of the planets also relates to signs and houses, creating a system of a 12-letter *alphabet* consisting of three parts to each letter: that of planet, sign and house. It is noteworthy that there are twenty such house systems: Placidius, Campanean, Koch and Equal, to name a few. Early house systems were based on the division of the circle by four and each tetrad further divided by three resulting in 12 houses.

The other school of astrologers prefers that its calculations be based on the planetary positions as they actually appear within the constellational backdrop. This approach uses the observable or *Sidereal* zodiac. Siderealists primarily place their interest with the planets' closeness to any or all of the four angles previously mentioned. They omit the Tropical signs and their meanings. In Sidereal astrology, the area where the cardinal houses *would* be, is known as the foreground, or as being close to any angle. The fixed house areas represent the middle ground and the mutable house areas contribute to background influences. It is agreed in both systems that a planet exerts its most powerful influence when closest to the angles.

These two very different schools of astrology, Tropical and Sidereal, have divided current practitioners of astrology and produced much spirited debate. Neither of these schools, however, can be related to the ancient observers. The ancients listed physical astronomical sightings, seen with the naked eye, as patterns and motions located primarily in the Sun's ecliptic and divided the ecliptic by using a generalized 30-day lunar reference.

In following this early procedure, all references in this book shall use the mathematics to find the Sidereal longitude in the observable zodiac, using either the more exacting Koch house system or equal house system for ease of use when rogressing the chart with Fagan/Bradley as the fiduciary Vernal Point.

Erroneous Views?

Astrology and astronomy never did mix well. All scientists throughout the ages had problems with astrologers and the application of astrology. That is because scientists and other empiricists view the Tropical sign and house system as little more than superstition. One of the many reasons for this is that calculations for Tropical astrology are not based on the planetary positions as they currently appear, but by their positions of about 2,000 years ago. Because of these dated placements, the Tropical zodiac is *out of synch* with the observable zodiac. Serious thinkers feel that a system based on an incorrect calculation of 24° of error must also be a fallacy. However, the Tropical zodiac serves good astrologers extremely well and they are adamant that the system works for them. Does this fall into the category of fallacy? Or enigma?

There are many such enigmatic puzzles, some of which derive from early cultures. One of the most puzzling texts from Egypt is Amenhotep's *Catalogue of the Universe*. It was written in B.C. 1100. It lists only five constellations, two of which can be identified; that of Orion and the Great Bear. Not much can be gleaned from such texts, other than a good deal of conjecture. Another curiosity of the text is there is no mention of Sirius nor any of the planets. Outside of this, the only accepted indications of Egyptian astronomy are references to star clocks and calendars. Thus, it has been said of Egyptian astronomy that "what little can be said seems to be enough." This quote presents a problem which seems to hold true for most of today's scientific arguments in understanding antiquity. Does this also fall in the category that Egyptian star knowledge is a fallacy? Our darkened room has another black cat.

The Problems with Contemporary Disciplines

Our current culture places importance on the left-brain thinking, which is listening and reading in sequential and/or quantified terms. Likewise, the English language requires subject and predicate to dictate the listener's mind into a set of fixed associations and classifications. While discipline of thought is required for interaction in today's society, the emphasis on it takes precedence over right-brain creative activity.

We need to look at a few examples of how many of today's astrologers fall into this same situation. While reading astrological glyphs, many search for left-brain subject and predicate instead of allowing a free form of right-brain association to emerge. Searching for linear thought forms forces too much left-brain function, thereby diminishing any right-brain intuitive communication that might otherwise develop.

For an astrologer it is necessary to encourage a marriage of reason and intuition, otherwise he cannot bring himself to the dialectical process necessary to blend ancient wisdom with his own. Astrological glyphs *require* the reader to combine reason with intuition and expand beyond the limits of modern day left-brain communication.

Today, we often place emphasis in a sentence by underlining or italicizing certain words or groups of words. Hieroglyphics may have been written with the same strict associations with subtle nuances indicated by color, a pictogram and possibly the layout of the completed sentence. Hieroglyphics appear to be pictorial "snapshots" which probably produced emphasis on integral concepts by the person who read them. They also expressed numerical values. This all suggests that the reader may have been allowed to contemplate and experience any message in combination with his own precepts.

Recent brain research has revealed that language parameters may be the underlying problem of stress. The so-called romantic languages ending with vowels allow the listener a relaxed juncture in conversation. The English, Germanic and Scandinavian languages use harsher consonantal endings which are more internally demanding for response. The difference in language styles indicates the different lifestyles among different cultures. Eastern philosophies have long known the therapeutic value of vocal mantras and quiet meditation for stress reduction. As for man's thought process, Pythagorean principles encourage the listener to muse and imagine, offering a variety of mental possibilities or processes. It has been shown that Euclidean geometry is not the final answer for solving geometric problems. For example, origami, the art of paper folding, can solve problems and equations thought impossible within the Euclidean system.

When we contemplate the limited number of 12 basic characters of the astrological alphabet, we begin to realize that hieroglyphics must hold a tremendous dimensional quality, perhaps still to be imagined or discovered. Even with its limitation, astrological sygils illuminate our mind, producing a quality of dimensional understanding unparalleled in contemporary thought. These astrological sygils represent a continuum of concepts that allow the astrologer to meditate and connect with both sides of the brain, experiencing the simultaneous and multidimensional content of his own nature.

Any astrologer will tell you of the empowering experience they feel when reading a chart. It is like an explosive thought-bomb of cerebral fireworks taking place as full intuition of the glyphical series reveals itself. This may well be what the Egyptians experienced while reading the medu-neter–hieroglyphs that embody the spiritual attributes of the object represented. Almost like musical notes in a song, the range of astrological glyphs shift and weave to form their own resolution. This is an experience that astrologers glimpse, while non-astrologers and the uninitiated can only dream.

The sygils of astrological lore may be the only real heritage passed down through the ages from our Egyptian and Babylonian ancestors. Within their paradigm, astrological sygils and glyphs reveal many nuances relating to the holistic view of cosmic life that the Babylonians and Egyptians seemed to know instinctively.

Star Systems and Cycles

There are repeated cycles in society, such as economic cycles, that coincide with the seasonal Sun-spot and Jupiter cycles. The Sun cycle still coincides with the coming of different seasons. Real estate cycles have been associated with the 19-year *Nodal* cycle, in which Sun and Moon intersect the ecliptic at the same latitude and longitude. The seven-year cycle of bone regeneration and the seven-year itch refer to the Saturn and, in some cases, the lunar cycle. The list goes on. Many more cycles can be observed throughout our daily lives if one only takes the time to look for them. After all, in the beginning, the sky was a giant clock for those who watched it. Is it not too different from the way we watch clocks on our wrist or wall? Do clocks *tell* us what to do or when, or do we use them to simply remind us of appointments and schedules?

Conclusion

After Alexander's conquest of Persia and Egypt, the Greek language became dominant throughout the conquered countries; hence, the Grecian scholar could communicate with the people throughout Persia and Egypt. There are many traces of Grecian manuscripts that boast of ancient teachings, but it seems that these scholars had to surmise and theorize large portions of such ancient literature. Much of what has been transcribed about Grecian theories was obviously developed from fragmented understanding or misunderstanding of the earlier cultures of Babylon and Egypt.

The simple fact remains that the original languages remained within the local communities and because they spoke Greek did not necessarily mean they imparted or revealed revered teachings. Nor is there implication that local scholars could easily read the early texts available to them. Many cuneiform tablets and hieroglyphs were written in different styles depending on the context or location of the scribe; if there was anyone alive who could read these ancient writings, their numbers were very few.

Also, keep in mind that occupations were directly passed on from father to son. Formal schooling taught the basics: reading, writing and mathematics. Learning, mostly by rote, was accomplished by copying from exercises and committing long passages of text to memory. Frequently, such instructions presented distinctly biased views which helped retain the philosophy of a culture and its trappings.

Warfare results in plundering and aggressive occupation. Under these circumstances, why would a people give up any of its deemed sacred knowledge to its conquerors? Retention of cultural morès and customs is always paramount to the success of a close-knit society. It is very doubtful that the Chaldeans were willing to give their jealously guarded secrets away. After all, human nature has not changed over the millennia. The idea of learned men of letters continuing in the tradition of their own culture does not die out because they were occupied or ruled by foreigners.

Much of what the Greeks said and wrote in their early texts about the Sun, Moon, stars and their relation to Babylonian astrological thought was guesswork and lacked continuity. Many long forgotten ideas and myths out of both Babylonian and Egyptian histories were dredged piecemeal, borrowed and eventually combined into what eventually developed into Grecian ideas about astronomy, astrology and even religion. Those ideas eventually became the basis for a new, hypothesized astrology. In this light, it is easy to conclude that Sun-sign astrology did not develop until 500 years *after* Alexander's conquest and probably *without any help* from either Babylon or Egypt, thereby losing many important early astrological concepts.

By the time of the Roman Empire, secret societies had really begun to flourish. Our own Bible supports this idea in as much as the letters and books of the apostles were codified by verse and number so the Romans could not recognize the true meaning of the messages.

CHAPTER 2

INITIAL BASICS

We can't run away or hide from who we are;
our destiny chooses us.

With certain exceptions, most people are born with the same sense organs and roughly the same ability to understand. Consequently, they all see the physical world in pretty much the same way. What they make of what they see depends on the manner in which their life force functions. Yet, many do not see their lives as being ruled by their emotional, physical or mental states. When we become aware of these three states of being, we at once notice these three states are constantly, in effect, fighting for complete control over the other two. Consequently, people find themselves being pushed and tossed about, either by emotional reactions, physical appetites or intellectual drives all in a confusing array of circumstances. As Shakespeare once remarked, "All the world's a stage" and, as the bard so succinctly pointed out, we are creating and directing our own passion play through these different states of being. Our behavior pattern usually indicates which state of being is precedent by our wanting to be either liked, right or in control.

The way in which we react to these three states of being entices other actors to enter our play. The other actors are directed by our performance ad-lib and then we in turn react to their reactions of our initial performance. In doing so, we create our subjective lifetime and wonder what is wrong with everyone else. Primarily, we believe we are separated from the All and, because of this illusion, we are *not in fact*, but *in effect*. Any belief of any condition held in the mind is converted into an experience in the physical world.

If we believe this external condition has control over us, it does. Within that thought frame our lifetime is measured by, and our life span measured within, our life flow. Recognizing the reactive "push me-pull you" quality which we call social interaction, places us in a much more desirable position of expressing self-control over our own lives.

There are many ways which allow us to become aware of our foibles, folderol and folie a deux. One such method is using the astrological techniques as set forth in this book. The basic precept of astrology is to view the objective template based on heavenly positions that represents our own experience. Within this template we find reflection of our life's activities and subjective beliefs. Correctly understood, astrology allows us to view our *belief-play* both internally and externally, to see our own script as others may see it.

The overall premise of astrology is relatively easy. The astrological template has 12 "departments of life" by which we can analyze and discover who the person in the chart is, where he is going and why. The ability to foretell future events correctly is what really separates a good astrologer from a bad one. Another problem that often arises with the novice astrologer is that he feels he should completely know the ins and outs of each department of life. Otherwise, in the process of doing business, how could an astrologer advise his client on eighth house investments without understanding investment procedures and principles, or 12th house medical procedures, ninth house publishing procedures?

Rest assured that this is not necessary because the client, by virtue of his actions, clearly shows the astrologer what is going on in his life. This is where the house system becomes one of many valuable tools. Not only do they indicate arenas of life but, as we shall see later, they show at what age to expect these arenas to play an important part in his life (see page 80).

Simple Myths or Reality Views

The mythological stories of gods and goddesses that characterize the constellations and planets all suggest that the ancients attributed much deeper meanings to these myths than just simple omina. Certainly there is more to the ancient cultures than what was believed by many of the earlier archeologists.

However, there is one archeologist who concludes in her work that the Osiris myth may have been deliberately encoded with the numbers 12, 30, 72 and 360. The numbers immediately catch the eye of anyone even barely associated with astrology or astronomy. There are 12 astrological signs of 30° each that equal the complete circle of 360° in the ecliptic. The number 72 relates to the precessional *slippage* of one degree every 72 years. Furthermore, by multiplying 30° x 72 years we find the sum of 2,160, which is the number of years it takes the Sun to pass through one entire constellation. This is called its *precessional age,* such as the age of Pisces or Aquarius. The number of years for a complete precessional cycle through *all* the constellations is found by multiplying the 12 signs by the precession of each constellation: 2,160 years is 25,920 years.

Different areas throughout the world are replete with the same numbers encoded in their myths as well. The mathematics are intact but the myths have lost their intrinsic meanings over the past 3,000 years. Perhaps it is time to dig even deeper into all myths connected with astrology and see just what valuable information has been buried for the past several millennia.

Is Psychology Astrology?

Over the last half-century, astrological parameters have again changed and are now being shoehorned and wedded into a psychological format. Psychology is defined as the study of mental processes of behavior: the emotional and behavioral characteristics of an individual, group or activity. This sounds like it belongs with the Moon or first house category. Astrology is the study of heavenly bodies and their synchronous timing with the affairs of man. The biggest misunderstanding about astrology is the claim that man is *influenced* and even controlled by the stars. True, a good astrologer can recognize the human being in the chart by the context of the planets and their positions. However, to an *aware* individual, the planets and their positions only show potential, admittedly some potentials are stranger than others, but still, for now, it is only potential.

Astrology as psychology can become confusing. The search for answers in this context becomes the search for the psychological axioms of Mars/Venus, Moon/Saturn and Mercury/Jupiter and how humanity fits into this mold internally. Furthermore, how do we organize the psychology of the world at large? What psychological myths do we hold today that relate to the colorful configurations of life as we know it. How would we develop a hero myth about our corporate "warriors" struggling to achieve his glory?

In my opinion, psychology is still in its infant stages of development and although it is called a science, it seems to be an art of perception and persuasion. The more serious problem to the astrologer is that the student of astrology is asked to also become a lay psychologist. The idea of practicing astrology *as* psychology does not do either field justice. The novice cannot possibly begin in two different fields and emerge with a complete understanding of either discipline within a reasonable time frame. This is probably why there are so many books on the subject rehashing old rhetoric.

To develop a psychological profile on their clients astrologers must *deduce* suggested planetary indices into a psychological response to *hypothetical external conditions.* Then, by examining a proposed response under the hypothetical situation, the astrologer must determine all possibilities and ramifications of the situation. This form of astrology does not deal with the basics directly; it becomes circuitous and indirect. The positive or negative power of the planets is reduced to "politically correct" terms which result in a watered down, tepid version of astrology. The result? We are left with *after the fact* astrology, whereas the condition is *not obvious* until after it has occurred. It is like trying to deduce the answer to an arithmetic problem by examining the esoteric meaning of numbers while doing simple addition.

Astrologers must first understand astrology. Then, and only then, can they apply it to their interest of research, which of course could be psychology. Teachers of astrology must understand the plight of the novice and help direct their student's thinking so they may recognize that the planets can be constantly synchronous with *different* activities and are not necessarily psychological in nature. Clearly, it is more important to teach the student how to think in astrological, rather than in psychological, terms. In this fashion he learns how to *analyze* an event and reduce it to astrological terms so he can later apply this thinking *to his chosen field of interest*. Psychology can have a field day analyzing the people who attend horse racing events because people who attend these events can be seen as having psychological needs, but the event in itself has nothing to do with psychology. It's a sports event and, as an old horse racing fan once told me, "In all games of chance, ya' pays yer' money and ya' takes yer' chances."

The advent of the model "astrology as psychology" is easy to understand. Both disciplines propose the idea that they recognize the fundamental elements that influence human circumstances but, they are two diametrically opposed disciplines.

Very basically, the bottom line is psychology proposes that we are not puppets and that we can change and alter our behavioral pattern by awareness and choices.

The same does not apply for astrology. Its message proposes synchronistic activities between the planets and the human condition: that we mechanically react to our emotional, physical and intellectual states in rhythmic accordance. We must accept this as a fact of life but the distinct difference is we can prepare for these activities in advance by knowing the timing of these rhythms and cycles.

However, by recognizing the intrinsic value of both systems, we can become the sovereign rulers of our own personal universe. The astrologer, as a psychologist, allows a deeper understanding of the human condition of which we are a part. The close association between psychology and astrology is this: psychology examines the individual *in relation* to his inner states of being; astrology examines the individual *by association* to his life events and circumstances. Such understanding releases us from the limitation of both systems, freeing us from the "push me-pull you" in our lives.

The Cook Book Course of Astrology

Of course, the question arises, do the inner states react to the planetary transits and aspects or do planetary occurrences and aspects create the inner responses? To help sort out this problem, a somewhat awkward but important practice developed in astrology: the use of key words. Today, most astrology books relate planetary meanings with a system of word associations. This is often referred to as *cookbook* astrology. In essence, the cookbook formulae should be used for reference only, much like a thesaurus or dictionary. Otherwise, "cook booking" may contribute to a problem that the beginning and intermediate student alike never seem to leave behind: a strict adherence to planetary meanings regardless of their association with the client's actual experience. "Cook booking" also limits the novice because it lessens the need to distill experiences into astrological terms and thought, not to mention stifling the client into a set of parameters determined "by the book."

Below, there are two illustrative myths. The first story relates to the basic planetary meanings and the second story is about aspects. These myths are the foundation for the cookbook references in the following chapters. Today's students would be wise to challenge the age old adage, "that's the way it's always been done" because it not only opens to new horizons but allows the astrologer to recognize important planetary associations in his clients mannerisms and activities. It is best to start working with astrology in one's own respect and experiences in relation to those cookbook analogies. Only *then* is the astrologer able to judge the experiences of his clientele. To accomplish this challenge, simply relate and create a parallel to the myths below. Replace the following activities with your own life experiences and adjust them to fit your personal story.

The Context—How Do We See It

To begin the illustration of basic planetary meanings, look back to when you were a child and recall when your parents told you to look both ways before crossing a street. You made it a big deal, you stopped, paused and physically turned your head in an exaggerated manner and looked both ways. It was sound advice but, as you became older, you approached street corners differently. While walking to a chosen destination, you began to listen for traffic, to "look" both ways with your ears instead of your eyes. Now that you are older and still out walking, you probably listen to the traffic subconsciously, bringing your attention to focus on the traffic only when you hear a vehicle while getting ready to cross the street.

This illustrates the point that the safety advice first given to you became reorganized to fit your growing needs. The same goes for the seeming oxymorons in astrological cookbooks that substitute words for planets. Understanding the basic *context* of an event allows you to find the right word-for-planet meaning. Depending on one's perspective (yours *or* your client's), planets seem to behave differently with different people. Once you have mastered the basic planetary meanings, it is important for you to personally conceptualize, reorganize, and isolate the meanings of each planet for yourself or your client.

This can be accomplished by interviewing your client as you rogress the astrological wheel to planetary aspects within the sunset chart. This practice will allow you to develop a planetary dictionary of your own. Astrology is experiential. As its student, you must develop your own planetary concepts and then adjust them to your psyche so the meaning comes forth as a flower bud beginning to blossom. Planets can act as nouns describing people, places or things. Other times they can act as verbs or an adjective describing its limits or other qualifications. Context is the keyword here. Once we understand the context of circumstances and describe events astrologically, we can define any situation and foretell which particular event may occur in the future with more certainty.

The graph below is read by looking at the planet on the left and cross-referencing it to the top of the list. For example, the *Sun* with Venus can be expressed as colorful light (sunset or sunrise) or staged lighting. However, pairing *Venus* with the Sun creates the ideal of a glamorous movie star or model. The following graph is an example of such objectivity. This is by no means the last word in planetary definitions but it does indicate how a planet may metaphorically be viewed with the other planets from its own perspective. Adjust your chart so *each planet* is placed *as* the Ascendant and try using that perspective for chart interpretation.

A great deal can be learned from placing each planet as the Ascendant for a planetary reference point. Notice how the planets change meanings by each different perspective and placement. For example, place natal Mars as the Ascendant. The relocation of each planet by house placement takes on a Martian meaning as indicated by the Mars line below. Thus, your Sun moves to a different location by house placement and that represents the objective that you desire to achieve in your life from the Mars point of view. Mercury's placement, from Mars' point of view, indicates the method or plans you make to achieve that objective. The Moon represents the people most likely to be used or the most likely to get hurt by your actions and so on.

	Sun	Mercury	Venus	Mars
Sun-	Light	Brilliant	Colorful	Glaring
Me-	Inspiration	Insight	Dreamy	Inquisitive
Ve-	Ideal	Eloquence	Disappointing	Coarseness
Ma-	Objective	Plan of attack	Weakness	Invincible
Ju-	God	Prayer	Devotion	Right action
Sa-	Investment	Marketing	Product	Expense
Mo-	Savior	Self doubt	Rescue	Antagonist

	Jupiter	Saturn	Moon
Sun-	Bright	Dim	Intensity
Me-	Tolerance	Wise	Reflective
Ve-	Luxury	Style & Grace	Comfort
Ma-	Show of force	Defense	Casualties
Ju-	Righteousness	Propitiation	Followers
Sa-	Profit	Useful	Consumer
Mo-	Indulgence	Melancholy	Helpless

After you read the two story illustrations below, go back and check the list again. See what changes you would now make. Take the time to make your own list. It will become quite useful as you read the rest of this book.

Another use for this graph is to directly relate the planets by aspect and notice how they relate to you. For example, if you had Mars square Jupiter in your chart, the cross reference from the Mars point of view is a show of force. This does not necessarily mean that you should approach your objectives in a belligerent manner. Quite the contrary. You should approach your objectives well fortified with an array of knowledge about the subject at hand. From Jupiter's point of view of Mars, right action describes the principle of following through and not becoming distracted or losing interest before an objective can be achieved.

I am sure you can think of many other cross-references. Taking the time now to prepare such a list gives you a much firmer grasp of planetary expressions. Often, only the Moon, Sun and Saturn will cover an entire situation. Spencer Grendahl's book, *Astrology and the Games People Play,* represents the three spheres of influence we all experience. The Moon is the child within us, the Sun as the adult, and Saturn the parent. An individual born with a penchant for only one of the planets will basically express his interest in life through that planet and see the world through those glasses, so to speak. Using his model, the other planets basically interact with only these three. There are other times, however, when nothing in the chart explains certain life experiences until you add a rogressed, secondary or tertiary chart. Then it all becomes crystal clear.

Remember to think about the above meaning of the planets while incorporating these ideas as feelings and experience. In this fashion they act as a background giving you a starting point from which you can adjust their meanings to fit your circumstance. This becomes more important as we progress through this book. As with hieroglyphics, a planetary symbol loses its essential meaning when assigned only a series of related words for description such as the preceding graph. Begin to expand your astrological vocabulary.

The story's design is two-fold, with emphasis on creating an image of concepts for the planets. Later, if you choose, the planetary meanings can be used as the astrological *signs* in Tropical astrology. This will help eliminate the confusion usually associated with the all too standardized keyword cookbook approach. The graph on the previous page sets forth in this story the basic planetary ideas and their meanings which you will find very useful in helping you to create your own keyword system. As a thesaurus, the keyword system will trigger your memory should you forget or need to contrive a meaningful dialogue between the planets. Review your own life history beginning in your childhood and modify the story by reason and comparison to fit your circumstances.

The Planets as Growing Awareness

Now imagine a baby as he lies in his crib, slowly developing an awareness of his surroundings. His world of experiences is a daily routine not particularly meaningful at first. However, as he becomes older, he begins to remember more and more about his mother, his crib, room, and the world just outside the windows. It's a world so vast, so new, that it's beyond his imagination. Months pass. His horizons begin to expand and eventually, room by room, his entire home becomes completely familiar to him. Soon, the backyard becomes the next horizon, then the front of the house with the street and whole block following. As he develops through his early years, his ever-expanding need for exploration eventually envelops the block, the surrounding neighborhood and eventually, the entire city.

Remember when you were a child? The sense of wonderment and excitement of learning about new things and exploring new places? The world was fresh, new and exciting to the senses! Your wonderful sense of innocence, naiveté and optimism was just waiting to be subjected to any new experience. During those formative years, your imagination was fertile and alive. The sense of wonder and curiosity was developing at a fantastic rate. You were eager to see what was beyond each new horizon. Even if you were locked in a closet, you would have eventually started talking to a new-found imaginary friend! All this wonderful experience takes place during the first sixteen years of life. The sense and feeling expresses the planet **Jupiter.**

The planet **Saturn** can be expressed as the emergence from innocent childhood into young adulthood. The personality becomes aware of the responsibility and discipline required in dealing with the social aspects of peers and the pedantic demands of executors of school and home. Learning to be responsible for his own actions, our protagonist, finds to be on *his own* is like climbing a mountain. He finds that he needs to rein in his once carefree dependent existence in exchange for one of independence.

His first job seems cold and filled with forbearance and responsibility. He must be punctual and perform his tasks correctly and in a timely manner. Saturn exemplifies that insecure feeling of always being under someone else's watchful eye and of waiting for them to pounce on any mistake. Yet, through it all, there are days of accomplishment, like the accumulation of good grades and friends. Of course, each payday also brings a sense of real achievement and the desire to at least stay on the job one more week. As the daily routine sets in, the sense of fulfillment at work diminishes and our young adult spends more time and energy improving his social life style.

His interests begin to broaden: a girlfriend, school dances, the team spirit with high school games, the excitement that comes with each team's accomplishment. One fine day the school team wins an important state championship game, or perhaps he receives a substantial pay raise or even a better job. Another possibility is that he may have graduated with scholastic honors or received a coveted college scholarship. For the moment the drudgery of his daily routine vanishes in the thrill of accomplishment, the exhilaration of recognition, of being singled out as unique, the best in one's field. At last, our hero is recognized as an individual, selected out of a whole group of peers.

The brief but exhilarating experience of **Uranus** has arrived: the principle of peer groups, uniqueness and sudden changes. Too soon though, the limelight grows dim, flickers and goes out. Again, our story guide has become just another name in the phone book. All too soon the exhilaration is just a memory. If only things had lasted, maybe a second chance is in order. If only he could relive the dream of **Neptune's** dichotic sense of euphoria, despair/inertia, his life would not seem so bad. Ever notice when things are going wrong they continue to do so until chaos reigns? There seems to be no way out of the doldrums and we just sink lower into self pity and low self esteem.

But, as life would have it, just when he seemed to hit bottom, a new acquaintance or new inspiration comes along and suddenly he bursts through his inertia into the brilliance of *Eureka!* Someone or something inside wakes up and stirs him into action, the **Mars** principle. Now it is the time to do something about the situation at hand. As his inspiration begins to unfold, its concept revitalizes and dazzles his imagination and, consequently, his enthusiasm becomes infectious to others. His despair, now forgotten, has been replaced by action, action to improve his new inspiration, to shape and mold it and lovingly develop it through the **Venus** principle of acquisition and appreciation.

Whatever the project, be it a new idea to get rich or the perfect love affair, it's developed with loving care. It is the powerful feeling of renewed vitality, of purpose revitalizing the once remembered feeling of exploration, responsibility; the uniqueness through achievement and even the despair have all been integrated in formulating something new and worthwhile. Our baby has emerged as an experienced young adult. Once the inspiration has developed sufficiently, he moves out into the world looking to convince a partner to help improve this wonderful idea through the concept of **Mercury,** the principle of shared interests.

After explaining why they should become partners, bonding takes place and the partnership becomes integrated through mutual consent. In a love relationship, a marriage may take place. In a business relationship, a partnership begins. Communication is the most important ingredient in any bond. As the relationship or partnership grows, its course may not be smooth. One or both egos may become bruised. Communication breaks down and is replaced by resentment. Eventually, these partners find themselves keeping secrets from one another, so much so that the union becomes fractured. The support and sense of sharing, once the hallmark of their togetherness, is sadly absent. That feeling of helplessness and vulnerability, the emotional **Moon** principle, has entered the picture. Emotional buffers and defense mechanisms come into play.

Neither partner wants to be in a weakened position or, the least desired result, out of control. The need for emotional stability becomes a desire not to retreat but to salvage something along the way. It is important that each partner keep something from past acquisitions. Strategic designs begin to form for self protection and preservation. Wanting to shed light on their situation, they both eventually seek outside help to work out their differences to reach a final settlement.

Coming out of a bad situation teaches many lessons; deferred payments, creative financing, and estate and investment planning all come into focus. With this established sense of direction, a new idea develops out of the old situation and a new interest takes hold. Again our hero begins a new venture. Everyone notices his new car, the new home, his style and manner. The way he speaks demonstrates an attitude of success. The **Sun** principle attracts success and invites others to *orbit* in his brilliance, serving as validation for his existence. This time, instead of partners, he has workers wanting to be on his team. More people seek him out, longing to be a part or even perhaps to catch a glimpse of the *lucky* potential he represents: success and achievement.

Throughout this process, a second, *more* experienced **Mercury** principle has developed. Our hero has emerged as the practical and critical business operator. No longer concerned with why he should have partners, he is now concentrating on finding the right partner. Communication is still very important, but now it is used in a manner of instruction rather than trying to be convincing. As his last experience taught, naive trust is no longer an important virtue in business. The business of knowledge and staying on top of things becomes tantamount to existence. It is necessary to scrutinize every detail in every department of life and business in order to survive. Every knock becomes a boost and every waking moment is spent in analysis. Staying in control is essential to maintaining his desired position. He now wants to know the *bottom line* and anything interfering with that success causes frustration.

To insure that his position remains secure, the *second* principle of **Venus** comes into play, which is that of the social networker. His social aspects of interplay are mostly with associates in his financial and business circles. The circle of friends and acquaintances is his primary source of information. As confidants and future influential resources, they are the leading supportive elements in his life. It is through them that he hears the latest news about his business and new lifestyle. As the close of life draws near, **Pluto's** intensity and anxiety come into play through self-analysis. A great mystery lies behind him, a greater one before him. Many questions about the purpose and fulfillment of his life arise and, no matter how deeply pondered, they still remain unanswered. Bringing us back to full circle, he approaches his transition. **Jupiter** once again beckons him to venture onto the new horizon ahead. Full of enthusiasm, he joyfully follows. He can only believe that what he left behind somehow made a difference. The end of life's sojourn comes about through dissolution into endlessness.

Tropical Usage

Tropical astrologers use the signs as companions to the planets. They do this by allotting the planetary nuances to its companion sign. This is referred to as *ruler ship,* such as Mars *rules* Aries. The term "rules" simply means associative energies, first house, the sign Aries and the planet Mars. They all mean the same thing: actor, action, (to be) active. To substitute signs for planets for the meaning of the Tropical signs in the above story, simply insert the astrological *sign* for the planet: Sagittarius for Jupiter, Capricorn for Saturn, Aquarius for Uranus and so forth. Continue to substitute each sign for each planet by following its natural order of succession to Scorpio. *The Astrologer's Handbook* by Zipporah Dobyns or *Moving with Astrology* by Maritha Pottenger describes the astrological alphabet rather succinctly.

Aspects

In our second illustration, the aspects are depicted in much the same way as the previous example. Aspects are the basic geometric configurations between the planets and stars and are thought of as the dynamic modifiers in birth charts. Traditionally, planets located a specific number of degrees away from one another are said to be in aspect. Major aspects are the angular relationship between planets and other celestial bodies.

Depending on the number of degrees apart, the major aspects are the conjunction 0°, sextile 60°, square 90°, trine 120°, and opposition 180°. The planetary relationships are considered most dynamic and powerful when exactly separated by these arcs. Aspects are recognized as the prime motivation for activity in any given chart. The current view, to which some astrologers rigidly adhere, is that the closer the configuration to the exact degree of separation, the more dynamic it becomes.

Picture this. In India there is a stringed musical instrument called the sitar. This instrument has two sets of strings, one set over the other. The upper set of strings consists of seven strings and the lower set has 12 to 18. The lower strings are tuned to each musical half-tone in the scale of a dominant key. When the musician plays a melody on the upper set of strings, the lower set will vibrate to the same note in direct sympathetic response. The notes that are not in synch with the melody do not respond but remain dormant. This sympathetic response is what gives this instrument its distinctive sound. Likewise, aspects differ in each and every chart and we respond to them with our own sympathetic vibration.

Let's say you are timing a client's chart. An individual born with two planets 110° apart has *that* position as his *personal* aspect; any traditional aspect between planets remains ineffectual for him. At the time of the traditional aspects mentioned above, there is no sympathetic vibration. It is only when the planets reach the distance of 110° that the motivational dynamic will take place in the form of activity for that individual. This brings up the idea of orbs of influence. Granted, there is a flux in the areas of planetary influence that gradually changes. However, a wide orb of 12° to the Sun does not allow much breathing room. With such a large orb it would be unusual for the Sun not to have some sort of aspect in the chart at any given moment, thereby diminishing any fluctuation of influence the Sun would normally have. Generally, one degree equals three months' time; 12 degrees equates to a full two and one half years of solar arc. It would be wise to establish the orbs of influence through your own experience.

For this reason, an orb of one degree applying (approaching) to individual aspects works best. Experience will demonstrate the gradations of aspects and how sensitive certain individuals are to them. There are many textbooks on the subject of aspects and each differs enough to create confusion. To help eliminate some of this confusion, the next illustration will demonstrate the dynamics of the aspects as seen from a holistic point of view.

The Aspects as Experience

As a young child develops his senses, he quickly learns about *good boy* and *bad boy* reinforcement. This controlling style teaches the child how to manipulate others as well and to recognize and qualify his existence. Manipulation requires special tools, both mental and physical. To attract attention, the development of such tools can be recognized as a gift, much appreciated by others, or the ability to have his peers follow his lead. Aptitude can be the inherent talent to draw, sing, perform or a capacity for athletics or mathematics. This recognition is considered the 0° aspect or **conjunction**. It is also a starting point, his beginning awareness of who he is and his developing interest or aptitude to attract attention.

As the child grows older, he continues to perfect his very successful *attention-getting device* and letting his mistrials fall into disuse. Eventually, he receives more reinforcement for his particular talent. The child's performance and subsequent praise satisfies certain anxieties he may have about his behavior with respect to peers and elders. This particular stage is the 30° aspect and the child develops self-worth with the second house **semi-sextile**.

This loop begins to develop further and at school he realizes that people outside his immediate family also appreciate his particular skill. The feedback the child receives may be positive but is probably negative through the teasing of his peers: However, the positive feedback pushes him to continue on his original path. This stage is looked upon as a 45° angle, the semi-square.

Because he is young, our youth's penchant has become a *talent* and he now seeks, with the aid of his parents, to further develop his talent into skill. They seek a mentor to teach and further aid in the child's development. This is the 60° angle, the third house **sextile.** The sextile initiates not only opportunities but introduces him to others who are also interested in the same field. During the sextile period, our youth will learn not only about his talent but how skilled others are and where he fits in the *pecking order* of his situation.

Encouraged by his elders, and in competition with his peers, the child, now becoming a young adult, begins to discover that there is a lot of work required in order to receive the same praise he did as a child. This is the 90° angle, the fourth house **square**. If the pressure is greater than he can manage, the easy way out is to quit. However, if the competition is not that tough, he may opt to continue in his training. In either case the square will present him with a choice. A decision will be made one way or the other. If the young adult decides to quit, he now faces a new horizon and has broken the loop he started as a youngster.

However, should he decide to continue perfecting his talent, he eventually develops a faculty, becoming facile and confident in its use. As a young man, he now has entered the fifth house **trine** position or the 120° angle. He sets his own goals for acquiring better and better mentors to help develop his now chosen career. His confidence heightened, he sets out to find other peers to interact with and to further his apprenticeship. This aspect is the fifth house **sesquiquadrate** or the 135° angle. It is a difficult and frustrating time because here he finds a lack of interest or discipline among his peers. He feels unwanted and possibly thwarted in his efforts to get organized.

However, once the right group of peers is found, he will interact with them. Together they will develop a working relationship while perfecting their individual abilities, each one suffering with the other's misapplications but working things out to fulfillment. This aspect is the sixth house **quincunx** or the 150° aspect.

By the time our young man has developed many skills, he becomes adept at pleasing others with his talent. He is also recognized and accepted as one specialized in his group's inner circle, both socially and professionally. Now he is sought after to join with other professionals in his field of expertise, either as a partner or highly esteemed co-worker. This is the **opposition** or 180° aspect. Once again, there is a choice to be made. The choice is now with whom and why, knowing full well that when his choice is made, he may well be burning a few bridges behind him.

Up to this point, aspects have moved outward or away from the Ascendant or zero point. They are considered objective aspects. Our protagonist has worked *toward* a particular goal. Once achieved, the progression of aspects begins to move from the opposition point *back* toward the individual. Aspects that are moving back toward the Ascendant are considered subjective, meaning our protagonist now wants to show his ability to the world while receiving some form of remuneration, award and prominence.

The aspects are still seen as 0°, 60°, 90°, 120° and 180° from the perspective of the initial house position. However, their reference is from the standpoint of a 360° circle. To continue in that fashion, the aspects are delineated by the actual degree of separation from the original point of departure. In this fashion, 270° is ten house segments from the first house, counting the long way around the circle, but only 90° the short way (counting from the 12th).

The aspect that moves away from the opposition becomes the next form of **quincunx** in the eighth house. The quincunx of 150° is like "seeking appreciation." It is an aspect that reflects the willingness to do anything for recognition. Counting from the Ascendant, this aspect is actually 210° from its point of origin. Our young man has become infused with the quality of his own ability and who is no longer *seeking* but *receiving* offers for work from others in his chosen field. The dilemma of this quincunx is that it has to solve problems through the process of deciding who he wants to work with. With this aspect, he often, but not always, seeks out others who are somewhat better than he but still recognize his abilities. In this manner our hero renders his work as part of a team effort, affording all to appear at their best. As an eighth house aspect, the 210° angle allows him to fine tune his ability as a partner with his peers whom he sought after in the 150° quincunx. This process can be viewed much like an actor looking for work (150° quincunx). When work is found (180° opposition), rehearsing the play (210° quincunx) follows.

From our initial zero point, the 225° aspect is the next **sesquiquadrate.** It is an eighth house position (may be seen as 135° starting from the Ascendant and counting backward through the 12th house). This aspect relates to the chaotic bee-hive like activity often seen in last minute preparations on opening night in the theater. The curtain rises as the returning trine of 240° from our initial starting point presents itself. The *ninth house* **trine** is the successful staging of our hero's ability with and among his peers. This trine, which is 240° (or 120°, depending on your point of view), is his next confidence builder. This is the "lucky break" or substantial promotion and, with this aspect, our hero widens his subjective perception of himself in a positive manner. He begins showcasing his abilities to an ever-widening appreciative audience and eventually, to the outside world.

The approaching tenth house **square** is the next major decision our protagonist makes. After his successful trine, he will now decide whether to stay in his current position or strike out on his own. In the lower 90° square, only a short amount of time has been spent and the decision was either to stay and develop his talent or start something new. With the 270° upper square, our hero has spent a serious amount of time in his profession and the decision must be carefully analyzed to create the best circumstances to further himself. He must now decide to what extent he is willing to exploit his efforts against his ethics. This square fully tests his belief in his ability to define success and what it means to him personally. Either way a decision will be made!

Once the decision to move on or stay becomes final, the next aspect is the eleventh house **sextile.** This 300° (or 60° depending on which house you start from) aspect is boastful. In the *earlier sextile,* moving away *from* the Ascendant or beginning point, initiates the opportunity to learn about a project or profession. This upper sextile is moving *toward* the Ascendant and creates opportunities for large projects using his previous experience as leverage and as a consultant. This sextile generates a feeling of expertise and exploitation to it.

Finally, the twelfth house **semi-sextile** of 330° is approaching the Ascendant or our initial point, as well as being nostalgic in nature. This aspect brings past experiences to light in the form of news items or gossip. Once again, he is reminded about his talent, but for his past accomplishments.

As the preceding story's show, any and all careers reflect these paths. However, it can be likened to one's own life path as well. In a manner of speaking, if we recognize and start with planetary conjunctions before we were born, we recognize that we begin our life with a set of aspects already under way by the time we are born. We "come in" during the play, in a manner of speaking. A lifestyle may be determined by the planetary aspects located by house sign and ruler ship positions alone, which in many cases is what contemporary astrologers do. In the case of being born with planets in square aspect, an individual may start many projects without seeing them through to completion because of distractions indicated by whatever planets are square. Or the individual may *take over* projects others have begun. However, as a person matures, the square aspect can develop into recognizing pitfalls and, if this were the case, the square becomes contingency plans in projects. As we can see, apects can define an individual's character, which is why the circular diagram with its angular relationships became so popular.

The most important point however, is that the planets and aspects can reflect *any circumstance* and it is up to the astrologer to recognize this fact and use it accordingly.

Many feel that horoscopic astrology covers the entire ontology of the planet. In this context, astrology is seen as the panacea of life and, as astrologers, we are supposed to cover all the variables but not unless we have college degrees in each area reflected by all the house meanings. My advice is to become a specialist in a given arena. Areas of special interest may include the positions of the Ascendant or Moon in the sunset chart or the planet with the highest degree of longitude and its house placement in the birth chart. Develop your aptitude by doing your homework. Become an investigative astrologer and develop your own unique astrological vocabulary and expertise. Research a specific arena in which you are interested! Soon you will find the planetary experience that works for you and your specialized field of interest. After all, astrology *is* for you...the astrologer.

The 30° Wheel or Stack

The next step is to recognize that no planet is ever less than zero degrees (0°) or exceeds 29° 59' by longitude regardless of the sign they are located (unless you use the Right Ascension). At any rate, list the planets by placing the highest degree on top of the list and working down to the lowest degree. Disregard the signs and houses for now. Once listed, the arrangement is divided into three groups similar to the decanates. Group one ranges from 0° to 10°; group two ranges from 10° 01' to 20°; group three is from 20° 01' to 29° 59'. Each group or decanate designates one of three main departments of life experience.

The first decanate represents the existential package that makes us uniquely us: our circumstances, talents, parental influence, and aptitudes. Planets located in this department are what we draw upon to reference our motives and categorize our experiences. Sometimes an individual has no planets placed here, such as Gandhi. An empty first decanate does not mean that there is no identity, but that the individual is more prone to work the middle section as their identity package. For these individuals, change is the hallmark of their lives. They are able to take in stride the changes in their lives. The type of changes depends on planetary placement.

The second or middle decanate reflects change and how we respond to it. Planets found within this arena are the schools we attend–the circumstances or obstacles that seem to keep us from advancing or the school of hard knocks. Once surmounted, they give us the insight and courage to achieve our goals. If this section is vacant, it generally describes an individual who has the "Midas touch." He simply moves from his personal ideas to achieving his goals without the hassle of having to fight for it.

The last ten-degree segment reflects the ideal or goals we seek. Planets so placed are what inspire us. The closer to the 29° mark, the more we will work for it. We are in a hurry to get there but reluctant to leave, for we want to savor the experience of late degree planets. A lack of planets, or a vacant position here indicates that the individual may be content with his lifestyle and not want to move beyond his present position. In this case the middle section becomes the goal with changes as the ideal. Without late degree planets, we often see people with "nomadic" lifestyles, whose ephemeral interests are dictated by transiting planets.

In addition, the stack arrangement allows us to further review the planets by intensity and modification. This is called the tri-planet configuration or triad. Each planet placed in the stack is between two other planets. In this method we can easily grasp how to judge the middle planet. This is done by degree. The closer a planet is to another by degree, the more influence it exerts. Conversely, the farther away it is, the less influence. The upper planet is seen as a positive influence, the lower more negative. For example, let us use Mars as the middle planet with Jupiter and Venus as the planets above and below. In our example, Jupiter will be the higher planet and Venus the lower planet. Should Mars be closer to Jupiter by degree, it will exert more of what is called "heart", similar to the will to win in the field of sports. If they are favorably aspected in the chart, there is a determination to finish what one has started. Conversely if they are negatively aspected. Should Mars be closer to the softened or compassionate subtleties of Venus, Mars becomes decidedly artistic, joyful and harmonious, even more so with good aspects. The artistic nature may look to the larger picture for expression. However, the lower Venus influence may indicate disappointment in an artistic field, either by commission or omission.

Other Influences

When looking at two individual charts for the purpose of compatibility, the stack presents a quick, no holds barred overview. Place each stack side by side and note which planets align by degree with each other and in what areas. The person with higher planets by degree, either in a section or the overall chart, has more control or influence in the relationship. More on this later.

The solar return may be used in the same manner. Set up a solar return chart based on your time of birth and place the planets that are near or on the same degree as the planets in your natal stack. DO, however, note the Moon's position at sunset and relate its rate of motion along with first and last aspect within 24 hours. The planets that align by degree will be the major influences for that year. A daily stack on the day(s) of the lunar return, giving a monthly overview, can also yield some interesting dividends. Daily influences can be watched in the same manner. It is important to keep a log of results during each solar, lunar and daily period. Gambling successes have been recorded within two to one hour(s) before the exact moment of the lunar return. This has proved to be very successful in many cases, the *exception* being when Saturn, Mars or, in some cases, Jupiter is *conjoined* by transit or progression to the natal Moon. The daily stack has to confirm to an auspicious time in synastry with the birth chart, such as similar planets in similar house positions or by favorable aspects to natal house (not necessarily sign) positions. Remember that the lunar return has proven to be the most beneficial time to start any endeavor with the exceptions mentioned above.

The Moon's Position and Lunar Mansion

Additionally, there is another interesting point concerning the Moon: the lunar mansion, a topic that has mysteriously disappeared into anonymity. Generally described, it is a 12° division of the zodiac or the distance the Moon travels in 24 hours. It can be very illuminating to determine the exact degree of the lunar mansion in your chart. Its importance stems from the notion that the first and last aspect made by the Moon imprints your emotional demeanor.

The Chaldeans described their every day life as running a 24-hour course from sunset to sunset. The very life of a Chaldean priest hung in the balance of his skilled interpretations of those periods. For this reason the Moon's daily progressive motion was recorded with the utmost of care. Planetary associations with the Moon were then interpreted and delivered to the king as the format for the following daylight hours. The procedure began anew at the next sunset.

The key to finding the lunar mansion in your chart lies in charting an equal house system cast for sunset of the previous day of your birth, if you were born *after* midnight. What we are looking for is the rate of motion the Moon traveled between sunset to sunset starting on or before the date of your birth. Check your chart and notice if the Sun is in the sixth, fifth or fourth house. This indicates that you were born *before* midnight. If this is the case, then cast a chart for sunset (Sun on the seventh house cusp) *on* the *same date* the day you were born . If you were born *after* midnight, with the Sun located in the third house, second, first etc., then cast the chart for sunset using the day and date before your birth.

The Moon's motion during the entire 24-hour period prior to your birth supplies you with your lunar mansion. When viewed as a *time* chart, the completed 24-hour sunset-to-sunset chart is the equivalent of 72 years. The Moon's general rate of motion in this context is equal to one degree every six years (see the chapter on the Moon for further details).

The Sun normally traverses 12 houses in 24 hours. This means that the Sun takes two hours to travel 30° or through an entire house. The Moon travels one degree every two hours, *or* for every house through which the Sun travels, the Moon advances by one degree. Starting at sunset, the Sun will travel in an apparent clockwise direction, that is, from the seventh house cusp to the sixth house cusp and so on. The Sun's clockwise motion through the houses describes the process of growth that you experience as you pass through each house cusp and angle. From the seventh to the sixth house describes the first six years of life; from the sixth to the fifth house cusp reflects the next six years or to twelve years old; and the process continues (see Sun chapter).

As the Moon advances one degree for each six years of life, the fourth house cusp represents the eighteenth year of life. Thus, the Moon will have advanced three degrees. Continuing this process, we find the cusp of the first house is your 36-year point at which time the Moon has advanced three more degrees for a total of six degrees. It is in this manner that the 24-hour period of your birth describes 72 years of your life! The Moon's 12-degree advancement sets the general undertone of the entire life experience. The changing house positions describe the departmental influences. Thus, at the age of 18, the entire chart has set up as a square to the original sunset chart. The angles reflect life changes, challenges and their results.

To reiterate, this style of lunar mansion falls into a new dimension of astrology. The entire 24-hour period on the day you were born, starting with the previous sunset, equates to 72 years. Thus, each house is equivalent to six years of life. For example, a birth time is early in the morning with the Sun in the third house indicating that the birth was *after* midnight and we find the Moon is 18 degrees Taurus. To find the Moon's sunset placement, go back to the previous sunset on the day/date *before* the birth time because our example birth is after midnight. In this case, the Moon will go *back* approximately four degrees because we are using the *previous* sunset. The *new position* of the Moon will be approximately 14° Taurus depending on its rate of motion. Cast another chart for sunset for *the same date* of your birth and calculate the Moon's motion for the next 24 hours. This is done by subtracting the Moon's previous position by degree of longitude (14° Taurus) from the following Moon position (26° Taurus) and you have the complete lunar mansion by degree. The average motion is 12-1/2°. We add this to the 14° Taurus we found at sunset for a total of 26°, which you probably would have found had you cast a chart for the following date. The example personal lunar mansion then is between 14 and 26 degrees of Taurus. The next step would be to note the first and last aspect made by the Moon and to what planet within the set parameters of 14° and 26°.

Every six years the Moon advances one degree starting with the Moon's position at sunset, and it becomes the underlying factor that explains compulsions that come into our lives without any other astrological clue. These factors are rarely revealed or recognized in standard Tropical charts. Often, transits in contact with your progressed lunar mansion position activate these strange circumstances that, again, are not otherwise visible. Of course, there is more to the Chaldean charting system and the following chapters will cover these concepts more explicitly.

Conclusion

In my experience, I find that the mathematical expression of longitude for the Sidereal zodiac is more accurate, this method is NOT at all satisfactory using the Tropical positions. Those of you who have worked in Tropical and switched to the Sidereal method will attest that it is hard to return to the Tropical way of doing business. If you are just starting out, have your chart done by one of the many charting organizations. Both charts look similar, but that is where the similarity ends. The Tropical chart is different by 24° 30' from the Sidereal chart. This is almost a complete constellation and the difference of Tropical planetary positions by degree of longitude or sign do not correspond with this work. This difference between zodiacs accounts for many problems astrologers have who use Sidereal methods in the Tropical form (solar returns, lunar returns, and the like). In this book, often you will read the word *sign* in place of the word constellation. This is used for the sake of brevity and does not refer to the Tropical zodiac unless stated. The constellations have the same name as Tropical *signs,* but Sidereal astrologers use them much differently.

My first 17 years as an astrologer led me down many blind alleys; blind because I wanted to believe in what I spent so much time learning. It became painfully apparent when I could not read my own chart with confidence. For the past 25 years, by careful study of ancient myths which are also the foundation of today's astrological beliefs, I developed a method of astrology without the wheel. I have deduced certain precepts which you are about to read. You will learn that you can use these precepts to predict the *timing* of everyday events or life-changing trends. During my research I have tried to find a completely neutral paradigm with which I could test these remarkable techniques, the most reliable and financially beneficial elements were derived from tests conducted at racetracks and casinos.

This work is not intended to replace the birth chart but to further support it. The ingenious system of casting the horoscope (Greek *horoscopos)* for the exact hour an astronomer wanted to chart the heavens, created the Ascendant as the basis for chart construction. It was originally intended as a tool for horary astrology (of the hour) and has become the astrological capstone that emerged from Greece. Although it was discovered at a much later date, it represents Greece's finest contribution to the art of astrology. As a horary tool, the time-of-Ascendant chart or the horoscope, answers questions set up for the particular moment when the question is asked. This is a wonderful form of predictive astrology. This technique is so powerful that the name and style of *horoscope chart* has lasted over the centuries as the form that astrologers still use for genethliacal purposes today.

Each of the following chapters is sufficient to give you, the reader, plenty of information to work with in each specific field of interest. As an admixture, they present a complete multi-dimensional perspective never before experienced with chart interpretation! We will then compare various contemporary techniques with the sunset-skymap technique and test our results in that fashion. With a little imagination you can then further explore and develop the sunset-skymap technique to your own fashion and liking.

But for now, let us jump back in time and locate pieces of the puzzle the ancients used to view the heavenly oracle. In part two we will explore the origins of terms and customs of the Babylonian and Egyptian cultures. It is through these ideas that we have discovered a new and different type of astrology that has been buried in the mists of time until now. With diligent research on your part, I am sure this work will inspire you, the serious student, to use it extensively.

CHAPTER 3

THE SUN

Do more than look, observe.

Many astrologers appoint the Sun as the native's chief significator in the chart. So with today's approach, anyone born on or after July 23 or before August 22, has the Sun in the sign of Leo. Secondly, if the Moon was located in Pisces it will have an *overtone* of Leo. However, if the native is born at night or the Moon is placed in a elevated position it is the stronger of the two. Then, the Pisces Moon carries the *undertone* of the Leo Sun sign. This same idea generally applies to the rest of the planets. This formula has basically evolved from the Ptolemaic discovery of the horary chart. Tropical astrology uses the Sun to indicate the person and their ego needs and to tell the native's general disposition by sign and house placement.

The sunset chart focuses on the Sun in rather a different fashion; it's the "time focus" around the wheel. We rotate the entire sunset chart in a clockwise manner using the Sun as the significator of age at the rate of five degrees of solar arc for each year of life. The rotating planetary positions will aspect themselves and describe our ever-changing life pattern, which in turn reflects the changes we experience while remaining in congruity with our sense of who we are in the birth chart.

The major difference is that we use the same chart based on the entire 24-hour period of the day of birth as well as the chart for the time of birth when available. In the Sunset chart, at the time of an event we, too, place a fixed point on the horizon but it never stays "fixed in place." It remains in motion as do our lives. The Sun indicates the various *times* in our lives by its changing position, just as the Sun indicates the hour during the 24-hour day. By rotating the sunset chart, we can designate not only an Ascendant, but an ever changing Ascendant to reflect the changes in our personality and our many changing viewpoints based on the changing position of the entire chart. In this fashion we can denote our life's experiences astrologically, all based on the original event–the sunset before birth.

This book discusses only the *Sidereal calculations* for the zodiac using the equal house system. The Tropical zodiac is ineffective using this method. To set up Sidereal charts, simply set your computer to Sidereal calculation; the Sun should be conjunct the seventh house cusp (actual sunset is preferable). If you do not have a computer, a quick, near accurate method for converting a chart from Tropical to Sidereal is to add six degrees to all the planetary degrees (including the houses) in the Tropical chart and fall back one sign. Thus, 14° Taurus in the Tropical chart becomes 20° Aries in the Sidereal chart and so forth.

The Chaldean Sunset Chart

The Chaldeans were simple and direct. They combined only seven planets against the patterns of stars. The timing of rising, culminating and setting for different planets and asterisms gave Chaldean observers the information they needed to establish their omens. They did this without using any elaborate house system. Yet the Chaldeans were famed throughout the world as the masters of the heavenly oracle.

In reflection of this thought, we also want to be simple and direct. The sunset chart method recognizes that each complete house, consisting of 30°, is equal to a six-year period. Therefore, when timing events, especially at the moment transits or rogressions are being considered, the cusps of the *equal house* system provide a quicker "read" than any other house system. The equal house wheel is a *time oriented* device only.

The general overview is that we want to start from the point of sunset which is symbolically represented by the seventh house cusp. To readily see the aspects between the planets, we use a biWheel chart system with the exact same sunset positions in each chart. We then rotate the smaller chart inside the larger in a clockwise manner (into the sixth house then the fifth and so on). Rotating the smaller chart clockwise within the larger is called **rogression**. *Each house has the value of six years.* The *equal house* system is used for mathematical ease to discern the "age of the native" during an event. This will be further explained in the following paragraphs. For now, cast a biWheel chart for sunset.

Setting Up the Sunset Chart

If you were born between sunset and midnight (Sun in the sixth, fifth or fourth house), calculate the chart for the *same* date. If you were born *after* midnight but before sunset, calculate the chart for sunset on the *previous* date. When the chart is calculated properly, the Sun will be placed on or near the seventh house cusp by degree of longitude. If you have a computer, cast a chart for sunset and duplicate it. Then call up the biWheel and print two copies. Cut out the smaller chart from one print-out and place it in the center of the other.

For those of you who do not have a biWheel format in your program, follow these instructions. Make two copies of the sunset chart and size one smaller so it will fit inside the larger chart, similar to the biWheel. Cut out the smaller chart and place it inside the larger chart. Make sure that the smaller chart is small enough to see the planets in both charts. Find the center of both charts and align the angles (first, fourth, tenth and seventh) to each other making sure that the Suns in both the larger and smaller charts line up on the seventh house cusp. You are now ready to rogress the chart.

We determine the timing of an event by advancing the smaller chart's Sun's position clockwise through the houses by solar arc. The average rate of motion for the Sun is one degree every 24-hours. Using this as the frame work for motion, 25' of solar arc in real time is equal to one month of rogression. Continuing; 1° 15' of solar arc is equal to 90 days and 5° of solar arc equals one year. Each house is equal to six years and each quadrant is equal to eighteen years of life. If you have access to a chart with 360 degree "hash marks" so much the better to distinguish exact aspects. The house meaning is read as you would any other chart except that you now have two indicators for each house: the sunset matrix and the moving inner chart as it travels within the matrix.

Some students have placed their birth chart inside the biWheel charts and, in effect, created a triWheel system. The biWheel sunset chart indicates timing while the birth chart shows the arena of events directly related to the individual through the birth chart.

The Birth Experience

On the day a baby is born, the entire 24-hour period becomes the whole potential for the time of birth. The circumstances that babies require for their lifetime are noted on the previous sunset of the date of birth. When the "right time" is determined by the child, the birth process begins. The time of birth coupled with the sunset chart is important because of the configuration of the planetary locations between the sunset and birth chart. The sunset chart becomes a fixed reference point that determines the base catalogue of an individual's "planetary DNA *experience* patterns" denoted on the day of the birth. It sets the stage. The birth chart indicates the location that experience will occur on the "stage" set by the sunset chart. The combined charts indicate the quality and *type of expression* the native will experience in his life by virtue of the planetary placement of the birth chart in relation to the sunset chart.

A note on Caesarean section births. Both Rudolph Steiner, the famous turn-of-the-century Christian mystic, and Edgar Cayce, "the sleeping prophet," often mentioned that the incoming soul knows well in advance the circumstances it will experience in its incarnation regardless of the length of time in the physical expression. It has been often cited by many spiritual and metaphysical leaders that the child "chooses his parents" for the purpose of their unique lifestyle and gene pool. This is a touchy subject at best but, in my opinion, one that should be looked at with a metaphysical viewpoint. My position is that the mother and child have entered into an agreement at the moment of conception. Whatever happens from that moment on, both the mother and child consent. If indeed we accept the notion that the soul has come here to experience life through the process of linear time, and is in agreement with its parents, then it may be *necessary* to either induce labor or extract the fetus through Caesarean section to comply with the chart of the day and the hour of birth.

Regardless of the type of birth process, one's life is still revealed by rogressing the planetary expressions within the 24-hour diurnal chart. This double chart system is like a compatibility chart for the baby and the outside world. It is the pattern on which he will base his reactions to the objective world for the rest of his life! Thus, by looking at aspects between both charts, we find the inherent propensity of planetary energies that will indicate and determine a deeper more meaningful expression for the native.

Rule. The integration between the planets' position on the previous sunset to their positions at the time of birth creates a basic aspect that is tantamount for forecasting events in each life.

What to Expect

Using th. Sun as an indicator and starting from the seventh house cusp, rotate the smaller chart into the sixth house clockwise using the rate of five degrees for each year. *As we rotate the inner chart clockwise, we relate past experiences by planetary aspects between both charts.*

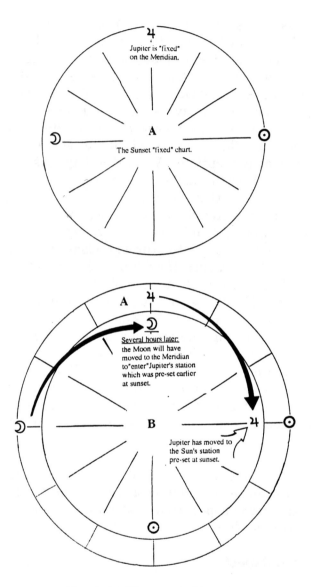

Figure 3.1 The sunset chart.
We have hypothetically placed Jupiter on the MC with the Moon
rising. By rogressing chart "B" three houses, we place the Sun on
the Nadir with Jupiter conjoining the sunset Sun's position and
the Moon conjoining Jupiter's sunset position

As the planets aspected *their own positions or each other*, we make note of subtle changes in their meaning as they pertain to us and our experiences (or how they described your client's past experiences). In this way we find how to personalize and relate the meaning of the planets through the expression of circumstances by aspects. One of the more exciting revelations with the sunset chart is how the events associated with the same aspect change in the rogressed chart. Planets rogressing or transiting your natal positions will, at some level, mimic earlier experiences later in life. The different levels of experience are indicated by the planet's house positions as we rotate the inner chart.

As the life progresses, planetary aspects in the early stages in one's development tend to reverse their influence later in life. They seem to change from "youthful" to "mature" aspects. Youthful aspects are like childhood diseases. They are simply experienced as events while mature aspects are seen as contingency plans or opportunities, depending on the aspect.

Squares at an early age indicate distractions, disturbances or obstructions which get in the way of achieving objectives. Hopefully, these frustrations teach the child how to recognize and prepare to avoid them later in life.

The consequences of those early aspects are not really judged but assimilated. During young adulthood, square aspects are uncomfortable choices generally concerning new directions and, more likely, they often determine distractions. With mature aspects there is more forethought. We are faced with making conscious decisions and, hopefully, are aware of the possible consequences of our acts. This is especially true by the time the rogressed planets reach an opposition to their original sunset configuration (age 36).

In both cases decisions must be made. Later in life, as an adult, squares can be seen as contingencies in a worst case scenario and with provisions for such circumstances they become useful in planning short-and long-term objectives. Trines and sextiles represent experiences that are taken for granted.

Aging the Chart

As we all know, the vernal equinox appears to move backwards against the backdrop of constellations at the rate of one degree every 72 years. Chaldean astrologers were aware of this motion. We know it as the precession of the equinoxes. We base our astrological ages such as, "the age of Pisces," or "the age of Aquarius," on the retrograde motion of the vernal point. The Egyptians and Chaldeans both referred to this motion as the Law of 72, a mathematical number that covered a multitude of synchronistic, rhythmic circumstances.

The most interesting fact is that the rate of 72 oscillations per minute falls exactly on the midpoint of a chart which scales all observed vibrational periodicity's, from ultrasonic, subatomic vibrations to galactic rhythmic frequencies. At the very center of all these frequencies lies our heartbeat, placing us at the center of the vibrating cosmos. The Egyptian pictogram of the "heart shaped" plumb-bob epitomizes this very thought, giving us further insight into the depth of their understanding of the thematic substructure of their philosophy of nature and spirit.

Taking this to the next step, this rule can also apply to the general statistical averages of man's approximate life span of seventy-two years (although we know any given individual may die at any age). Using this principle we divide 360° by 72°. The result is five degrees. This is why we age the chart or advance the inner wheel clockwise by five degrees of solar arc for each year of life.

As stated above, the rate of five degrees of solar arc is equal to one year of life. Each house consisting of 30° represents six years of life. Using the equal house system allows us to quickly and visually calculate the aging points between planets. For example, if planet "A" is 35° from planet "B," then at the rate of five degrees per year, it takes planet "A" seven years by rogression to reach planet "B." At that time an event will take place related by the nature of the interacting planets. Described below is the method for aging the native in the chart, it is based on the Babylonian universal "Law of 72" which also corresponds to Fagan's pentade theory.

Rule: The outer sunset chart is the *fixed* reference. The rogression refers to a double sunset chart matrix. One chart is placed inside the other and *rotated clockwise* to determine the age of a client during an event. The age rate equates to the Sun's solar arc of five degrees for each year of life.

This clockwise rotation of the inner chart, called rogression, equates the age by degree to the various experiences noted by the positions of the planets throughout the entire chart. Major events are recognized when the placement of any planet on the smaller chart comes into contact with planets in the outer sunset matrix chart, either by sextile, square, trine or any other aspect the astrologer finds important.

The standard meaning of the house positions remains the same and intact. All planets currently transiting through the houses keep their contemporary meanings and are judged by their positions in both charts. That is, both the house position in the sunset chart *and* its advanced position in the "aged" rogressed inner chart, are used. In the case of adding the birth chart, forming the triWheel, all three are used in combination.

Any event experienced during childhood identifies the nature of the event by the planets involved, and often the planetary nature is not a textbook circumstance. From this, each planet can then be identified, and its personal experiential nature recognized for later events during the aging process.

Using the biWheel sunset chart and rotating the inner chart you can now analyze, sort and label your own "cosmic DNA experience." From this neutral fixed standpoint, the events are similar to tumblers in a combination lock. The *personal* planetary timing derived from rotating the chart clockwise staring *from the time of sunset* predicts the events for the entire lifetime within this 24-hour period. This procedure clearly indicates the association and timing of experiences by the planetary placements. It is important to interview the client and his events in the early years of his life using this method. You will find that *each planetary experience* always repeats itself by transit and rogression at later time periods.

For example, using only the biWheel sunset chart based on February 26, 1932 (the day before her actual birthday), Liz Taylor moved to America when she was seven years old. By rotating the inner chart Sun 35°, her rogressed Sun/Mercury was approaching Saturn. Although I have not read anything about the move, my guess is it was for health purposes. The reason I say this is because, from that moment on, any rogressed or transiting aspects to, or by Saturn, has seen her battling with some illness. It would be safe to say that anytime Saturn makes an aspect or is aspected by another planet she becomes ill. With her last hospital episode (February 27, 1998), she fell from a dizzy spell thereby knocking her unconscious. Transiting Neptune was conjoining her *natal* Saturn by eight minutes of arc and *transiting* Saturn conjoined her natal Uranus by three minutes of arc. There are other factors but this will suffice as our example.

This method relieves the astrologer's stress of timing future trends because upcoming trends can be readily seen from past experiences previously examined and noted. In this manner the sunset chart permits astrologers to forecast future events with complete confidence.

The house meaning is read as you would any other chart, except that you now have two indicators for each house: the sunset matrix and the moving inner sunset chart. As you rotate the smaller chart clockwise against the static larger one, notice that the houses and signs start to "play against each other," becoming a dual house system. This is extremely useful for determining answers to the most frequently asked questions; money, marriage, career and health.

For example, if a client asks about finding a new working situation. As an astrologer, we would ask the client what he thinks is the most important factor. Is it a career move? Check the 10th house sign in the sunset chart and note its new rogressed location. Is it just another job? Check the sixth house and its new rogressed location. The best money lies in the location of the rogressed second house. Watch for the rulers of each sign and their interplay as aspects, house positions, harmonious and inharmonious signs and transits as they do alter the chart. Astrologers who have worked with the sunset method have been astounded at the information they have been able to discover, even circumstances and events which were not found using conventional chart analysis.

House Meaning

Over many years, the major question has arisen; "How did each house come to be considered as a particular department of life; how was its influence recognized?" The natural placement of the Sun at sunset is on or about the seventh house cusp. For the next two hours in real time, its clockwise motion will carry it through the sixth house, two hours later the fifth house, then the fourth house and so on.

Rotating the Sun clockwise, start from the seventh house and rotate it into the **sixth house**, the entire sixth house represents the first six years of life. It represents the "toddler stage" where the child learned to not only walk and climb, but to do all the other wonderful yet distressing things one does while learning about life at this age. It is the house where all the childhood illnesses are worked through to create the necessary antibodies to ward off later infections. During this period, the child, in most cases, experiences close parental care, all in the house related to health and health-care. Any planets placed in this house at sunset indicate noteworthy experiences by the native which are not necessarily related to health.

Traveling clockwise from the sixth-house cusp through the **fifth house** represents years 6 through 12. This formative period relates to childhood peers (children) and stimulates the creative instincts. It is a period when one starts being a "child of experience." With the onset of self-awareness the child learns how to become a social animal through schooling and other things children do during this time. It is very likely that the child will experience (parents aside) his first crush on someone of the opposite sex.

Moving on, from the fifth house cusp through the **fourth house** relates to the twelfth year through the eighteenth year. During this period the child moves into adolescence and becomes more aware of his roots and responsibilities. The fourth house represents the age where one becomes a young adult and begins to examine his place in the outside world. All the while the adolescent considers leaving the "home ties" for independence and exploration.

By the eighteenth year the Sun has reached the fourth house cusp and enters the **third house**. This is *a major angle* and the first square to the sunset Sun's position. Objectively, and at an early age, squares are indicative of distractions that move us from one sphere of influence to another. During this period the young adult may decide to leave home and venture into a different lifestyle. This new lifestyle may be college, a new job, joining the service or even getting married. Leaving the fourth house cusp we find our adolescent "coming of age" during his next six years. Whatever choices he made during his first square, he must now learn to live with. In the third house he learns new and different ways of thinking and communicating, all connected with his new lifestyle.

By the time he is twenty-four years old, the Sun has reached the **second house** and we find the young adult has become a college graduate, or a young spouse with children, or is experiencing new possibilities within the workplace. He has become firmly fixed on his values and begins to really concentrate on his money-making abilities. This is the period where self-reliance, serious responsibilities and earlier values taught at home are put to the test

By thirty years of age, the Sun has reached the **first house.** During this time he will develop a strong sense of identity as he continues to develop his lifestyle. For the next six years he will examine his personal motives, maturing further in his character and sets his sights on furthering his ambition and career. This is an important period to the native and often major changes take place between twenty-nine to thirty-two years of age. All the planets throughout the entire chart is in opposition to their sunset position.

By or about the age of thirty-six, his Sun has reached the sunset **Ascendant** and is in opposition to the seventh house sunset Sun. The sunset Ascendant represents one's core being, the innermost ideal one fantasizes about. Relating to a play or motion picture, it is the character with whom we identify. Often, a reliable clue to this "secret self" is the type of books one is interested in reading. This position in the chart symbolically represents the "dawn" of our life. Many aspiring leaders of the past have often written their manifesto during this time. It can be a very deep and often a soul-searching period.

By thirty-six years of age he reaches the gateway to the **twelfth house.** He begins to recognize values about himself that he never before realized. During the next six years something in him stirs and he suddenly understands that the old rules he has lived by all these years are outdated and no longer apply. He sees himself in the light where more universal principles seem to apply. He now views his life in terms of a broader scope. New horizons are visualized and the entire lifestyle he was living is now in complete jeopardy as his new insights and experiences spur him on to new objectives.

By the time he has reached forty-two, the Sun has rogressed from the twelfth house and is now entering the **eleventh house**. The former years of rediscovering himself have led him to recognize his own mortality. During this period he tries to recapture and relive the years of his youth. He may sell the sedan he has driven for the past few years and buy a sports car; thinning hair and weight gain may become enough of a problem to urge him to be more aware of his physical fitness. He becomes concerned with attracting "the right people" and being seen with them. His chief concern is to find friends who will help him achieve his hopes, wishes and desires.

As he enters the **tenth house**, he is forty-eight years old. Having acquired his eleventh house resources, he can now focus on his professional status and how he may gain a more powerful position among his peers. During this period, he is now concerned with how he may become a distinctive entity and set himself apart, not only from his friends, but the rest of the group in his age bracket.

By age fifty-four, the Sun has reached the upper square position to his sunset Sun. The rogressed Sun enters the **ninth house**. His innermost thoughts may turn to religion, personal spiritual values or forms of altruism. He may want to right some of the wrongs he believes he may have committed in his earlier, carefree years. By now he has become entrenched in his world and has learned the specialized techniques of his profession and lifestyle. He feels that he is in his "prime" years, where he is old enough to know better about dangerous ventures but still young enough to be tempted. The danger lies in his becoming pompous, as he will now want to express his views to colleagues and perhaps the world. During this period he may write his memoirs about his life's work.

As the rogressed Sun reaches the **eighth house**, he is now sixty years old and feels that he is at the pinnacle of his "game." His major concerns are how he is perceived by those he feels are significant people in his world, and to maintain his "position" and uphold his principles. Facing inevitable retirement, his main fear is becoming extinct in his field. In his mind it is clear that the bottom line is that he will have to eventually step down from his position. Even so, he insists on "being of some use" to those who will replace him. But through his resistance to leave, he is contemplating "doing all the frivolous things he always wanted to do" that might also be enjoyable. Hobbies may emerge as avocations.

By the age of sixty-six, the Sun has rogressed into the **seventh house**. This transition may bring about widowhood. Often he hears about some colleague or friend who has passed away and this saddens him. Health concerns have become a part of his daily routine as well as maintaining contacts with those he still admires. The years have gone by all too fast. He is now retired and he pursues new interests with a renewed zeal.

By the age of seventy-two, the Sun has completely rogressed through the entire wheel. Having come full circle there is a form of "second childhood" that takes place as the rogressed Sun enters the sixth house for the second time. Although health concerns have become issues, he realizes that life goes on.

Solar Birth to Sunset Positions

The section on aging the chart describes the life process as the Sun is rogressed through each house. If the time of birth is unknown, understanding the nature of the Sun regarding its position in each house is a good indicator of where the Sun might be placed at the time of birth. At times, and coupled with good reasoning power, chart rectification can be accomplished by recognizing this factor and by how the client responds to the circumstances in his life. More seasoned astrologers might easily recognize energy patterns the native exhibits by understanding this procedure. One process of rectifying a chart is that an astrologer can approximate the birth time by using the sunset chart as the base matrix. Question the client about his lifestyle. Is he aggressive? Place the Sun near the first or tenth angle. Is he passive? Place the Sun near the seventh or the Nadir. Does he like to teach? Maybe his Sun is in the third or ninth house. This type of questioning alerts us as an indication, at least by quadrant, what the approximate birth time might be. With further examination we may discern, quite appropriately, the approximate location of the Sun's placement in the birth chart.

Using the sunset method not only supports conventional astrological processes, but the astrologer can easily accumulate a great deal of knowledge from just the sunset positions. In many cases chart rectification has been a real will-of-the-wisp process for many astrologers. Additionally, with only an approximate time of birth, an astrologer can easily rectify the chart within a few minutes of the actual birth time. This is done by first determining the "type" of Sun a person expresses by its probable house position (which will be discussed in the next portion of this chapter), followed by the timing of an incident using the age method. When a rogressed planet (or Sun) reaches an aspect to a planet activating an incident, match the incident with the "type" of house related to the event with the sun in the triWheel placed in the appropriate house. There is a good possibility that the chart can be "backed up" to the sunset position for a reasonable birth time.

Rule to remember. When working with the sunset chart, we use the equation $360° \div 72° = 5°$. To age a chart, advance the Sun in the inner wheel clockwise by five degrees of solar arc for each year of life. Each house represents six years of life, and using the equal house system gives a "quick look" to discern approximate ages at which events will occur. A 90-day period is equal to 1° 15' of solar arc. Thus, the average solar arc rate of motion of real time is 25' per month. Planets located by house imply *events or experiences related by degree to the age by years*. Questioning the client about significant events that coincide with time periods in relation to the planetary locations in the chart will further aid the astrologer in determining future events.

On one level with the sunset charting method, the entire chart is the person in the horoscope. At another level, it becomes the chart of the event the person in the horoscope experiences.

Comparing the Birth and Sunset Charts

Now cast an equal house biWheel chart for the actual birth time and place the smaller birth chart *inside* the larger sunset chart. This is crucial! *Judge the position* of the planets in the birth chart *in relation to the sunset chart.* Notice how the planets aspect each by house placement and by their general planetary positions. Viewed from this perspective, the seeming conjunctions and other aspects are a clue as to why you chose that particular moment to be born. It also gives an insight to your particular destiny.

This may also be accomplished by either placing a *transparency* of the birth chart over the sunset chart and aligning the two Ascendants. If the birth Sun is conjunct the fourth house cusp, the overall birth position to the sunset chart is in square aspect. If the Sun is on the Ascendant at birth, then the charts are in opposition to each other and so on.

The placement of the birth chart in comparison to the sunset chart indicates your *personal* astrological energies as they apply to only you. In this fashion we eliminate the idea that any planet has a distinct "set meaning." And, at the same time, we find out whether or not the planets are "*in* or *out* of sync" with each other. To be in sync is harmonious and easy going. Out of sync has a sense of agitation, misdirection, frustration and/or extravagance, depending upon the charts and their angular positions to each other.

Planets that are in negative aspect to each other, such as Mars squaring its own position from the birth chart to the sunset position, indicate that the Mars energy pattern will be expressed in a negative fashion or until the individual recognizes that the pattern of behavior is not beneficial for success (unless his idea of success is antagonism or pugilism). In a square pattern there is a need for easy aspects to assist him toward a successful life venture. On the other hand, birth planets that are easy, such as a trine or sextile to their sunset positions, show the native will use his energies with ease. There is a need for "hard aspects" to help stimulate the individual into a successful life venture.

Natives with trines and sextiles between their birth and sunset charts need inter-chart squares (either in the birth or sunset chart) to get out of the state of ennui and into a more aggressive mode of activity. Those born with trines and sextiles to sunset planets generally are referred to as "late starters" because they find themselves experiencing "a little more of life" before settling down to the serious application of a career.

When rogressing a chart, pay close attention to the position of the Sun in the birth chart. The Sun's position by house and degree indicates the age of great change marked by a flash of sudden insight or increased awareness. This insight may lead to a deeper search for self-understanding through the house in which the Sun is located. Often the native leaves his present circumstances and changes into a new lifestyle. Generally speaking, natives born with the Sun located from the third to eleventh house either get married or divorced during this time.

In the section above, we discussed the house meanings as we rogressed the chart through them. In this section we want to analyze the Sun's position with the time of birth in relation to the sunset Sun. It is recommended that you exercise your observational powers and look at the energy level of the person for whom you are doing a chart. The position of the birth Sun, compared to the position of the sunset Sun, signifies, by aspect to itself, a planetary description: a quality of life based on the aspect between the two charts. This can be referenced as a **"type"** of personality trait. Each position is explained as if the Sun were on the house cusps.

For instance, for an individual born two hours after sunset, the Sun is on the sixth house cusp in **semi-sextile** position. The birth Sun position is 30° from the sunset Sun and indicates an information-seeking lifestyle, where there are never enough answers. In this position one feels less informed, making it difficult to move or get started. It is a life with many associations, and there is a friendly energy flow. When an individual's time of birth is close to sunset, the energies are somewhat similar to the sunset pattern thereby reflecting world events but more so of the local area. Sunset births generally follow the trends set by their generation. They will either work hard to set examples indicated by their generation (Sun in the sixth house position) or will find assistance from those in power to do so (Sun at birth located either in the eighth or sixth house position). This reflects the age of six. At times, the client is unaware of the circumstances preceding his birth. If this is the case, put him to work and have him ask his parents for the details about the period during his mother's pregnancy. You may be startled by the similarity between those circumstances and his experiences.

The birth Sun located 60° from the sunset Sun in **sextile** position indicates that there are many opportunities in this lifetime. The negative side may be that there is too much to do or too many irons in the fire. There is a love of children, an interest in creative or artistic endeavors; there is an easy energy flow. This relates to about the age of twelve.

Individuals with the birth Sun at 90° from the sunset Sun in **lower square** position feel vulnerable and are easily influenced. They need someone to need them. They seek associations with people for guidance (intense energy flow). People whose time of birth have the Sun placed on the Nadir are born with an energy square to the sunset pattern. Sometimes this will tell us about an enigmatic individual, one who seems at odds with, or does not understand, the trends of his generation. Early in life, individuals with Nadir Suns are shy and often unquestioningly follow the lead set by others. There may be a sense of vulnerability associated with this birth time. The native will have to learn to take care of himself before he can get on with life. The Nadir Sun position relates to the eighteenth year of life.

Those with the birth Sun at 120° from the sunset Sun in **lower trine** position can be a guiding light. They like to be informed so they may inform others. Here are people in the "know" who are glib and friendly. Their energy has an easy flow. These people are "quick studies" and learn rapidly. This position relates to the twenty-fourth year.

When the birth Sun is 150° from the sunset Sun in a **lower inconjunct** position, this life is one of constant re-organization. There is a need to either fix oneself or the outside world. There is also an understanding of values but difficulty in maintaining them, both externally and internally. There is an erratic flow. It relates to the thirtieth year.

Those with the birth Sun in **opposition** to the sunset Sun exemplify a willingness to go against the grain. We see rebellious, ambitious, calculating and designing people. Persons born with this are aware of their personable influence. There is an easy but intense flow. Sunrise is the opposition to the sunset position. This pattern indicates that later in life, the native will act against the prevailing movement of his generation and do things on his own terms. His focus is on redefining the circumstances with which he was born and change them according to a more personal Utopian ideal. This position relates to the thirty-sixth year.

Those with a birth Sun in the **upper inconjunct** position experience life similar to the lower inconjunct. Their re-organization of values pertains to living up to the standards of others more than the self. They often seek solitude for self reflection and to "straighten things out." This position relates to the forty-second year.

Upper trine: Similar to lower trine only its orientation is toward group activities rather than individual accomplishment. This position relates to an undertone of constant but friendly competition—a need to excel among peers. The native thinks it necessary to belong to social groups or clubs who will either benefit or further his desires. Often the native has many friends but there is a sense of expectancy or wanting and waiting. The individual is hopeful, positive and generally helpful toward his fellow man, energy flow has a quiet undertone. Relates to the forty-eighth year.

Upper square: This represents activity from the sense of position and power; one seeks and expects others to support his aims and ideals; recognizes what is needed in situations. The tenth house Sun is success oriented, the entire chart is in a tenth house square to itself. There is an innate sense of being in charge. In general, tenth house Suns are undaunted by failure and see it as a reason to continue rather than to quit a project. Energy flow can be demanding and intense, often there is a sense of "royalty" with the person who has this position which relates to the fifty-fourth year.

Upper sextile: Here we find a willingness to serve and share; selfless; recognizes the needs of others. There is a proud childlike bearing; sense of inherent kingly "rights;" seeks attention and recognition; looks to the future; exploitive; ebullient energy flow. Relates to the sixtieth year.

Upper semi-sextile: The native is interested in seeking acquaintances with strong personalities and people who are in power; there is a feeling of strength and a quiet sense of confidence; the need for accolades and recognition. The native has a friendly nature which is almost "too polite," the energy flow has various levels of intensity. Relates to the sixty-sixth year of life.

The above descriptions give us a method with which we can recognize the base matrix pattern of the sunset chart as it relates to the birth chart. The patterns are based on the "exact degree of the house cusp" but you must recognize that these parameters are not hard lines. They blend into each other by degree. It is up to you to determine how your clients relate to these energy patterns by your observations based on the interview with them. This planetary variance may explain why we often see the classic energy patterns differ with each individual. The time of birth pinpoints the Ascendant and Midheaven which also presents the personal "points" for the birth and sunset chart system. Once the planetary positions are known in both charts, their internal aspects reveal a subtle modification of meaning as they pertain to the individual, giving us a heightened insight to the chart we are evaluating.

Rogressed Sun

As mentioned above, we begin from the seventh house cusp and rotate the chart clockwise. It is important to recognize that the Sun, by rogression, will square its own position both in the sunset and later in the birth chart. For example, a person born with the Sun located *exactly* on the *fifth house cusp* will express a first period of crises at the age of eighteen years when the rogressed Sun squares its sunset position. The child may choose to leave home to go to college, get a job, get married or become involved with a pregnancy or any other sundry experience. The next period of crises will come at the age of thirty when the rogressed Sun reaches the cusp of the second house now in square position to the Sun at birth on the cusp of the fifth house. This birth position creates an enigmatic problem because at the age of thirty there is a square to the birth Sun but a sesquiquadrate to the sunset Sun. It is important to recognize that for everything desired there is an emotional, physical or mental price to pay. Always question the client further about his contingency plans related to the circumstance at hand then look at the chart to see if there is support for those plans.

84

As another example, the Sun at birth placed exactly on the third house cusp. The first period of crises will occur at the age of six when the rogressed Sun is 90° from the third house Sun at birth. Those of you who are born after sunrise may have the Sun placed in the twelfth house. In this case your first experience of crises is an opposition to the Sun before the age of six (by whatever degree the Sun in the twelfth may be) and at eighteen years the square follows and then another square when the Sun squares itself from the third. Those of you who were born at sunrise face a "T" square at the age of eighteen when the Sun has rogressed to the Nadir, squaring both the sunset Sun and the birth Sun near the Ascendant. It is important to question prior events to get a firm understanding of what your client's reaction to these aspects will be in the future. They will be repeated at some other level when the Sun makes another aspect to itself.

The same applies to the softer aspects of sextile and trine positions. The sextile presents itself as an opportunity at the age of twelve years (two houses or 60°) from the sunset position. As in our example chart with the Sun exactly on the fifth house cusp, an opportunity for some form of success appears at the age of twenty-four when the Sun rogresses to the third house cusp in sextile to the birth Sun and in trine to the original sunset position. Another trine aspect comes into play as the rogressed Sun reaches the Ascendant in perfect trine to the fifth house Sun and in opposition to the sunset Sun.

Rotating the inner biWheel chart for rogression confirms the timing for major events to take place. When any rogressed planet makes an aspect within the two charts, the aspect illustrates a clear influence and we can easily determine what secondary progressions or transits are meaningful. Many times a favorable transit takes place without any direct results. The reason for this is that the transiting planet is not "connecting" by aspect within the native's chart or with any rogressed planet. For Jupiter or Venus to come to a favorable fruition, they must be favorably aspected by sunset rogression, otherwise they just happen without any results.

At other times, a transiting planet will activate all sorts of responses with no visible aspects in the birth chart. By consulting the rogressed sunset chart, we often find the rogressed or birth Ascendant or Midheaven being activated. Another hidden aspect is the phantom Moon in the lunar mansion. As you will see in the Moon chapter, the Moon advances one degree every six years and often the advanced Moon reflects transiting aspects that seem to come completely "out of the blue." More about this follows in the next chapter.

Courtesy of W.H. Kennedy

Cylinder seals came about by 3500 B.C. and were an important form of record keeping in early Mesopotamia. They were of exquisite craftmanship and their rolled impressions on tablets, boxes, jars etc., served to mark and protect the belongings of its owner against theft. Cylinder seals were made with durable materials such as stone, bone, shell, ivory, metal and sometime glass. Many of these seals were no larger than big beads and were often worn as pendants or bracelets.

CHAPTER **4**

THE MOON

The size of our Moon is an enormous, $1/80^{th}$ the mass of the Earth. It circles the Earth at a distance of 9.54 times the circumference of the Earth's equator. When we look at the outer planets and examine their satellites, we see that the orbital distances to their mother planet remain rather insignificant. In effect, this ratio makes our Moon this solar system's largest satellite by comparison to its host. The gravitational effect the Moon has on the Earth is greater than the effect of other moons orbiting their host planets.

Another extraordinary feature is the remarkable relationship between the Moon's relative size with the Sun during an eclipse. From the Earth's perspective, the Moon appears to be exactly the same diameter as that of the Sun. If the diameter of the Moon were a hundred miles smaller or larger, or placed in an different orbit about the Earth, its eclipse effect would indeed eradicate the effect of viewing the corona discharge from the Sun. When we stop and realize all the possible ranges (by size, position in space, or orbit) of the Moon, each solar eclipse becomes an extraordinary event.

Additionally, the Sidereal rate of monthly motion is 27.32 days around the Earth, which is close to the speed of the Sun's rotation on its own axis of 27.3 days. It is as if the Sun and Moon were rotating in an eternally synchronized ballet with one another.

Other facts: We know that the Moon is slowing down the Earth's rotation with its constant gravitational influence on the tides. It is the Moon that shuts out the light of the Sun during an eclipse. It is as unique in its lifeless form as our Earth is unique with its teeming life. The Moon's orbital position acts as a counter balance to the Earth's orbit around the Sun. By comparison, our Moon is the most enigmatic satellite in our solar system.

Lunar Effects

Due to the gravitational pull between the Earth and the Sun, there are many inequalities to the Moon's motion. Its "wobble" is due to its slight oscillation and registers in both longitude and latitude; it has held astrologers' attention for the last decade or two. Another inequality, known as "variation," is primarily allotted to the Sun's gravitational pull and has its greatest effect when the Moon is 45° (semi-square) and 135° (sesquiquadrate) in longitude *from* the Sun (as viewed from Earth).

On an astrological basis, another unique fact about the Moon is that half its orbital journey around the Earth is between the Earth and Sun which, in effect, makes it an *inner*, personal planet (beginning of the last quarter, new and end of first quarter) while the other half of its journey is between the outer planets and Earth placing the Moon as a trans-personal *outer* planet (beginning of first quarter, full and end of last quarter). Recognizing this lunar position in the chart often indicates whether an individual is subjective and introspective or objective and outgoing.

The Early Moon

In Babylon, the Moon god Sin was referred to as the *Lord of Wisdom* and *He Who Would Open the Gate to Heaven*. At first glance this is an incredible statement. How is heaven defined? Is it "a condition or place of supreme happiness?" Why does that description apply to the Babylonian Moon? In their view wisdom and thus happiness resulted from acquiring invaluable knowledge, gained not by following the Sun or planets, but primarily by the Moon moving across the sky.

In Egypt the Moon was associated with an eye because of its association with the retina and its appearance to blink over a period of time, opening after the new Moon and closing after the full Moon. The Moon was known as Khons, the Eye of Horus, Osiris, Ptah and was sometimes associated with Min [60]. The Egyptian Moon symbolized the goddess power and was believed to be transmitted *to only those on Earth who understood its magic.*

The ancient Egyptian preceptors believed that there were two minds within the human being–the solar and lunar. The solar mind represented the autonomic system regulating the heart and blood, intestines and glands that comprise the sympathetic and parasympathetic nervous system. The lunar mind regulated the hypothalamic and cranial glands and functioned in terms of reflected light through the retina.

Today we know that the ever-shifting patterns of light are received and translated into frequencies through the retina so the optic and cerebral nerves can translate the light frequencies into images in our brain. The initial reaction from the objective world of light patterns is internalized and reflected as mental images. The Egyptians believed that the Moon symbolized the brain because of its function as our internalized receptor/reflector directing us through comparative perceptions in the world of objects and color.

The Egyptians also thought that the perceptive, mirror-like lunar mind had the power to eclipse the solar mind of singular purpose. The mirror-like perceptions in the brain were considered distractions from the outside world around them. Like looking at a barren landscape or a placid lake, one would immediately notice any movement. As a matter of fact, the Egyptian hieroglyph for the word mirror and the word for life are the same, *ankh.* Many hand-held mirrors were crafted in the shape of the ankh, still another reminder of the Egyptian idea of the reflective nature of the cosmos.

To the ancient Egyptians the Moon, Sun and Earth were all regarded as a perfect triad where each was in balance with the other. The cycles of the Moon symbolically represented the idea of subsequent replication of natural vibratory forces which coalesce as fertility, renewal of vitality, and the transient creation of life and death. It was believed that the Moon reflected the Sun's life-giving stimuli and governed all growth of life forms here on Earth through their *involuntary motion* of liquids. Also, the larger part of humanity (royalty and its entourage excepted) was thought to be nothing more than mechanical, *reactive* automatons governed by the Moon. With all the influence the Moon exerts upon the Earth, it is rather mystifying why astrologers use Sun sign rather than Moon sign astrology.

The lunar view is maintained in this book. The Moon represents our impulses to react rather than act, to follow rather than lead and to allow others to control us. The Moon symbolizes, for whatever reason we may justify, our weakness in dealing with other human beings.

Lunar Power

Today, there are many views regarding the significance the Moon's movement. M. Gauquelin's research suggests that a person with the Moon immediately following the cardinal angles (the cadent houses) has a propensity and a talent for writing. Of course, the "ready rhetoric" written about the tides and human reaction at a full Moon has already been overdone. *The Farmer's Almanac* has followed the course of the Moon for planting and harvesting crops since the time of Ben Franklin and, obviously, he got it from someone before his time. The fact that it has been published for so long certainly implies its success. The scientific study of Sidereal Moon rhythms by Thun, Kolisko and Fyfe revealed a definite correlation between plant life and the position of the Moon in different signs. These and other studies support the idea that the Moon has an influence that is readily felt here on Earth. Additionally, lunar research by various astrologers has demonstrated that when properly applied to predictive work, the Moon is indeed the power behind the chart.

Historically, the Chinese, Hindu, Arabic and Babylonian societies all relied heavily on the Moon for their predictive work and omina. Today, even though Hindu or Chinese astrologers may ask about the Ascendant, they are much more interested in the Moon's position than any other planet. What is really amazing is that early literature about the Moon is very rare and nearly impossible to find even though the concept of the daily lunar mansions (motion) must have been used extensively in ancient astrology.

With all this, there had to be more than just watching the Moon at night. Through the millennia the Babylonian/Chaldean culture and, to some extent the Egyptians, continued to adjust their entire way of life to the whimsical lunar calendar. The Babylonians followed the Moon's irregular course for over 40 centuries and yet the Moon remained their Lord of Wisdom. Why the Moon? What magic and what wisdom does it have to offer? The lack of available information, either contemporary or ancient, is surprising because lunar progressions are a powerful predictive tool. Any astrologer who is unaware of the power of the Moon is missing a very important facet in his predictive work.

The Addictive Moon

All the above ideas relate to the ancient belief that the Moon was the Earth's offspring. For this reason the ever-changing Moon became symbolic as a child. If we look at the Moon in the Egyptian cosmology chart (page 496), we notice the Moon is located near the "out of control" angle of the fourth house cusp. This position of the Moon symbolizes the idea of seeking guidance and/or being a guide.

Of course, the nature of the Moon is such that in order to be reflective it needs the light to do so. In this fashion we see the Moon's position in the birth chart as that of an addiction in seeking nurture and protection to preserve its own nature. This is readily seen in the case of the performing arts. Its position in the chart indicates a basic need and inclination to please people, wanting to be liked and accepted by them. On the other hand, in both the birth and sunset charts, an afflicted Moon by association to harsher planets, such as Mars, Saturn and sometimes even the Sun or Jupiter, manifests as a marked propensity toward an antagonistic or even a shy attitude toward people. In either case we voluntarily give up some form of our sovereignty and go out of our way to please or displease others, because at the moment it seems the right thing to do.

A strong or prominent lunar placement, such as near perfect aspects or those close to angles, is often recognized as easy going, good natured and affable with predictable mood changes. And because of this, someone with a strong chart who has the Moon either conjoined, square, trine or in opposition to one of our planetary placements has the power to influence and dictate our actions in some manner. The people who come into our lives with planets in close proximity to our Moon, either by sign or location in their chart, will either say, do or be something that enhances or distracts us in some way and, for whatever reason, we will want to respond favorably.

The ever-changing Moon in the lunar mansion, either by rogression or transit, is the weak link in our psychological make-up. The Moon's location requires us to recognize, by its placement, our vulnerability and decide what must be done for our own preservation and protection. When influenced by synergy or transit, its effect is similar to that of the fourth house cusp. We feel that we are placed in a hostage-type situation where we have little or no control in the matter. Under these circumstances we trust others to do for us what we feel inadequate to do for ourselves, like hiring real estate agents, accountants or lawyers to help us work through an unfamiliar system. The Moon's house position also indicates where we would really like to excel but feel inadequate. Activities represented by the house the Moon is located are the principles we need to learn so we can take the initiative and extend ourselves. Fulfill the Moon and you fulfill your deepest emotional need.

The Emotional Moon

The Moon's subtle yet ever-changing nature is most likely the reason why it has always been associated with the emotions. If we were to define emotion, we would conclude that it is a strong *subjective* response to a given situation. The natal lunar position is the *most vulnerable position* in the chart. Basically, it represents your emotional reaction to outside influences. It pulls us into circumstances where we feel we have no choice. These outside influences come in the form of demands from others whose needs we think, for whatever reason, are more valid than our own. Resistance is difficult because of the fear of loss and, because of this, the Moon also represents a guilt factor.

Keeping this in mind, the Moon's placement in the chart suggests that the native seeks emotional stability in his drive toward his subjective ideal. It is where we pinpoint our weak link with respect to close friends, relatives, and our connection with society. There is an old saying about business: "Should we depend on friends and relatives for its success, we would all fail." The reason for this is they all equate material possessions with emotional nurturing and expect discounts because they think they are the special emotional favorites. Too many discounts equals no profit; no profit equals no money to buy merchandise; no merchandise equals no sales which equals no business. This saying is very apt about the description of the Moon which demonstrates all aspects of human needs. One cannot simply keep on giving without receiving something in return. We need Saturn's reciprocal maintenance principle to stabilize the Moon's all too willingness to please.

As all planets are attracted to their own seventh house ruler, Saturn, the ruler of Capricorn and the Moon's natural seventh house, is therefore the Moon's chief attraction. By learning to follow Saturn's principle, we can change our reaction to the Moon's position in our chart thereby curbing our need to be overly generous and thereby averting the "doormat" syndrome. Once we recognize that the Moon's placement represents our weakness, we can learn how to break away from our need to indiscriminately satisfy someone else's bidding.

Lunar Awareness

The degree of one's sensitivity is registered by the Moon's position by decanate. The Moon's influence changes by virtue of its degree of longitude. The Moon in the first ten-degree decanate, indicates the development of understanding "emotional buttons." The child learns early to assimilate knowledge concerning emotive reactions.

In the second or "teen-degree" decanate, the decanate of change, the native feels that that his emotional needs may never be filfilled, this Moon placement its most risky position. The Moon in the second decanate is "constantly inconstant," or change for the sake of change. This restlessness is reflected in all parts of the lifestyle as a constant search for an ephemeral "something." The native often avoids close personal relationships because he feels if someone really got to know him they may find that, emotionally, "no one is home."

In the third decanate of goal-seeking, the Moon higher than twenty-degrees reflects as "seeking guidance" to find answers to satisfy emotional objectives. Often an individual with an ideal Moon placement will rarely reveal any weak position in a given situation. At times, when involved in conversation, the native may not be "up to par" on a given subject. With this Moon placement he will probably wait to see if further conversation will reveal more information without having to ask for it. In this way, he feels that he is in control and maintains his idea of self-esteem. The Moon in this decanate usually reflects as the "perfect student" who synthesizes his mentor's doctrine with his own ideas and in return challenges his teacher's original ideas intellectually. As with the other planets, we should scrutinize this arena very carefully.

The Moon is your main source of information in recognizing emotional responses. Review your own past circumstances or that of a client to show patterns of behavior which reveal future tendencies. Examine the first and last aspect the Moon makes. It is *most important* to note the *initial aspect* the Moon makes by rogression and as well as all the Moon's aspects throughout the rogression. This is the lunar mansion as stated in this work. Pay close attention to the Moon there will *always* be *some* lunar aspect in connection with events that are important to you.

Rule. The Moon is a weak link in our psychological make-up. The Moon's nature is not to be different but to avoid the pressures of our peers; to yield, fit in, and *go along* without creating any disturbance. The position of the Moon indicates where we feel it is our duty to comply with the wishes of others or otherwise feel guilty. Unchecked, people who have any planets close to our Moon's position, either by trine, square or conjoined can exert undue influence over us.

By recognizing that the Moon's placement reflects weakness, we learn to break away from indiscriminately satisfying the needs of someone else over our own. Learning that you do not have to sacrifice your own happiness for the happiness of another is very rewarding.

The Tertiary Lunar Progression

Although not directly connected with this work, lunar progressions are a part of lunar astrology. Two distinctly different forms of predictive lunar astrology come to mind. The first is the *Tertiary Lunar Cycle* developed by E. H. Troinsky (the term secondary progression is reserved for the Sun, therefore tertiary refers to the Moon). This method is calculated from the *Moon's exact position* on the day of birth; each 24-hour period thereafter equals *one month* of life. This is equivalent to 13 to 14 days in the ephemeris. Therefore, the 13 to 14-day period is equal to *an entire year* of life. This method is not as popular as the minor progression because the mathematics are laborious as one must constantly adjust the Moon's rate of motion for accuracy. Calculating a period of forty or more years would require an extensive amount of time and labor. The minor return is much easier.

The Minor Lunar Progression

The other lunar progression is known as a minor progression, also calculated from the Moon's exact position at birth. The difference here is that the minor progression is calculated *like* a lunar return. That is, in the ephemeris, the Moon travels through *all* the signs in one month's time. The 12 signs transited in the ephemeris during a lunar month equal one complete year; each sign the Moon transits equals one month. A person at the age of forty years and three months will equal forty lunar months plus three signs in the ephemeris.

When looking at the ephemeris, we see that the Moon enters a new sign approximately every two and one-half days. This two-and-one-half day period equals one month of real time. Thus, if one is born with the Moon at 3° Taurus, 3° Gemini is the next sign and *equals one month* of real time; 3° Cancer is two signs or two months away and so on. This procedure is followed until we return to 3° Taurus once again on the following page of the ephemeris. The end of the actual lunar month in the ephemeris equals one year.

As an example of a minor progression, look at the birth on May 14, 1960. The client is thirty-eight years of age with the Moon in Sidereal Sagittarius. Using the ephemeris, count the number of lunar returns equal to his age which is thirty-eight. The date in the ephemeris will fall on March 19, 1963, with the Moon the same degree as the birth in Sagittarius. If the reading is on the client's birthday, the Moon will be in the sign of his birth which establishes the beginning of his next yearly period. Each additional sign that the Moon changes equals a period of one month. Make notes on planets changing signs, and check whether or not they are changing directions (retrograde or direct) also what aspects they are under. This will give us a clear example of what to expect for the year under the lunar influence.

In predictive work, learning to use either method of lunar progressions can be likened to the old adage of giving a man a fish and you feeding him for a day, but teaching him *how* to fish and feeding him for life. Lunar progressions are that powerful and may allude to the Lord of Wisdom and the *Open Gate of Heaven,* as the Chaldeans cited.

In using lunar progressions, hard aspects by the Moon such as the conjunction, square, trine and opposition to natally sensitive points or planets, work especially well with both the tertiary and minor progressed charts. Equally important are planets going in or out of retrograde motion. They must be noted by which time frame, sign, and month in which they occur. This indicates when important changes may take place. Location of events is denoted by the planet(s) and its respective positions both in the birth chart house placements and in the sunset rogression.

A careful look at *lunar and solar eclipses during the nine-month gestation before birth* can reveal important event trends triggered by planetary transits. Additionally, *transiting* solar and lunar eclipses conjunct pre-natal eclipse points, as well as other sensitive points, can reverse one's circumstances rather impressively.

Rule. *Starting* with the exact degree of the *birth Moon,* each sign the Moon occupies in the ephemeris equals one month, and each lunar return equals one year. Thus, approximately forty-five pages (months) in the ephemeris is equal to the forty-fifth year of life. Hard aspects to natal as well as pre-natal eclipses of either the Sun or Moon are considered important. When using either style of lunar progression, retrograde planets determine changes in the individual's lifestyle. These changes are noted by planetary influence in the house where they are located and by whatever aspects are involved.

Rule. A minor progressed Moon, as well as the lunar return entering a cluster of planets (stellium) either in the birth or sunset chart, indicates a very auspicious time for successful ventures and accumulating money through such endeavors noted by the house.

Lunar Returns

The lunar return described in the *minor progression* above relates to the page-by-page lunar return in the ephemeris that takes place each month immediately after birth. The actual real time lunar return refers to current monthly transits that occur every month. The return is just that: the transiting Moon will sometime during this month reach the exact same degree as it did in the birth or sunset chart. This is approximately one month in time (actually 27.3 days). Therefore, we have a current lunar return every month throughout the year.

Another form of lunar return falls in the category of a solar progression. When working with secondary *solar* progressions, the Moon advances only one degree per month and takes approximately twenty-nine years to return to its exact birth position.

The transiting lunar return is considered an auspicious time to begin new projects or just, generally, a *lucky* period. Note any supportive planets by any aspect, either by transit in the natal or sunset chart, especially conjunctions. When the Moon is either crowded or traveling through a constellation with another planet, in either the transiting or progressed natal position, it is an auspicious time to begin any new endeavors. This is because the Moon has support and can receive assistance from the other planets with which it is conjoined.

Rule. The Moon loves a crowd, even in the natal chart. The Moon's position is affable, wanting to please. There is a note of caution–the Moon in hard aspect to the South Node or Saturn is a difficult one. Both are attritional and we can expect setbacks. On the other hand, the Sun and Jupiter might be likened to royalty and the Moon in favorable position to these points is *very* favorable. Enterprises during these times may have a feeling of enthusiasm, but planets that get too close to the Sun or Jupiter are not always favorable. They do not conjunct or square well and reflect this through the individual. When the transiting Moon conjoins either the Sun or Jupiter, it can produce results quite the contrary to what was expected. Conversely, when the Moon transits our natal lunar position, it may be a "lucky" time for us provided the South Node or Saturn are not involved.

The 24-Hour Lunar Arc

The numbers eighteen and twenty-eight have long been associated with the Moon. Additionally, during a Saros cycle of eighteen years and eleven days, there are no less than twenty-eight eclipses during that period somewhere on the planet. The daily motion of the Moon is found by observing the Moon's motion measured by longitude from the beginning to the end of each 24-hour period.

We note that the Moon travels about one degree of longitude every two hours, also known as its rate of motion. However, for a more accurate measurement, it is better to calculate the *actual rate* of motion of the Moon's movement than just using 12° as an average motion. This is accomplished by the usual procedure of deducting the Moon's longitude from the *previous day* of birth using the exact time of day on both occasions. You will find the rate of motion by subtracting the longitude of the previous day from the longitude of the birth day. The distance the Moon travels by degree during that 24-hour period is called the lunar arc or, in this work, the lunar mansion. When we divide the average lunar motion of 12° 51' into 360°, we receive roughly 28 as the estimate, the number of assigned lunar "stations" or mansions used in contemporary analysis.

The Lunar Mansion

Today, there are three systems correlating to the twenty-eight lunar mansions. They are called Nakshastras in the Hindu/Vedic astrology system, Sieu in the Chinese system and Manzils (mansions) in the Arabic system. Their fixed positions are appointed by dividing the twelve constellations into segmented arcs of 12° 51' in length. Each mansion begins with a fiduciary or reference star as its starting point. To list these fiducial points would be meaningless and would require too much space. Additionally, this idea of positioning the lunar mansion as fixed points of reference reduces the Moon's emotional influence into a static and boxed state without any personal consideration of the client. That is definitely something the Moon is *not*. The origin of fixed lunar mansions is probably derived from the term "Manzils," the Arabic term for mansions by al Biruni, the tenth-century Arabian astrologer.

The rate of daily lunar motion can vary from as little as 11° 36" to as much as 15° 06". One's *personal* lunar mansion is described by the longitudinal motion the Moon travels during the complete 24-hour period of the day of birth. This format is the probable Chaldean lunar mansion which was not fixed but measured by the Moon's *variable* distance of daily motion as it traveled through the zodiac from sunset to sunset.

In this work we, too, measure the lunar mansion by the variable daily motion and distance the Moon travels through the zodiac during the sunset to sunset period.

However, there are those of you who will want to look at the distance that the Moon travels from sunset to the actual time of birth. In this case, the distance by degree of lunar arc is NOT the lunar mansion, as it will vary depending on the time of birth. Those of you who were born just after sunset will have a much smaller lunar arc by degree than those of you who were born late in the afternoon. This difference of motion by lunar arc does not seem to have any direct bearing on an individual's life although someone may try to assign esoteric meanings to such differences. *This is not the intent of this book.*

Rule. The lunar mansion is always based on the complete 24-hour period starting at sunset *before* birth and ending at sunset *after* birth. Once the sunset chart is in place, it is necessary to calculate the Moon's daily rate of motion. To do this, simply look into the ephemeris for sunset preceding the day of your birth and subtract the difference in longitude of the Moon on the following sunset. The difference in longitude is the daily rate of motion and this *distance is your personal lunar mansion.* Next, divide the daily rate of motion into 24 to obtain the hourly rate of motion.

The law of celestial mechanics can also relate the Moon's motion with the motion of the Sun. The Sun requires approximately two hours of *real time* to travel the distance of 30° in longitude or one house. The Moon also requires approximately two hours to travel one degree of longitude. Based on the "aging" process (see page 73), the Sun will move one house every two hours and the Moon will advance by approximately one degree (preferably by its calculated hourly rate). This is important to remember for rogressing the chart.

The *personal* rate of motion of the lunar mansion describes the emotional demeanor of the person in the chart noted by the first and last aspects the Moon makes. It is also a very important indicator of the person's emotional journey because it is a clear indicator of life's state of affairs. The directional "urges" are best described as an inner recognition or basic need that is imprinted on the child during the early years. *This is shown as the planet or angle the Moon first aspects by degree.* The last planet or angle the Moon aspects by exact degree indicates *the characteristic manifestation,* the individual's attitude in acquiring the Moon's first aspect's basic need. Those with Jupiter as the first *or* last aspect just expect good things to happen, regardless of their situations. Those with Mercury feel that they can think or talk things through to resolution. Saturn, as the first or last aspect, promotes a reluctance to see things positively or the need to control them. With Mars, the native thinks with his fist or has a "might makes right" macho attitude.

The lunar mansion, coupled with the lunar progressions, clearly dictates life's emotional "urges," direction and changing circumstances. This is easy to follow because the Moon will aspect the other planets as it advances one degree every six years. Very often, *transits* will *trigger a situation* based on the Moon's sunset *rogressed* position only.

In this way we find these first and last aspected planets indicate the quality of emotional life and the emotional needs for fulfillment, both in giving and receiving. During the life, aspects made by the rogressed Moon represent the conditions and circumstances to which the native feels drawn. A powerful, ill-aspected Moon indicates a restless nature. This is like a "jack of all trades" who is in constant need of change, both in mood and environment. The process of life itself is an issue with him. They are often emotional conditions to which the native is subject. But often we find a different person who has the same ill aspected issues with the Moon but acts on them in reverse. Look at the chart to see if there is a strong Saturn, he may be a "stick in the mud" wishing he had the courage to break away from a dull routine. Or check and see if Venus is strong, often, a prominent Venus produces someone who is too lazy to do anything about his situation. One person may follow his instincts and become quite nomadic, wishing he could settle down while another is very settled and wishing that he could get out and see the world. Talk to your client, it is up to you to discern the difference.

Imprinting: First and Last Lunar Expression

Note that the Moon advances one degree every six years. In working with the lunar mansion, we are primarily interested in watching for two items: (1) We want to find out in what time frame or how old the individual was when the Moon reached its *first* aspect to another planet by the exact *same degree* and the nature of the aspect. (2) What planet does it *last* aspect by exact degree and its nature within the 24-hour period on the day he was born.

As a recap, the last planet aspected by the Moon indicates how the native expects his hopes, wishes and dreams to manifest. The Sun, Venus or Jupiter represents more of a sense of ebullience than that of Mars or Saturn. The last aspect also indicates the overall emotional state and the *inner sense* regarding the conditions at the end of life and death itself. The Sun, Venus or Jupiter shows a willing or peaceful transition.

Rule. The Moon's first aspect identifies the most basic emotional urge for satisfying one's self-expression designated by the planet aspected. Planets placed between the first and last aspects represent changes in the lifestyle or experiences during the life. But *always* keep in mind that the Moon's first aspect is the native's *imprint,* a deep-seated desire for emotional fulfillment. This is ascertained by the nature of the planet and its type of aspect. The last aspect represents the characteristic manifestation–the *expected end result* of his desires as signified by the planet and it's aspect.

For example, say a client's Moon makes its first aspect to Mercury. His emotional nature would be Mercurial and changeable with the need to express himself, either verbally or in writing. Should Saturn be the planet last aspected by the Moon, this would be toned down by intellectualism or perhaps even labored. With Jupiter as its last aspect there is more vitality and fervor.

To determine the individual's emotional state when viewing the age of an incident by year, advance the sunset chart to the house that represents the age of the event. By counting the number of houses the Sun has rogressed by age, add the *number* of houses to the degree of longitude of the Moon, then look for any planet that has the same degree, either by rogression or transit. Note the planet's enclitic influence as the Moon assimilates those energies as if it were its own process.

This can be likened to an earlier astrological custom of the translation and collection of light where the Moon picks up the energy pattern from the last planet it was in contact with and transfers that pattern of energy to the next planet it aspects. We call this function enclitic.

For example, should the Moon aspect Venus by conjunction and later sextile Jupiter, the now enclitic Moon will act as if it were Venus-oriented when it aspects Jupiter. This circumstance, taken alone, would describe someone either with an abundance of charm, a loving, charitable person or possibly someone with an artistic nature wishing to express it in a global way. If Venus and Jupiter were the first and last aspect respectively made by the Moon, with a harmonious Sun and/or planet placement(s), we would notice a distinctively warm and friendly individual. With a negative Sun or inharmonious planet placement, we might notice an inclination to laziness, conceit and perhaps even negligence. In either case the individual would have "film star mannerisms" with a tendency to gain in popularity in spite of himself.

In the charts that follow (Figures 4.1, 4.2 and 4.3), notice the Moon's first and last aspect in the lunar mansion. It is the chart of a personality we would consider extremely well known. The air of mystery is to see if you can guess who it is using only the lunar mansion.

For ease of reference, arrange the planetary degrees in numerical order starting with the highest degree and work down. We will use this method throughout this book and it will often be referred to as the 30° wheel or stack. An important point to remember is that the highest degree is related to the lowest degree as if the stack were a wheel, similar to house degrees. Whereas 30° of a sign is the same as 0° for the next sign.

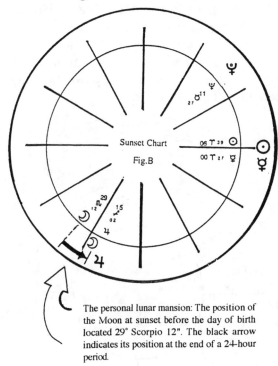

Sunset Chart

Fig.B

The personal lunar mansion: The position of the Moon at sunset before the day of birth located 29° Scorpio 12". The black arrow indicates its position at the end of a 24-hour period.

Figure 4.1
The example chart has the Moon placed 29° 12' Scorpio.

In figure 4.1 the Moon's arc for the lunar mansion is 14° 27" long. The Moon's *constant* influence is its first contact to Mercury. The Moon reached 11° Sagittarius moving toward but not completing its *near* conjunction with Jupiter before the following sunset. In this case Pluto is contacted last because this individual achieved fame and *it is the planet last aspected by exact degree within the 24-hour lunar mansion.* In 24 hours the Moon will be 13° 34' Sagittarius giving us the rate of motion as 14° 27'. Pluto's influence by last aspect is the more powerful but the *hint* of Jupiter may be associated with the incredible display of political power and grandeur associated with his mid-life successes.

As we rogress the chart clockwise, the Sun conjoins the sixth house cusp (Figure 4.2 below). The Moon had advanced to 0° Sagittarius 39", highlighting Mercury by exact degree with a trine aspect–the ability to arouse emotions and inflame people either as an orator or in the art of lying. This also speaks of a powerful and intense (Pluto) need for self preservation.

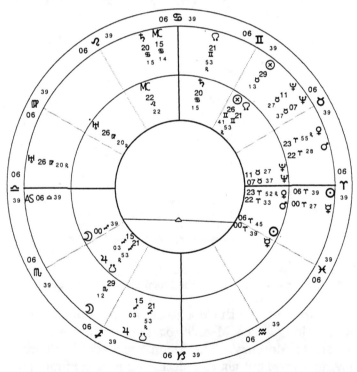

Figure 4.2 Moon's first aspect to Mercury at age six.

In figure 4.3 below, the Moon advanced by 1° every six years. Notice that by the age of thirty-five Mercury, closely followed by the Sun, had rogressed to the sunset Ascendant; the Moon was becoming a tight aspect by virtue of nearing the same degree as the Sun (six degrees). It was during this time that Hitler began to write his manifest destiny while in prison. Six years later, at the age of 42, the Moon had reached the same degree as his sunset Sun and he had firmly established his position of power.

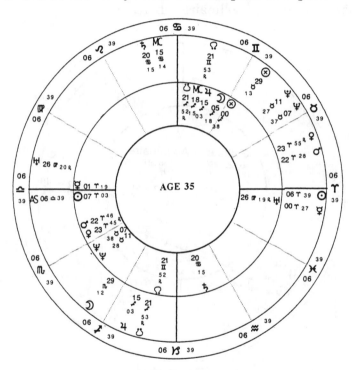

Figure 4.3 Writing of his manifest destiny

The examples above are not considered to be "classic examples." By using the lunar mansion method we provide a clear image of each individual's needs described by the planets contacted and by what aspects. The following charts will further demonstrate this procedure.

The sunset chart below is for the poet, Guillaume Apollinaire, born on August 26, 1880, at 5:00 A.M. in Rome, Italy. This chart reveals two good examples of how the sunset chart points out unseen aspects that, in other astrology techniques, are never seen until after the fact. These "after the fact charts" leave the astrologer trying to force the issue by "fitting" different aspects in the birth chart to match an event experienced by the native. The first good example is the rogressed Sun's position for different events in Apollinaire's chart.

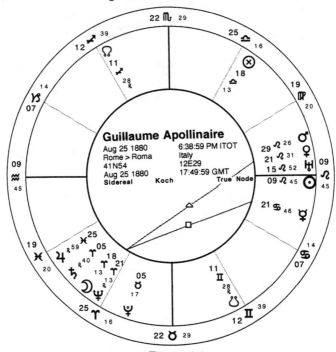

Figure 4.4
Apollinaire's sunset chart. Note his Moon is exactly three degrees from Neptune, Venus and Mercury.

Three lunar degrees (90° by solar arc) reveals that 19° is significant and played an important role in his life. Second, his lunar imprint discloses a powerful planetary alliance in his lunar mansion. This major imprint/alliance happened when he was nineteen years old by rogression.

The first lunar aspect by exact degree conjuncts Neptune, then trines Venus and squares Mercury, all of which are the same degree but in different signs. This happened between eighteen and nineteen years of age.

Apollinaire was a French poet whose fame blossomed by 1913 when he wrote his masterpiece *Alcools,* poems about reliving his past experiences. In his short life, his poetry was filled with experiments of technical writing which were considered daring and outrageous techniques. When he died in 1918 of Spanish influenza, his rogressed Moon was approaching the degree of Jupiter by semi-sextile; his rogressed Ascendant was 19° Leo.

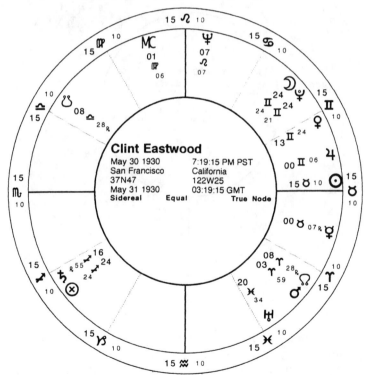

Figure 4.5 Clint Eastwood

Clint Eastwood above, was born on May 31, 1930, at 5:35 P.M. PDT, in San Francisco, California. We cast the sunset chart for the day earlier. Note the Moon's close first aspect to Pluto at sunset to the last aspected Mars. Known for his early roles as a lone, reluctant hero who was always "vengeful with a purpose," Eastwood has mostly played his characters with a "tough guy image." He has starred in many films that personify this "Dirty Harry" Pluto/Mars type of character.

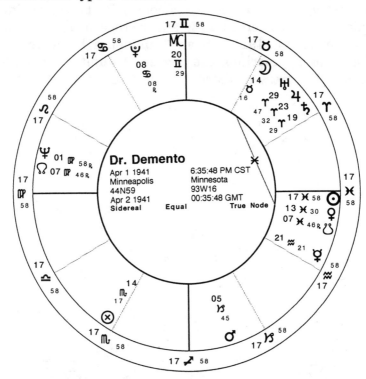

Figure 4.6 Dr. Demento

Famed musicologist and radio personality **Barret E. Hansen,** also known as **Dr. Demento,** was born on April 2, 1941, at 10:48 A.M. CST Minneapolis, Minnesota. His Moon, although sextile Venus, makes its first exact aspect to the Sun by sextile and the last aspect (semi-sextile) to the midpoint of Jupiter and Uranus. The sextile to Venus does carry some influence giving the enclitic Moon a Venusian trait which accounts for his artistic career in music. His interest in music began at an early age by listening to Spike Jones' records and classical music played on his parents' state-of-the-art Victrola. By the age of four, his parents allowed him to handle the fragile 78S and play them on the record player without any help from them. As he grew older, his passion further developed into collecting old records, odd tunes and comedy recordings. Today he has an outstanding collection of wax, vinyl and compact discs that number near the 300,000 mark and his collection is still growing! An icon in music for the past quarter century, his specialty is finding *rare and unusual* comedy recordings to play on the air.

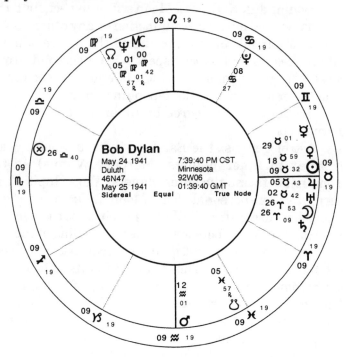

Figure 4.7 Bob Dylan

Bob Dylan, May 24, 1941, at 9:05 P.M. CST, in Duluth, Minnesota. We cast this chart for the same day because he was born *before* midnight. Note the close enclitic conjunction with Saturn carrying the saturnine quality to his first aspect (semi-sextile) by exact degree with Mercury. The last aspect the Moon makes by exact degree is a conjunction with the Sun but it is moving toward Pluto (sextile). Dylan, who displays brooding, somber, "all alone against the world" characteristics, is best known for his philosophical songs about hard times and the immorality of war.

At times, you will find the Moon has just passed by a conjunction with another planet, in these cases the Moon is referred as "enclitic" in nature. Very often there is a planetary "carry-over" by the Moon with the past conjunction and is NOT the Moon's first aspect, but the planet last visited either by conjunction or any other aspect does play a partial role in imprinting the native when it finally makes its *first* exact aspect. The degree of orb is generally no more than 1° (which is equal to six years) although it may vary a little depending on the rate of the Moon's motion and its degree by lunar arc depicting the lunar mansion.

Astrologers use the Earth as their mid-point when they refer to inner planets (Mercury, Venus) as the personal planets and the outer planets (Mars, Jupiter and Saturn) as non-personal. The Moon falls in a unique category because during half of its orbital journey around the Earth, it acts as a personal planet (beginning of the last quarter, new and end of first quarter) because it is between the Sun and the Earth. The other half of its journey, the Moon becomes an outer planet (beginning of first quarter, full and end of last quarter) because it is between the outer, non-personal, planets and the Earth. The inner planets are called personal planets because they orbit between the Earth and Sun. They relate to "the how to do" internal considerations, the native considers how to care for his personal requirements by deciding what types of schools, proceedure and academics to choose for his lifestyle.

More research on the Moon's inner and outer planetary placement is needed but initial research suggests that the Moon, while acting as an inner personal planet, reflects in the native as searching inward to find resources for expression and associates his expression with Mercury (learning protocol) and Venus (social activities). The outer placement of the Moon would reflect Mars, (competitive) Jupiter (enterprising) and Saturn (processing) as external resources for expression.

Any book of charts will allow a quick synopsis of any individual you may choose to research. In each case, based on sunset period prior to birth, the native's lunar temperament is quickly revealed by first and last aspects made by the Moon and its personal or non-personal placement in the chart.

Two final notes. The Moon plays a particularly important role using horary charts. Horary astrology is the practice of answering specific questions from a chart erected at the moment the question is asked (see chapter 11). The Moon is always considered the co-ruler of such a chart.

Once determined by our sunset chart, the synodic arcs between the Sun and planets stay fixed in place. The difference of arc between our birth time to that of sunset is very small by degree *except for the Moon*. With sunset as the "fixed" position, the Moon becomes prominant not only for its size and brightness but by virtue of its motion during the entire 24-hour period. When a child decides to be born it is the Moon's position that will define his lunar mansion. Under this concept it is easy to understand how the Moon would come to be considered the significator of childbirth and the baby in general.

CHAPTER 5

THE PLANETS

To get a clear picture of Chaldean cosmology, we must first examine the concept of what the planets and stars probably meant to them. As early as B.C. 4300, the Sumerian cosmogony enlisted the Earth as a flat disc enclosed within a hollow space. The space was thought to be inside a solid surface shaped like a vault that contained heaven. Between heaven and Earth was a substance called *lil,* a word that reflected the characteristics and movement of the wind. At other times it also referred to breath, air or spirit. The Sun, Moon, planets and stars were thought to be made of lil but somehow endowed with luminosity. Surrounding heaven and Earth was a boundless sea that kept the universe fixed and immovable.

These were obvious and indisputable facts to the Sumerian thinkers and philosophers who invented a doctrine that not only the Babylonians, but the entire Near East, inherited and followed as dogma. Many of their theosophical concepts were not developed as a systematic treatise. The Chaldeans were simply content with metaphysical inferences which explained why the gods created the cosmos and kept it running without confusion or conflict.

Many scribes, unlike the philosophers, were not interested in theological explanations or cosmological truths. They were simply content with writing about the glorification and exaltation of the gods, their kings and their deeds. These scribes were the pseudo-historians who gave us a mythical glimpse, although confusing, about the accomplishments of their gods and kings. They wrote in an inspiring, appealing and entertaining manner. The scribes, who were more interested in current theological notions and practices, became priests and astronomers. Their interest lay in the intellectual pursuits concerning the origin and

114

operation of the universe. It was they who listed the heavenly deeds and glorified the gods in the form of planetary motion against the backdrop of stars.

Planetary Cosmogony

The scribes noted the planets by their appearances both by their heliacal rising and their periodicities. The heliacal rising is any time a planet appears on the horizon during the course of the evening after being hidden in the Sun's corona. In this case, planetary periodicity does not refer to cycles, although synodic cycles relating to the planets and the solar arc were noted.

The Chaldeans observed the stars and planets at face value. Like children, if they could see them, they were involved in their omens, if not, then they were not involved. In other words, out of sight, out of mind. Therefore, the Chaldeans recorded each planet in the fashion of periods of visibility and non-visibility.

Venus, Mars and Jupiter were often observed by their waxing and waning phases. There are texts that speak of these phases as planets with horns (in crescent form). At other times they related to them by their magnitude (brightness or dimness), their superior or inferior position to the Sun. Exactly what the phases or brightness meant to the Babylonian astronomer is not clear as there is little information on the subject. A possible conjecture is that these planetary phases might have been associated with planetary energies becoming more or less powerful depending upon their phase–increase in light toward full (as in full Moon) or decrease in light as they waned.

Another astronomical observation noted planets within 15° of a conjunction with the Sun. A planet was said to be in its exaltation when it was first seen rising on the edge of the Sun's corona or 15° from the Sun. Any planet closer than 15° would be in the Sun's corona, which rendered it invisible to the naked eye. This is probably where the idea of "via combust" and exaltation originated.

Mercury was the most difficult to observe because of its nearness to the Sun and its subsequent periods of invisibility. As such, Mercury would appear, then disappear within weeks (sometimes longer if Mercury went into a retrograde period while in the Sun's corona). However, when it was observed, Mercury's movement was thought to resemble that of a jumping jack.

Venus was not quite as difficult but posed some of the same problems of invisibility. The visible outer planets were observed and noted by their advancing and retreating movements, as well as their disappearance when in conjunction with the Sun.

As stated earlier, sunset determined the entire course of events for the following 24-hour period. During the course of the evening, omens were established by noting the different times and the order of each rising planet or star pattern, presumably against the sunset matrix. At different times during the evening watch, various planets and star patterns would modify the omens originally fixed at sunset, much like an adjective modifies a noun or verb in a sentence. The observer would note and then interpret the entire evening's course of planetary events to determine which omen he would discuss with the king the next day.

To date, only thirty-two astrological genitures have been discovered on cuneiform tablets. They are dated as early as B.C. 410 (page 451). The most curious factor about them is their lack of information. One possible explanation for their meager text, both in number and in writing style, may be that they are just notations the scribe made for himself as a memorandum for later references, similar to writing a grocery list today.

Many other non-planetary occurrences were considered as part of the omens, such as barking dogs, halos around the Moon, clouds, weather conditions, etc. However, in Chaldea, it was the overall position of the planets that dictated their omens. Planets that were not visible in the clear sky simply did not fit into the scheme of things, nothing more.

116

The Chaldeans pragmatically enforced and strictly adhered to all manner of civil laws, customs and religious procedures. It was their custom to simply copy tablets previously written by other scribes who, in turn, copied tablets of the many scribes before them. Often, after a lengthy discourse, texts would end with "such is the procedure" followed by the name of the scribe who copied it. These copied tablets were probably the "calculations" mentioned in other ephemeride tablets when the sky was obscured by dust storms, rain or clouds.

The 30° Wheel or Stack

The origin of the 30° wheel is unclear, but texts in cultures east of Chaldea lend support to its theory. To date, no Babylonian tablets have been discovered to directly support the following procedure. However, in view of their lifestyle, the Babylonians recognized, by possible analogy of their political organization and the human state, that the hierarchical order of the gods was not equal in rank. In ancient texts these gods were numbered: 60 was reserved for Anu, the chief god, with the numbers 50 assigned to Enlil and 40 to Ea, Sin (30), Shamash (20), and Ishtar (15). They were often referred to by their number instead of their names. It is very possible that the Chaldean astrologers rated the planetary positions in the same regard they rated their gods, by a numerical system. It is more than likely that the Chaldeans saw this reflected here on Earth; that life was pre-ordained by gods and everything and everyone fit into a graded, caste-like system. Whatever one's position, it was to serve the the highest ranking individual i. e., the king.

In the same light, whatever planet held the position of the highest degree in their system may have been the prominent planet for the day. We do know that Jupiter was considered the overall "king" planet. At any rate, the 30° wheel system or stack has proven itself time and again to be effective and is placed here with considerable respect to its accuracy.

Today, we can use the planetary longitude for similar purposes. The planet occupying the highest degree of longitude is regarded as the reigning ruler of the horoscope and its nature the chief attraction to the native.

Procedure

List the planets by longitude in numerical sequence. Place the highest degree planet at the top of the list and work down to the lowest degree. For now, disregard the signs in which they are located. Once listed, divide the list of planetary longitudes into three groups of 10° each; these are called decanates.

Start with 0° to 9° 59', this is the first decanate. Planets found in the first decanate indicate those aptitudes with which we are born and represent childhood; this is called the way of Ea. The planet closest to the tenth degree is considered the major influence of this decanate. Next, the second decanate from 10° 00' to 19° 59' indicates the primary lessons and changes we face in life; this is known as the way of Enlil. The planet closest to 19° 59' is considered the major influence of this decanate. Finally, planets from 20° 01' to 29° 59' comprise the third decanate and indicate how to satisfy goals or achieve ideal circumstances in one's life. This is known as the way of Anu. The planet with the highest degree is the overall influence of the stack and is representative of the main objective in the life.

This procedure allows us to quickly determine the personality traits of the first decanate (Ea), changes to expect in the second decanate (Enlil), and the goals we wish to achieve in the third decanate (Anu). Note in Apollinaire's chart below, the Sun is at 9° 45' and above Saturn and (then yet to be discovered) Pluto. His origins were kept secret and his father did nothing for him. He was left more or less to himself and by the age nineteen to twenty he went to Paris to lead a bohemian life. His Moon is located in the decanate denoting change. It was not until he visited the Rhine land in Germany that he awakened to his poetic calling. His unrequited love for a woman inspired him to write his famous *Chanson du Mal Aime*. Mars, is the overall ruler of the chart supported by Jupiter, which indicates that Apollinaire was a person of action who enjoyed doing things on a large scale. His interest in poetry is shown by Mercury, Venus and Neptune all occupying the same degree (not sign). The department heads, if you will, of each decanate is the Sun, Moon and Mars. They describe a passionate individual who would want to associate himself with strong personality types, which he did.

The numerical arrangement of longitudinal degrees is known as the *stack* and will be referred to as such from this point forward. Of course, the entire list will never exceed more than 29° and 59'. Determine the birth time and be sure to include the Ascendant, the Node and Midheaven as well as the trans-saturnian planets for a total of thirteen. It is interesting to note that many Edgar Cayce readings often made reference to planets having the highest and lowest degrees as being the most influential.

Rule. Arrange a list of the planets from the highest to the lowest degree, disregard the signs. Divide the stack into three groups of 10° each. Note the highest planet by degree in each group.

Once the planets and mathematical points are numerically categorized, take note of the distance between each planet by degree. Each planet will have a planet above it and one below it. This is called the *triadal* planetary position or triad for short. The planet closest by degree to the center planet is the more influential.

For example, if Saturn were located between Mercury and Jupiter and it was closer to Jupiter by degree, then Saturn would be influenced by Jupiter's relaxed tone. It will become less organized than if priggish Saturn were closer to Mercury

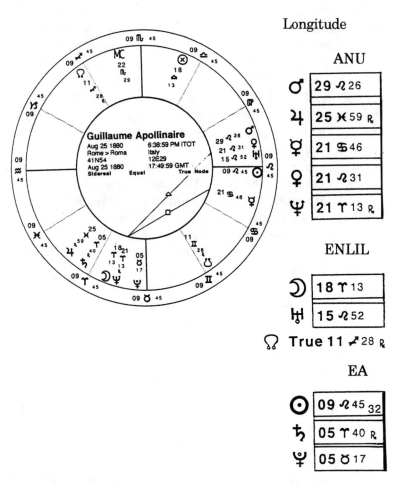

Figure 5.1
Poet Guillaume Apollinaire - the 30° conversion chart.

The highest planet by degree of longitude represents the motivation or *chief attraction* in life, that which the native desires most or wishes to achieve. The planet setting after the Sun combined with the highest planet indicates what the native *must know or do* to achieve his life's goal. Conjunctions of different planets that lie in the sunset seventh house are mutually influential. However, the planet closest to the setting Sun in the wheel (Uranus in Apollinaire's chart) is always the chief character indicator, and is the planet with which the individual most identifies with as himself.

To recap the 30° stack, any planet is further defined by the nature of the planets immediately above and below the planet in question. This is called a triad. It is very important to notice which two planets in the triad influence the planet setting immediately after the Sun. In Apollinaire's case, Uranus is between the Moon and the North Node. The Moon has more influence because it is closer by degree to Uranus than the North Node. The setting planet's "planetary triad" indicates what an individual honestly thinks of himself OR what the native may expect from his associations with others. In Apollinaire's case, he surrounded himself with "bohemian types," (Uranus) artists who approached their profession with a distinctly different style; much in the same way he wrote.

The most desirable *solar* influence is, of course, planets that are *exactly* 15° in longitude above or below the Sun–this position in particular was considered the point of exaltation by ancient astronomers. In all cases, when relating to this type of exaltation (or the planetary triad), look at the house position associated with the planet(s) for its affinity and arena of expression.

In addition, it is important to remember that all planets seek their fulfillment through "pairing" with their natural "seventh house" ruler. The principle of polarity becomes the principle of identity. An example of this is the Moon and Saturn are opposites in the natural wheel (Cancer/Capricorn). This natural opposition is known as the planet's maximum or chief attraction. When viewing any planet, its natural attraction must always be considered. In this way, we can see that the expression of the Moon's vulnerability, regardless of house location, is either satisfied or not through the influence of Saturn's stabilizing position. Again, this is true irrespective of their house positions or aspects in the chart. A planet should never be viewed without considering its chief attraction as well as the planet above and below it in the stack.

Unfortunately, we often find planets in opposition that are completely different than their chief attraction. When this happens the continuity of resolution by the natural attraction is disturbed by whatever planet is in opposition. The native who has "unnatural" oppositions in his chart tries to resolve the energy patterns of both planets by seeking the planets' natural attraction as well as having to go through the opposition in the chart. The challenge of this type of opposition is that the native has to contend with the opposing energy pattern as being "in the way" of such fulfillment.

For example, consider an individual with the Moon in opposition to Jupiter. Both planets' energy patterns are "unnatural" to the other. In seeking resolution, Jupiter is generally expressed as being a happy, optimistic and generous individual with an obliging and helpful demeanor. Much of what the individual has learned in life through Jupiter's principles needs to be expressed through its natural partner, Mercury. However, in this case where the Moon taking Mercury's place, the expression is more influenced by feelings rather than through the intellect. Also, this particular aspect indicates there is a strong need for guidance, often to the excess. On the other hand, from the Moon's point of view, Jupiter's dynamic nature is far too expansive for the sense of close protection and security the Moon naturally seeks through Saturn's position. So, the opposition between the Moon and Jupiter metaphorically "get in the way" of each other's search for identity through their natural "partner." The native may express himself in a more religious tone because his Moon may seek comfort through Jupiter's religious expression. Also, the focus from Jupiter to the Moon, the native may be too uncertain to express itself with the air of a teacher's assurance that Jupiter naturally has through Mercury.

However, there is a way to resolve the matter of unnatural oppositions. In the above scenario, if the Moon were in a stronger position, through elevation or by more favorable aspects in the chart of our client (client's chart "A"), he can seek a significant other (chart "B") with a Jupiter/Saturn configuration either by conjunction, square or trine. In this way Saturn is involved by proxy through the partner's Jupiter in chart "B" and will tend to satisfy the person's Moon in chart "A." However, should Jupiter be the stronger by position in chart "A," then the native can seek a significant other with the Moon and Mercury in some form of configuration in chart "B". In this way the "unnatural" opposition in chart "A" can be focused and channeled through the pairing with a partner's planetary positions in their chart "B." Fulfillment in these cases can often be achieved by finding a partner who has similar planetary configurations which combine the chief attractions with the planets in opposition.

Planets in Decanates

In many books, planets are all too often written in such a way that they become the last word as a focus for their energy patterns. Often we read, Jupiter represents joy and goodwill in a chart and Saturn places hardship in the department it is placed. A more practical outlook is to discover how each planet's energy works best for the individual through an interview. On occasions we find people who do not associate with specific planetary meanings that traditional charts express—such as the Sun behaving similar to Uranus or Mercury behaving more like Jupiter. Conversely, there have been many who have. Why is it that the same planets differ for different personalities? It is quite possible to understand this enigma when we look at the metaphorical position of the Sun in reference to the Sunset chart.

•

Sun. Seeks self enhancement. In the rogression it is the point of focus, the spirit of creativity, sense of self. It symbolizes a new idea, healing and renewal, the act of judgment, recognizing what is needed for one's growth and development. Like Jupiter, the Sun does not want any planet in conjunction with itself. Other aspects are good but trine is best and the square is antagonistic. Maximum attraction is to Saturn which promotes the attainment of personal goals in whatever manner is deemed necessary. The Sun likes to work with Saturn.

In the first decanate, planets are particularly influenced by the other planets that make up the triad position, that is, the planets above and below it. The planets above and below the Sun in the first decanate indicate the determining factors of how the ego is realized. For example: Apollinaire's chart shows the Sun between the more influential North Node, which is closer by degree, and Saturn. Remember, Apollinaire was left to himself as a child (Saturn) and later he sought companionship (Node) in Paris.

In the second decanate, changes are brought about by bruised egos. Often the native will leave a situation if he thinks he is not recognized as being as important as he thinks he should be.

In the third decanate, the ideal is the self. It is the pure expression of the ego. The native with the Sun in this position wishes he could marry himself. In addition to the decanates, the first planet located just above the sunset Sun, by any degree or distance by house, will fall into the following categories:

•

Mercury. Seeks information. Those with this configuration are quick in spirit. Vocal and/or mental expression is important. They may seem nervous. It is a neutral planet that acts like a chameleon by taking on the energy patterns of any nearby planet; loves all aspects. "All planets are stumbling blocks or stepping stones." The maximum attraction is the jovial Jupiterian type or Jupiter.

Mercury in the first decanate of Ea is chameleon-like. The native's mind is quick to grasp the implications of how to fit in with the external world. This placement of Mercury indicates that the native learns by watching and observing.

Mercury placed in the second decanate indicates the native views the world as ever-changing. This placement of Mercury places great value on the native being mentally prepared to take advantage of these changes.

In the third decanate, Mercury's placement indicates that the native is intellectual and places knowledge as the ideal. "Chance favors the prepared mind" would be a good motto.

•

Venus. Seeks beauty. This is an artistic and social expression. With a negative Venus the native expresses vanity and seeks self gratification; "sexy and lazy." The native is also chameleon-like; it has an enclitic nature that often takes on another person's characteristics; "to copy another is the best form of flattery." The native's nature is affable, attractive, charming, considerate, flattering, obliging, pleasant, seductive and wants to be with any one the native feels is important. Venus' higher octave is giving or caring "with no strings attached." Otherwise, it is usually associated with disappointment. The energy pattern of Venus works well with conjunctions. Maximum attraction is to Mars or the martial type.

With Venus in the first decanate, the native is attracted to different artistic views, music, dance, painting and, when coupled with Mercury by degree or rogressed aspect, there is a possibility of an interest in writing.

With Venus in the second decanate, the native views life in a more opportunistic way, often expecting others to do more than their fair share to help the native. Changes are brought about by loss of important associations.

Venus in the third decanate—the native depends on his social standing. The ideal here is to get to know the right people and befriend them. The native with this position can develop an attitude of "is that all there is?" when the friendships cool.

•

Mars. Seeks action. Here we find a warrior, a native who is combative, daring and dynamic. He is valiant and willing to champion other people's causes. He is quick to act. This planet indicates a lively, tireless, reckless and spontaneous individual. He has an unpredictable nature and prefers confrontation, likes squares and oppositions. Mars-oriented people will work for Saturn types, Sun types and sometimes Jupiter types. Maximum attraction is to the Venus type.

Mars in the first decanate, the native may be gruff. In this position one associates with the "tough-guy" attitude. Up-bringing may reflect the attitude and importance for the native to "do things like a man" and "take it like a man" either from his peers, siblings or his father.

Mars in the second decanate produces restlessness; changes are brought through the lack of discipline or inconstancy. An outlet for this placement may be reflected as a career in motion—the airlines, shipping, the motion picture industry or any profession that requires a constant change of pace and locale.

Mars in the third decanate is exemplified by competition with competitive practices as an ideal. This may be reflected as athleticism, interest in medicine, the police force, military or any profession that requires competitive struggle for success.

•

Jupiter. Seeks expression. The native acts as self-righteousness, ambitious, warm, witty, social climber, initiator of change. It was called the king planet by the Chaldeans. Jupiter's slogan is "I'll help you help me." Jupiter's expression symbolizes the idea of appearing to help others while achieving one's own end; laid back. The native struggles to express himself well if he has any other planet in conjunction with it in the chart; works much better with trine aspects only. He is willing to exploit the lunar type, but maximum attraction is to the Mercurial type.

With Jupiter in the first decanate, the native expects good things to happen; he has a Pollyanna attitude and feels well supplied with the proper needs as a child.

In the second decanate, the native will usually over-extend himself on a smaller scale. The attitude is one of being busy with many little things to do. Positive changes are brought about by recognizing his failure to reach for higher stakes on a larger scale and learning to work "smart," or more efficiently. Often, ill health is associated with Jupiter in this placement (through over-indulgence).

With Jupiter in the third decanate, the native recognizes that the only thing that holds him back is himself. This placement usually bestows an attitude of successful conclusion to his undertaking. It is the king or queen maker.

•

Saturn. Seeks organization. The native has an interest in law and order, is cold, conscientious, discreet, introverted and a lover of truth. His sense of justice is deliberate and premeditated. This planet symbolizes the principle of the seed. The native understands the need to preserve the present for the future. The native expresses Saturn in the chart best through sextiles and squares. Through Saturn's influence, the native recognizes the ego's purpose and is willing to hide unfavorable circumstances; he loves to observe, organize, and be methodical. Saturn types enjoy the Mercury and Venus types but their maximum attraction is to the Moon.

Saturn in the first decanate reflects a mistreated child, someone whose ideas or dreams are squelched. As a result he becomes a somber, quiet and studious type, who takes himself seriously. There is a love of orderliness and organization.

In the second decanate, Saturn's influence brings about changes through hindrance or negative and unfortunate losses. His efforts seem to be blocked by fate's command. The positive changes that Saturn may bring about are through undaunted efforts, slow but sure. The native needs contingency plans.

In the third decanate, Saturn indicates a person who is learned, wise and provides good councel. The road to success is deliberate, with planned execution as its counterpart.

•

Moon. Seeks guidance. Its placement indicates a sense of helplessness, vulnerability, weakness. The native expresses a willingness to please but not in the sense that Venus pleases. The person expressing his Moon in a pleasing manner is often seen as ineffectual, subservient or fawning and needy. The Moon's influence is amiable, dreamy, easy-going, generous, helpful, impressionable and tolerant. The Moon symbolizes the act of exploitation, either by being exploited or looking for someone to exploit. The native may have a sense of good timing in the area of the Moon's position. It symbolizes and also recognizes past conditions. Any aspect is good; oppositions are nice but the conjunction brings out a sense of identity. The Moon needs company and any planet will suffice. The Moon reflects the trait of a socialite and likes Venus and Jupiter types, but maximum attraction is to the Saturnine type.

Pay close attention to both the Moon's decanate and decanate of the planets the Moon aspects to evaluate the first and last aspect the Moon makes to them. By associating the first and last aspects, then combining them with their placement in the decanate, reveals considerable information about the individual.

In the first decanate the Moon's trait reflects a shy and demur person, often afraid to express himself for fear of ridicule; usually appears to be well behaved.

The second decanate placement is usually the weakest placement for the Moon. Here, changes are brought about by the native being too willing to accept other people's interests and ideas over his own. Often the native is abandoned by those he has adopted as his caretakers or directors. A restless placement for the Moon.

The Moon in the third decanate indicates a search for an ideal or a stable emotional attachment. A native with this lunar position may tout loyalty as a reason for his attachment. Older partners are sought after as guides who "know the ropes" or for "soul unions."

The above outlines can, of course, be modified or enhanced by other planets in various positions such as— planets on the MC, the first planet to reach an angle, the lunar mansion, triadal positions, the latitudes and the aspects between the planets.

Trans-Saturn Planets

The trans-saturnian planets are higher octaves of the first six planets in the solar system (Sun not included). They represent our gateway to success on a grand scale. For the moment, the general population can only react through the outer *visible* planets and their influences. Likened to an artist, the first six planets represent the learning process (Mercury/Venus), ability (Moon/Mars) and execution (Jupiter/Saturn) to achieve the status of an artist. Once achieved, the trans-saturnian planets become a gateway for expression: Uranus, for uniqueness of approach; Neptune, for inspiration by subject matter; Pluto, for intensity and message to the world. However, not everyone is an artist. Unless an individual finds himself in a unique leadership position, he will probably never have the need for, or the ability to, work directly with these higher planetary energies. The trans-saturnian planets represent the larger picture; the hard work and organization that the public, in general, fails to recognize on a personal level. They are the planets that offer uniqueness, inspiration and the intensity that lead to large scale public success. Many may not hear the call or take up the challenge to follow that path even though they think they express desire to do so.

Those of us who do not hold a high profile, such as the general public, are swayed and induced by the people in power. With this understanding, the planets Uranus, Neptune and Pluto are not fully activated until a person becomes either famous, notorious or gains a position of influence over large groups of people or the masses. Such individuals have influence over their generation and therefore *pro-acts and / or reacts* relative to the influence of the trans-saturnian planets. The general public simply and *indirectly reacts* through its personal planetary combinations that make up Uranus, Neptune and Pluto. It is important to remember that only the leading echelon of each country and its captains of industry are the trend setters. This is a fact of life and is performed in quiet and unobtrusive ways through the media, written word, laws, motion pictures, television, radio, etc. Generational influences and trends can be produced by public demand but are brought about by those who are in the position to make things happen.

When the trans-saturnian outer planets activate the native's chart by transit, the native will generally respond to these planets in a personal way either through the Moon, Mercury, Venus or through the transpersonal planets of Mars, Jupiter or Saturn.

In effect, the combined influence of Mars, Jupiter and Saturn are Plutonian. These planets represent intensified action or reaction by their planetary house positions. The same rule holds true for Uranus and Neptune which is described below. For example, the planet **Pluto** is comprised of Mars, Jupiter and Saturn (see below). Should Pluto rogress or transit a personal point in the natal chart, say, the Moon, the reaction would be a combination of Mars, Jupiter and/or Saturn influences combined with the Moon. One would look to see if any natal aspects were made by the Moon to either Mars, Saturn or Jupiter. Under the influence of Pluto, Mars, Jupiter and Saturn are subject to activation in the chart and the one aspected either by the Moon or Pluto has more influence and would be the reactive planet to the Pluto/Moon transit. However, if the combined energies *of all three* planets, (Mars, Jupiter and Saturn) are energized by rogression and/or transit, then the position of Pluto in the chart becomes the *reaction point* according to its house placement and the house placements of Mars, Jupiter and Saturn. A transit of this magnitude would indeed be a powerfully transformative one.

•

URANUS. The three planets that express the same energy that we associate with the planet Uranus are the combined energies of Mercury, Mars and Saturn. The resultant planetary reaction depends on which planet has the more powerful influence either by planetary contact or by virtue of its position in the sunset chart.

Should **Mercury** be the most powerful, then a new ideology [Mercury] induces the activity of forcibly destroying [Mars] the social order [Saturn] through revolution.   This is accomplished by forcibly [Mars] changing the boundaries and limits [Saturn] formally accepted [Mercury] as society's laws of the land.
Me= Ma/Sa

If **Mars** is the most powerful, then the destruction [Mars] of the existing form [Saturn] must be changed by developing a more contemporary design [Mercury] and structure. This is accomplished with regard to keeping the existing foundations and also through a more agreeable change.   Here we see the activity of upgrading present circumstances and conditions by agreement and re-design.
Ma=Me/Sa

With **Saturn** as the most powerful, the status quo [Saturn] is questioned by innovative [Mercury] acts of discord or demonstration [Mars] against authority [Saturn]. This is accomplished by recognizing known boundaries and physically extending oneself beyond them. Society sees this as being different or *marching to the beat of a different drummer*. <u>Sa=Me/Ma</u>

When additional planets are involved, either by transit or rogression, the changes further define themselves by the planets involved, such as **Uranus** with:

Mars. Here we find the exuberance of exploring new possibilities with unlimited boundaries: to boldly go where no one has dared to venture.

Venus. Look to exclusivity as the definitive pride of the privileged. The first on the block with a new, but expensive, antique toy.

Mercury. The answer lies in defining the question properly. State of the art processing produces extraordinary results.

Moon. Organized services are provided for those in need on a personal basis. Sudden success. Tendency to exaggerate. Interest in metaphysics.

Sun. Dynamics in personality result in unique expressions. Revolutionary spirit. New conditions.

Jupiter. Here we find the concept of taxation and insurance: how can we tax them, have them pay for services and make them think it is voluntary.

Saturn. There is always an alternative: The only difference between a dugout canoe and an ocean liner is size and the concept of necessity.

•

Next we look at **NEPTUNE.** The ancient formula for the planet Neptune would fall under Moon, Venus and Jupiter. It is defined as our full potential, which is hidden from view by our self-doubt or self-interest. With Neptune we can achieve goals even beyond our expectations.

Neptune is the scope of history that lies behind its circumstance.

A more powerful **Moon** would sense a feeling [Moon] of helplessness or vulnerability in a social, [Venus] larger than life atmosphere [Jupiter]. It is often seen as somewhat shy. Mo=Ve/Ju

With a prominent **Venus** being more powerful, one realizes pleasure by taking advantage of a weakness [Moon] in another person by manipulating [Jupiter] relationships or social functions [Venus]. It is negatively seen as a con artist and is seen positively as the social leader. Ve=Mo/Ju

With **Jupiter** as the most powerful, one seeks honor, glamour, beauty and style. It is the feeling of meeting and developing one's ideal relationship, often felt as love. In a social sense it is the politician winning an election! Ju=Mo/Ve

Neptune reacts to planetary transits either by rogression or progression as follows:

Mars. It is the need to hide one's experiences for fear of discovery of one's true purpose. There is the necessity to change and reform one's lifestyle in fear that the past may catch up, such as an exposé.

Venus. As all things have weak points, there is a sense of debasement about one's inner values. The seeming ideal union of internal with external affairs may create a false sense of independence. A lack of discipline can create heartaches and disappointing relationships.

Mercury. Alternative solutions to uncomfortable situations are sometimes seen as excuses. Or it may be *creative thinking* that does not agree with the facts or figures. Unclear motives and lack of foresight allow problems to occur which will later demand self-examination for justification.

Moon. There is a feeling of being unaware in demanding situations with no excuse for failure. One must gather information and details on how to monitor and attend to personal needs and the needs of loved ones. Acquiescence to one's own desires without any thought of another person's position eventually creates discord and degeneration.

Sun. One's self importance can be blinding, especially when reflected on oneself. This makes one susceptible to inactivity and weakness; a lack of vitality; the longer one waits, the harder it is to make amends or to correct past mistakes that were created by neglect; may be easily influenced.

Jupiter. Complacency can lull one into believing that the task at hand is just too great for one person to accomplish; but within the proper perspective, one may attract many followers and friends for assistance. A great position to organize help for the needy.

Saturn. One understands how past attitudes can create turmoil. It places one in the unique position of being able to facilitate change where it is thought to be impossible. There is concern with universal principles and goals which may be coupled with the ability to see problems clearly. This also indicates that one can delegate "the details" to the correct subordinates. The ability to materialize dreams.

•

The last planet is **PLUTO.** It represents the intensity of power and the magic of subtle influences. Pluto is represented by the tri-planetary configuration of Mars, Jupiter and Saturn. Since Pluto was discovered in 1930, when delineating a chart on people born before that year brings up an interesting question. Does the planet Pluto (now relegated as an asteroid) have any influence in their lives? When pre-Pluto birth charts are reviewed, the intensity that is known as Pluto shows up in a variety of ways but always as the influence of Mars, Jupiter and Saturn. Hitler had Mars square Saturn with Jupiter conjunct his South Node. Gandhi had Mars in opposition to Jupiter with Jupiter inconjunct Saturn. The more contemporary Nixon had Mars conjunct Jupiter, inconjunct Saturn rising (sunset chart). Each of these tri-configurations reveals some form of Plutonian intensity not necessarily found by the position of Pluto in the chart.

Saturn. With this planet as the most powerful focus, the experience is one of fear [Saturn] through intimidation [Mars] by some force or overwhelming experience [Jupiter]. Such an occurrence could manifest as a negative experience with the police department or government agency. Sa= Ma/Ju

Mars in the foreground relates to sudden insight and personal [Mars] transformation [Jupiter] that changes former negative traits of a cruel taskmaster [Saturn]. This is usually caused by extreme circumstances, such as near death experiences or surviving some life-threatening experiences. Ma= Sa/Ju

Jupiter in the most powerful position places one's personal [Mars] safety [Saturn] at risk. We bravely face our dragons or *worst case scenarios* but often with disastrous results. Ju=Ma/Sa

Transits, to **Pluto** by rogression or progression activate the planets in the following way:

Mars. Represents the significance of one's personal value system. This perpetuates clarity of purpose and is often seen as fanaticism. The negative expression usually does not align with society's principles and laws. The positive expression is often seen as the war hero. At any rate, the personality is intense and confrontational.

Venus. Relationships without a clear blueprint of reciprocal considerations result in misunderstandings, disappointment and dissolution. It is through recognizing the cost of past mistakes that allows one to choose a proper course of action.

Mercury. Inner research is required to examine one's own rationalizations and mental habits. The power of oration can alter the judgment of those who listen.

Moon. Awareness of underlying principles can reveal why one will place oneself in situations in which seemingly there is no control.

Sun. The focus is on recognizing the emotional or physical cost of habits, associations and activities that we feel we need to enhance our self-image. If we do not want to pay for them, then they are best left alone.

Jupiter. Here there is courage to recognize and change, with seeming clarity, vague principles that make one's life an undirected, uninspired and meaningless act. The ability to focus large amounts of energy into projects; the negative side is to initiate change with political doublespeak that leaves confusion in its wake.

Saturn. Obstacles that seem difficult must be endured with a sense of humility and duty. A determined, unemotional destruction of obstacles is necessary if they stand in the way of success.

The previous descriptions are brief and are only suggestions. They are by no means considered final. Each generation develops new standards which may be different from the generation before it. Influences continually change and restructure themselves into patterns that fit more contemporary viewpoints. It is wise to question the client when first viewing the sunset chart. Discover the distinct meaning of any planet's influence by reference to earlier events triggered by trans-saturnian planets. In this fashion the astrologer can understand how trans-saturnian influences may later pertain to the client's life and direction.

Planets in Retrograde

A planet is said to be retrograde when its apparent motion appears to be traveling backwards along the zodiacal belt. Many astrologers interpret retrograde planets as sinister or malefic because they are going against their natural course, thereby creating negative energy patterns. Helio-centric astrologers ignore retrograde planets because in reality, they are not actually going backwards at all. But for our intent and purpose, and to the Chaldean astrologers, they appeared to be traveling backwards and were said to hold less power or none at all. It is important to note, however, that retrograde planets are moving towards the planet with the lesser degree of longitude in the stack. This movement toward the lesser planet is like a demotion, the planet is stepping down toward its negative side and the native's response will probably be negative as well. Pay careful attention to the energy pattern of the triad while the planet is retrograde.

In the birth chart, retrograde planets seem to work in the same way. The planet is stepping down toward the lesser planet. It's like repeating the lessons one has already learned. Those born with retrograde planets have less energy available until the planet goes direct and then the native seems renewed with vigor. This is clearly seen when using secondary progressions and, more importantly, the tertiary or minor lunar progressions. In secondary or tertiary charts, retrograde planets represent a change of attitude or perspective in a client's current life pattern.

Personal observations with your own charts will reveal that retrograde planets do seem to lose their power while in transit. It is almost as if they have stepped outside to take a break from every-day activities. When the planet once again resumes its direct motion, the native will notice that it returns with some impact as if it had renewed energy.

During the Summer Olympics of 1996, all the outer planets from Jupiter to Pluto were retrograde. The only outer planet not retrograde was Mars. In the astrological view, Mars is said to govern athletics. With Mars as ruler "pro-tem" during the Olympics, it is easy to see why the activity was at an all time high with festivities and record-breaking events.

Additionally, the bombing incident was contained in a small area with minimal overall damage, if the loss of one life can be considered minimal. Still, there could have been greater damage if one of the outer planets had not been retrograde. Later on October 6, 1996, there was a giant blackout in the western United States when Pluto went direct stressing the point that planets coming out of retregrade renew their energy.

A retrograde planet in a chart represents little or no power by that planet. However, the native may regain that power sometime later as awareness increases through rogression. This generally registers as renewed interest or a surge of activity in relation to the planet in question. For example, one born with Mercury retrograde may have problems with communication early in life and later when Mercury goes direct or opposite its position in the sunset chart, serious study in communication begins to make up for the noted deficit experienced earlier.

One way to recognize the balance of power with planets in and out of retrograde is to correlate current events from the perspective of the everyday diurnal sunset chart. Another tool is to watch the daily sunset charts with respect to your personal activities and pay attention to any rising planet at sunset. Rising planets located in the twelfth, eleventh or tenth house modify the influence of the lunar mansion along with the first planet that reaches an angle.

Personal Interpretation

Our *kingdom* here on Earth is symbolically demonstrated by the planetary positions in the chart as follows:

Sun. The castle of the self and boundaries of one's kingdom.

Mercury. The propaganda, both incoming and outgoing. But more significantly, the chronicles of important events for further reference.

Venus. Gives diplomacy, aesthetics, grace and shows the world how one wants them to see their kingdom; what one wants for physical comforts in his kingdom.

Mars. Applies the forces to defend the kingdom and conquer its enemies or further build, develop and expand its boundaries.

Jupiter. The king or queen in residence who will go to extremes to exploit whatever is necessary for the upkeep of the kingdom.

Saturn. The execution of power through organization and laws, the need for reciprocal maintenance when dealing with others is necessary for safeguarding one's resources.

Moon. Where the Sun as king (or queen) needs protection; the weak link in the chain of command; one's alliances to individuals, a false friend who will take advantage of a situation for their own benefit.

Node. The ideal purpose the kingdom serves both philosophically and symbolically.

As the above list illustrates, any subject can be broken down into basic components with each planet representing an activity *within the system* of each subject. To represent every aspect of Babylonian life, the seven planets must have been listed in such a fashion. In this way they could perceive and predict the outcome of any event. The list below is an attempt to place general meanings to the planets in a mundane circumstance. They are examples and are by no means final.

> **Sun.** Event, Objective or Circumstance (E.O.C.).
> **Mercury.** Generic idiosyncrasies or required policies to understand the E.O.C. What it is, how it is done, where, when and why performed.
> **Venus.** Participants and their roles. Actors or spectators. The false favorite in a gaming situation.
> **Mars.** The primary function, process or activity in an E.O.C.
> **Jupiter.** The expected outcome of the E.O.C.
> **Saturn.** Parameters and location of the E.O.C. Its rules and regulations. Organizers of the E.O.C.
> **Moon.** Conditions of failure or the vulnerability of its participants or actors. Coupled with Venus, the crowd. The weak link.
> **Node.** The attraction or appeal of the E.O.C. Beware, the North Node represents acquisition, or accomplishment, the South Node represents attrition or loss.

The above descriptions will serve very well as interpretation of planets for the entire personal, business, organizational or any other sunset chart.

The "evening star," or planet just above the Sun in the sunset chart, will generally follow the suggested meanings. However, sometimes the sunset planets are modified by a planet on an angle or through the time-of-birth house position when compared to the house position in the sunset chart. Other times, modification is noted by planetary clusters and conjunctions. Each planet's level of importance and functional ability will be found by the degree the planet occupies in the 30° stack and by both its upper and lower neighbor.

CHAPTER 6

PLANETARY EXALTATION

The purpose of this section of the book is to give you an outline on one of many methods used in the attempt to distinguish which planet is the most powerful in a chart. Its main focus, however, is not Vedic or the Tropical Sun-sign meaning but in the sunset method at the end of this chapter. This format is presented for the purpose of comparing the sunset method with the technique you are about to read. At any rate, you are encouraged to review this section for the many useful insights and valuable nuggets that are used in the Hindu/Vedic system of astrology. It is my conviction that this form of planetary analysis works very well in both Vedic and Tropical astrology and should be used by astrologers who use those systems.

In today's astrological circles the process of planetary exaltation has fallen into disfavor and is considered archaic. To allow this form of astrology to fall into neglect seems rather limiting to astrologers who use the Tropical system. Was it a lack of understanding? Or does it fail in the final analysis? Whatever the case, I suggest that astrologers review this old idea and find ways to re-establish its presence in today's Tropical delineation process.

The development of planetary exaltation through the various constellations is most likely early Greek in origin. Ancient Babylonian astrologers had long known about this useful tool and used it extensively but by degree only. They considered the exaltation point as any planet rising 15° before sunrise or setting 15° after sunset.

In earlier centuries, Tropical astrologers used this system to identify the strength of a planet. Early astrologers described a planet as exalted when it exerted its most powerful characteristic (not influence) by degree and sign, and more importantly, it's house placement in the zodiac. Its influence is displayed through the sign it rules and the house that sign occupies. Thus, Mars located 28° in the sign of Capricorn is considered in deep exaltation and the house placement of the sign of Aries becomes a very powerful house.

Cancer is the seventh house position of this Mars placement. Thus, the native with powerful Mars exalted in Capricorn could be gathering a work force to provide the opportunity for individuals (Aries) to support the needs (Scorpio, ruled by Mars) of their families (Cancer). The product being produced is best found to be related with the house position in which Aries (and Scorpio) is placed. Another example is Venus. The influence of Venus is most favorable in the form of dispensation and we find its exaltation placed in 27° Pisces. Under this placement, Venus seeks to secure a place of comfort (Taurus, ruled by Venus) to gather (Libra) the infirmed (Pisces) in order to heal them (Virgo, seventh to Pisces).

Normally, a planet seeks its fulfillment through its natural seventh house ruler. But when using the technique of exaltation, the natural seventh house of the sign (i.e., Mars in Capricorn) becomes the sign of debilitation (Mars in Cancer). This is probably based on the idea that if Mars were to take on the Moon's vulnerable nature, Mars would not display its competitive nature but act in more of a weakened and recessive manner. I have not seen this to be the normal case with Mars in Cancer and perhaps this is the reason it has fallen from grace in the astrologer's toolbox.

By B.C. 300, the Hellenization of both Egypt and Babylon started to replace valuable empirical knowledge with idealized Grecian philosophy. Among the many new changes, the idea of exaltation and the pronouncement of planets was absorbed into the Greco-Roman way of thinking. The zodiac was reconstructed into ruling signs and spherical geometry rather than the original heliacal rising and synodic tables.

The Athenians proclaimed that planets are considered essentially *dignified* when posited in their own signs. Any planet placed in the opposite sign of its dignity was said to be in its fall; the same idea for any planet opposite its exaltation would be debilitated or at its worst. Planets squaring the sign they rule are said to be in detriment, and considered weakened.

According to Hellenistic tradition a planet is said to be dignified when it resides in the sign over which it rules. Furthermore, to say that a planet rules an entire constellation may seem absurd but, in this context and among professional astrologers, one must consider synchronicity. In other words, the effects of a planet are similar to the effects of a sign. Because the planet is faster in motion than the constellation, the term ruler is applied to signify relationship between the planet and sign.

The term exaltation is used when a planet is in the constellation where it essentially displays its characteristic qualities more powerfully and dramatically than it would being only dignified in its own sign. In similar fashion, a planet residing in the opposite sign of its exaltation is said to be in its debility or at its worst. Throughout the centuries that followed, astrological terminology and concepts were collected, revised and systematized by Arabic and late medieval astrologers. All this was later referred to as Ptolemaic astrology under the direction of Ptolemy's work known as *The Tetrabiblos*. Oddly enough, Ptolemy, even at the onset of his writings, had very little original input. His writings were mainly compilations of earlier traditions that he himself scarcely understood.

By the 17th century, Western astrology had changed completely. The original Sidereal or fixed star zodiac's apparent retrograde motion, known today as the precession of the equinox, went unnoticed or ignored. The Ptolemaic system had mistakenly diverged into a second system known as the seasonal or Tropical zodiac first named by Ptolemy himself. As such, most Greco-Roman and Ptolemaic astro-logics have remained intact to this day. The Hindu or Vedic system adhered to the teachings and precepts of the East by remaining with the mathematics of constellational astrology.

A planet in its exaltation is similar to a world leader, someone who has a great deal of power or political strength. He is able to influence others to bend to his desires, planets in exaltation influence the other planets in the same fashion.

The Place of Exaltation

The planets are said to be in exaltation when placed in the following sign and by degree:

Sun	19°	Aries
Moon	03°	Taurus
Mercury	15°	Virgo
Saturn	21°	Libra
Venus	27°	Pisces
Mars	28°	Capricorn
Jupiter	05°	Cancer

One of the many problems faced by the ancients was getting their calendar in order. Many different cultures began their year at different times due to their calendar process or local politics. By the time Greece developed into a world power, it was obvious that a standard calendar had to be calculated to meet the growing needs of trade and commerce schedules. It was determined by Hellenistic astronomers that the Egyptian calendar was to be used and that the Spring equinox would initiate the first of the year. The obvious reason for the Sun to be in its exaltation at 19° Aries may be due to the fact that the Sun was about this degree when the changes in the Hellenistic calendar occurred. Interestingly, the closest star, Sidereally, is Upsilon (v) located between Hamal, "to follow one's own path," and Botien. Combined the two stars have the energy pattern of Mars conjunct Saturn and are considered unfortunate.

The Babylonian calendar was decidedly lunar. During the early Babylonian period, the spring equinox began with the Sun in the sign of Taurus and the first *new* Moon would be considered a magnificent moment, just because it appeared. Today, the first new Moon, as well as the first full Moon after the spring equinox, is still considered an important event by many religions. The equinoctial new Moon was probably considered the proper time for planting, and this could have possibly taken precedence at a later time in Greece when the **Moon** happened to be 3° in the sign of Taurus commencing the spring equinox. The closest star, Alcyone, is located at 5° Taurus 12', the brightest of the stars of the Pleiades. It is said to have the nature of Moon conjunct Mars (impulsive and forceful). The Babylonians referred to it as "Temennu," the foundation stone. Alcyone was considered the central star or Sun in the Babylonian universe and one of the most important stars in ancient lore. Of course, this probably stems from the fact that Taurus traditionally marked the beginning of the spring equinox in the Babylonian culture.

Mars in exaltation spoke of the cold hard nature of "might makes right" in the sign of Capricorn. Its placement at 28° might have been because, Sidereally, 28° Capricorn 45' marks the end of that constellation with the star Deneb Algedi which has the nature of Mars and Jupiter (success, resolution). With Jupiter noted as the "king" planet added to the viciousness of Mars, we can readily see the meaning of this degree of exaltation. Additionally, Sadalsuud, located at 28° Capricorn 36', is nearby and marks beginning the constellation of Aquarius, with just nine minutes of arc difference, its meaning in Arabic is "the luckiest of the lucky," very fitting for the kings who conquered their domain with impunity.

Venus is said to be in exaltation at 27° Pisces and presents itself in the form of compassion. The nearest star in the constellation Cygnus, located 28° Pisces 15', is Azelfafage, and is considered dreamy, cultured and adaptable, with unsteady affections, love of art and swimming. Scheat, located 28° Pisces 30', is considered malevolent. Venus here apparently applies the balm of Cygnus to the destructive nature of Scheat and its victims.

The only mechanical sign in the zodiac depends on the fulcrum point to maintain its integrity. However, **Saturn's** point of exaltation is 21° Libra, six degrees off the Tropical balancing fulcrum point of 15°. Perhaps the extra six degrees indicates that in order to tip the scales of justice in our favor a little extra "something" is needed. Or, on the other hand, justice is best served with the understanding that a little more than "an eye for an eye" is in order. Sidereally speaking, the star Zubenelgenubi lies 20° Libra 17' and marks the beginning of that constellation. It is said to have the nature of Mars conjunct Saturn (overcoming difficulty) positive social reform.

Jupiter has long been recognized as the reproductive chakra (one example is seen using pomegranates representing the ovum or fecundity in early paintings). Jupiter located 15° of Cancer could mean that fifteen minutes of sexual fun could turn into twenty-five years of caring. However, in ancient times a fertile wife who gave birth early and often meant there would be plenty of help with the farm within a short time. The Sidereal location of 15° places Jupiter near Asellus Australis, a Mars/Sun influence considered fortunate. Why exactly 15° was determined is another mystery unless the ancient exaltation of 15° from the Sun's corona was considered.

Approximately five to six months after the spring equinox, **Mercury** travels to 15° of Virgo. This must relate to the ancient crop pickers. However, using this point for exaltation may be somewhat outdated. My observation indicates that the axis of 10° Leo and 10° Aquarius may be better points of exaltation for Mercury. In my opinion

Mercury on the Ascendant is its place of debilitation. Sidereally speaking, 15° Virgo 09' is the location of Vindemiatrix, the "grape gatherer," and is said to have the influence of Mercury conjunct Saturn (depth of thought). The star is related to disgrace, falsity and folly. Why Mercury was said to be exalted here is any body's guess.

Planetary Strength

To indicate the strength and power indicated by each planet, we will use the place of exaltation to establish a point system. When placed on its *exact* degree of exaltation, a planet is allotted 20 units of strength. We will diminish the alloted points on a sliding scale as a planet moves farther away from exaltation toward its opposite sign and degree of debility. Thus, a planet in square aspect to its exaltation point will have only 10 units of strength (half the distance). The point of debility is the same degree as its exaltation but in the opposite sign. The degree of debility has the value of zero.

Conversely, as a planet departs its point of debilitation, it gains in value. For example, Saturn placed in the sign of Libra 20° longitude is in its deepest exaltation and would have 20 units of strength. Any planets in the constellation of Capricorn become associated with Saturn by its exaltation and likewise exert more influence than they otherwise would. However, should Saturn be placed in its own sign of Capricorn, its unit of strength would be diminished to 10 units. This is because Saturn is halfway (90°) or between its debilitation point of 20° Aries and its exaltation point of 20° Libra. To further illustrate this point, Saturn placed at 20° Aries would be allotted no units of strength because it is opposite to its exaltation. In this case Saturn's defiling nature weakens the constellation Capricorn and any planets therein—guilty and weak by association so to speak.

To determine the value in strength of a desired planet, simply subtract *one unit* of strength for *each nine-*

degree segment between the planet's placement from that of its exaltation point. The reason for using nine degrees is due to the fact that we are using the sum of 20 units as a measure between 0°–180° (180° divided by 20 = 9). Conversely, add one unit of strength for every nine degrees as it moves away from its point of debilitation.

For example, the Sun is 28° Cancer 38 minutes (or 118 ° 38" of arc from Aries). Divide the degree of arc (for the Sun's exaltation using 10° Aries as fiducial) by 9. The distance from the Sun's point of exaltation (10° Aries) is 108 ° 38," divided by 9 equals 12.07 units. Now subtract 12.07 from 20. The result is 7.93, or roughly 8 units of strength.

The Vedic method sets about the same conversion in this manner:

To subtract the debilitation point from the Sun's position, we must first add 360 to the Right Ascension (using 0° Aries) as follows:

Sun 28° Cancer 38' converted to Right Ascension. The right ascension of 0° Cancer from 0° Aries is 90°. Therefore 28° (of Cancer) is added to 90° Right Ascension for a total of 118° and 38" .

$$360° + 118° \ 38' = 478° \ 38'$$
$$478° - *190° = 288° \ 38'$$

Because 288° 38" is higher then 180°, it must be subtracted from 360° i.e., 360° − 288° 38' = 71° 22' Divide 71° 22' by 9 and the result is 7.93 units of strength.

 * We are working from 10° Aries, so the debilitation
 point is 10° Libra or R.A. 190°.

The graph on the next page will facilitate this procedure. Starting with any planet exactly on the same degree as its exaltation has a value of 20 points. As it moves away from its exaltation, its value diminishes on a sliding scale. The graph below indicates the variance by degree and its consequent numerical value. Remember, we are moving away from the point of exaltation toward the point of debilitation.

Right Ascension is defined as *how far around* the equator we are moving. This is symbolized by the rim of the zodiacal wheel starting from zero point of Aries. Thus from zero Aries, zero degree Cancer is 90° or, zero degree of Libra is 180° (from Aries) and zero Capricorn is 270° (from Aries). With exaltation, the same holds true. But instead of starting with 0° Aries, we start from the point of exaltation of the planet in which we are interested. With Mars, we would begin with 28° Capricorn as its exaltation is our zero point and our beginning reference.

Exaltation

Planet Exactly on the Degree of Exaltation = 20

01° - 09° = 19 points	91° - 99° = 9 points
10° - 18° = 18 points	100° - 108° = 8 points
19° - 27° = 17 points	109° - 117° = 7 points
28° - 36° = 16 points	118° - 126° = 6 points
37° - 45° = 15 points	127° - 135° = 5 points
46° - 54° = 14 points	136° - 144° = 4 points
55° - 63° = 13 points	145° - 153° = 3 points
64° - 72° = 12 points	154° - 162° = 2 points
73° - 81° = 11 points	163° - 171° = 1 point
81° - 90° = 10 points	172° - 180° = 0

Notice in the graph above that the orb at debilitation (9°) is a considerably larger orb than that of exaltation which is exact. This further emphasizes the lack of strength when a planet is placed near or at its point of debilitation.

With the exaltation method we find, as the planets move through the zodiac, that they are either helping the native advance by traveling toward exaltation or working toward re configuring the existing thought structures and/or patterns by traveling toward debilitation. Thus, we can see that a person born with Saturn moving from the sign of Aries to Libra is advancing his ability to judge matters in a more mature manner and in harmony with the external world and blending easily into the constructs of society. Conversely, when Saturn is traveling from Libra to Aries, the judgment may be more "me first" and thus less mature. He may find commitments and decisions a little more difficult to live by. It is important to note here that the planet in debilitation is in a difficult position but not necessarily completely restricted. The lack of maturity and unwillingness to cooperate may be readily noted by others but not necessarily by the native. In the case of Saturn, the closer a planet is to its debilitated point, the more self-centered and egotistical the individual will appear.

This does not mean that a debilitated planet is completely devoid of any positive attributes, but that the native born with planets in debilitation will have to work harder to acquire the finesse necessary to integrate oneself into the community. The answer toward success lies in using the energy pattern opposite of the planet's sign placement in the chart.

Often, a planet in debilitation can be offset or canceled either by our own recognition of its negativity or through planetary dispositorship either by sign or placement. As most of us know, a dispositor is the ruler of the sign in which another planet may reside i.e., Mars in Leo is disposited by the Sun.

When these mitigating factors occur, we find that a person with a debilitated Mars in his chart can overcome his easily hurt feelings and actually add to the mix in relationships. The Sun in Libra can overcome the constant need for company or the feeling that others are always right by becoming more self confident and expressive by noting the placement of Venus (or *acting* as if their Sun were in Aries). Likewise, a person with the Moon in Scorpio can overcome sensitivity and vulnerable feelings and develop a deeper understanding of the psyche by looking where Mars (or Pluto) is placed (or acting like a Taurus). Those with Saturn in Aries can develop a strong sense of leadership, purpose and strength of will. Likewise, debilitated Venus in Virgo can overcome shyness and enhance the artistic sense or learn and teach interactive social skills. Jupiter in Capricorn can develop into a well respected political leader or captain of industry. Mercury on the Ascendant can have many ramifications. Often, a native born with this Mercury placement has "the sense of being overwhelmed" with many different projects. This can be overcome by having friends help ease the workload or by developing a systematic discipline. At other times, the native with Mercury/Ascendant tries to function by splitting his concentration, this is generally developed by abused children. (Give a friend permission to squirt you randomly with a filled water pistol. Now defend yourself while you try to read a book.) Individuals with debilitated planets can always recruit the help of others to lessen the load by looking for people represented by the dispositor and its placement.

In judging the nativity, this system will reveal which direction the native is going, either building or revising his/her lifestyle. Exaltation gives us a quick look at the functional direction planets move and may offer insights into why the native builds upon or sabotages his own efforts (as applicable). Rather than describing the degrees by number, such as the constellation Aries as 0° to 30° or Cancer as 90° to 120°, the use of constellations by name will serve to represent each 30° segment. At times, the word "sign" is used in place of constellation.

Planets in Exaltation

The descriptions that follow are stated in their most ideal and undisturbed manner. They are listed *as if* there were no other planet in the chart to modify them. Of course, in reality they are always modified in some manner because their position may place them in a weakened state or other planets may aspect them or take precedence over them by virtue of their position. Remember, the descriptions that follow can always be modified into a softer or harsher description as indicated by other planets in the chart.

•

SUN

The **Sun** is the center of our solar system, so too, a pronounced Sun in the chart wants to be the center of attention with everyone and everything revolving around it. As a personal point of focus, the Sun's attribute in a chart indicates tolerance but does not particularly work well in a chart if conjunct other planets. However, the native expresses himself best with others when the Sun trines other planets.

Aries. The Sun is in its exaltation in Aries. The Sun is springtime in nature, an expression of this Sun is powerful and gentle in its ways, this is reflected in the abilities of the native. The Aries person is best described as the perfect idea and embodiment of creativity, physical dignity, self reliance and is often described as generous and affectionate with a commanding nature. He makes a good leader.

Taurus. The person with the Sun in Taurus is strong, yet willing to share the limelight to a small degree even though the Sun's influence does not like to share. The native with this Sun placement exerts a more responsible, quiet display of power, steady and on course, willing to do the work necessary for his own achievements.

Gemini. The individual with the Sun in Gemini loses some power as the Sun is further removed from its exaltation. Still, there is an influence that is distinctly solar in nature. With the Sun in Gemini, the individual senses that his power is in a decreasing mode and so exerts its influence in an intellectual way, hoping to diminish the power of others with glibness. This influence is achieved by the Gemini native convincing others of the Gemini's intellectual prowess and seeming ability to lead. It is in this constellation that we start noticing the solar energy becoming more negatively self-centered as it begins to square its source of initial effulgence.

Cancer. With the Sun in Cancer, the native exerts more energy by enticement than in the preceding constellations. To acquire followers, there must be some form of inducement available as an attraction. The power of the native's leadership quality by this Sun's placement is lessened by half and here there is a diminished sense of self reliance. The acquisition and use of *goods* and *things* so other people may enjoy his company is how he can establish a form of leadership; to influence fellow companions to come to the native for their needs to be filled.

Leo. When the Sun is in Leo, the native becomes aware of the necessity of doing something that will create a following. The solar energy is warm and aware of the politics of influence. Self reliance is weakened and staging is important. It is here that creativity is demanded of the self to attract leadership.

Virgo. With the Sun in Virgo, the native feels diminished to the point where recognizing his power lies in being needed by others. This Sun position will acquire knowledge that other people do not have the time to learn. Virgo's fulfill their own needs of leadership by being of service to others. This is accomplished by being *in the know* in specialized fields and involved with service-oriented agencies. It is here that the inner self-esteem is fulfilled by helping others and developing a following of those who demand service.

Libra. The Sun in Libra is in deep debilitation at 19° Libra. It is here that personal power is weakest and real power is recognized vicariously through other people's achievements or their abilities and skills. A native with a Libra Sun develops his leadership through involvement in the social aspects of power. Aware that it is *who you know* in life, Librans strive to align themselves as partners with people in powerful positions. It is here that the power of the Sun is willing to relinquish its initial self expression to be able to share and be close to those in prestigious or controlling positions; leadership is sought through social recognition of those with whom they associate.

Scorpio. The Sun begins its movement toward exaltation and the individual recognizes the power of power itself. He begins to turn toward more selfish ways and understands the importance of personally attaining a position of power. The Sun is climbing out of debilitation and is much like a person who has come up the hard way through the ranks and who also recognizes the need to control by force. He empowers himself by associating with organizations and becoming extensions to those already in power. Leadership is sought in order to control others.

Sagittarius. The Sun in Sagittarius has now emerged even further from debilitation and the native recognizes the power of being important. Sagittarius wants to be involved in a teaching capacity or as part of the management team. His power lies in the knowledge of ritual, pomp and circumstance and the teaching of same. Leadership is achieved through teaching others the ropes to reach the inner circle.

Capricorn. The Sun is half way to exaltation and the native recognizes his personal power of enticement through organization and disbursement. Capricorn recognizes that the ability and potential of others can be

154

exploited. The "agent" personifies the perfect concept of Capricorn, they involve themselves in the talent business and help performers achieve their goals. The Capricorn's empowerment is to have others envy their position and perpetuate the myth of being a person in *the inner circle* or one who knows how to get there. Leadership is sought through organization and the administration of laws and regulations with the need for security.

Aquarius. The solar energy of Aquarius expresses itself through recognizing the need to fulfill ambitions. The Sun is moving toward exaltation and the goals and dreams of life are very clear. Natives of this constellation recognize the importance and power of developing influential friends to attain personal goals. Aquarians recognize what other people need in order to reach their own goals. Aquarians know the avenues where provisions may be acquired and how to organize the production of, and/or outlets for, such accouterments. The quality of leadership is the feeling of unique independence through abundant human resources.

Pisces. Pisces power? The term itself seems to be an oxymoron. At times, his power lies in martyrdom but this is not always the case. Two fish swimming away from each other is not what Pisces is about. It is the *cord that binds* the fish that produces tension and stress from the internal "tug-of-war" going on inside the Pisces person. They seek relief by attempting to metaphorically "cut the string" from whatever opposes their idea of individual freedom. Leadership is acquired by joining organizations that require learning protocol and customs to achieve rank.

Summary. In observing the Sun's transits through the constellations, one can easily see the emergence of Sun sign astrology. Its succinct approach can explain away the seemingly basic characteristics of an individual simply by the Sun's position in each constellation during the seasonal year. The Sun's position, however, only points out the area of life and what knowledge the native will acquire as a means of gaining recognition and power. However, it takes much more than just the Sun to define us.

Many times, a negative situation comes about when the Moon is ill aspected or weakened by being away from exaltation position or by poor placement. The Moon symbolizes helplessness and vulnerability. Those with a debilitated Moon are seen by others as a target for exploitation. In charts of those with exalted Moons, there is some form of rescue or guidance that helps avert unpleasant consequences. Later we will learn in the sunset method that the rogressed Moon very much likes any aspect to itself.

•

MOON

The **Moon** has been associated with protection, nurturance and motherhood much earlier than the time of Ptolemy. Exaltation of the Moon in the constellation of Taurus probably came about because of the Babylonian association with the spring equinox. Today the Moon symbolizes helplessness, vulnerability and our foremost needs but, in its exaltation, the helpless factor may be feigned. It is in Taurus that the Moon' demands to be nurtured. The Moon works in Taurus best because the ground rules point to placing oneself in the position of self dependence. From what I have observed, the placement of the Moon by sign and house is where we need to excel by developing self reliance.

The individual with the Moon in **Taurus** tugs at the heart strings without even trying. He needs help but it is generally not openly expressed, wanted or appreciated. Others still respond by coming to his aid regardless of the lack of expression. Helplessness or seeming naiveté bring out the parent in all of us. Remember, a person with this Moon position knows the power of planting one seed to later reproduce many. The wisdom reflected by this lunar position is represented through interest bearing accounts. Self reliance comes from persistence to achieve goals for future benefit.

In **Gemini.** The Moon is expressed in a cerebral way. This is accomplished by observing who will respond, how and by what button. Helplessness in this constellation can be demanding and designed by machination. Many with this placement when ill-at-ease may play dumb or talk baby talk. A good motto for this Moon placement is, "More...all is not enough!" The wisdom of a Gemini Moon lies in the form of the written or spoken synopsis such as magazines and illustrated reviews or the quick overview. Self reliance comes in learning communication skills, grammar and the ability to trust one's own intellect.

In **Cancer.** The native with this Moon has a quality of helplessness with a brand new approach. This native is generous but openly demanding of his needs. The feeling is he is either a baby looking for his parents to help him or he is a parent looking for a child to nurture. The native with this Moon placement often appears to be like a brave lost child who attracts a helping hand from others. The wisdom of this Moon placement is represented through day-care centers. Self reliance is developed through understanding that denial of another person's demands may have its benefits.

In **Leo.** Individuals born with this Moon placement are generous and not as demanding as those in the preceding paragraph. People born with this Moon thinks everyone is psychic. They expect you to recognize what they need and have you give it to them without them having to ask for it. If you do not give them what they need, they will simply take whatever it is they want, thinking you owe it to them anyway. They can be a great ally who will overlook naiveté and become a powerful protector to those whom they feel are less fortunate. Their motto is, "Lend a hand here, I'll help you later." The wisdom here is in the "pomp and circumstance" of giving awards to those who deserve them. Self reliance comes from becoming an authority in a field of interest.

In **Virgo.** Any native with the Moon in this position takes on the flavor of Taurus and Gemini. These individuals are able to recognize what is needed and for whom. They are aware of the need to help and be helped. Moon in Virgo is the promise to fix problems that other Moon placements would use to their advantage. Virgos recognize the fact that there are those who are "in the know" and those who do not know. The individual with this Moon position wants to be the one who is "in the know." This is simply recognized by him as a fact of life. It's a great Moon placement for business, as the native can exploit those who are vulnerable or in need of some service. The wisdom of this Moon lies in recognizing the importance of expedient schedules, concise records and catalogs. Self reliance is developed through dependability and careful attention to detail and continuity in any given project.

In **Libra.** The Moon is still moving away from its exaltation point. The idea of helplessness takes on more meaning and becomes more dependent. A native with a Libra Moon seeks people of means and power for comfort and protection. Often, Libra Moon people allow the exploitation of their resources because they are unaware of the machinations of others. This can be the baby looking for the parent. Whoever invented the suction-cup probably had this Moon position. The wisdom of a Libra Moon lies in knowing who's who in their field. Self reliance rests in becoming "indispensable" with one's associates.

In **Scorpio.** The Moon is debilitated. Here the person with a Scorpio Moon prides itself as recognizing reality and considers "nature is as nature does" a way of life. A person with a Scorpio Moon detests helplessness and sees it as a great weakness. He seeks to find answers and establish safeguards. This placement can sometimes be obtuse. These natives may want to have a party but, as the party plans unfold, it develops into potluck, and the party ends up at someone else's home. Exploitation comes in all packages and the old adage applies: "Heaven helps those who help themselves." The wisdom of a Scorpio Moon lies in the upkeep of social agencies through insurance and taxes. Self reliance is developed by joining organizations requiring power and force in their routine.

In **Sagittarius.** "Heaven helps those who help themselves" may be the Scorpio adage, but the person with a Sagittarius Moon will add the ending, "*get to heaven.*" This placement of the Moon recognizes the foibles of mankind. This individual outdoes the Gemini Moon by not only knowing what button can be pushed and when, but will then tell you that your response was wrong! How to exploit the exploiter becomes an interesting affair. The wisdom of this Moon position recognizes the necessity for religion as food for the soul. Self reliance stems from becoming a teacher in one's chosen field of expertise.

The people who have the Moon in **Capricorn** appear to let you take advantage of them. They can endure arduous circumstances in a quiet and unobtrusive way to advance themselves. However, their seeming discomfort is the system in which they, in turn, take full advantage of you. After all, isn't turn about fair play? This form of exploitation does not want the disadvantaged to know that they have been taken. As a person with the Moon in Capricorn wants the people he has taken to be happy about his having done so, his exploitative and controlling nature is often done with a soft touch and with the appearance of help. This is much like an agent who receives a healthy percentage of somebody else's hard work in exchange for a phone call or a handshake. The wisdom of this Moon recognizes the public's need for representatives in specialized fields. Self reliance is developed by learning how rules of organization lead to understanding one's place in the chain of command.

A person with the Moon in **Aquarius** can argue a point with a look of innocence even a five-year-old could not muster. This person's exploitation game runs in the order of obsequiousness. A good waiter will probably have the Moon placed here. At the other end of the spectrum, we find emotionally independent personalities who are friendly but distant in some fashion. This Moon placement may well be the origin of the phrase, beware of "a wolf in sheep's clothing." Self reliance comes from knowing that we are all unique without having to join the "look alike" unique club.

The **Pisces** Moon in the form of exploitation is to make you feel sorry for those who are born with this position in their chart. After all, you are getting their best performance. Of course, if you try to beat them at their own game you become trapped into being their slave for life. A Pisces Moon person will probably call and let you know that their hard-to-reach light bulbs need changing. They will not say it in that manner. What you will probably hear is they are sitting in the dark while trying to read. People with the Moon in Pisces believe that you really want them to behave that way. The wisdom of this Moon position lies behind the idea of the health care profession. Self reliance is developed by understanding that it's all right to "not fix" other people's problems.

An **Aries** Moon person is like Robin Hood, and understands the phrase, "what goes around comes around," particularly the "comes around" part. He appears to straddle the fence but most of the weight is on his own side. An Aries Moon will help others but generally has his eye on the recipients as future supporters. The wisdom behind this Moon position recognizes the importance of knowing that the other party understands the process of reciprocal exchange. Self reliance is achieved by developing détente, diplomacy and the art of graciousness.

•

JUPITER

Jupiter was known as *the King Planet* to the Babylonians. The Egyptians referred to Jupiter as *the abundant provider* when rising in the east. As Jupiter is the largest planet in our solar system, its physical size suggests that any association with it will be expressed in a larger than life form regardless of the situation or circumstance.

There are many reasons Jupiter was associated with the king. Its motion through a constellation was considered unhurried and one that never strayed off course thereby associating its movement with stability and strength. To the Babylonians and Assyrians, Jupiter was always considered a benefic planet. At one time Jupiter/Marduk was considered the savior and supreme ruler of all the universe, suggesting the belief and worship of one god. Jupiter, in many omens, appears to be protective as one text clearly states that Jupiter, when seen with eclipses, negated the necessity of magical spells such as Namburbi. Many texts declare that the presence of Jupiter during the spring festival meant protection of the kingdom, peace, plentiful rain and flooding for an abundant harvest. With its rising or, "standing fast," Jupiter heralded the promise of an abundant spring.

Jupiter's later association with the constellation Sagittarius probably stems from the amount of rain that occurred during winter when this constellation was setting. However, an interesting aspect regarding Jupiter and Sagittarius is that the Babylonians believed when Jupiter entered that sign "war and destruction would devastate the land." With such ill omens associated with Jupiter it makes

Sagittarius. Jupiter was also regarded as ill-omened when transiting the constellation Taurus.

Jupiter transiting through Cancer during the winter solstice probably gave rise to the many other references to good fortune. Remember, the Sun has to be under the Earth to see the planets at night. When the Sun sets in Capricorn, Jupiter in Cancer would simultaneously rise. Such an event was held in reverence.

In later centuries, Jupiter in Cancer was said to be in full exaltation during the deepest part of Winter. Jupiter promises big things and, like children at Christmas, we expectantly await our gifts with zeal. Jupiter in the chart works best with trines for ease and does not do too well with other aspects.

In **Cancer**. Jupiter is perfect at the politician game. Well aware of the position of power through its seventh house sign Capricorn, this placement helps others to help the native achieve his own end, much like the Moon in Sagittarius. With nurturing, what better place to have Jupiter placed? With an abundance of food and care taking, this placement would be like living in the garden of Eden.

In **Leo**. Jupiter is a "show business" game. The native extols its importance and is willing to help or entertain you for a price. This Jupiter looks for an audience to teach its principles. The native with Jupiter in this placement is like a precocious child who expects adoration for acts accomplished.

In **Virgo**. It's the game of planned obsolescence. Being business oriented, Jupiter in Virgo is good at the negative sales pitch, the less said the better. When it breaks, the native will fix it for you. It is only a limited warranty though, do you want extended coverage? The other side of Jupiter in Virgo is the amount of work coverage an employer did not expect to receive in a given project. These natives will give a lot more of themselves just to prove they are invaluable.

In **Libra.** Jupiter says, "I was there when you needed me, now it's your turn to help me." The more people the native knows, the better the chance for survival. The native with this placement probably has lots of ideas about someone else's project. What have you got going (can I get in on it)? Hopefully there is success if a project catches on. Remember how Jupiter in Libra helped you? This placement is very good for attracting social contacts. The politician.

In **Scorpio.** Jupiter plays the insurance game. Jupiter is willing to bet against you while using your money. This native recognizes the foibles of humanity and is willing to leverage those character flaws into the business of rescuing those in need, provided they pay for it first.

In **Sagittarius.** Jupiter plays the monastery game. The trick is gathering people in and keeping them at bay through some form of belief system. There is a lot that humanity does not know and the native with Jupiter in Sagittarius will tell them, but it will take time. This placement recognizes the importance of the entourage; they may have to bear with the native but it can be worked out. This native has a lot to say about everything. Jupiter was considered most maligned in this constellation.

In **Capricorn.** Jupiter plays the shoestring game. The native with this placement probably has a business that is barely scraping by but, for those who are interested in joining or buying the business, "it's worth several million," or "the chance of a lifetime." This native is aware of the importance of the showcase presentation. Make anything look good and someone will buy it. P.T. Barnum comes to mind.

In **Aquarius.** The native has never met anyone he did not like. In the natural zodiac, Aquarius is the eleventh house and, counting from the sign of Aquarius, Sagittarius is *its* eleventh house, "a friend in need is a friend indeed." An individual with this placement is somewhat of a bohemian type and could live under any condition until his "ship comes in". This native has such a slick method of conversation that before anyone is aware that they have done the native many "favors," he is gone. Those he left behind will miss him.

In **Pisces.** Jupiter will play the hospital game. People need a place of care when they are sick. If you build the hospital on this individual's property, he may even allow the purchaser to hire him to help run it. This is a very generous native who understands the principle "it is better to give than to receive" because those on the receiving end are in need of what is given. Those on the giving end are in abundance.

In **Aries.** Jupiter plays the "you can depend on me" game. The native with this placement probably cannot stand the idea that someone may need a helping hand and is unable to find it. These are the people who speak up just to end the nervous silence when a volunteer is needed from a group. One may often hear the native say, "You can count on me, but start without me, I have an errand to run." As soon as the native returns, the work is probably finished. The other end of the spectrum is that once this native decides to help, often it will be to the detriment of his own schedule.

In **Taurus.** The "if you're so smart why aren't you doin' it" game is played. With an eye on material possessions and the future, this native works toward the end of his autumnal years. To the Babylonians, Jupiter in Taurus was considered an omen of aggression because of the need for other kingdoms to acquire gold and human resources. Security becomes the mainstay for anyone born with the Moon in Taurus. His idea of fun is having stocks, bonds and money in the bank. Listen to the plans of the person with this Jupiter placement. He has something going for himself.

In **Gemini.** This Jupiter placement reflects as the "knowing someone who can get it wholesale" game. Desirous of many contacts and connections, this person is sociable with pleasing mannerisms. In all the signs of the zodiac, Jupiter in Gemini has a carefree attitude in life and is the most superficial and changeable–the Puer (and Peurella) Aeternis. The tendency here is to be lighthearted and sunny, often addicted to planning and play.

•

MERCURY

In both the Babylonian and Egyptian cultures, the scribe was considered both priest and politician. He was the most important subject to the Pharaoh or king. It was the scribe (Mercury) who kept the required business records which insured their success. In Babylon, to become a scribe was a very important goal because of the prestige it brought. In the pragmatic Babylonian vernacular, it was a prestigious and well-paying job.

Mercury is associated with and considered a planet that exhibits quickness. To the early observers it seemed to dance in and out of view, the Babylonians called it *the one who jumps* and the *herald of the king.* The Egyptians symbolized Mercury as a scribe possibly because of the quick movements made by the hand when writing, or a baboon because of its quick movements when frightened.

In my opinion, Mercury's debilitation is in the constellation of **Gemini** or on the Ascendant. Individuals born with Mercury placed in Gemini need to understand *why* things are the way they are. This enables them to categorize and store their input of information for later reference. Although this is considered one of Mercury's ruling constellations (mentally quick), it is also the other end of the mental spectrum when compared with Virgo. The Gemini placement continually searches for the "why" of things. Why are we here? Why does humanity act the way it does? The philosophy of "why" can become a trap, a Gordian knot that mentally ensnares its possessor to search for the answers to unanswerable questions. It is here that Mercury becomes the "monkey mind" which mentally jumps quickly from one idea to another and often without full comprehension. This placement inherently works in abstract ways and methods. It's good for design and understanding spatial concepts. Mercury in Gemini often is indicative of the parrot mind. It is also good at mimicking and plagiarism.

Mercury on the Ascendant will often depict an individual with his mind a lot faster than his mouth. As a result, we find individuals who stutter, or who jump from one subject to another without completing sentences. At other times, we find an individual who starts talking "out of the blue" or in a disjointed manner with no relation to the context, situation or ongoing conversation. On occasion, he may speak about a subject that may seem bizarre and over the heads of others. In general, he seems to be "out there" with his powers of reason and often his basis for motivation may seem trivial or even odd to others. *He* knows exactly where he is mentally and what he is doing. It's just that the people around him are having a problem understanding him.

Mercury in **Virgo** is in its traditional dignity and exaltation. Much more pragmatically placed, this Mercury position relates to the world in the language the world can easily recognize and assimilate. This is the placement of the scribe: how to be at one's best as a scribe or to herald the king properly; how to best acquire knowledge and record it. In the constellation Virgo the individual seeks to understand *how* things came to be the way they are. He needs to know procedure or protocol in order to do what is expected. Mercury in Virgo indicates the "scribe mind" which knows the proprieties and importance of knowledge. This placement inherently works in analytical methods, good for understanding mechanical procedures, mathematics, journals and schedules.

The Mercurial midpoint *axis* of 10° Aquarius to 10° Leo is the balance between the two minds of Virgo and Gemini. The Aquarian scientific mind gives its possessor pragmatic attributes with a quickness of intellect that many would recognize as genius. Mercury here exhibits its full potential of what the planet signifies. The other end of the axis, that of 10° Leo, may not be a mental giant in the material realm but this placement is considered the seat of God, the domain where we hold dearest and deepest thoughts of spiritual purpose. With Mercury in this placement, we find individuals with a set mind or purpose with little or no reservation to speak their mind regardless of consequence.

•

SATURN

Saturn is considered by many to be a vile planet that should be taken very seriously. However, the myth of Saturn speaks of bravery and courage. In ancient times Saturn was considered a brave warrior. In the creation myth it was Saturn who, when no other god would undertake the task of subduing the underground goddess of chaos, went underground and recovered the "Tablets of Law and Order" which at that time returned peace and tranquillity. For his efforts he was awarded the prize of controlling destiny through law and order. Saturn understood the principle of preserving seeds for future generations and was always associated with the Sun. A native with Saturn placed in sextile is discerning, brave in opposition and judgmental by square aspects.

Saturn is in exaltation in the constellation of **Libra.** A loyal partner with a strong sense of duty regarding partnership. Saturn is at its best when ruling a cardinal (angular) *and* a trinal house (ninth and tenth [Taurus Ascendant] or fourth and fifth [Libra Ascendant]) at the same time. In Libra, Saturn works with full judgmental faculties. It is not that these people do not make mistakes, they do, but, their plans are well thought out and Saturn knows that mistakes can be corrected. People born with Saturn in Libra seem to advance automatically into positions of management even if they are considered as being ditsy or strange. Interestingly, they perform well and often make the right decision when called upon to do so. Saturn in Libra recognizes that the law is for the benefit of all and that justice should be swift; "let the punishment fit the crime."

In **Scorpio.** This placement of Saturn is probably where it got its vileness review, not for its own distaste but from those who would rather not have had to deal with the person with whom Saturn has this placement. This placement understands the real world and the harshness of life—good judgment and truth are an ideal and the enclave to power. At times, the individual with this placement can become dictatorial. The attitude is, "a good offense is the best defense." It is here that a person is called upon to rely solely upon his own resources to keep his integrity intact. Like a muskrat caught in a trap that chews off its own leg to regain its freedom, an individual with Saturn in Scorpio will go to extremes for the resolution of conflict. For this placement, it is important for these individuals to understand the truth of a matter so they may remove themselves from feelings of entrapment in a situation they do not like. When it comes to law and justice the Saturn in Scorpio person believes in serving it themselves; "revenge is a dish best served cold." The psychologist.

In **Sagittarius.** Saturn sextiles its exaltation point and we see Saturn's power of diplomacy. In a positive light this position can lead to sainthood if the individual has the resolve and courage to carry on. The native can point out other people's problems in such a positive light that he impels them to follow his philosophy. Like Saturn in Scorpio, the truth is somehow a banner and is very important to the native. A negative Saturn can exploit the suffering of others to attain his own ideal of truth and justice. The major difference from Scorpio is that Saturn in Sagittarius trusts that there is a higher power that will see that justice is served.

In **Capricorn.** Saturn relates to self expression. The truth will out: whether or not it is fully revealed is another story. The individual born with this Saturn recognizes the need to bite the bullet and preserve the future. He encourages others to do so as well. This placement of Saturn indicates a person who advocates that law and justice should be stern at times. The native is cognizant of mistakes in history and the need to avoid repeating them. We could say that, metaphorically, Saturn in Capricorn supports all the weight at the base of the pyramid. Law and justice are seen as the glue that is necessary to keep the fabric of society functioning in a civilized manner.

Aquarius. An Aquarian Saturn is creative in practical ways. This person recognizes that established rules are not what they seem and is willing to extend his boundaries to suit his own needs. Established traditions are looked upon from different viewpoints and Saturn in Aquarius believes that there are unique ways to follow established rules and decisions. The individual with this placement of Saturn often looks at his own truth with mirth and finds that all that glitters is not gold. Law and justice are seen through democratic principles where the majority rules.

Pisces. Many born with Saturn in Pisces are modest and reserved and tend to go about their lives in seclusion. The trait of a Saturn in Pisces person is to stay in the background and not compete because he would rather not disappoint the loser should he win. In this sign, Saturn is weakened and diffused, but experience can discern new avenues to overcome such weakness. Often reflected as lonely and depressed individuals, this placement encourages one to explore new horizons if the old ones seem impossible or improbable. A Pisces Saturn, reflected correctly, can use determination and discipline to develop self-esteem and courage. Law and justice are seen as regulations that allow one to feel protected against the tension and uncertainty of uncharted waters. Similar to feeling fearful while walking through a rough neighborhood and suddenly seeing a policeman on the corner.

Aries. Here Saturn is in opposition to its exaltation point. Even in complete debilitation the native can be brave. This individual has a need to control others, which is generally accomplished through mirth and comedic disguises. He thinks that as long as others laugh at what is presented, they cannot laugh behind his back for reasons that are undisclosed to him. With his Saturn in Aries, most of the individual's respectable qualities are diminished here. Good judgment and discernment are often laid to rest for more selfish reasons. Law and justice does not apply to the native, only to others.

Taurus. Here Saturn is lazy and selfish. This individual would rather take the easy way out of a situation, but he works harder at avoiding work than actually accomplishing the task at hand. The attitude is that one really good effort at something should be enough, like a songwriter who enjoys his one hit record. Once accomplished, one's laurels should speak for themselves. A person with Saturn in Taurus is often a good boss, as he looks to others to get the job done. Saturn in Taurus signifies a persevering and deliberate individual in anything he does. Where there is a will there is a method to find the way. Law and justice lie in the reward of a job well done.

Gemini. This is probably the one placement where the native honestly *tries* to tell a joke. Often, it's told in a rather slow, dry and droll way with the punch line often forgotten. This is a cautious individual who sometimes loses direction and seems scattered. Saturn here exemplifies the concept that "a deal is a deal" and stays with its promise. "Monkey mind" Gemini is under control with some values and good judgment but that, too, can be laid aside if some forbidden fruit is desired. This placement of Saturn likes to solve problems, is thorough and logical. Unlike the usual Gemini trait, change in this case has little appeal to the native. Law and justice are respected in the term "put it in writing," a good reference to remember.

Cancer. Saturn is *a stranger in a strange land.* Saturn is weak and vulnerable here, this individual often has bad judgment and seeks scapegoats for his own lack of success. When this individual seeks control, he can make half truths into ideals. He will often relate to others by distinguishing his own concerns as everyone else's, the poor me "look what they have done to *us*" attitude. The individual with this placement of Saturn recognizes weakness in others and can turn their depression into anger, then exploit them with damaging results. Good judgment is needed here, more so than any other placement. Strong friends who are emotionally reserved with a love of independence and virtuous moral fiber who are wise in council should be cultivated and emulated. The

171

individual with Saturn in this position knows laws are made to be manipulated and the people in control use them best.

Leo. Here Saturn is seen as a person who finds little fun in life. He takes on the holy man syndrome. Saturn is moving toward its exaltation point. The individual with Saturn in Leo follows the gnostic point of view and believes that life here on Earth is a struggle to be overcome. "Karma spoken here" is the placard that hangs around their necks. Saturn in Leo people usually have the healing touch, but do not call it an art in front of them. Generally reliable and often loyal to individual friends and acquaintances, there may be a dislike for social contact in general. Saturn in Leo defines the person who believes in divine retribution.

Virgo. The native with Saturn in Virgo is rarely adrift but searches for answers to the many difficult situations that life presents. He is not as morose as the Saturn placement in the previous constellation but is just as concerned with his well-being, both physical and moral. The individual with Saturn in Virgo is a good honest researcher and believes that the truth is out there and it needs to be told. This placement is pedantic and exhibits good business judgment and is generally honest. His pact with his clients is done with integrity. The person born with Saturn in Virgo knows that virtue and intelligence are their own reward. The native recognizes that it is a only a matter of time before law and justice catch up with any perpetrator of wrongdoing: "Give 'em enough rope and they'll hang themselves."

•

MARS

In the ancient world, **Mars** represented the most vicious of natures. This planet, along with Saturn, was associated with death and destruction and the carnage of warfare. The Egyptians and Babylonians alike had magic spells designed specifically to weaken the destructive powers of Mars. The Chaldeans physically observed the arrival of the spring equinox with the Sun in the constellation of Aries and, by sunset, Libra is seen rising on the eastern horizon. Taking this to the next step, the Vedic scholars formulated this theory: When Libra is rising, Scorpio is on the second house cusp with Aries on the seventh house cusp, both are ruled by the planet Mars. From the beginning, Hindu/Vedic astrology used the *second* and *seventh* house as indicators of death in their charts. Mars associated with Saturn in the Babylonian canonical texts indicates destruction and famines.

According to Babylonian myth, Mars is the brother of the other warrior planet, Saturn. Both were considered to be the planets of deliberate destruction. When joined by hard aspects, they were their most brutal and pernicious selves with indefatigable energy for destruction. Mars loves squares and oppositions. The chart reflects the enjoyment of conflict in its exaltation and avoidance of conflict in debilitation.

Mars in exaltation is placed 28° in the sign of **Capricorn.** The person with this placement is considered hard hitting, defiant, ambitious and success-oriented. He is always willing to fight and endure hardship for his own principles, leadership and independence to the end.

Aquarius. Mars in Aquarius looks for new and unique ways to perform his duties. This person has a sense of fairness and is willing to take up and champion causes for reform. However, even though he is the knight errant, he can sometimes be contradictory, mercenary and superficial.

Pisces. The quiet warrior who enjoys secret societies and campaigns, and can be quietly vengeful.

Often seen in a negative light by companions and in love unions as unreliable.

Aries. Mars in Aries reflects a person who is impatient and irascible with the urge to do something, whether it's right or wrong. A fighting spirit with a zealous nature. This person is often energetically wasteful like rocking a chair when sitting or making too many moves while performing a simple task.

Taurus. This person has physical endurance and strength; the persistent warrior who refuses to give up. A better friend and a terrible, vengeful enemy.

Gemini. We find a quick thinker who loves a battle of the wits rather than a physical conflict. Here the warrior is mentally and physically adroit with the psychology of war, the best defense is a good offense.

Cancer. An individual with Mars in Cancer generally lacks self-control concerning the physical appetites. A poor warrior, he is often seen as an easy mark, acts on instinct, fears retribution, and seeks protectors.

Leo. The person with this Mars can be timid but his appearance is one of self-confidence and assurance. He is very enterprising and avoids physical battle as though he cannot be bothered with the trifles of disputes. A better administrator than warrior.

Virgo. Mars battles behind the scenes, is also good at strategy, does things in a methodical manner, and prepares well for projects and campaigns. He is the strategist who designs the plans of attack or defense.

Libra. The native with this Mars uses diplomacy and detante as its battleground. The person with Mars in

Libra seeks alliances to gain his own ends. Love of teamwork and its social aspects are dominant.

Scorpio. There is a heightened awareness for self-preservation, a gang type, quiet when alone, ruthless with peer groups. Persistent goal orientation and critical of his actions, Mars in Scorpio represents power and its relentless urge for attainment.

Sagittarius. An individual born with Mars here is often considered an instigator, the rabble rouser who will enthusiastically exploit the fields of conflict. It represents a "producer" whose self-interest is best served by promoting contests. The love of physical extravagance, over- exercise or grand energetic displays; showcasing.

•

VENUS

Long associated with love and art, **Venus** has a dual nature. It is at its best when giving, helping or dispensing comfort but, when used for selfish ends, she becomes covetous of someone else's love, money or anyone else's possessions. Once the goal is acquired, Venus becomes either dissatisfied or disappointed. Many times Venus, as the highest planet by degree, gives up on a project or love affair because of some disappointment in the matter.

In Babylon, women lived in the temple of Ishtar (Venus) until they were bought for pleasure. Many times a woman was not considered acceptable for marriage until her stay in the temple was completed. The Venus energy is very aggressive when seeking to acquire what it wants and becomes lazy or listless once the desired object is acquired. Venus can be the most enigmatic planet in the chart and will reflect the overall nature of any combined planetary picture by aspect. An old adage that fits Venus very well is, "Venus makes you chase her until she catches you." Those

175

with Venus in water signs serve others well, they speak well in air signs but are generally more selfish in fire signs and warlike in Earth signs.

The chase for Venus fits extremely well in the form of exaltation in the sign of **Pisces.** This individual is demur and tantalizing. She smiles beckoning with one hand while assuming a posture of resistance with the other. The positive influence of Venus in the chart is that of comfort and ease. It is a person who aids those in need and generally is involved in securing assistance for those less fortunate. One who longs for true love and companionship.

Aries. The individual expresses this Venus attribute the same as he does in Pisces, only more aggressively. The posture of resistance is lessened or altogether gone. This position is often associated with romantic dreaming; being swept up off one's feet into an affair of passionate love. Negative aspects to Venus increase the aggressive nature, with the desire to experience "the good things in life" at the expense of others.

Taurus. The individual with this Venus has a strong power of attraction who may be the epitome of sexy and lazy. This position of Venus fit the Babylonian concept of the temple sister best, if you want something pay for it. Venus in Taurus is often seen as a constant, faithful and conservative individual. However, if we could ever be fortunate enough to hear this individual throw his tantrum, we might hear, " I want it, I want it, I *want* it...is that it? Where's the rest of it? There's got to be more for later!" Lover of luxury and ease.

Gemini. The native recognizes that there are so many lovers, so little time, too few excuses. You never know whether this individual is serious or joking. The native is charming and seeks the company of anyone who enjoys other "party time" people. Negative Venus in Gemini often finds it difficult to say no to requests.

Cancer. The person with Venus in Cancer instinctively knows just how to please, just the way, when and where you like it. This placement often expresses itself as a strong urge to lean on his partner. An appreciation of family ties. Artistic surroundings.

Leo. The native is outspoken about another' person's performance or duty yet refuses to be outspoken about what he desires, hopes for or needs. His quick reaction to uncomfortable conditions is often misunderstood and attracts resentful situations. He desires ease, wants to be pleased as well as pleasing. This condition expresses a person with a warm heart who loves pleasures and games.

Virgo. Venus is in debilitation here, and the person, although compassionate and moral, is rarely soft and mushy. Love is seen with practical considerations and may be considered too emotionally draining and demanding; however, companionship is desired.

Libra. We find the native to be a wonderful actor and socialite! Charming and graceful, this person knows how to live. Venus in Libra indicates an obliging nature that makes it easy to establish contacts quickly and easily.

Scorpio. We find a direct drive Venus, whatever the native wants with this Venus placement, he gets! This placement runs the gamut between extreme self control to licentiousness.

Sagittarius. A good Don Juan or Juanita can exploit the best of them. This placement suggests the song, "Just a Gigolo." This placement has an infectious buoyancy with idealistic notions about love and romance.

Capricorn. This native knows just what he wants, just the way he likes it. Sometimes a good fight sets the mood for making up. Responsibility coupled with self control is important in relationships.

Aquarius. This placement is gregarious. It indicates a love of friends while retaining an aire of independence. A lover of unique "artistic bohemian type" friendships and a supporter of the work they do. Venus in Aquarius generally has eccentric views on love relationships or an eclectic series of partners. A lover of anything state of the art or, on the other end of the spectrum, antiques. Attachments are considered cumbersome and anything the native has is for sale. However, do not expect this native to just give it to you.

•

Conclusion. With the Vedic or tropical method, always note the sign and house in which a planet is placed, because its influence is "regulated" by the sign's ruler (like living in an apartment and abiding by the rules of the manager). In other words, planets behave differently in different houses and signs. A planet's influence is two-fold: it represents what you will receive from the house of experience and it represents what you must learn to do in that house to expedite your success or fulfillment.

Whatever the nature of a planet, it will exhibit its nature in the arena of the sign in which it resides. And, whatever position the planet, it is expressed through the house it is associated or rules. For example, Saturn in Gemini, located in the tenth house, produces a Saturn "regulated" by Mercury in the arena of life's objectives. We are now interested in two things: the location of Mercury by sign to recognize the "attitude" Mercury possesses in its regulation of Saturn in Gemini, and the location of the sign Capricorn for where the placement of Saturn is best expressed.

Saturn in Gemini suggests that the native learn to express himself in a clear concise manner for proper communication because Saturn/Gemini-tenth-house indicates a battle of wits with superiors in the professional work place. The native's expression is best served through fifth house matters, i.e., creative but practical application in his approach to persuade superiors to subtly recognize his point of view. The same holds true for planets with a contrary nature to the sign in which it resides. As always the above descriptions are modified by aspects and other planetary and house position factors.

The process of planetary exaltation and debilitation is an important resource for those of you interested in Tropical astrology. A chart explored in this manner can be very rewarding and revealing. Mars conjunct Venus in Pisces might make a compassionate assassin, providing the rest of the chart supported such a notion. However, if Saturn is in Pisces as well, we might recognize a charismatic champion overcoming tremendous obstacles while at the same time encouraging others in a similar situation to do the same.

On the other side of the coin, we often find an individual with a Mars/Venus/Pisces configuration who has great potential but is lax in his efforts and lets the "chips fall where they may." Often individuals with this configuration do as little as possible for themselves but this attitude often creates an interest in others to do things for them. In addition, an individual who knows how to use the principle of "Pisces power" may become wealthy using his "seemingly helpless dilemma" to attract people who feel the urge to help him get rich.

In another view, the same conjunction of Venus, Mars and Saturn in Leo might produce someone who might be likened to the adage: "When life hands you a lemon, make lemonade." Tropically, every planet so placed is additionally altered by its sign, position and ruler's placement. Thus, if Mars is exalted in Capricorn, Tropical astrologers need to look at Cancer, Aries and Scorpio and then find the sign in which Saturn is located and that ruler's sign placement and so on.

The generic exaltation/debilitation graphic scale at the end of this chapter will help to determine the process of the planets in chart delineation. In using the scale, the *starting point* for each planet begins *from its own* exaltation point by degree and sign. They are then judged by degree of separation from their exaltation point. However, the beginning portion of this chapter is intended to compare it with the position of the overall planetary placements in the stack which is presented next. Having described the Tropical views, we now want to examine the exaltation points using the sunset method. You will find that both sources of information are valuable in discovering the character of the person in the chart. However, you will find that the sunset method is quicker.

The Chart for Gandhi

In view of Gandhi's exaltation graph (end of chapter), Saturn and Mercury are high on the scale and so is the Moon. Jupiter, Mars and Venus are moving away from debilitation toward exaltation, placing further emphasis on his ability to achieve his ideals. For Tropical aspects discussed in Gandhi's chart, it is important to notice the house placements of planets that have any aspect combination to Mercury, Saturn or the Moon and how are they interact with each other.

In the sunset chart system, the reference to house positions is basically to determine the age at which events will take place. Gandhi will undoubtedly exert quite an influence in the time-frames indicated by their planetary house placement in the sunset chart.

The Sunset Method

Many new astrologers make the mistake of observing charts as if they were photographic snapshots of frozen points in time. As no point in time is completely static, neither is the horoscope. Astrological charts must be considered as living and evolving entities reflecting their counterpart's lives. As with life, their motion is constant. In the final analysis, we are not interested in observing just a *single planetary point* by place and aspect, but the overall changing positions as suggested by the rogression.

For example, in the sunset second decanate of changes, Gandhi has the Moon located in the fifth house and Saturn in the ninth house. They both have the same degree but Saturn is the most influential planet in the decanate because it is higher by just 23 minutes of arc. However, the Moon is also influential because of its close proximity to Saturn. These two planets indicate the age at which major changes would occur in the rogression. They are trine to each other which indicates the age of twenty-four, also they both sextile the Sun and a sextile is 60° of arc or twelve years of real time. When Saturn rogresses to the Sun, the Sun will in turn rogress to the Moon indicating the first major event of his life at age twelve. Another major change in Gandhi's life would take place at about the age of twenty-three to twenty-four because Saturn would reach the Moon's placement. Within the time frame of those events, he would either change the world around him in some manner or the planetary influences would reflect a personal change in him and his outlook. The changes would come about by the nature indicated by the planetary influences.

At birth, he has no planet 15° away from the Sun. However, in the chapter "The Moon," we discuss and emphasize an advancement of one-degree for each six years of life. With the Moon's rate of motion of 13° 25' in 24 hours or, to be exact, 1° 07' every six years, we advance the moon to find it has moved to the position of exactly 15° from the Sun in the stack (Chaldean exaltation) by the age of 60 years 3 months. This is about the time he encouraged India's chief negotiator, Nehru, to declare that India's goal was complete independence from British rule.

The 30° Stack

Review the sections on the 30° wheel or planetary stack on pages fifty-three and eighty-nine. The 30° stack completely eliminates the above method and process of exaltation but its usefulness in this work lies in comparative reference. Using the Sidereal mathematical formula, we look for the planet that is the highest by degree of longitude. It is often placed in the third decanate between 20° 00' and 29° 59'. Any planet located therein, by its nature and influence, indicates the overall ideal an individual seeks to achieve. More planets located in the third decanate indicate complexities as to what one wishes to accomplish. The planet closest to, but under 20° in the second decanate, is most influential in problem solving, while the planet closest to, but under 10° in the first decanate, indicates the more influential planet for developing the native's personal ideal situation as noted by the planet at the top of the stack in the third decanate. With many planets located in any one decanate, the native places emphasis in that decanate. The tri-planet configurations further diagnose the "harmonic" sensitivity of each planet by the placement between the upper and lower planet.

Conclusion. The sunset positions give us a quicker read with basically the same results as the extensive Vedic charts. We immediately recognize, by numerical value, the planet with the most influence by its location in each decanate. The planet with the highest degree by longitude is the ruling planet of the chart. The highest planet in each decanate is basically the chief influence of that decanate and subject to the highest planet's overall influence.

Long	
♅	28 ♊ 45
♃	27 ♈ 17 ℞
♆	25 ♓ 30 ℞
♂	25 ♎ 05
⚷	24 ♈ 44 ℞
♀	22 ♎ 50
♄	19 ♏ 24
☽	19 ♋ 01
☉	15 ♍ 27 29

☊ True 12 ♋ 48 ℞

☿	10 ♎ 30
MC	02 ♋ 56
AS	02 ♎ 49

The outer trans-saturnian planets lie dormant until the native develops his leadership abilities. In Gandhi's case, the principles of Jupiter, not Uranus, represent the ideal he "sought after" in his youth. Gandhi's mother was very religious and, consequently, he was brought up in a religious atmosphere. However, between the ages of twenty-four and twenty-five, Uranus, the planet of revolutionary activity, began to manifest in his life and soon he began to reflect that energy relating to Uranus as the overall planetary ruler.

The configuration of Saturn ruling the second decanate with close support from the Moon generally reflects as self-control and/or "controlling"–two of Gandhi's strong traits.

The lowest decanate has no planets but it does contain the mathematical points of the Midheaven and Ascendant. The mathematical points generally reflect as being absorbed more in the mental rather than the physical realm.

Once Gandhi recognized his calling as a revolutionary, Uranus became the exalted planet. His early training under Jupiter's religious principles became his main theme in leading his countrymen out from under British rule. His vows of poverty and fasting are reflected perfectly in the decanate of change under Saturn's influence while still in keeping with the exaltation of Uranus. The lower decanate, ruled by the Midheaven, also supports Saturn and Uranus in the decanates of change and ideals.

Figure 6.1
Gandhi's sunset exaltation chart

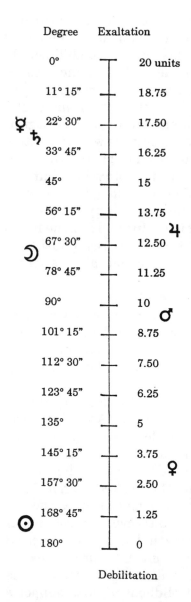

Degree	Exaltation
0°	20 units
11° 15"	18.75
22° 30"	17.50
33° 45"	16.25
45°	15
56° 15"	13.75
67° 30"	12.50
78° 45"	11.25
90°	10
101° 15"	8.75
112° 30"	7.50
123° 45"	6.25
135°	5
145° 15"	3.75
157° 30"	2.50
168° 45"	1.25
180°	0

Debilitation

The outer trans-saturnian planets are not used in the Vedic system, only the planets that range from the Sun to Saturn. On the right side of the chart, Venus, Mars and Jupiter are leaving the point of debilitation and are ascending toward exaltation. These three planets, by sign and house placement, reflect the native's ideals and aspirations. Saturn, Mercury, the Moon and Sun are moving away from exaltation indicating an awareness of the material world and the native's requirements to meet its conditions. Notice Saturn and Mercury are less than thirty degrees from exaltation, together, both planets reflect determination and resolution–something easily recognized in Gandhi's lifestyle. The Moon is between exaltation and debilitation and is rendered less important than the sunset chart revelation. The Sun is debilitated indicating that Gandhi's physical health may be weak in Virgo. Also, Virgo Sun generally expresses the service to other people's needs rather than his own.

Figure 6.2
Gandhi's Vedic exaltation chart.

This table is designed to enable you to determine the exaltation value of each planet. As the scale is generic, all planets begin with their own sign and degree of exaltation. Do not get confused, 0° **represents** the starting point of each different initial degree of exaltation. Start at the point marked "20 units" or "0°" count the degrees from exaltation (or debilitation) and work downward (or upward if you are starting from the place of debilitation).

For example, should the Moon be placed 23° Libra, count from 3° Taurus to 3° Libra. The distance is five signs plus 20° or 170° from its point of exaltation (from 0° on the chart). In this case, we would allot the Moon only 1 unit of strength because it is 10° from its place of debilitation, which is 3° Scorpio. The same holds true if you were to start from the debilitation point.

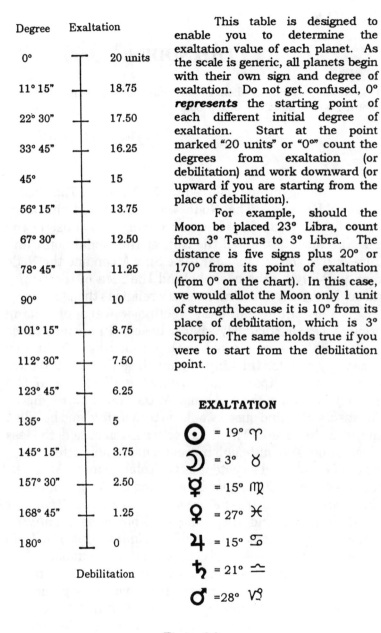

Degree	Exaltation
0°	20 units
11° 15"	18.75
22° 30"	17.50
33° 45"	16.25
45°	15
56° 15"	13.75
67° 30"	12.50
78° 45"	11.25
90°	10
101° 15"	8.75
112° 30"	7.50
123° 45"	6.25
135°	5
145° 15"	3.75
157° 30"	2.50
168° 45"	1.25
180°	0

Debilitation

EXALTATION

☉ = 19° ♈
☽ = 3° ♉
☿ = 15° ♍
♀ = 27° ♓
♃ = 15° ♋
♄ = 21° ♎
♂ = 28° ♑

Figure 6.3
Generic Vedic exaltation Chart

185

CHAPTER 7

THE NODES

The most important ingredient in the formula of success is
knowing how to get along with people.

Theodore Roosevelt

The Egyptians referred to the Node as "The Hidden One" in Heaven. The Node was considered the most powerful heavenly force because during an eclipse of the Sun the Moon conjoined the Sun at the Nodal point and appeared to shut off its light. The Sun, Moon and the Node may possibly be the basis behind the idea of the trinity throughout early and contemporary religious thought.

For the Chaldeans, eclipses were menacing occurrences, particularly solar eclipses. In ancient times such events were viewed with foreboding. This was especially true for the king. So much so that for 100 days after a solar eclipse, a *substitute king silently ruled* the country in place of the real king. At the end of his reign, the substitute king and queen would go to *their fate* and be killed to fulfill the omen. The lunar eclipse was considered less threatening and, although it drew considerable attention, it was not considered as potent as the solar eclipse. At times, lunar eclipses could be seen as favoring the king, but only if they were altered by the presence of Jupiter, Venus or magical spells and incantations known as *namburbi*. Nearly forty percent of the tablets *Enuma Anu Enlil* are devoted to the discussion of eclipses and their omina.

However, as we have seen in tertiary and minor lunar progressions, transiting eclipses aspecting planets in the birth chart portend major changes in life circumstances. Often, when a progressed angle falls on one of the prenatal eclipse points, the possibility of "death" arises. This does not necessarily mean the actual demise of the native but rather drastic changes of circumstances. Sometimes the configuration produces lottery winners, possibly an inheritance or other fortunate circumstances giving rise to the death of the previous state of affairs. Of course, other characteristic elements in the chart must support this possibility. On the average large events will include large planets in the birth chart to support such changes.

Nodal Mechanics

The Nodal point at which the Moon intersects the ecliptic is actually two points. The northern latitude is the *ascending* North Node. Conversely, the southern point is the *descending* South Node. The North Node is often referred to as the dragon's head and the South Node as the dragon's tail. The Node's speed is approximately three minutes of daily arc and takes a little less than 19 years to complete its cycle around the zodiac. The Nodes travel in a *stutter step* manner. That is, they are retrograde for a period of time, then turn direct in motion, then back to retrograde again. During the solstice periods, their two motions are about equal in length. As the Sun approaches the equinoxes, the direct motion of the Node becomes very short in duration but nevertheless occurs. Many astrologers have chosen to ignore the true node and only follow the Node's mean motion. However, with this custom it is always considered retrograde—an astrological practice that seems questionable. To ignore even a portion of the mechanics of celestial motion brings up the debate of what else may be overlooked.

Uses of The Node

From an astrological point of view, the Node is probably the most enigmatic point in the chart. We seem to be directed by an "indefinable something" within us that

187

pulls us toward different circumstances which determine our lifestyle along with the people to whom we are attracted. The Nodes represent our affinity to people and situations. The Nodes represent everyone we meet—our employers, our teachers, both formal and informal and anyone else who will disseminate their opinions, ideals and ways of living to us. And, as we shall see, when placed between two planets in the stack, the Node's direction becomes extremely important and gives us a clearer picture of our inner urge to attract people to us represented by the planets above and below the Node. It is my conviction that the Node represents curiosity, the "soul's" interest in learning about the life principle through our inner drives. The Node is *not* the same inner person as "the hero" we identify with in movies or books, that is the meaning behind the Ascendant. The Node represents the real people with whom we wish to identify with and their message.

There are different techniques that one can employ when working with the Node. One such technique is using the *Moon's North Node* of the birth chart as *the Ascendant* and reading the planets from their newly assigned positions. This method is often referred to as the "draconian chart" and many practitioners adamantly claim that this chart reveals the destiny of the individual. Quite a distinct chart, but if the native has the Moon located on the fourth house cusp, it would be in the best interest of the native NOT to follow the destiny of this chart.

Another technique employed when working with the Node is finding the ideal place to live. This is done by using the longitude of the Moon as the Ascendant and then placing the birth chart on a map of a city or any other area of interest. Along the line of direction by which the North Node lies is the most ideal spot   The direction of the South Node is the less desirable place in which to reside (Saturn conjunct either Node is undesirable). However, the Moon represents vulnerability and a desire to please, so the question of being easily swayed in one's new environment does arise, even more so when it is placed on the Ascending angle. Such an influential Moon placement demands that the native living in such an area must stay grounded.

Anyone who decides to do this should be aware that he may be excessively influenced by others. Unchecked, the native may be swayed to the degree that he would be too busy helping others to live his own life.

Often, when a client is in a state of indecision, you may observe that the minor or tertiary lunar progressed Node is changing directions. If this is the case, look to the planet in the direction that the Node is traveling for a clue to your client's solution.

When located in the fifth or ninth house, the North Node promises enlightenment or refinement. The Nodes are said by Hindu/Vedic practitioners to work most favorably in the constellations of Gemini and Virgo or in the third or sixth houses. Examine the charts of famous personalities with whom you are familiar and see if any of these techniques describe their life circumstances. The Hindu/Vedic view of the unrefined South Node is generally prone to coarseness in the house in which it resides and the people represented by the South Node are usually limited in some capacity.

In Vedic astrology, both Nodes are considered negative. The North Node is said to exhibit a Martian quality while the South Node exerts a Saturnine influence. This holds true if we keep in mind that the sunset system views the North Node as outgoing and acquisitive while the South Node is attritional. Those of us who are South Node types need to manage our affairs with some form of a contingency plan or insurance policy in mind. In this way losses (if any) would be held to a minimum.

The Metaphysical Node

A nodal point in physics relates to the zero point in a system. In mathematics, it is the point at which a continuously curved line crosses itself. The Node is defined as "the intersection or terminating point of two or more lines or curves." Egyptians viewed existence in this fashion. They saw all existence as different combinations of intersecting energy patterns that permeated the universe. The result of these intersecting vibrations was the world of material form. The fields of energy, as they saw it, pre-existed outside the material world and were three-fold in nature: neutral, active and inactive, all behaving in wave-like patterns. The *active* energy patterns were considered conscious life force: *inactive* patterns were considered *inert*.

The interplay of the consciously active and unconsciously inactive energy patterns produced, at their intersecting nodal points, a vibratory force that became static. Within the static field, a third force was created, its result was the physical existence of matter. The interplay of stronger inertia or inactive fields resulted in inanimate objects, such as the various geological metals and ores of the Earth. *Animate* objects, such as all living flora and fauna, have *more life force* than that of inert objects; human beings are at the apex of creation and have the most conscious life force. Given the Egyptian view, the *entire* expression of existence is through the different levels of *nodal* vibration.

Should we extend the Egyptian point of view, the Node in astrology may reflect Rupert Sheldrake's treatise on *pre-existing archetypes* which are genetically coded, predetermined forms lying dormant in the form of seeds or eggs. These codes determine what makes a horse a horse or a tree a tree—it is what the DNA code fashions itself after.

With this outlook, the Node can then be expressed in the astrological chart as a pre-existing archetype, the coagulating force and the indicator of the current incarnation. With a general esoteric view, the Sun (our masculine side) symbolizes the life-giving force while the Moon, that of inertia (our feminine side), symbolizes the reflective forms of life. By placing the Node between the planets in the stack, the combination forms the third point in the chart that well expresses the idea of the religious trinity and how we express it by creating our life pattern.

Many astrologers think that the North Node is the point in the chart where the client expresses his higher resources for achievement and the South Node forces retreat to a less ambitious mode. Under this frame of reference, the Node becomes the only sygil in the chart that does not have complete expression as do the planets, Ascendant or Midheaven. I find this simple interpretation of the Node to be too restricted. The idea of a limited Node forces astrologers to box the person into the horoscope thereby confining our understanding of his truer potential. However, the above interpretation on ambition may hold true if the triadal energy pattern determines such a life style.

North Node - Transits

The *transiting* Node aspecting a natal planet, especially by conjunction, in either the rogressed or birth chart, is *not* part of the inner core of our being and it must be interpreted differently. The transiting Node is often experienced as meetings with individuals or situations which inspire and/or create the sense of opportunity. The result of this conjunction produces the feeling that the *chance of a life time* is at hand depending on the nature of the planet involved.

This transit often brings with it an imperative urge for the native to drop current projects and put forth extra effort to either assist, interact or just to be with the individual represented by the planet that the Node is aspecting in the birth chart. The transiting South Node works exactly the opposite. The people we meet under the South Node influence quickly fall into the category of "loser" or "flake" and we either drop them or they move on. Usually best laid plans under the South Node influence disintegrate and nothing comes of the matter.

Interpretation of planetary **transits** by the **North** Node with the following planets:

Mars. There is inspiration or a sense of opportunity brought about by a male figure. A quest that has often been pondered and, during the transit, the native is encouraged to act upon it. It's the ability to endure much discomfort or anguish while allowing no thought of diversion or retreat.

Venus. There is inspiration and opportunity brought about by a female figure or organization. In a man's chart it may represent the girl of his dreams and marriage becomes a possibility. This transit also represents the ability to recognize and possibly exploit the current trend and style of society's attachments. Usually the native will follow the concept "when in Rome, do as the Romans do" and join in some trendy vogue at this time. Potential for growth lies in understanding the innermost core of a group's consciousness. Disappointment in expecting too much to come of this transit may be experienced.

Mercury. This may represent a youthful person of either sex. Using and understanding the power of the alchemy of the mind supersedes all earthly treasures. A new philosophy, study or research, or a new friend may inspire interest in a mentally stimulating project. At some point, the native will come to the realization that acquiring knowledge allows one to achieve the status of a *beacon* to those in darkness. A thousand years of darkness is dispelled by a single flash of light. Before one sets sail, it is important to know the capabilities of one's vessel.

Moon. This may represent a matronly woman who has the capacity to understand one's deeper needs. A sensitive person with the ability to teach techniques to overcome feelings of vulnerability; a time to recognize one's own inner power and potential by showing others who feel helpless how to gain self-empowerment. The opportunity to help other people. The timing of this transit may coincide with the reorganization of a project thought finished. New insights may come under way.

Sun. This often typifies meeting a prominent male figure with a strong sense of purpose. It is a person who desires childlike acceptance from those who will follow and not question his lead. The creative spirit may be set free. Situations occur which foster recognition of what has been lacking in one's life, yet there may be the desire to hold back such information from the native. What Earthly treasure can ensnare the soul as to abandon the love of self in its quest? A possible religious quest.

Jupiter. A male figure may appear in the native's life encouraging change to satisfy his own end. In a woman's chart there is the desire to become married to the individual represented by Jupiter. There may be the excitement of exploration or trying something new. One must be careful not to bite off more that he can chew; exploitation in some form must be avoided. Often during this transit false hopes and expectations arise without justification.

Saturn. Either an older man or matronly figure may appear to present a task which, once accomplished, will bring recognition. Set procedures and planning are in order; any alternatives outside the norm are denied. A conventional plan of action creates success in one's state of affairs. There is success through organization.

The South Node

The attritional South Node entices us to take defensive action. It represents the fear of loss that motivates us to create contingency plans. One recognizes a need for protection and insurance for the protection of what has already been gained. The South Node is attritional by nature; dissolution occurs gradually. We may find ourselves asking, "How is it that the accumulation of the world's material stuff can retard one's ability to take proper action? Do my possessions own me? What devil torments me by day and renders my nights sleepless?"

Mars. A new male acquaintance may inspire a physical fitness program to firm up aging muscles. The need to keep pace with competitors may begin to flag during this transit. Self acceptance is important during this transit. Losses through a male associate.

Venus. One may recognize that the aging process occurred too suddenly and youthful members of the opposite sex now refer to the native more with respect than interest. Treasures may be stored and security strengthened during this transit. The need to invest for the future comes to light. Losses through a female associate.

Mercury. The thought of losses and separation may create such anguish that one may find himself drawn closer to a situation in order to avoid experiencing its losses. During this transit the best laid plans often go awry; contingency plans are necessary. Nuisance lawsuits come to mind. Advice at this time may prove costly.

Moon. During this transit one may be influenced by a person in a much weaker position than originally thought. The native may rely on help from those who actually cannot help him at all. There is a strong need to find that which was lost, yet to actively set about for its retrieval requires too much effort, so its chance of recovery is gone. A con artist comes to mind; one should guard heirlooms.

Sun. This is a quality which lives in the soul and produces a longing for approval from others by working harder, being more efficient or trying to become indispensable to a significant other. During this transit one may seek the accumulation of material goods as if his very existence depended upon it. During this transit a good insurance policy could be drawn up. Overexertion of the physical body may produce illness; it is best to pace oneself and get plenty of rest.

Jupiter. One should not overindulge or spend like a drunken sailor. One's ego may like it but the wallet will have to endure the pain. Care should be exercised so as to not *over* purchase one's insurance policy; know exactly what is needed. Exploiting others for worldly success to validate one's existence produces soul retardation. Negative habits should be reviewed at this time; gossip may prove disastrous.

Saturn. Separation from a condition, person or thing makes one feel uncomfortable and sad. It is important to remember that every knock is a boost. Through loss, what violation has taken place that makes one feel empty? The best time for a health check-up and general "fence-mending."

The Birth Node

The first objective concerning the Node is to decide which one is the more influential. To do this, look at the wheel in the sunset chart and notice which Node has more "traffic" or planets near it. The Node with the most traffic in the sunset chart is the Node of choice and is the Node that the native is working with in this lifetime. Next, in the stack, the North or South Node will be placed between two planets, this triad represents the type of persons to whom the native is attracted and/or repelled. Use the true Node and note whether it is retrograde or direct in motion.

In this discussion, I will use the term "soul" to describe the inner "something" that impels us to associate

195

with the people we do. In many cases I have found couples who have fallen in love at "first sight" have the Node and its triad positively reflected in each other's charts.

The Node's position between two planets is the initiative for the soul's birth and describes influential people and their teachings which we will meet throughout our lifetime (Venus - artists, Mercury - communicators, Saturn - ambitious types and so on). Its direction represents the inner need for experience and that need is described by the direction and planet toward which the Node is traveling.

The planet which the Node is leaving represents the type of experience the soul has already sustained and has an intrinsic knowledge thereof. The planet the Node is traveling *toward* is the new *style* of experience and general lifestyle that the soul is seeking. Pay close attention to whatever planet the Node is traveling toward–its qualities are the chief indicator of what the native needs to know to achieve his goal indicated by the planet that is the highest degree in the stack.

Of course, any new lifestyle will reflect the planetary lessons learned from the planet which the Node is leaving. With any form of progressed charts during the lifetime, the Node will occasionally change directions (retrograde or direct). It is during these times that the native may meet a new friend and develop an interest in the friend's field of expertise. Sometimes the native's lifestyle changes altogether. Again, pay attention as to which planet the Node is moving toward. Also, in the minor return, note the period of time the Node will remain in whatever motion it is in when any changes occurred.

Which Node

Occasionally, both Nodes can be active if each has conjunctions or traffic within exact degree and minute separation of arc. The chances of working with someone having this type of chart is nil, as they are very nomadic and are too busy searching for their own answers to be bothered by someone else's ideas about who they should be or what they should do.

Once the Nodal type is determined, the entire chart takes on an *inherent directional style for learning,* which establishes success in relation to the highest planet by longitude, the planet immediately setting after sunset, the lunar mansion and the sunset Ascendant. The other planetary configurations are directed by and subject to the style and influence of the nodal triad. By using this perspective, review different charts and you will find that the other planets and angles support and reflect the Node's position as life's compass. If they do not, this is the direction to which you, as an astrologer, want to alert your client. For those of us who do not incorporate the planetary lesson, (the people the Node indicates) are subject to confusion and lack an important factor in establishing our success.

As an example of this process we will review two charts. In Gandhi's sunset chart *wheel* we use the North Node because he was born with the Moon close to his North Node; the South Node is void of any traffic (see page 316).

In the *stack,* the North Node is *numerically placed* between the Sun and Mercury. The North Node is closer to Mercury by degree and it is also retrograde traveling toward Mercury. Therefore, Mercury has a strong influence by closeness of degree, motion and the planet setting after the Sun; trans-personal Uranus is the planet with the highest degree with the personal outer planet Jupiter supporting it. Hence, Mercury is the more powerful planet in the triad of Uranus (see page 131) and it is easy to see its Uranian influence. Furthermore, with Jupiter (ruler of his sunset Ascendant) being the highest *visible* planet, we can recognize that its principle of religion and consideration of others was Gandhi's childhood ideal. Between the ages of twenty-three to twenty-four, with a bruised ego (Sun), he recognized the social injustice against his people instigated by the ruling class; the energy of Uranus became the new principle, his new ideal. His prominent Mercury would become the voice of the Indian revolution (Uranus).

Known more for his "soul force" (Jupiter), and his revolutionary (Uranus) message (Mercury), Gandhi eventually claimed the limelight (Sun) of leadership through the unique and difficult circumstances of his protests; his life became his message suggested by such a strong Mercury. The tri-planetary picture of the North Node, Mercury and Sun, combined with the influence of his lunar mansion, very clearly describes his leadership abilities as a caring spokesperson for his people and the heads of state with whom he came in contact to further his lifestyle and purpose. Gandhi used the principles of both planets in his Node pattern (triad) by learning to communicate with the heads of state in his country.

The opposite end of the spectrum is exemplified by Adolf Hitler (see page 300). We choose the *South Node* from the *wheel* because of its planetary traffic near his natal Jupiter, hence the Node has a grandiose Jupiterian effect. Once the Node is ascertained we place it in the stack between Mars and Saturn which are within an orb of 2° 13' in square aspect. At this point, we discount Jupiter's influence because we are now concerned with the South Node placement in the *stack* which is closer to Mars than Saturn. Mars is also the planet setting after the setting Sun. The Moon is the planet with the highest degree, and Saturn is the first planet to contact an angle (the MC). As a team of planets, this affinity is very articulate in regards to negative circumstances.

To the ancients any combination of Mars and Saturn was considered deadly. The picture of Hitler's evil purposes through the South Node tri-planet configuration is very clear. Mars setting wants to be the knight in shining armor but in this case Mars is negatively influenced. The Moon seeks guidance in early life and later develops the need to be a guiding light but, with so many negative configurations, the Moon will reflect the negative patterns mentioned above. Cruelty and disaster followed in his wake.

Hitler only used the positive principles of Saturn (law and justice, self control) as a means for his rise to power.

Even though our interest lies with only the first seven personal planets (Sun to Saturn), the outer trans-personal planets are also placed in their natural order by degree. As mentioned in the chapter on the planets, the outer planets express the experience of a generation and do not *necessarily operate* in an individual's *early* life although the *promise* of their influence is in the background. In both cases above, we find no trans-saturnian influence exerted by either individual until they both gained wider recognition and a public following.

As an aside, in Marilyn Monroe's chart, we find that Pluto's position is closer to the North Node. This involvement suggests the final decisions in her life may not have been completely her own. The North Node is direct or traveling toward the Moon while retreating from Pluto and the Sun. Marilyn was born with the North Node between the Sun and Moon (vitality and feeling) with the Moon having more influence by degree (her roles of sexy innocence and vulnerability). Study the charts of famous personalities to determine how, after they became public figures, their trans-saturnian planets altered the Node's journey.

Rule. When calculating the primary Node of expression, we look at the *wheel* in the sunset chart and the Node with the closest planet by degree or the most traffic. This determines the primary influential Node for the native. In the *stack*, the closest planet by degree to the Node is the planet of influence and the Node carries with it the inflection of the closer planet. Whichever Node the individual operates under is considered the inner and basic urge. Its direction indicates the principles for success. The complete triad is almost a psychic calling when working with different issues and circumstances concerning the people in our lives (different from the highest planet which equates with desire or the Moon which is emotional or the Ascendant which is our fantasy self).

Planets conjunct the North Node either by transit or in the birth chart are more positive in their effect, and are associated with the vulnerable lunar inflection. The transiting North Node is magnetically influential, like the Moon. The adage, "If you see the Budda on the path, kill him," is an apt expression for both Nodal transits and lunar types. Its enigmatic message points out the danger of allowing something or someone else's influence to take over your own belief system and lead you astray. The South Node and planets conjunct it are always detrimental. They associate with the *negative influence* such as too much Sun (dehydration or sunburn) and relate to an excessive attachment to the material world. Often the health of the individual may be adversely affected by the South Node through the influence of the planet with which it is associated.

Destination Node

The following is a brief description of the Node placement in the stack as it travels on its course of destiny either by retrograde or direct motion. With the exception of Mercury, the expression of the personal planets is written in reflective prose to convey a sense of inner compulsion rather than firm direction. The planet indicated by *all caps* is the planet the Node is moving *away* from while the *subheading* is the planet of the Node's destination. As always, the planet which is closest to the Node by degree is the more influential. The Node we are reading about relates primarily to the North Node. The South Node indications are reversed.

•

SUN. It is our personal light. Our inner thoughts that often reflect who we believe we are. It also represents the powerful people we meet and interact with and our desire to expand our influence upon others. The Sun's strength is also our ability to recognize what we believe is needed from others for personal growth and development. We gather our life experiences in the same way a spinning wheel gathers wool. Then, we ask ourselves what dreams to pursue so the world will value our accomplishments.

Mars. Vitality. As I am the center of my world, to whom do I owe this existence? I can champion any cause to those who swear their allegiance to me. Leadership is nothing more than strength and survival of the fittest. I am aware of my physical being and its power.

Venus. The ideal; strong social attractions, glamour. What would become of me if I were unable to find someone to help me fulfill my dreams and ambitions?

Mercury. Common sense. Shall I ponder life's mysteries or simply accept existence as it is? Do I think in my innermost being that the challenge is too great for me to handle or not great enough? I observe my intellect. How do I use my knowledge to further myself? In what arena do I reveal my brilliance?

Moon. Instinct. With so many changes how can there be constancy? When all is well, whom do I thank and whom shall I curse when all has gone awry? Surely there are others who will hold my hand. I manage my emotions as I search for joint successes. I need someone to need me.

Jupiter. Recognition. I am special! I will first seek sponsorship and then pay handsomely for loyalty and allegiance as I am the rightful heir to the throne. There is a sucker born every minute and I inwardly hope it's not me.

Saturn. Modesty. As my life progresses, how can I take advantage of the things that interest me? How do I judge its value? Is that which is attractive good for me or more so for others?

•

MOON. The Moon is our weakness; any burden thrust upon us we accept. We can only know the situation but not the force behind it. One often asks, in whom can I place trust for help and succor? Are my adversaries and antagonists so powerful that I am to lose control? Are the needs of my friends above my own needs? How can I demur requests in a diplomatic way without hurting the feelings of others? The following list reflects the Moon in combination with each of the planetary energies.

Mars. Honesty. Impulsiveness leads to disaster, I must develop inner strength. Should I lead or follow? What if others are right and I am wrong? Caution here would be the best advice. In what way do I eventually learn the identity of my allies, maybe their wives can help. The influence of power and enterprise.

Venus. Affection. Touch me, hold me, caress me. I need to feel that I am loved. Why is so much demanded of me? Is there no one who will help? Why can't we do what I want sometime? The influence of diplomacy.

Mercury. Thoughtful consideration. Why is it that I always think of the perfect comeback after the conversation is finished? How can I get a clearer definition on the situation? Will I ever know enough to remove myself from the same old drudgery and grind? The influence of exchange and information.

Sun. Balance. Other people always seem to lead well. What if they don't like what I've done? I'll have to start all over again. I hate to be in charge when I have no idea what I'm doing. The influence of marriage.

Jupiter. The sense of false confidence, like whistling in the dark. Feelings of being overwhelmed by insurmountable odds. This is the most uncomfortable I've ever been. I'm so confused. I had better find someone who knows about these matters. Why does opportunity knock so softly while reality kicks the door down? The influence of success.

Saturn Reserved. I must find ways to gain self-confidence or self control. Isn't there any end to this situation? Things are never the same: up one minute and down the next. Where can I find stability? The influence of a woman in business.

•

MERCURY. If one will not admit that there is something to learn, one cannot be taught. The following reflects Mercury in combination with each of the planetary energies.

Mars. Inquisitive; critical. The thought process is defensive, argumentative. Just what did he mean by that? If I follow his instructions, will he laugh at me later? What is the correct course of action? Is there another Anne or shortcut that will result in the same outcome?

Venus. Artistic; romantic. The right words and phrases, diplomatic. Thinking influenced by a sense of beauty. There may be a better solution for all concerned but what do I get out of it?

Moon. Reflective; sensitive. My thought process is influenced by feelings. Perceptions are easily influenced. I have always had a quick mental grasp; facility in learning.

Sun. Direct; knowledgeable. I have the answer to any question. Where there is a will, there is a way. Common sense is about perceptive reasoning.

Jupiter. Philosophical; optimistic. My life is a mental banquet; intellectualism; I'm a teacher who teaches through understanding and not by rote. I understand what "walk a mile in my shoes" really means.

Saturn. Serious; logical. I know that there is a method or example for anything desired. I need to know the bottom line; search for options. I have the ability to learn from someone who has gone before and succeeded.

•

VENUS. The planet of giving with no strings attached can be a disappointment when we try to manipulate by gifts. In this light, she represents the disappointment of failing to find the support or promise of security within the social structure. There is need to be aware of one's own social position before support can be given. Indiscriminate associations should not be fostered. The following reflect descriptions of Venus in combination with each of the planetary energies.

Mars. Sensitivity in relationships. Coarseness becomes an issue. Having sex appeal, not just good looks, increases one's self worth. Softly stated yet strongly opinionated, it is important to be in control.

Mercury. Appreciation of eloquence. Failure to keep one's promises is non-productive. Charm and the soft-spoken word are effective social tools. Knowing the territory can put one in a position of avoiding disappointment.

Moon. Devotion to comfort. Self gratification comes first, but maybe I should consider the needs and desires of those close to me. Perhaps I will, later.

Sun. The ideal harmonious self. I want to gain the respect of others, but should I not have substance besides pleasant personal appearance and poise? Do my friends like me for who I am or what I offer?

Jupiter. Luxury. Friendliness and goodwill towards others create great expectations. However, I choose friends as assets with selfish aims in mind, and I may receive the compensation but you must see that it was all done for you.

Saturn. Dissatisfaction. I strive for positions of power yet downplay its value to others. For me, style and grace, this is an admirable trait. I want you to sacrifice while I pamper myself outrageously, "Do you have a problem with that ?"

The Outer Planets

Unlike Mercury or Venus, the outer planets, Mars, Jupiter and Saturn express themselves as objective or external influences. Our inner association to them is reflected by what we must do to mold, care for and protect our own personal environment. This would be the same as a farmer who, by following the guidance of the inner "how to do" planets, arrives at his decisions concerning planting. The outer planets relate to "the what to do" when considering all the possibilities of *what* crops to plant and for what purpose. The planet heading in all caps is the planet the Node is heading away from.

•

MARS. Energy. Mars represents the primal force that propels us toward our destinies. It is the excitement of clear and decisive action. It is the application of consistent force to effect or alter a situation.

Venus. Impulse. Associates are receptive to any new ideas you have. This may be the leader who promises to promote a project to others. Dependence on others often proves disappointing. Search for weakness in others.

Mercury. Tactical. Developing plans for approach or attack whichever is necessary. It is important to seek wisdom in any matter and to clarify its many facets.

Moon. Excitement. Hasty actions can often create remorse through unexpected casualties. This may be the urge to dominate others who are in a weakened position or who are open, giving and supportive to the needs of others.

Sun. Will power. Hard work is required to eliminate past indifference that has created discord. If truce is necessary to establish one's directives, then truce it is.

Jupiter. Enterprise. The jack of all trades who diffuses his energy by trying to be something to everybody; wasting time and energy. The amassing of assistance or helpers for the purpose of the exploitation of other people's efforts. The show of force.

Saturn. Resistance. Here we are actively seeking effective self sufficiency, correct action and defenses to resist or overcome our foes. What must be assessed to deny adversaries their power over ourselves.

•

JUPITER. Kingly. This often bestows honors and may operate in an expansive or impressive ways. A director would speak first to the administrators of the ruling class to enlist its efforts in recruiting volunteers.

Mars. Allegiance. Right action means to join forces with the activities and traditions of others and then defer their activity in favor of advancing oneself. The emerging hero.

Venus. Gain. The quality of one's lifestyle will quietly impart similar values to others. The native seeks to exploit popular sentiments in society. These are his expectations of support and devotion.

Mercury. Influential. This is the ability to express and inspire the desires of others which will attract able and enthusiastic helpers to assist in one's own aspirations.

Moon. Connections. There is an overblown sense of self importance, high expectations are dismally short. One pays too much for the goods or services received. It is necessary to find followers to support one's follies.

Sun. Self confident. This is often seen as an overly enthusiastic demeanor, such as grandiose expression and well-staged histrionics to accomplish deeds. One often sees himself in an association with God.

Saturn. Insightful. There is a drive to define new concepts to fit with steadfast ideas of others or an ascetic desire to achieve spiritual insight and wisdom.

•

SATURN. Consolidation. Learned principles and techniques. After many years of preparation if one fails to attain one's goals or objectives, this planetary combination inspires us to seek alternative measures for success.

Mars. This often indicates a heavy-handed means of persuasion and creates no end of annoyances. In order to enlist the assistance of others, it is necessary to focus on more subtle psychological approaches. Experience is a necessity for decisive action. Often one invests his time to see an enterprise come to fruition.

Venus. Experience. Prospects for business are alluring but the partners are not capable, nor is the product packaged correctly. Cooperative and loyal relationships require good judgment, openness and painful honesty.

Mercury. Logic. Learning the "ropes." Arguments and ultimatums accomplish nothing; small reforms with a restrained approach generate trust. Diplomacy is the key to successful alliance. Interest in proper marketing procedures.

Moon. Need. How does one break into the state of perpetual self-restraint by our potential customers to place our product into the consumer's hands? The act of trying to gain the confidence of others while in a weak position.

Sun. Observant. A serious attitude suggests that one re-evaluate and study the examples of success of those who have gone before. A quiet, calm demeanor may often be confused with aloofness.

Jupiter. Prudent. Enthusiasm about new projects or relationships eventually is bogged down with delays. To work one's way out of entanglements, a good administrator will distinguish parameters and organize the chaos; a poor one will submit. The bottom line, what's at stake?

•

OVERVIEW

In this work, the planets beyond Saturn (Uranus, Neptune and Pluto) are viewed as combinations of the first six planets, those between and including Mercury to Saturn and is covered in the chapter on the planets. This is not to say that the trans-saturnian planets are of no influence. To the contrary, now that they are used in today's world of astrology, it is impossible to avoid them, but the ancients did not work with the trans-saturnian planets.

One last note: remember the influence of the North Node is acquisitive in its expression. It gathers experience in positive, quiet, peaceful ways. It is symbolic of innate understanding of how to achieve one's desired goals by working for them without having to suffer. The South Node is attritional and thus symbolic of the prevention of losses or the need for contingency plans like an insurance policy. Planets associated with the South Node are like an infection that must be taken care of before the problem becomes a major one. For example, suppose we find the configuration of Moon/*South Node*/Saturn in a chart. We certainly cannot tell the native that he must never marry because the women in his life are only temporary affiliations. The problem is solved by suggesting that the native work in a field where women are transitory–the airlines, teaching or counseling to name a few. In the preceding discussion, planets associated with the North Node can be interpreted with their cookbook meanings in a positive way. Those associated with the South Node should be viewed as a negative influence.

As we rogress the chart, the *changing angles* (by sign and degree) also work extremely well with the lunar minor return. Also the Node will change direction many times using either the tertiary or minor progressed methods. Keep a watchful eye for such changes as they represent a change of direction or attitude in the native.

CHAPTER **8**

ANCIENT CHALDEAN SYSTEM

Life isn't a dress rehearsal.

Why the Sunset Chart?

Sunset. The Chaldeans began each new day with sunset. This fact is our basis for the following speculation on how the ancient Chaldeans may have conducted their heavenly observations.

When we view the birth chart combined with the sunset chart in a biWheel fashion, we immediately notice aspects between them of which we were previously unaware. For example, consider a person born four-hours and forty-eight minutes after sunset. We would find both charts relating to each other in an aspect called a quintile. This relationship between the two charts might explain a level of inventiveness that might otherwise not be indicated elsewhere. Another feature of the sunset chart is its use as a timing device between planetary arcs. The "ground rules" for events are described by the nature of the planets while the timing of such events is regulated by the distance of longitudinal arc from each other. Any and all personal aspects, regardless of degree, indicates the nature and timing of events, both by transits, and/or rogression.

As astrologers, we believe that our destiny is absolutely written in the stars, but at this time our current knowledge seems to fall short of such understanding. Any astrologer knows that the planets and their aspects pre-define and categorize the human condition which, hopefully, extends our horizons of predictability. However, many astrologers feel that their conclusions are only educated guesses, mere speculation through limited knowledge. Something is missing in the existing system. We all too often hear the term "there are no absolutes in astrology" suggesting either a lack of understanding or failure to properly categorize charts. Yet we continually see repetition of occurrences as cyclic events in our lives, in some instances we call them habits.

Astrology, as does life, does not respond well to the purely mathematical, yet it is within that realm that we base our analogies. In the present astrological system, there needs to be some method of classification that eliminates our lack of scientific definition; even though astrology fits within a criteria of science i.e, that of observable rules and principles which can be repeated. With our present understanding of astrology, although observable rules are part of the criteria, controlled repetition and/or duplication is unavailable. If this were not true, astrology would be placed in the same scientific category as the other sciences. This is the main reason astrology has not become a practiced science, such as psychology or meteorology (of which both are definitely based upon educated guesses and on probability).

There may be yet another reason why many people view astrology as non-scientific. Humanity is not ready to relinquish the idea of free will or that we personally live in an imperfect world. We do not accept the fact that we react to external influences in a mechanistic manner like so many sheep who jump because the one in front did. How many times have we left an uncomfortable situation wishing we had said or done something differently? To change reactive patterns we need to become proactive and decisive. We need to learn to take the initiative.

But how is this to be done? Not by believing we are acting in a proactive manner while still behaving in a reactive fashion. That is called denial. With this form of action we create an interesting Catch 22 because, in actuality, this performance clearly shows that we do not possess free will but a reactive will. By accepting this as fact, then and only then can we take the necessary steps to achieve true autonomy. The first step toward self-awareness is to observe the mechanical nature of our reactions which was dictated on the day we were born by our astrological configurations. Here is one example of how astrology can be most useful—learning how to recognize our own reactions in given situations.

It is our own subjectivity, our false evaluation of ourselves within our own mind, that tends to get in the way of true self analysis. Our subjectivity is the reason why many astrologers find it difficult to read their own charts. In the matter of "choices" what we actually do most of the time is decide between the lesser of two painful options. In this fashion we have become *somewhat* subjectively aware of ourselves which, according to very early literature, seems not to have existed in ancient cultures. Our subjectivity is where the term "free will" enters the picture—the all-inclusive escape clause for "psychics" who err in their predictions. At any rate, if we could objectively *categorize our subjective input* through examination of our own past *and* present circumstances, part of the problem of subjectivity would be solved and the work of deeper self-understanding could begin.

A thorough analysis of the sunset chart permits us to re-evaluate our old habits and then merge them with fresh, new ideas. The sunset chart, combined with the birth chart, contains many basic descriptions of ourselves with all the information we need for self observation. By analogy, the sunset chart becomes our *external planetary DNA.* Just like our internal sub-molecular code, the physical DNA prescribes our bodies' growth and characteristics, the external planetary DNA code is our prescribed pattern with which we can view our experiences and activities objectively.

Astrologers need to take a lesson from doctors and other professionals who require personal histories. Taking a personal history allows both the astrologer and client to learn what the planetary aspects personally mean to the client and how he is likely to respond to them at a later date. This is accomplished by choosing one planet at a time and rotating it around the chart and listing each aspect it has made to other planets and then relating the planet, aspect and position to past events. We do this with each planet to determine its meaning.

Double Chart System

As our lives evolve, we can now see that incidents and events are indeed presaged by planetary positions and their aspects, as located in various houses. At the risk of repetition, but for the convenience of the reader, this is found by casting two charts for sunset which places the Sun on or near the seventh house cusp. Using the equal house system, in a biWheel fashion, the Sun becomes the indicator of time while the active planet determines the event for the period.

To determine the time and influence of an event, we rotate the inner wheel at the rate of five degrees for each year of life (one complete house is equivalent to six years). By rotating the biWheel chart clockwise, the distance between planets by longitude presages the timing of future events described by the nature of the planets involved. Continue the process. As the different planets "come into play" and aspect each other (at times their own sunset position), the active planet(s) become the planetary "ruler of the period" indicating the event by its symbolic reference. Check the transits and minor progressions and note which planets are acting on the indicated rogressed planet. To further refine your interpretation, note the exact degree of solar arc from sunset to the planet coming under aspect. The event indicated *by transit* will take place at the time of year when the Sun is within the identical orb of degree as it was on the birth date.

As we will see, the rogression is where the sunset chart can be of most service. We rogress the inner wheel and determine past planetary reactions and how they relate to an event. The Sun's mean distance of arc from the sunset Sun depicts the native's age at the time of the event. Once determined, the astrologer can look for their cyclic recurrence at different levels (houses) in the future.

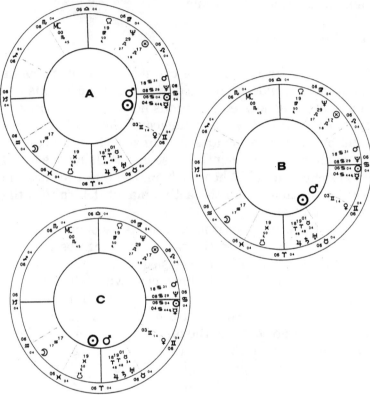

Figure 8.1

Example charts A, B, and C show Mars rogression to sensitive points in the sunset chart. In each case the native moved to another state. Therefore, Mars represents moving and will be in aspect every time the native changes residence.

With this knowledge, the astrologer is placed in the unique situation of knowing exactly how the native reacted to planetary aspects in the past. Past references about illnesses, accidents, change of locations as well as honors received give us a clear insight about future trends. This method takes the guesswork out of "what, when and where" by retrospective reviews that provide information prognosticating probable future experiences. Research using the sunset rogression method has shown that once astrological aspects and their personal meanings are confirmed, *the native will respond in a similar manner to the same configuration later in life.* However, similar to becoming aware of a bad habit, once the cyclic patterns and tendencies are recognized, a complete reversal of these circumstances may occur.

A good example of a reversal might be Mars square Jupiter. In a youthful chart the individual may be reluctant to follow the dictates of authority and become rebellious, extravagant, hasty and prone to exaggeration. As he matures, and having experienced these negative traits early in life, he may become aware that these traits have become wasteful distractions and are ineffective for a productive life. As a mature individual, his Mars square Jupiter may be seen as possibilities of future problems in his projects. His mature square now proposes contingency plans to offset such problems should or when they occur. His extravagant and rebellious nature is now put to more productive uses, and his hastiness is subdued to a more methodical approach to ensure success in his actions.

A New Starting Point

In developing the sunset chart, the first task was to take cuneiform text at face value rather than using mythological or philosophical references or trying to fit contemporary ideas into their texts. The Chaldeans held to the premise that the day began at sunset and ended on the following sunset. Within the course of the 24-hour period, the Babylonians watched for natural phenomena that would depict omens to describe the course of coming events. The Chaldean's extraordinary ability to scientifically observe and catalog heavenly phenomena is repeatedly cited by those who have taken the time to examine their culture.

Joseph Campbell wrote in *The Masks of God,* that the "arithmetic that was developed in Sumer as early as

B.C. 3200, whether by coincidence or by intuitive deduction, so matched the celestial order as to amount in itself to a revelation." O. Neugebauer cites that some (earlier) plan had to exist because "it is impossible to devise computational schemes of high complication without a very elaborate plan." Further, Mr. Neugebauer found that the Babylonian calculations were not those of the Babylonian observers but were "prepared from some fixed arithmetical schemes which were given and were not to be interfered with." Additionally, in *Tablets from the Archives of Drehem,* (records of the ruler of Ur, named Dungi), Stephen Langdon tells us that the Nippurian calendar selected a certain body of star patterns by whose setting *against the sunset* (author's italics) it was possible to determine the exact moment of the new year's arrival.

Obviously, by these statements we can see that the Babylonian people were sophisticated and intelligent when it came to celestial calculations. However, it is obvious that the Chaldean observers used the zodiac (lu-mes-mes) signs (singular lu-mas) as regions for their computation with no other meaning attached to them. One solar day equaled one ûs (degree of longitude) in the heavenly band of Anu (ecliptic). Babylonian ephemeride texts describing planetary motion of heliacal and achronychal stations are more mathematically calculated rather than depicting the arc as parts of a full 360° circle.

Omens, such as those below, clearly indicate such stations. These omens established "fixed" positions in relation to the planets' placement in the heavens.

"When the Ram by Jupiter will be entered,
* when *Venus enters the Moon,* (author's
emphasis) the watch will come to an end."
Other cryptic descriptions:
"When the Sun stands *in the station* of the Moon."
(author's)
"The Moon set and Mercury in its place fixed."
(W.A.I. 59,2)
"The Moon sets and Mars is fixed." (W.A.I. 59,7)

"The Moon sets and the Sun in the place where the Moon sets is fixed." (W.A.I. 54,1)

* If we embrace the term at face value, "Venus enters in the station of the Moon" refers to the same phenomena. Furthermore, simply by its rate of motion, Venus is a much slower planet than the Moon. It cannot possibly catch up with the Moon unless the scribes were talking about the previous position held during an earlier time frame (perhaps synodic). In our new proposal we set the time frame as sunset. That way, as we rotate the chart, Venus *can* catch up to the Moon's position and we can equate the event and its timing by the distance of arc between the two planets. Omen after omen refers to the Sun, Moon, constellations and planets being fixed in place. A "fix" refers to converting data from a floating or moving point to a fixed point. It is evident that these fixed celestial placements were of different planetary synodic periods and not of daily motion and must refer to the date and location of an earlier synodic phenomena or events.

Any navigator can tell you when using a sextant (a device for ascertaining the positions of stars relative to the position of the observer), he takes a "fix" on the planetary or stellar locations. This navigational "fix" determines the moving position of his ship or aircraft in relation to the star or planet observed. This is accomplished by determining the positions of celestial bodies then relating them to their time difference based on the distance the local meridian is from GMT—exactly what we do when we cast the astrology chart.

An example of synodic phenomena would be Mars rising two hours before the Sun. Let us say that Mars is located zero degrees in the constellation of Taurus and the Sun is zero degrees in Gemini. The exact synodic period (the next date) that these two planets will be in the same *exact* position (the synodic arc) both by constellation and degree (of longitude) is 32 years plus 11 days (same aspect same signs).

Another example is that the *exact* synodic arc and time for Jupiter to conjunct Saturn in the same sign and degree is roughly 2,383 years! If we only *approximate* the Jupiter–Saturn conjunction using a two degree orb rather than the exact degree, we can lessen the synodic period considerably, to about 170 years. An even wider orb of five degrees will lessen the synodic period to only 59 years; and finally *any* conjunction of Jupiter with Saturn in any sign regardless of orb is about 20 years.

Using this time frame it is easy to recognize that we do not have many synodic periods within our lifetime. As you can see, by relaxing the orb and/or the constellation "fix" of synodic phenomena, we find the aspect repeats itself but in different constellational signs (we know that the Sun will be exactly 30° from Mars in a little more than a year's time but in different constellations).

Recognizing this, I have scaled down the synodic arcs and their extended periods into the much shorter time frame of 24 hours, thereby keeping our personal synodic arcs at birth. Once determined by our sunset chart, the synodic arcs between the Sun and planets stay fixed in place. The difference of arc between our birth time to that of sunset is very small by degree except for the Moon. With sunset as the "fixed" position, the Moon becomes prominent not only for its size and brightness but by virtue of its motion. When a child decides to be born, it is the Moon's position during the entire 24-hour period that will define his lunar mansion. This may have been the concept that related the Moon with childbirth and babies in general.

Another important point is the "pseudo phenomena" that occurs when relating the time between the sunset chart and the natal chart. As we rotate the wheel in a rogressed manner, the changing aspects of the Sun and planets, *in relation to themselves with the sunset chart,* will do exactly what the Chaldean scribes noted in their diaries about synodic phenomena, only within a shorter amount of time.

Throughout Babylonian texts, synodic phenomena, along with sunrise and sunset, remained a constant reference for first and last sightings of stars and planetary appearances and/or disappearances along with significant omens and seasonal changes. But with the sunset formula we can duplicate in 24 hours what the Chaldeans did over many years, decades and even centuries.

Our Current Astrological Model

Since the time of Ptolemy, astrology has attempted to describe planetary patterns in set symbolic sigils and their configurations into deterministic expression. This was all based on Grecian formulas that would have been completely foreign to the originators of astrology. To date, we still use those time-worn patterns that have persisted throughout the centuries.

In any philosophy it is often said that there is no, absolutely no, absolute. The same is said of astrology. At best, the astrologer can make an educated guess as to the outcome of proposed events and, if the astrologer is right, both client and astrologer are happy. But more often than not, we find ourselves asking "why didn't the proposed outcome occur?"

Until now, predictive work has been unsatisfactory because current techniques are inadequate. Many astrologers do not know where or how to build a foundation. When reading a chart, they depend on perpetually stale rhetoric handed down to us over the centuries, such as the Ascending sign, Moon sign or the even more popular Sun sign. The search for a different view of astrology is supported by the fact that there has been a tremendous interest in the convoluted Hindu-Vedic methodology which, by the way, must have some problems too, because many Vedic astrologers are interested in learning the Western form of astrology to fill in their deficiencies. What is really needed is a neutral matrix, a "fix" by which we can judge the rest of the chart. The answer lies with the concepts based on the sunset chart.

Once the planetary synodic distances located in the chart become apparent, the entire chart will "come alive" and reveal information on any context of interest by time and/or condition. However, all aspects reflected in the chart must be duplicated by the transits and *with the rogression* for any event to take place with certitude.

At any rate, it is time to once again to look extensively to the heavens for a new direction. Today, we can thank Kepler, Ebertin, the Hubers, the Gauquelins, and many others too numerous to mention, whose scientific research has announced that planetary influence agrees with what original astrologers knew 3,000 years ago—that astrology is a tool that directs us toward a better understanding of the world within and outside ourselves.

The Astrologer

It has been said that the Egyptians were theorists while the Persians were practitioners and the Greeks philosophers. In earlier times each name for any object or phenomena was identified and derived from experience and intuition. Today, modern man has been given many sets of parameters with which he may learn. In this fashion the student should emerge from his studies much wiser than his instructor. A student of astrology must become a nouveau scientist, an empiricist who is willing to *actually test* theories he reads or hears about. To do that he must be relentless in his effort, much like Aristotle and his neophyte scholar.

Aristotle was approached by a young man who wanted to be a scholar. After much discussion, Aristotle agreed to tutor him and promptly handed the boy a dead fish. He told the boy to study it and explain his findings when he returned the next week. The boy did as requested and, upon his return, when questioned about the fish, he proudly spoke of its size, type and in what area it was indigenous. Aristotle only replied with the question; "How many scales does the fish have?" Of course, the boy didn't know and was given another fish and was told to examine it and give his report when he returned the following week. Upon his return the boy promptly announced the exact number of scales on the fish. Aristotle then asked how many spines did the fins and tail contain. Of course, the boy didn't know and was given another fish and told to report to him when he had finished examining it. Many weeks had passed before the boy exhaustively studied, examined and inspected the fish in every detail he thought imaginable. Confident he could now answer any question about the fish, he returned to his mentor. When asked about the taste the boy didn't know...and so the story goes.

To press the point, imagine the word automobile. "Auto" means "self" and "mobile" means "capable of movement from one place to another." When combined, they suggest a self-powered vehicle of conveyance. The *word* is descriptive but it does not imply status, horsepower, comfort level, ease of handling or a multitude of other possibilities. These nuances greatly modify the idea of an automobile. Thus, in a similar fashion, research will modify your idea of astrology. Learn to be an empiricist.

Below there is a brief synopsis about a discussion concerning the ability of two different astrologers. Written in cuneiform, some 4,000 years ago, it succinctly points out that the ancient peoples approached life seriously and based their existence on results.

A much older astrologer accused the younger more brash astrologer of being incompetent. When the argument ended, the younger astrologer lost his credibility. He petitioned the king to allow him to continue his work. The king denied his petition and ordered the young astrologer to make bricks for a living. The other court astrologers felt the young ex-astrologer was very lucky because the king had spared his life.

It is important to recognize that we never read a chart but actually engage in quantitative analysis. We first qualify the chart by an overview and then dissect it for its supportive fragments to find where it does and does not correspond with the synopsis. Fragments that do not support or seem to be at odds with the basic overview are indeed problems the individual is faced with in life.

Fiduciary Points for Observation

The early Babylonian observers were true scientists, empiricists who had no real interest in theories. They wanted results. The only proof necessary was practical, tangible, workable formulas. As the above story suggests, their observations had to serve them well or the outcome could be disastrous.

There were many omens in Chaldean antiquity, but one stands out as the most important—the simultaneous rising and setting (acronychal) of stars or planets or any combination of each. This probably stems from the fact that Babylonians noticed that the star Aldebaran in the constellation Taurus and the star Antares in Scorpio were *exactly* opposite one another and, on a given night, rose and set simultaneously. Both stars are precisely in the center of their respective constellations. This discovery led the Babylonians to divide the heavens in half, allowing them to observe either of these two bright first magnitude stars as the fiducial axis any time of the year. We can easily see the magnitude of this discovery and the excitement it must have caused. *It gave them a starting point,* a system by which they could relate and measure other planetary and stellar placements and their positions at any time during the year.

Conventional astrology today upholds the traditional ideas of the Ascendant, Sun sign, and Moon sign as the ideal points to begin delineation. However, the astrology wheel is inadequate. The mandala is limited and incomplete, it is confusing to many, has no scientific value and until the research of Kepler, Fagan, Ebertin, Gauquelin and the Hubers, to name a few, there has been very little serious astrological research to render it more precise. Astrology has stayed the same for over 1,800 years.

Astrologers today use the time of birth as a starting point, but the question remains; what influences *urged* the baby to enter the world at that particular day and hour in the first place? The secret lies in sunset before birth. After reading the chapter on the Sun, we can easily understand and determine why the second house became the natural house of money even though the time relates to pre-dawn hours or that sunrise relates to the 12th house of sorrow. These points of reference have had no obvious foundation until now (see page 80).

On a another level, and aside from aspects, how can we determine if the overall influences of planetary directions are positive or negative? Indicate change? Set an ideal? Astrology today works around these problems in much the same way as a sentence written without any punctuation:

itcanbedonebutimaginetheprocessawholebookwouldrequirer eadinganentireessayorjustbyreadingthisoneline.

By breaking down the Sunset chart into components (like adding the appropriate spaces and punctuation to the above sentence) and combining it with the birth chart, we have our initial point of reference all neatly packaged.

Periodic Energies

The following is an overview of the principles of the sunset chart.

The **First** item to determine is the energy pattern of the historical date of the year of birth. In ancient times "Happy New Year!" didn't arrive as we know it. The Egyptian year began with the rising of Sothis in mid-July. The Babylonians were happy to see the new Moon each month and the years were not recorded as we know them but singled out by special events, such as coronations, war victories, weddings and births of notables, festivals of the spring equinox, and other sundry events. Great years were noted by the new king coming to the throne or by the destruction of a neighboring enemy. Often, many of these calendrical events were simply local happenings without any meaning to other settlements.

This ancient tradition can still be used today by noting the occurrence of different events during the year of a person's birth. Although this may require a little thought on your part, it is important to know that world events subtly flavor the charts of those born during such times. The premise of astrology is that it is a symbolic stellar language reflecting synchronistic events between heaven and Earth. During gestation, different events in the external world are reflected and imprinted upon a child's nervous system by the mother. This is accomplished through the mother's mental and emotional outlook of different events. Her trials and errors, self esteem, her position or standing in the community, her physical reaction to world events are communicated to the child through the nervous system creating a *general influence* on the child while still in the womb. Whether the child is receiving *cosmic vibes* or *physical imprints* is not the issue. Research has shown that the child *is* being imprinted by the mother's physical and chemical reactions during pregnancy.

The following discussion points out the importance of the events taking place during pregnancy and the eventual birth itself. Look at the suggestions denoted by certain years and see if you can relate to them. More often than not you will see the synastry between the child's birth and his relationship with worldly events.

Energy by Geographical Location

One's geographical location presents different perspectives to historical thought depending on his point of view. For example, let's examine a birth between the years of 1914-1917. People born in Europe before and during World War I experienced the war with a different perspective than the Americans did. The Europeans were directly involved from the very beginning. The general European population born prior to 1914 was inundated with the possibility of, and preparation for, war. Its world reflected the fear of constant threat of invasion, especially if surrounding countries were not allies of the Germans. On the other hand, the German children raised during this period reflected their emotional nationalism and felt it was their right to fight, if necessary, for what they believed in. Conversely, American charts will reflect the energy of *jumping on the bandwagon* and *going "over there"* to set things right. So we can see that babies, while in gestation in different places throughout the world, were imprinted with different perspectives which effect chart interpretation.

Periodic Energy by Years

An important year for those born in America was 1917, the year America became involved in World War I. When the war ended in 1918, there was a victorious mood of celebration and the feeling of getting back to normal. On the other hand, Europeans had a feeling of relief and were ready to return to peaceful times and rebuild their war-torn countries.

As you can see, each period of history has its own particular form of energy pattern and it is important to understand these influential patterns before we begin reading a chart. The following is a quick list of world events which set the tone for those born during those times. These are by no means final but will serve as a basis for getting started. We will look at the American point of view beginning with the first World War. See if you can associate any of the years with the birth of celebrities:

1917 These people are visionaries. They feel they need to set things right.

1918-20 People born during this period have a positive "yes, I can" attitude.

1921-28 This period is one of prosperity and abundance; those born within this time frame feel that life is basically good.

1929-32 The depression years, there is a need to conserve; money is important to people born at this time.

1932-38 People born during this period are set in their ways and are mostly interested in power, structure and machinations.

1939-40 People born in these years are not content with the way things are; they have ideas for changing the world.

1941 These people are diligent, wary and guarded. They act as if they are waiting for the other shoe to fall.

1942 These individuals have self-righteous personalities, tolerant and mildly defensive.

1943 These people are always seeming to prepare for something.

1944 Energies here are expansive and aggressive, goal oriented.

1945-46 The energy here is building and reforming; those born into this period want to restructure and re-organize.

1947-48 People born during this time have a serious side, the winding down of karma. They are tolerant, willing to step aside; a sense of spirituality. Life does not seem to be fun to them.

1949 Such individuals have a high degree of spirituality. They identify with loving and caring. A deep sense of personal mission.

1950 These people are suspicious but quick to grasp subtleties and implications.

1951-53 Those born during this time struggle with personal decisions regarding the rules of society versus their individual freedom of expression.
1954-56 These people work out reversals in life. Change is a necessary element to them.
1957-58 These are "walk ins" who feel that they don't belong on the planet. Often they think that they are in the wrong family and that they are not really their parents' offspring.
1959 These are willful people with an "in your face" attitude. As they mature they "mellow out" and become more socially responsible.
1960-62 These are the years of the genius. In some fashion the brain power is noticeable either in its abundance or lack.
1964-66 These individuals are general protesters, the "no before yes" group.
1968-69 The people are organizers, concerned with group efforts and the big picture. Yuppies that may well be over-achievers.
1971-72 This birth year seems to be the nemesis of the people born a generation ago during the late 40s.
1973-75 This group may be subject to "the conspiracy idea," believing that any source of management is not to be trusted. The X-Generation.
1976-80 The advent of the personal computer marks a strong influence with this birth group. Mentally quick with the need for faster personal gratification, these people seem to be on the fast track.

It is important to note: As people develop, they either align themselves *with* or *against* these energy patterns. All energy patterns listed above are generalizations and *undergo modification* throughout each 24-hour period by the changing planetary positions. An individual born in 1949 suggests one with a spiritual affinity who may decide to follow a dedicated reverent path, but only if the individual is born with a harmonious chart arrangement such as a trine or sextile with sunset. On the other hand, if his birth time is inharmonious (square or opposition to the sunset positions), such a person may feel that his contemporaries are "too soupy" with a distinct dislike for that kind of personality. Each pattern is a double-edged sword, like the old quote, "Isn't the jailer in jail as well?"

The more you dig into contemporary history, the better you will be at understanding the foundation of an individual's birthing energies. Get to know historical background and use it when erecting each chart. You won't be disappointed.

The 24-Hour Diurnal Clock

Second step: The 24-hour period represents a complete cycle called the Circadian rhythm. Many organisms live an entire lifetime within a 24-hour period. It seems highly unlikely that the Babylonians would not know about this cycle as they constantly observed nature for their omina. In view of this we will use the Circadian rhythm of 24 hours to represent our "cosmic DNA experience cell" which describes expected events during our lifetime.

In today's world, astrologers use Greenwich Mean Time (GMT) to calculate chart delineation. In ancient times they used *local mean time* or local space for the same purpose. Sunset was considered the starting point for each new day, very much in keeping with their religious views. It was in this fashion that they established a *neutral matrix* upon which all divination was based. Astrologically, the time of sunset places the position of the Earth directly opposite the Sun, i.e., right on the Ascendant. Throughout the ages, the Ascendant has been known as the giver of life, quite the fitting description for Earth.

The time required for omens was determined by calculating the amount of time a planet had taken to repeat any synodic period. In this fashion the Chaldeans were able to make their predictions based on previous experiences depicted by each synodic phenomena. This process designated a major part of their omens.

Based on this information, the sunset charting system has been developed by fixing the stars and planets in their sunset position (casting a chart for the time of sunset) to form the matrix from which our analysis and forecast can be made. Once the sunset planetary matrix is set, we have, in essence, devised our own synodic period based on the distance by arc from the birth chart to the sunset chart.

We have taken a process that required years, decades and even centuries to acquire and reduced it into a 24-hour system. This 24-hour period replicates a lifetime! We are about to observe the human experience based on previous experiences as depicted between the birth chart, the sunset chart and present time. In a biWheel format, we rotate the smaller sunset chart within the stationary larger sunset chart and ask our client about his experiences as each planet aspects the sunset positions.

Repetitive phenomena occurs as each planet and asterism, by virtue of *its own diurnal motion,* conjoins, sextiles, squares, trines or opposes its *own fixed position* designated at sunset. The original aspects in the chart remain the same and, as it rotates, keeps the sense of "sameness" through each experience. In this way the chart replicates the way we experience our lives.

Rule: The very first thing you must understand about this technique is that the wheel is basically a *timing* device for progressing events and evaluating overall planetary conditions for a lifetime. *During the course of the nightly watch, each star, constellation and planet will sextile, square, trine or oppose the position it held at sunset.*

This format indicates how early events in the life will, at some future time, repeat themselves under different circumstances (similar to synodic returns). Furthermore, by using contemporary astrological principles, there is information within the sunset chart that correlates with the psychological makeup of an individual in question. This is readily demonstrated when stacking the planets by virtue of their degree of longitude. Overall, the sunset chart can certainly be used as a complete tool for personal exploration as you will see for yourself. But for now, the equal house wheel's primary purpose is to time events.

Once we understand how the planetary energies are expressed between the birth chart and the sunset chart, we are able to anticipate events as they occur throughout the life. Keep in mind that basically harmonious energies, when combined with squares, promote an outlet for the square and encourage positive activity.

When a planet is in both a square and trine aspect, the trine acts as an outlet thereby relieving the square. When we look at the sunset and birth charts in Figure 8.1, the whole configuration of Mars square Jupiter/Saturn is relieved by a trine aspect *to itself* between both charts. The trinal position indicates that these energies will be expressed harmoniously rather than the dire circumstances expressed in contemporary astrology.

Birth Chart - Sunset Chart Interaction

The following example explores the natal with the sunset chart. The distance between the two charts by arc demonstrate that the charts are in trine with each other. A trine position works in an easy "laissez-faire" way. An individual's birth chart with only trines *and* in trinal aspect to the sunset chart may find that as the person grows older, he will probably spend his entire life telling everyone that he is "going to do something someday" but never finds the time to achieve his goal. Trines need to have energetic squares to get things going as shown in the example.

Uranus and Neptune are trine in the natal chart and, although indirectly active, they represent avenues for success. We immediately note a seemingly wide conjunction of sunset Uranus to natal Neptune. Furthermore, natal

Uranus is in opposition to sunset Mercury and natal Mercury sextiles both Uranus trine Neptune which places emphasis on Mercury and its part in the triad of Uranus. Mercury's focus on Uranus makes Uranus a possible doorway to success. Furthermore, aspects to Uranus also represent interest in antiquity, history and astrology. The individual was born into a family who were astrologers for three generations.

The opposition of sunset Mercury to natal Uranus is related by sextile to each other in the natal chart. This indicates sudden perception with flashes of insight giving the native a mental adroitness to quickly grasp and evaluate situations. It is only in the light of the combined charts that we see this complete activity between Mercury and Uranus. However, notice natal Mercury conjoined with the sunset South Node indicating problems in communication and writing. With this configuration the native has his road to success challenged by the weakened Mercury. The native grew up in an ethno-eclectic neighborhood with as many as seven different nationalities all speaking their native tongues. There was little or no English spoken in his community. As he grew up, objects were named by any playmate who pointed to them first. Thus, the children created a language only they understood.

The Mercury/Uranus opposition further expresses the idea that set parameters are simply boundaries that invite crossing. This planetary configuration also focuses on a revolutionary understanding and/or an innovation in any thing that seems stagnant. The negative side of these two planets speaks of too many irons in the fire (Ebertin).

When we disregard the sunset chart and view the natal chart, there are no oppositions, only a major square from the fourth to the twelfth house. Current cookbook interpretation would find this configuration extremely depressing. However, the opposite has been the case. It is only with both charts that we recognize how the square works in a positive manner. It is almost as if the native has been on vacation his whole life.

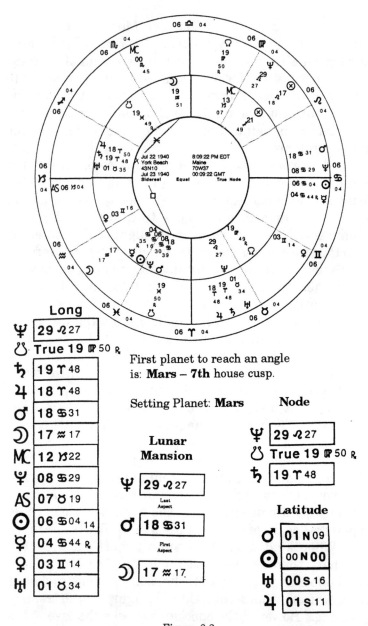

Figure 8.2
The sunset chart compared with the birth chart.
The outer chart is sunset. The inner chart is the birth chart.

232

In light of the combined sunset and natal charts, we find an important opposition (sunset Mercury opposing birth chart Uranus) coupled with the overall trine aspect between the birth chart with the sunset chart.

Personality Expression

Third step: The next level of evaluation consists of locating the planets *at sunset* immediately above and below the Sun (sixth and seventh house). Planets located in the **sixth house** portray an individual's physical appearance and personal expression. This position conveys the impression we get when we first meet someone or what we have heard about the individual before we actually meet him. When reading a bio on someone in a magazine, notice how the photographs agree with the following descriptions.

With **Mercury**, the focus is on the vocal expression or what you hear about the person before you meet him. Like a singer or orator whose lecture or performance you have just attended. He would be thought provoking, a teacher who likes to express himself in a thoughtful manner.

With **Venus**, we find attractiveness an issue. Either the individual feels that he has good looks or is homely. Often artistic, soft spoken, and generally appealing in some manner with a sense of style and grace. Attracts others through his possessions or abilities.

With **Mars**, the native has a sense of coarseness about him. He is often athletic, lithe and impulsive, carrying himself with a sense of urgency. Generally, there is a combative-like stare as if he were thinking about "taking you on" in a fight.

With **Jupiter**, the individual exemplifies showmanship, clown-like antics; he is the likable politician. There is a "larger than life" expression about him and we feel that he knows a lot more than he says.

With **Saturn**, the native is quiet and reserved with a sense of seriousness; he seems "more real" and has depth of character. He has presence and authority. We feel that if we make a mistake in front of him we would regret it for the rest of our lives.

With the **Moon**, the native is engaging, warm, charming and possesses a vague sense of mystery. You may feel that you want to do something for him. He follows a conversation well and reflects it to the speaker in such a manner that anyone listening would believe he brought up the subject.

The same planets as they might appear in the seventh house (above the sun at sunset) in the **seventh house** have a similar meanings but their expressions are more *introverted*. Rather than depicting these qualities outwardly, the native uses those qualities as a form of self-identification. For example, Einstein had Jupiter in the sixth house with Mercury conjunct Saturn in the seventh. He was light-hearted and a showoff for the press and to those who were close to him. But with Mercury and Saturn in the seventh, he identified with his own depth of thought as a scientist.

Returning to the example chart above, Pluto and Mars are above the Sun. Although Pluto was not used by the ancients, it is noted here for clarification. Basically, Pluto exemplifies transformational energy similar to the combined energies of Mars, Jupiter and Saturn. Mars in this position also indicates transformational energies (square Jupiter conjunct Saturn) and implies the need to rescue others from limiting or self-destructive actions (to transform Saturn's restrictive energy into a more expansive Jupiter style of energy). The mode of action with Mars and Pluto identifies with making a contribution that will change the circumstances of those around him or, on a larger scale, a contribution to the world. Mercury is in the sixth house indicating vocal and/or written expression. The individual enjoys talking about astrology, metaphysics and spirituality.

The natal Sun is located in the third house, the house of communication, in trine with its sunset position, and indicative of eighteen to twenty-four years of age. The natal Sun's position located here announces his most significant "solar return," when the sunset Sun reaches the point where the natal Sun is in the natal chart. This suggests that this period would be the most influential period of his life. He closed his past and entered into a completely new lifestyle when the rogressed Sun reached this position; he got a divorce from his first wife, entered college and remarried.

The double Sun positions, combined with Mars and Pluto above the Sun and Mercury below, indicate the desire to teach and inspire others toward self-motivation (rescue the world through communication). With this combination of Pluto and Mars, the individual wants to be a knight in shining armor. Jupiter conjunct Saturn usually suggests an interest in the non-material world or spirituality. In earthly matters it suggests integrity, responsibility, and a willingness to accept one's duties, however, the square from Mars suggests the native may take his time in acquiring these attributes. The native may not be as responsible as he would have others think. Still, the overall configuration indicates the native wants to be instrumental in changing people's lives for the better (his idea of better, that is) through communication.

Based on the above descriptions we easily recognize one of the driving forces that motivates the native. In the following section we will see how an angle plays its role.

The First Angular Planet

Fourth step: The next step is to find the planet that is *coming forth*, i.e., the first planet to conjunct *any*

235

angle after sunset and any planets advancing through the quadrant containing the Ascendant, twelfth, eleventh and tenth house.

Advancing the example chart's outer wheel clockwise by 12.5°, Mars conjoins the seventh house then Jupiter (square to Mars) will conjoin the fourth house angles respectively (Pluto conjoins the seventh 2° 25' earlier [age six months] but at such a young age we discount it). At the rate of five degrees equaling one year, the 12.7° of arc is equivalent to two years and eight months, Mars had advanced to the seventh house cusp before Jupiter to the fourth by seventeen minutes. Mars (coming forth) is the first planet to contact an angle after sunset.

Event: By the age of two years and eight months, the parents divorced and relocated. The native was left with his aunt and various other caretakers while the mother worked.

The nature of the seventh house is *reactive*. Events occur while the native is passive. Planets by rogression or transit to the seventh house cusp indicate events that are not of the individual's making; therefore, he can only react to the situation, like being caught in a sudden rain shower. Rogressions or transits over the fourth house cusp indicate vulnerability, where the native has no control over the situation whatsoever, like being kidnapped.

Analysis: The "first planet" imprint with Mars at an early age is that of change and/or losses due to an influence outside the native's control which negatively impressed him (square aspect). He would naturally endure the loss of his parents but his experience enabled him to later develop empathy with those experiencing similar feelings. In this case it is reasonable to estimate that the configuration of Mars square Jupiter/Saturn would reflect in the native's awareness of his sense of impending threat of loss in life. These responses could be directed at understanding and trying to care for and help heal the suffering of others, even at the expense of securing his own future. The Mars square Jupiter/Saturn aspect bears the signature of becoming involved with friends and clients whose lives typify separation or loss (divorce, death, business, etc.). Over the years this has indeed been the case.

The next planet to conjunct an angle is the Moon. By the age of eight, the Moon had advanced to the Ascendant. The Ascendant is proactive; the native initiates processes and solutions. At that time, and through the native's urging, he became re-acquainted with his mother. The Moon, from that time onward, had become the significator of unions and reunions. Analysis of this event determined that the Moon is the significator of his mother and any aspects to the Moon will signify future forms of partnering or have a nurturing signature. At the age of fifty-two, the native lost his mother to cancer. The native suspected her situation because his *rogressed Moon* had advanced to semi-square his sunset Pluto (Pluto is used here because of his tri-planet configuration of Mars square Jupiter/Saturn). This set up a "T-square" to his sunset Moon opposing his sunset Neptune (Neptune is used here because Moon, Venus/Jupiter were configured in both charts at the time).

Something Different

Before we begin this next segment, it is important for the reader to understand that this is, admittedly, the furthermost system directly relating to the Chaldean concepts. However, within this next concept lies a rich field of research for the astute astrologer who wishes to undertake such a venture. It has proven itself time and time again when describing the person in the horoscope and, although possibly not of Chaldean origin (Egyptian? Vedic?), it fits extremely well within the context of this work.

While there is no empirical evidence to support the following concept of the 30° wheel, there are subtleties in early texts that allow for its alleged conjecture favoring its presentation. They are as follows:

First point: We do find a form of this concept in the Hindu-Vedic system. Whether the Hindi astrologers formulated the idea or it came to them by cultural exchange, is difficult to determine.

Second point: When we read more notable astrological charts from Chaldea, they are sparse and lack sophistication not only by today's standards but by their own standards. Their astrology records are almost childlike. Yet, all other records indicate a high level of intelligence. What emerged from early Sumer are thirty-nine accountable historical "firsts:" the first tax cut, the first system of law, the first educational system, a very sophisticated mathematical system, the first love song, to name a few of a long, notable listing.

However, in explanation for the reader, cuneiform texts were written in monosyllabic terms. Only one syllable expressed a complete word such as AN for Earth and KI for sky. Two syllables were used as a compound word to express larger concepts such as AN-KI (Earth-sky) for universe. Today, contemporary translations of cuneiform texts are made by creating "bridgework" that fills in gaps, missing lines or because the clay fragments have only a small portion of written content on each piece.

The Babylonians left us records by memorializing social events that give us insights from early Babylon to the time of Chaldea and later. These texts are of considerable value as their records of celestial events were faithfully reproduced by succeeding generations. But there is a catch: Babylonian astrological texts found to date do not match the intelligence displayed in other aspects of their writings. Much of what has been learned from earlier ancient writings comes to us not from historical records, but by inference from their epic poems that contain historical truisms. From this we can surmise that either the early astronomical scribes did not proclaim the obvious (which seems to be the case in many instances) or that they wrote notes in shorthand fashion for their own references later (diaries). Possibly much of what they knew was passed down orally and committed to memory. Regardless of their method of transmission, it is difficult to imagine that, although they were brilliant in their data compilation, they were somehow illiterate in their own field of expertise.

Today's scientists use the intellectual tool known as epistemology; the philosophical method that investigates the nature and origin of knowledge, definition and generalization. Sumer and early Babylon apparently lacked this intellectual tool and yet they offered many concrete examples operating under the law of cause and effect without ever formulating it as all pervading.

Third point: It is more than likely that the Chaldeans developed some form of astrological structure reflecting their pragmatic lifestyle, that of a hierarchical monarchy. The Babylonians had what we would call a bi-cameral congress which consisted of a seat of elders and an assembly of arms-bearing citizens. All of this, of course, was overseen by a king. Their government was hierarchical: from the supreme ruler down to the peasant. And after all, the power structure of their gods was assigned and ranked by numerical order, a format inherited from their Sumerian ancestors.

By following this strict adherence to hierarchy, even the inhabitants of Babylon held various rank within their civilization. With all this, it is a reasonable supposition that the gods who traveled through the heavens may have held a similar hierarchical order in the Babylonian mind.

To reiterate, although there is no direct confirmation that the Chaldeans used this device, the 30° wheel or stack has proven itself as a valuable tool numerous times in the charts of clients, mundane circumstances, electional charts and horary charts.

Stacking the Planets, the 30° Wheel

Fifth step: List the planets from the highest degree to the lowest. This is referred as the "stack" and will serve as an easy guide for locating planets. Each sign in the zodiac begins and ends with 0° or 30° as the same degree of reference. The stack is similar to this. It is considered a circle containing only 30°, the highest (29° 59') and the lowest (0° 00') wherein 0° and 30° are the same reference point. The planets are also viewed as if there were no signs and are simply listed in numerical sequence. Be sure to add the Ascendant and Midheaven from the natal chart.

As each planet in the stack lies between two other planets, the middle planet is always the one in consideration. An axiom in astrology has always been; the closer a planet is by degree, the more influence it exerts. Although influenced by both upper and lower planets, it is *mostly influenced* by the planet *closest* by degree.

The highest planet by degree of longitude is the chart ruler and represents the overall goal that the native yearns to accomplish in his life. Often, the highest planet by degree also displays a style of presentation with which the native expresses his mindset or displays his ego. It is how one wishes to be seen. It also influences and interacts with the planet immediately before and after the setting Sun.

In the example chart, Pluto is actually setting immediately after the Sun but we use Mars to represent the Pluto energy. Thus Mars is the energy pattern the native reflects and it is in the seventh house setting after the Sun and Mercury in the sixth house which is just below the Sun. Neptune's influence (expressed through either the Moon, Venus or Jupiter) is the highest degree by longitude; the native wishes to keep his true actions somewhat of a mystery and may express his abilities and achievements in an exaggerated manner. The Neptune influence also describes an artistic penchant for the music and motion picture industries.

The 10° Decanates

The next step is to note the planets by ten-degree segments. The keywords below apply to all situations located within the stack. The first 0° to 10° refers to basic traits and the self interest with which one is born. Planets so placed are the emotional, existential package. These planets are the fundamental elements that represent our parents' guidance. We attempt to express ourselves according to our parents' teachings and usually against our own desires. It defines the child's personal interest and response to his environment *according to his parents' wishes*. Planets in this position influence how, why and what one does and the manner in which he does it during childhood. Often, when major planets such as Mars, Jupiter, Saturn and sometimes the trans-saturnian planets aspect the first decanate planets, the client is facing some issue that is antagonistic to his upbringing. When working with a client, any rogression or transits to the first decanate refers to childhood issues taught by the parents.

The middle decanate (10° 01' to 20° 00') represents the arena of life's challenges. Planets in this location help develop and hone planetary vibrations located within the first decanate. Planets here act as stepping stones or stumbling blocks to our success.

The last decanate (20° 01' to 29° 59') indicates the ideals, by their planetary nature, to which the native aspires. Furthermore, the planet by highest degree influences the other planets in the middle and lower decanate as an ideal result, like spokes to a hub. Soft planets (Moon, Venus, Node, sometimes Mercury) tend to make the native lazy with the desire to have his associates do the bulk of the work. Harder planets (Sun, Jupiter, Mars sometimes Saturn) are self-motivating where the native wants to do the work and get the credit for his accomplishments.

In *each* 10° portion of the stack, the planet with the highest degree has influence over all the other planets below

241

it. Metaphorically, all planets work through a chain of command while at the same time seeking to satisfy the "king" planet (the highest degree) as well as having to satisfy the highest planet within each decanate. This is similar to three different foreman on three different job sites working toward the completion of one project under the direction of the contractor.

Rule:

29° 59' to 20° 00'
Personal ideals and/or goals set for oneself.

19° 59' to 10° 00'
The changes and challenges we meet in life.

00° 00' to 9° 59'
The teachings we relate to in childhood.

Keep in mind the nature and characteristics of the planets. The planets act like a clique. The Sun, Moon, Mars and Jupiter work well together and prefer each other's company while Mercury, Venus Node and Saturn work well together and prefer only their own company. Any planet foreign to the clique creates problems because these planets operate against each other.

When evaluating transits, be sure to remember the original planetary placement in the birth chart by decanate. The placement by degree not only "colors" the transiting planet's personal meaning for the client but refer to the section of life coming under the transit's influence. A client coming to you and wanting to know if it is a good time to start a business would be hard pressed if the transits only related to the first or second decanate without any planet relating to their proper goal-related decanate. It would be best to encourage the client to choose a commencement time that balances the influence of the decanates without too many negative influences such as too many squares, retrograde planets, a "stuttering" Node or wrong decanate activity.

The Trans-Saturnian Planets

As we are in general review, the mention of the planets in the following section is cursory. To evaluate how they influence the decanates turn to page 123 and review that section. As many of you will be working with celebrity's birth charts, we will start with the outer trans-saturnian planets first. Those of you who are not celebrities, and are working on your own charts or clients' charts, might look at the trans-saturnian planets as your "potential for achievement." We have discussed the trans-saturnian planets in an earlier chapter (page 129).

Pluto:
Pluto exemplifies the power over oneself or others through psychological exploitation. There is an extreme intensity applied to anything with which the native associates or wishes to accomplish. There are associations with well positioned or high-ranking persons. Its perspective is power, force, intensity with powerful motivation and a total regard or disregard for the sublime.
Negative expression would be ruthlessness and brutality.

Neptune:
Neptune speaks of the ideal fantasy. It involves wishful thinking about one's associations, commitments, or purpose. There is a feeling that no one can really know what is going on, thus associates can be easily deceived. It represents natives who are attracted to the performing arts. Often they search for "something missing in life" depending on the position in the chart. Its perspective is like looking underwater without eye protection or through a thick fog.

Negative expression of Neptune would involve fraud, deception and a lack of clarity.

Uranus:
This planet typifies the awareness of boundaries and a signature of one carving out his own niche from set parameters. It marks the ability to notice what is needed or missing in a given circumstance and to create solutions. It is inventive. This planet pertains to the ability to focus exclusively on specific aims. There may be technical interests or extraordinary mathematical ability. Objectives are pursued with zeal and intense ambition. There is also an interest in historical facts and antiques. Its perspective is to be, do or say something in a different fashion.

Negative expression develops by having too many irons in the fire, scattered energies, and a bold, shocking, flippant demeanor.

The Visible Planets

Saturn:
Saturn demonstrates self restraint, reliability, perseverance and a tendency to focus extensively on any given subject of interest. It indicates a slow, steady climb towards success. Generally there is a somber demeanor with great organizing abilities. This is could be a professor or one who teaches from experience. Its perspective is contraction, laws and regulations. The outer form and structure of matter.

Negative expression involves a fearful and negative demeanor, restriction and losses through negligence.

Jupiter:
Jupiter represents the desire to accomplish or build in an expansive way upon the ideals of other people with a sense of self-imposed responsibility. There is a keen perception of the larger picture and an understanding of the plight of others and their needs. Its sole perspective is "the

more expansive the better;" a teacher who seeks to educate.

Negative expression involves reckless exploitation of circumstances, hasty reaction and effusive behavior.

Mars:

Mars is ever mindful of competition. It is the warrior type, who seeks to achieve success in an independent way. There is an ambition to physically and energetically *do* something. Here is a willful, fighting spirit who, like a knight in shining armor, will champion a cause and defend another person's position. Its perspective is "do *something* even if its wrong." The warrior who ventures where no one dares to go.

Negative expression of Mars involves impulsiveness, destructiveness, and lack of self control.

Earth:

This is the position of the Ascendant at sunset or the opposite position of the Sun in any chart. This position relates to one's penchant or the inner urges generally attributed to the sub-signature in contemporary chart analysis. By being aware of our interests through the books we read, music we like, movies or plays we attend, we can recognize our deepest ambitions. More often than not our ambitions will correspond with the highest planet in the stack. The Earth-point associates with the "hero" in movies or novels. It is the base nature of the native, the *natural interest* and *base instinct* for survival. Metaphorically, it is the actor's assigned role on stage directed by the two planets above and below the Node. In association with the latitudes, it is the overall style and interest of life; going back to our metaphor–the actor's intensity and activity according to its sign placement.

As all of life's expression takes place on this planet, no negative expression is considered.

Venus:

In its purest form, Venus represents softness, artistry, beauty, grace, charm and a healing, soothing nature. However, the ambitious side of Venus has a sycophant nature and is obliging; sympathetic to the needs of associates for personal gain; very social; and, is a lot like Neptune in the sense of beguilement. Venus can produce negative, disappointing results, by encouraging one to rely too much on others to "recognize one's inner beauty and value." Its perspective is allure, comfort, ease, artistry.

A negative sense of personal fulfillment through Venus is often reflected by minimizing the ability or pride of others, calling a beautiful home a shack, referring to a new outfit as an old rag or any other indirect way of stating; "Can't you impress me any better than that?"

Venus represents both the desire of the warrior to win and the victim's need to be rescued; the original "double-edged sword" in ancient literature.

Negative expression involves empty promises, disappointments and is sycophantic, and often lacks morality. For reasons stated, Venus cannot have "any strings attached" to its nature. A prominent Venus tends to agree with whomever he is with at the moment regardless of his position on the matter. It is Jezebel or Machiavelli dressed in alluring attire.

Mercury:

Mercury represents the consultant who is the authority in his field, the decision maker. The native's ambition is to be polished, facile with one's abilities, similar to a stage magician's ability to perform with ease and dexterity. There is a desire to astonish with one's mental dexterity or to be the last word with a profound expression. Its perspective is analytical, questioning, deductive and inventive. The student who yearns to teach.

Negative expression is the desire to boast, tease and taunt. A one-up-man-ship individual, a know-it-all who is quick to say, "I told you so" in a derisive manner. A negative Mercury relates to the old saying, "a little knowledge is a dangerous thing" meaning, of course, the person who listens to someone with this aspect may be ill-advised. A negative Mercury also implies: a lack of concentration, diffused thinking or working the line of least resistance.

Moon:

The Moon represents both our receptor base for evaluating external stimulus and our internal reaction to such stimuli. The Moon exemplifies the search for "inner truth" and emotional stability. There is a desire to be knowledgeably prepared for, or shielded from, our vulnerabilities. It is like trying to identify and protect oneself from any or all awkward or potentially threatening situations. The Moon's expression is one of searching for the "correct" teacher for guidance. Once this knowledge is acquired, the Moon's influence turns to ambition and a desire to express oneself in a public manner. Its perspective is yielding, cowering and wanting to be in the place of caring attention and protection. Often one seeks associates to fulfill "chores" undesirable to the native.

Negative expression includes impressionability, lack of self motivation, and susceptibility to external influences. A seeker of comfort and ease; a carefree attitude.

Sun:

The position of the Sun is where one recognizes what is needed for growth or further development. Its perspective is that of a child needing attention. The Sun represents the native as becoming "a shining example" in some field. There is a desire to be in the forefront of situations or recognized as being the favored one in a group, such as the best friend, the best student or being in the leading role in a play. Its placement by sign is indicative of the ideal qualities and type of individual with whom one truly seeks to associate. The Sun often indicates the search for religious experiences.

Negative expression involves the need to prove oneself totally blameless. The ego needs to impress others, usually with an overbearing nature.

The Mathematical Points

The following discussion is about the abstract mathematical points more commonly known as the Ascendant and Midheaven. They are calculated to define an intangible position in space, unlike the planets, that are calculated by their visible, physical locality. They cannot be decided upon until a time of commencement is declared. Therefore, they relate to the mental plane only.

The Midheaven can be considered the memory of past action from the last incarnation; hence, the desire to achieve what was successful in the past. The Ascendant is seen as the condition of the physical form required by this incarnation. Combined, the Midheaven and Ascendant are the "core being" of the individual. In association with the Node they represent the inner penchant, passion or driving force each individual follows throughout his life. The Node is chosen because its mathematical expression clearly represents the law of three: an active force (Sun) interacting with a passive force (Moon) creating a neutral effect (Node). Until a *time is declared* (such as an event or birth) and the chart erected, the Ascendant (body) and Midheaven (memory of past action) only exist in the collective.

The Node is more in tune with the MC. It is very important to determine the direction the Node is traveling, to which planet and its influence. This will indicate how the native develops his lifestyle, with whom and his relation to the MC and its ruler. His mode of action toward success.

The Ascendant is related more to the latitudes. It represents the physical nature and interests of the native necessary to achieve the Node's life-path. The Ascendant, combined with the latitude triad, indicates the physical level, stamina and interest related to the native's ideal noted by the highest planet. Always associate the Nodal triad with the MC and the Ascendant with the latitude triad to get a more complete view of your client's interests.

Ascendant and Midheaven:

Often these placements, when they are the highest degree by longitude, allude to abilities rather than desires or ambitions. This is observable in people who have abilities in sports, craftsmanship or tradesmanship who are always competing, creating or mending objects. Think of an inventor working on practical solutions to mechanical problems, or a sports figure who understands the importance of teamwork. There is a quick mental grasp in understanding how the physical universe works. The ego is simply seen as the emotional bridge that connects one person to the rest of humanity in relation to its "pecking order." Both perspectives relate to manifestation (Ascendant) and accomplishment (Midheaven).

Node:

The Node represents the soul's inclination or sense of direction or duty to achieve one's ideal. It is awareness, often expressed as awakening to reality at an early age. A young child could display talent or an aptitude for learning in relation to the planet in its direction or by close proximity. This is not necessarily the child prodigy but has the same sense of expression. The North Node openly seeks to elicit the world's support to achieve the ideal and MC. The South Node is attritional and makes contingency plans to insure and maintain its position in the world. Both nodes have the perspective to desire experience, the underlying doctrines of religion, the expression of higher principles or higher octaves of the planets with which it is associated.

Planets with Emphasis

A person born with a cluster of planets noted with the same degree (regardless of signs or house positions) has a cosmic stamp of fated circumstances. When this happens the native will be drawn into situations described by the planets involved. Two planets with the same identical degrees in any position of the stack place emphasis in the area of life indicated by the houses. Three or more planets with identical degrees are considered an intense destiny that cannot be ignored or denied. The indication is single mindedness with an absolute drive for success. The planets' nature will be expressed in the combined areas indicated by their house positions in the chart. Their influence will be determined by the triad, the planets immediately above and below them. The timing of such events shows in the rogression by way of the Sun's solar arc and current transits. Review Joseph Stalin's chart: January 1, 1880, Zone 2, 44E05 X 42N00.

The Node Technique

Step six: The **Nodes** of the Moon are the diametrically opposite points created by the intersection of the path of the Moon with the plane of the ecliptic (path of the Sun). This is called the North Node in northern latitudes and the South Node in the southern latitudes. The Node was known to the ancients as the Hidden One and it represented the third part of the sacred trinity. It later found its way into many religious cults and sects.

The Nodes also symbolize the animation process or meeting place of the soul/spirit with the material world. It is the reason why we incarnate into this plane (see chapter on the Nodes). The placement of the Node in the stack represents our mentors and determines the type and style of associations the native seeks or feels comfortable with during his lifetime.

It is very important to use the true Node and not the mean Node because the true Node often travels direct in motion. Together, the Nodal points act as a chart axis. The North Node is the *influence of attraction and accumulation;* it is outgoing and positive while the South Node is the *influence of attrition and elimination;* it is negative and like Neptune, erosive.

Look at the horoscope wheel and find the Node having a planet placed near it naturally. The busy Node is the more influential Node and the one we use in the stack. The North Node represents associations that assist us in reaching out to the masses for support. Associations under the influence of this Node tend to last longer. The South Node drives us to create contingency plans as well as reserves and insurance policies to offset anticipated losses. Associations under this Node are of the short-term variety. In connection with karma, the North Node begins new karmic debts while the South Node eliminates them.

The North or South Node, depending which one has the most traffic, is not only the soul point but the "people desire" package as well. Associations will fall into the category relating to the decanate in which it is placed by degree along with the planets above and below it in the stack. The Node is also *enhanced by* the Midheaven at birth (sometimes sunset) and rulers. Combined, they form an internal recognition of whom we want to identify and associate with, and why. For this reason it is important to note whether or not the direction of the Node is retrograde.

The planet the Node is traveling *away from* is similar to potting soil for a plant, and can be likened to the native's innate root intelligence about himself and like roots in a plant seeking nutrients. The native seeks what he needs or wants from other people. The planet the Node is *traveling toward* represents the type of people to whom the native is drawn, as a plant reaching for the Sun. The closeness of a planet by degree of longitude indicates the motivational intensity by whatever planet is closer to the Node by degree.

Returning to the *wheel* in (figure 8.1), we can instantly see that the South Node has more influence because of the traffic (planets) surrounding it. Neptune is closer to the North Node but we do not use it until the native becomes either a celebrity or a captain of industry. The triad of the Moon/SNode/Saturn configuration suggests that there are many separations from friends in his life. This is supported by the fact that the native was raised in a military family and relocated numerous times. Remember, it is important to have as much information about your client as you can. It will help you put his astrological timeline together for better predictive results. Our native seeks sad, melancholy types of people to apply his Mars square Jupiter/Saturn energies; he has a need to rescue them with words of wisdom and cheer. (This configuration also suggests that he is happy in quiet surroundings.)

The Node's motion indicates, by direction, the soul's interest. In our example chart, the South Node is retrograde, traveling away from Moon *toward* Saturn. Earlier, we found in our example chart that the Moon represented a re-acquaintance with the mother at the age of eight. This Moon has an undertone of the loss of female companionship coupled with the joy of re-acquaintance. From this standpoint, the native will either consciously or subconsciously develop female associations primarily as an insurance factor in the case his chosen significant other chooses to abandon him. More significantly, and in the workplace, he has had a female boss most of the time.

His sunset Ascendant or Earth point (internal desire) in Capricorn opposes the Sun and Pluto. Capricorn, and its association with Saturn, represents the development of knowledge and assurance; the Moon seeks guidance for his development and well being. In his sunset chart, Pluto and Mars are above the Sun indicating a need to rescue others. The Sun's opposition to his sunset Ascendant in Capricorn is like a spotlight focusing on his Nodal associations of Moon and Saturn, Capricorn's ruler. This also repeats his leanings toward rescuing lonely people, those who are considered saturnine, strange or eccentric, with encouragement and by guiding them (Capricorn) through knowledgeable remedies (Saturn). However, by doing so, his attention to one group of companions may be construed as a lack of interest by another group. This may backfire and produce bitterness from those whom he sought to rescue in the first place. Unchecked, a situation like this could develop into the problem of trying to care for too many people, or "biting off more than one can chew." With so many demands being placed on the native by too many associations, we often see a state of overwhelm and the native's own needs going unfulfilled.

The best advice an astrologer could give this client is to learn to take control of situations by placing personal limits on himself and his clients. The chart repeatedly stresses the influence of Saturn. His sunset Ascendant is ruled by Capricorn and the Node is placed between the Moon and Saturn, Mars is in square aspect to Saturn and the conjunction of Jupiter with Saturn, all of which point to Saturn's overall influence—self-control and discipline to acquire self-fulfillment (Node).

The positive side to South Node's position is the promise of success (birth position trine sunset position). This can be accomplished by being more mindful of his own needs and how helping others to meet their needs can be accomplished through a conscientious sense of duty, not by continuous care and attention. In this way all parties gain self-control and thus soul growth. On the other side of the coin, with the South Node being closer to Saturn than the Moon, we can readily see that the native often feels lonely himself and may seek the company of his associates. There is a sense of impending loss that is always present. With the South Node between the Moon and Saturn, a possible interpretation could be that during his life, the native focuses on avoiding emotional losses through associations with other lonely and eccentric individuals who are also influenced by different forms of emotional privation.

Squares to the Nodes represent distraction from the native's true intentions. Associations under this configuration can be more detrimental than good. In this case the native may often give himself "away" by being overly compliant or give up prized personal items to "prove" his value in trying to elicit or maintain friendships. At other times the native may feel inadequate and will devise indirect ways to invite potential friends to visit him to see something new he just acquired or something different about his home.

Solutions to this and other negative aspects lie in self-observance. It is important to advise clients to remember to watch their own personal natures, to mentally observe their actions and reactions to situations, as if our client were watching a motion picture of their lives and was the "projector." In this fashion the client begins to learn more about his own actions from an objective viewpoint thereby eliminating negative reactions to situations. The process takes practice and is rather entertaining if one does *not* judge oneself but simply watches, allowing the folly to unfold while under scrutiny.

The Latitudes

The **Seventh step.** Up to this point we have been discussing the *longitude* of the planets. We now move to planetary Latitudes. There is a distinct difference between latitudes and declinations. The astrological latitudes are defined as the relative distance of the planets north or south of the *Sun's ecliptic*. With *latitudes,* the Sun is always the focal point and is noted at zero degrees. With the exception of Venus and Pluto, the latitudes rarely exceed five degrees off the ecliptic. On the other hand, declinations are measured from the celestial equator and may reach a maximum of plus or minus 27° above or below the equator. We do NOT want to use declinations.

Look at the planets' latitudes and note them in the same stacking order as you did the longitudes. Using the

Sun (zero degrees) as the focal point, note the planet that is immediately above the Sun (north) and the one immediately below the Sun (south) in the latitude stack. This triad will explain the physical comforts one can expect to attain through one's own efforts and the physical nature and "tone" of the individual. The planet above the Sun (north latitude) describes the effort one is willing to put forth to live the lifestyle indicated by the planet located below the Sun (south latitude). The latitude also describes what the native is prone to do in given situations. The latitude triad, combined with the Ascendant, also describes our physical body and its susceptibility to any possible physical problems or injuries.

The latitude, then, is the persona, the physical ambiance or sense of presence about the person; his physical attributes, strength and propensity to action. Look at the wheel and determine the aspects of the planets' in the latitude triad. When affected (good or bad) natally or by transits or rogression, the physical body is the reacting agent.

Planets in close parallel by degree to the Sun show a marked *attitude* of what is expected and accepted in the lifestyle. The soft planets (Moon, Venus and Jupiter) in north latitude are easy going and lack intensity. Their effort is minimal; these individuals seek others to provide their creature comforts. The native wants to be surrounded with "the good things in life." When the soft planets are in south latitude, the native is interested in refined entertainment and lifestyle, the arts, social standing, style, grace and what is expected from others by mannerisms: the genteel. Negative aspects in the wheel may indicate what the native wants but is unable to receive.

The hard planets in north latitude (Mars, Saturn and the Sun [when no planet is located in the south latitude]) are more aggressive and intense. Their expression shows an individual who expects to work for what he receives. Often, accepting charity is viewed as a character flaw or weakness. Therefore, these natives will tend to make a point of their independence and try to provide (no matter how meager) for themselves and their dependents. The same planets in south latitude are expressed in more physical forms of entertainment, such as boxing, football, hockey and other contact sports: the proletariat. Negative aspects may indicate that the native acts in a manner a little more to the extreme to those indicated above.

The above scenario is written in the extreme sense and must be modified and judged through other planetary situations in the chart. Very often you will find a chart that reflects style and grace in some areas with the coarser planets in the latitude layout. This may allude to a poor background with the desire to "better himself" by refining his expression, or an artistic type who likes to go out and "raise hell." In any case you will notice these trends immediately once the chart is complete and you meet your client.

In working with latitudes, the planets immediately above and below the Sun also have an additional, subtle modifying influence to the planet that sets immediately after the Sun. Latitudes are like electrical transformers that increase or decrease the energy flow.

The *meaning* of the planet setting after the Sun *by longitude* can be likened to the words of a song: they convey its message. The *latitude* modifies the planet setting just after the Sun like the musical key frames the melody or tune. When the latitude of two planets is near perfect or perfectly parallel by degree of separation (such as each planet by latitude is exactly one degree north and one degree south of the Sun), the native is either very determined to succeed or is precise in his methods regarding life projects. In other words, his energy is balanced and more intense.

Each facet is like adding spices to the mix when cooking. It is just a matter of remembering the different ingredients and in what proportions they are used. As we look at each facet in the chart, it adds a little more to the interpretation. In this fashion you, the astrologer, are delivering "tailor made" charts, not just generalized readings. Often there will be triads such as the latitudes or the lunar mansion that appear to rebut each other. Not only do they create havoc in the chart, but planetary contradictions are situations to be resolved by your client during his lifetime.

Compatibility in the Chart

Now let us look at compatibility charts. The sunset method is probably the easiest form of synastry. The term synastry stems from the Greek "synastria" meaning similarity of stars. It denotes the study of how two or more people's charts compare with each other for the purpose of describing their relationships (like the birth chart compared to the sunset chart).

Charts between two people, in any kind of relationship, will have certain planets in common. The more popular method is somewhat complex and requires a great deal of time and effort to evaluate properly. The sunset method is simple and will provide a great deal of information.

With compatibility charts it is advisable to use the natal charts whenever possible because in these charts the Ascendant and Midheaven are known. Additionally, the Moon is in its "critical point" at the time of birth. If the time of birth is unknown for one of the two charts, then use the sunset charts for both individuals. Always use similar charts when comparing your client's chart with someone else's chart. This is admittedly not as desirable but, under general circumstances, will still help evaluate the relationship. We will use the trans-saturnian planets (Uranus, Neptune and Pluto) because the charts are of famous people and they speak to us of both their private and professional lives. However, in using these planets, it is fair to state that they are not fully activated until fame is achieved. These planets are non-operative in the pre-fame years but are gateways to success. However, upon acquiring their new found status, pre-fame marriages usually dissolve into divorce because the trans-saturnian planets are activated in the chart of the successful person and not the spouse.

The Process

To view the compatibility of two or more charts simply stack the planets in numerical order starting from the highest degree of longitude to the lowest. Next, for *compatibility purposes only,* list the *sign* with the degree of longitude for the purpose of establishing planetary aspects. Obviously, if two charts have planets that are the same degree but are in different signs, it is important to recognize what works well (trine and sextile) and what type of work (square and opposition) must be done to maintain the relationship.

The more planetary contacts the better. Lack of planetary contacts between two charts indicates a weakened relationship. If your client has just met someone and there are only transiting planets contacting natal planets, the relationship will be short lived, probably for the duration of the initial contact only. No planetary interplay whatsoever indicates that there is no chance for a relationship to develop. For example, in sports, we often see a great player who will not stay with any one team for any length of time because of a few weak aspects between the player and the team's franchise date. Often when the player finds a team with the "correct" franchise date, one that matches his chart in synastry, he is happy and will stay with that team.

The following relationship is that of Adolf Hitler and Eva Braun. Their association was more difficult for her as she was never allowed to accompany him or be seen with him in public. Hitler met Eva through his photographer. She worked as the photographer's assistant. By comparing the stack, we can see that there was quite an attraction for Hitler even though it was negative.

HITLER aspects with **BRAUN**

VENUS 23° ARIES 29' square **SUN** 22° CAPRICORN 59'.

MARS 23° ARIES 11' square **SUN** 22° CAPRICORN 59'.

SATURN 20° CANCER 16' square **SATURN** 20° ARIES 14'

JUPITER 15° SAGITTARIUS 03' conjunct **VENUS** 15° SAGITTARIUS.

MOON 13° SAGITTARIUS 22' square **MOON** 15° VIRGO 31'

All the aspects above, except his Jupiter and her Venus square one another. Squares denote problems as well as impetus toward completion of a union. The list below shows only those planets just outside the orb of one degree.

NEPTUNE 7° TAURUS 39' conjunct **MARS** 8° TAURUS 47'

SUN 7° ARIES 36' semi-sextile **MARS** 8° TAURUS 47°

MERCURY 2° ARIES 28' sextile RPLUTO 3° GEMINI 38'

JOHN LENNON with **CYNTHIA LENNON**

SUN 21 VIRGO 21' semi-sextile **SUN** 22° LEO 16'

PLUTO 10° CANCER 15' semi-sextile **MERCURY** 10° LEO 45'

MARS 8° VIRGO 04' sextile **PLUTO** 8° CANCER 22'

URANUS 1° TAURUS 40 trine **MARS** 1° CAPRICORN 54'

From the moment he saw her, John was attracted to Cynthia although he considered her a "bit snobbish." She was as polite as he was aggressive, but she understood John's lack of consideration for others. When he first met her, his appearance was unusual, compared to the rest of the college students. He had a "scruffy," tough-guy image.

However, with Cynthia's gentle influence, John managed to alter his image to be more in keeping with the school's more accepted "arty" look. He changed to using scarves, black slacks and loose fitting jackets. He even changed his hair style from the greasy duck-tail fashion he usually wore to the more fashionably long-hair "dry look" style. His influence on her was pronounced as well. At his urging, she started to wear doe-eyed make-up and began dressing like Brigette Bardot. When we examine their compatibility charts, there was undoubtedly a need for each other's company. There were favorable aspects between them. Although they were both pleased when Cynthia became pregnant with Julian, they both admitted they probably would not have married if the pregnancy had not happened.

JOHN LENNON with YOKO ONO

MOON 26° SAGITTARIUS 54' square URANUS 26° PISCES 41

SUN 21 VIRGO 21 trine MARS 21 LEO 41'

MERCURY 13° LIBRA 18' trine N.NODE 13° AQUARIUS 58'

MC 11° SAGITTARIUS 30' sextile MERCURY 11° AQUARIUS 58'

URANUS 1° TAURUS 40' oppose MOON 1° SCORPIO 14'

John was quoted as saying, "When I met Yoko, I had to drop everything" (for her). He describes their first meeting: "Imagine two identical cars racing toward each other at a hundred miles an hour on a head-on collision course and slamming on the brakes just before they hit each other, where they stop with the bumpers just inches apart with smoke everywhere." It is surprising that the first time they met she did not think much of him. Of course, this may be attributed to her being seen with another celebrity at the time. Later, she relentlessly pursued John with letters and phone calls that both annoyed and fascinated him. Yoko stated that there was "electricity in the air" when they were together and that they had a "very tempestuous relationship."

STAN LAUREL with OLIVER HARDY

		PLUTO 13° TAURUS 49'
PLUTO 13 TAURUS 38'	conjunct	
		NEPTUNE 13° TAURUS 14'
MERCURY 12° TAURUS 15'	inconjunct	URANUS 1 2° LIBRA 38'
NEPTUNE 11° TAURUS 52'	inconjunct	MERCURY 10° SAGITTARIUS 56'
MARS 6° SCORPIO 53'	sextile	SATURN 6° VIRGO 50'
SATURN 5° LEO 49'	inconjunct	SUN 5° CAPRICORN 08'
SUN 2° GEMINI 22	inconjunct	MARS 3° SCORPIO 04'
VENUS 2° CANCER 11'	trine	MARS 2° SCOPRPIO 04'
N. NODE 0° GEMINI 37'	inconjunct	S. NODE 0° SCORPIO 31'
	square	MOON 0° VIRGO 23'

Stan Laurel was raised in the theater and felt he always knew what he wanted to do. Note Mercury's triadic position between Neptune (theater) and Pluto (determination). On the other hand, Oliver Hardy had always been hampered by a feeling of inferiority to the point where he even dreaded watching himself on the screen. Note his Mercury squaring Saturn. They were complete opposites in every way, except that they were both "unfailingly courteous" to everyone they met. At first, Stan was not too keen on the idea of them working together. However, it was Oliver who saw their potential and was anxious for them to work as a team. As they developed their routine, each played the perfect straight-man for the other. It was Stan who became the more dominant of the two. He always wanted to direct and wrote most of their scripts. He also insisted on "only one take" to maintain their spontaneity. Oliver always trusted Stan's judgment and studied the scripts each night so he would know what the scenes were about. In that way he would be able to ad-lib his scenes the next day knowing that the dialogue would be changed during the shooting.

The above discussion gives the reader an idea how to look at chart synastry. For a more in-depth review there are additional considerations which can be added to the mix: in viewing either the sunset or birth chart note how the planets that make up latitudes align, in what sections and by what degree; how the decanates (Anu, Enlil and Ea) influence the overall patterns; the Nodes and how they fit into the soul's scheme. By reviewing the entire chart in this fashion, a lot of the "weaving and unraveling" within the circular diagram can be dismissed, making it easier to come to conclusions about the individuals involved by use of these "checkpoints".

Summary Rules and Conclusion

(1) For an individual client always check the natal chart in comparison with the sunset chart to establish and analyze the intra- biWheel aspects.

(2) To determine the timing of significant circumstances or changes in the life in the sunset chart, note the difference of arc by degree; remember, five degrees are equal to one year of time. Place the smaller, identical sunset chart inside the larger chart and rotate the smaller chart clockwise for the timing and aspect depicting an event. Take note when a planet reaches an angle or another planet by a seeming conjunction or aspect.

> (A) Five degrees equals one year and each house is equivalent to six years.
> (B) By rogression we have two signs indicating the same house; look for their rulers.

3) Check with your client about any earlier incidents located in the sixth, fifth or fourth houses. Relate them to the first decanate. These events and how they relate to your client by planetary expression, decanate and age, will

pinpoint the entire event. They also denote a psychological statement, and its expression will reveal future trends by the same planet(s) involved.

(4) When viewing the age process by rogression, it is very important to remember the degree and decanate of the planet when noting and relating experiences.

Take note of which position the planet occupies by degree:
The first decanate or the first ten degrees relates to childhood experiences, teachings and desires (Ea). The second decanate (Enlil) relates to changes brought about by outside pressures (like being uprooted by a change of residence or fired from a job). The third decanate (Anu) relates to the dreams and aspirations held by the native.
Count the degrees from the sunset Sun to the planet to equate the time of life when different events occur. Transits, as well as the rogression and minor progressions, play an important role here. Remember, the Moon advances approximately one degree for every six years of life.

(5) In the sunset chart, the style and influence of the planet immediately setting after the Sun may not be located in the seventh house, but may be further away by house placement. The procedure remains the same, except that you may not immediately recognize the expression of the planetary influence. Case histories have shown that planets can be located as far away as six houses and still flavor the chart, although weakly. When this occurs, the native is usually uncertain of his position in life and may continue to operate from the first decanate planetary influence. Often, natives who fall into this category become perpetual students until they have acquired enough degrees to validate their place in the world.

(6) Take note of the two important positions:

(A) the first and last planet the Moon aspects by exact degree.

(B) the first planet to *conjunct any angle by rogression.*

Both circumstances describe the abilities for which the native has a natural affinity. This is modified by the latitudes, the planet of highest degree and the one setting after the Sun.

In closing, it is very important to recognize three solar factors in the chart that are revolutionary and often life altering. The first factor is the aspects between the positions of the sunset Sun and the natal Sun. Furthermore, as you rogress the chart, the rogressed Sun will also aspect the natal solar position as well. During the course of life, the Sun will sextile the sunset Sun at the age of twelve, square the sunset Sun at age eighteen and trine the sunset Sun by twenty-four and so forth. The rogressed Sun will aspect the natal position as well, however, in the natal chart, these aspects will not necessarily fall in any exact order because the timing of the natal chart places the Sun in any number of different houses.   It may be necessary to do a tri-wheel chart placing the birth chart in the very center to recognize the entire pattern of activity.

The second factor is noting the age when the Sun will rogress to the point where the Sun is located in the birth chart. This is the true solar return! Those of you who were born later in the day or afternoon will experience the sunset Sun-to-Sun square or opposition before you experience the Sun-to-Sun conjunction. As mentioned, these pivotal points are powerful. The timing of these events will revolutionize the overall lives of those who will experience them and recognizing them can be of great assistance in directing one's life or career, yours or your clients. Awareness of one's own potential during this rogression allows one to make the most of it. It can literally be associated with a sudden interest in forms of spiritual assessments and practices, completely new changes in direction or, if timed with a project, a tremendous experience of success or failure depending on the aspect.

In each case with the individuals interviewed, either the square (upper or lower), conjunction or opposition of these solar points in the sunset chart represented some inner, sudden recognition and an inner drive that motivated powerful changes. These major aspects usually indicate a time when the client became influenced by a powerful personality and the native had probably "taken on" and mimicked the traits of that person. The timing of these events should be scrutinized "to the max" to glean the impact of both the positive and negative aspects of such changes. Until this discussion, the importance of these periods (Sun to Sun square, trine, opposition and conjunction to natal Sun) were not known and could not have been utilized to take full advantage of them. It is during these times that counsel is greatly advised to further the potential of the person in the chart.

In daily mundane charts (diurnal or quotidian charts), the Sun-to-Sun position, either by square, opposition or conjunction, represents a "turn around" point. This is useful in predicting major changes in a given circumstance or project.

To further your own personal experience in the matter, start with sunset each day. Place your natal chart inside the smaller of the two diurnal charts and *align your Ascendant* by the same sign and degree to the diurnal chart. Rotate the internal charts (natal with sunset) and note the time different events occur. Look at the planets involved and how you handled the situation. Keep a daily journal and record these activities.

The third factor is chart *rogression*. In both sunset and natal charts there exists, at all times, the possibility for powerful changes to take place during rogression. As the planets in one chart approach the positions of the other chart, the aspects "tighten" either to the planets or angles. The planets emerging with the closest aspect become the "ruler of the period" until the rogression has passed. Pay close attention to the "ruling planet" in transit; favorable aspects create ease for the native while adverse aspects are indications of "challenges" the native will have to work through. Be sure to note which decanate is activated.

For example, at about the age of thirty-six, the Sun reaches the exact opposite point of the Sun's Ascendant in the sunset chart. Symbolic of sunrise, it represents our dawning awareness that we are standing on the threshold of new experiences yet to be discovered or lived. Many notables have written their manifest destinies during this time, sooner if there are planets located in the sunset sixth-house. A favorably aspected Sun in all three charts, the sunset, natal chart and current transits during this period is definitely desired. Also look at the aspects to the transiting planet currently in rulership.This is not to say that the thirty-sixth year is the only year that this happens; other planets will be passing other angles during the lifetime.

For those of you who have passed these earlier periods, look back and take note of your experiences at those times the rogressed Sun made aspects to itself. Reviewing your chart about the goals you set in that time frame using this system can be quite revealing .

CHAPTER **9**

CHART INTERPRETATION

If you don't know where you're going,
when you get there you'll be lost.   Yogi Berra

Below is the complete outline for the sunset chart system. At this stage it is important for you to understand the procedures used to process the sunset chart. The primary goal is to establish the *context* of the chart. This is accomplished by combining the natal chart with the Sunset Chart. Using the sunset chart as the backdrop, then process the individual elements in the horoscope. The natal chart further individualizes the general context found in the sunset chart, but as you will see, the time of birth is not necessary because a great deal of information can be gleaned just using the sunset chart. However, the time of birth is very important because it adds the Ascendant and Midheaven–critical elements to the process. By combining the birth chart and the sunset chart they both set the context by which we can understand how our clients express and experience themselves.

As an astrologer you develop an understanding about your clients as you research their charts by levels of a systematic "layer-like" process. And as you uncover each section, you eventually discover the person in the horoscope. In this fashion you evaluate each segment of your client's chart and, rather than trying to construct an analysis, the information is revealed. With this method you do not have to interweave the aspects with the planets, by house, sign or mid-points and, although these techniques do have their uses, the sunset procedure clearly shows you what you need to know for a complete delineation. We will start with the outline and follow it with charts for you examine the procedure further.

Chart Procedure

We start this procedure by obtaining the following information:

NAME
DATE OF BIRTH
TIME OF BIRTH
PLACE OF BIRTH

Cast the *one* copy of the *natal chart* using the KOCH HOUSE system. Using the biWheel technique, make *two* copies using the EQUAL HOUSE system.

    A. Note the *Ascendant* and *Midheaven*.
    B. Note the energy patterns of the year
       of birth.
    C. Note the Moon's rate of motion. Determine
       the first aspect the Moon will make to   another
       planet or angle.
    D. List planets by numerical degree of
       longitude (stack).

Next, cast the *sunset* chart using the EQUAL HOUSE system in a biWheel format. Use the same date if the individual was born BEFORE midnight—the previous date if born AFTER midnight. Make two copies.

    E. Note the planet setting just after the
       Sun.
    F. Note the first planet to hit any angle
       (i.e., 10th - 7th - 4th - 1st cusp).
    G. Note the first *and last* planets the Moon
       aspects by *exact* degree.
    H. Note all lunar aspects using the
       stack.

From the equal house *biWheel* charts, carefully cut out one inner chart from the birth chart and one from the sunset chart leaving the other one intact. You will see examples of this technique later in this chapter.

Place the SMALLER natal chart inside the larger sunset chart; align Ascendants of each chart.

I. Make a special note of the Sun's position at the *time of birth* and how it relates to the sunset Sun. This will serve two major functions. The charts will determine:

> **I–1.** The level and general tone of the aspects of both charts.
>
> **I–2.** The time of life (denoted by the position of the Sun in the birth chart) when a true solar return will signify what might be termed as pronounced self-awareness or "wake-up call." It is the time when major introspection occurs and (generally speaking) the native begins a new path in his life.

J. Note the positions of all the planets. The basic aspect between the natal Sun and the Sunset Sun sets the overall tone for the entire chart. It indicates the *level* at which the native may seek to solve his problems.

> **J–1.** Opposition or conjunction indicates focus and the need to clear away confusion between the planet in opposition and the planet of maximum attraction (see Chapter 5). The native must observe the planetary energies and follow through for a fulfilling life. The ratio of the opposition is thirty-six years (six houses).
>
> **J–2.** The square is difficult, the native has to learn to ignore distractions. Concerning reincarnation, there may be a higher degree of spirituality. The native has come into this life to work through difficult problems. The ratio is eighteen years (three houses).

J–3. The trine is easier. The native may either have a sense of mission he wishes to achieve in this life or he maybe a "young soul," getting his feet wet in the material world. The ratio is twenty-four years (four houses).

J–4. The sextile indicates many lifetime opportunities for material success. The rogressed ratio for success lies within the Jupiter cycle of approximately twelve years (two houses), the time it takes for any planet to reach another planet to fruition by sextile.

J–5. The lesser aspects are quintile, semi-square, inconjunct and so on. Their general meaning still applies to set the tone for the native's lifestyle.

K. The next step is to locate and note the planet that makes first contact to any angle.

K–1. The 10th house angle or Midheaven is concerned with control issues.

K–2. The 7th house angle is reactive, our response to outside stimuli.

K–3. The 4th house or Nadir indicates the native's vulnerability and self-esteem.

K–4. The 1st house or Ascendant is proactive or the motivating principles.

L. The next step is to determine the planet's patterns in the "stack." Be sure that the stack includes the natal Ascendant, Midheaven and Node from the natal chart.

To note the planets by 10° decanates:

L–1. 00° 00' to 10° is the first decanate; planets placed here denote the formative teaching by the parents.

L–2. 10° 01' to 20° is the second decanate, denoting the type of changes or challenges.
L–3. 20° 01' to 30° is the third decanate, denoting the individual's ideals and goals.

M. The next step is to form the planets into triads. Starting from the *top,* list the planets in groups of three. There will be 13 groups. For example, as any planet may be on top, we will generically indicate each planet in alphabetical form. For this purpose we will call the top planet Mars and determine this planet as "A," the second planet Venus as "B," the third planet Jupiter as "C" and so on. List planet A, planet B and planet C as one group; then list planet B–Venus, planet C–Jupiter, and the next planet D, as the next group. Then list planet C, planet D and planet E in the next group, continuing in this manner until you have completed the entire stack.

I recommend the use of Ebertin's book, *Combination of Stellar Influences,* for quick reference. Look up the combined planets, the upper and lower ones of the triad. Then look at the middle planet on the following page. In our example we would look up Mars combined with Jupiter and then refer to Venus on the following page.

N. The above information allows you to establish the style of each planet's energy pattern within the middle triad, as in the example of Venus, Mars, Jupiter influence. The native's form of reaction depends on how the energy patterns are determined by the triad, the arrangement by each decanate and where the planets are located by arc in the rogression.

N–1. The planet that is closer by degree has more influence.
N–2. As a planet naturally increases by its degree of longitude, the upper triad planet has a more positive nature while the planet in the lower part of the triad is considered negative.

271

N–3. Retrograde planets move toward the lower planet in the triad i.e., negative.

N–4. Planetary transits will activate each group. It is important to recognize the energy patterns and their placement in the decanate.

Planets located in the first decanate relate to childhood issues. Transits to these planets may bring understanding of these issues or the same issues may be repeated at a different level. Transits to the second decanate indicate changes or challenges the native will work through. Transits to the third decanate relate to goals and ideals.

O. Look at the planets' *latitudes* and note them in the same stacking order as you did the longitudes. Using the Sun as the focal point, note the two that are immediately above (north) and below the Sun (south). This triad will explain the physical comforts the native can expect to gain through his efforts and his physical characteristics. The planet in the northern latitude is the effort one is willing to put forth to earn the lifestyle indicated by the planet located in the southern latitude (see page 254).

P. Taking into consideration the planets above and below the Node, combined with the ruling planet of the sign opposite the Sun, we can learn a great deal about the people we associate with and what influence they have in our lives. The Node describes the characteristics of our unions, the type of people we are attracted to and their personalities. It primarily indicates, by the description of planetary influence, our affinity to instructors, employers or the people with whom we are willing to associate.

Rogressions

Rogression: a coined phrase to reference a small chart rotating inside a larger chart. You "age" the chart by starting with the Sun on the seventh house cusp and rotating the smaller chart clockwise. Each five-degree increment denotes a year of life.

Rogressed ratios are determined by dividing the number of degrees in the aspect by five (sextile = 60° ÷ 5 = 12 years). The following is a schedule for timing events. For the ease of the reader, a table of ratio is set forth as follows:

    i. 12 months is equal to 5°
    ii. 6 months is equal to 2° 30'
    iii. 3 months is equal to 1° 15'
    iiii. 1 month is equal to 25'
    iiiii. 1 week is equal to 06' 01"

By using this method as a time frame, each house of 30° covers six years of life. The equal house system allows you to clearly see the approximate age and event at any given planetary location. Thus, if a planet is exactly four houses from the Descendant, you will know the individual has reached twenty-four years of age when the rogressed Sun reaches that planet (4 [houses] times 6 [years in each house]). Likewise, you can also determine different times for your client's chances for success by looking at the distance of arc between each planet to the tenth house meridian or the MC.

Lunar Mansion

The lunar mansion is defined by the distance of longitude the Moon travels in 24-hours. It commences from sunset on, or before, the day of birth to the following sunset after the birth. You are also interested in the aspects it makes during that time frame.

    a. Our first concern is to find the Moon's rate of motion. This is the distance the Moon travels by longitude from sunset to sunset or 24-hours. This is called its rate of motion (ROM).

b. Next, you want to know the very first and last aspects the Moon makes by exact degree. This information allows you to understand the basic imprint the individual acquires during the time these aspects occur–it is the native's personal emotional demeanor.

c. It is important to understand that, as you rogress the chart, that the Moon will generally increase its longitude *by an average of one degree* every six years, more or less depending on its ROM. The rate of advance equates to one degree for each complete house the Sun travels.

For example, a sunset chart has the Moon located 29° Aquarius. By age eighteen, the Sun will have moved to the fourth house cusp and the Moon will have advanced three degrees (two degrees Pisces).

Getting Started

With the above procedure and information from the former chapters in place, you are now able to look at charts and analyze them. If, for any reason, you are not readily conversant with the material, it would be advisable to reread portions that you do not completely understand. Refer to the planetary meanings (Chapter 5) to help determine the outline of the following charts for John Lennon, Adolf Hitler and Mohandas Gandhi. These charts are chosen because they exemplify similar interactive elements with different outcomes.

We will review each chart in the sunset fashion and see how similar planetary influences are modified by aspects, the lunar mansion, placement by decanate and/or degree. In the chart of Hitler and Gandhi, there is a conjunction of Venus and Mars in the same sign. John Lennon's chart has Venus semi-sextile Mars by same *degree of longitude* in two different signs. The Venus/Mars conjunction alerts us to an impulsive and/or artistic nature but one that is not always artistic in the fine arts sense. Lennon and Hitler both had artistic aspirations with Lennon achieving them. Gandhi's artistry manifested in the craft of spinning and weaving his own clothing.

The Moon's first and last aspects further define the planet setting immediately after sunset. In Lennon's and Hitler's charts, the Moon is the strongest influence by virtue of its high degree in longitude, denoting the desire to influence the public in some manner. In Lennon's chart, the Moon's first aspect conjuncts the Midheaven, demonstrating his inner need for success through soulful communication modified by his setting Mercury. In Hitler's chart the Moon's first aspect is a trine to Mercury, modifying his sunset Mars and denoting his gift of communication (Mercury) to incite and sway public opinion into a state of war (Mars square Saturn).

The effect of the Moon in Gandhi's chart is not as dramatic. But, in the lunar mansion, its significance lies in its first aspect, a trine to Saturn which modifies his setting Mercury. Saturn's positive influence on Mercury denotes reflection, prudence, thoughtfulness and a sense of duty. He used his gift of communication to correct and heal India's immoral laws. In each case the lunar mansion is significant because its initial aspect creates a lifelong imprint based on the planetary influence. This analysis is <u>VERY</u> similar to the way the Sun sign is used in astrology today.

The first planet reaching an angle by rogression adds yet another subtle modification to the lifestyle and its direction. With Lennon, the Moon was the first planet to cross over the empowering Midheaven. With Hitler, a troubled Saturn crossed over the Midheaven. With Gandhi, it was Neptune contacting the proactive Ascendant. In each case we can clearly define a lifestyle within the sunset chart with just these two moves: the first aspect by the Moon and the first planet to cross an angle.

By aligning the birth chart with the sunset chart, we combine the influences of both. The outcome is a concise description of an individual's destiny. Within the parameters set forth in this book, we will find similarities with three vastly different world figures. With their personal styles these men followed the energy patterns indicated by their planetary positions, all with the influences described at sunset on or before the day they were born.

Make copies of the charts of each "personality reference" and keep them handy for quick reference. And, using an author's right to the redundancy clause; go back and study the areas with which you are not familiar.

JOHN LENNON

Our first chart for analysis is that of John Lennon. He was born on October 9, 1940. A good deal of controversy surrounds his time of birth; the chart on which we will base our analysis is calculated for 6:29 A.M. 53N25, 02W55. This timing is chosen because both the sunset and birth charts agree with the fact that he was cared for by his aunt which began when he was about six months old (solar arc difference of two degrees with his natal Saturn approaching the sunset eighth house cusp). Furthermore, the nature of the 6:29 A.M. chart, opposes the sunset chart, indicating that he would distance himself from contemporary views held at the time of his birth. The opposition corresponds to John Lennon's personal nature. It was in direct counterpoint to the war-like nature of his year of birth and contemporary views of his peers at school. At a later age he was able to act on his ideas and influence an entire generation.

1940 energy pattern:

The pace of the whole world was rapidly changing, both philosophically and technologically. The world became smaller with the advent of advanced intercontinental communication. This was also a time of uncertainty as the world prepared for the growing threat of war against the Axis Alliance between Germany, Italy and Japan. The Jupiter/Saturn conjunction has always marked the beginning of changes in world history and, for those who are born into its generation, the effect is always a marked one. It was a powerful year in which to be born.

Individuals who were born during 1940 are subject to aggressive and counter aggressive influences and may *act on* or *counteract* the principles of such energy patterns in the future. As they mature, these individuals may later influence global socio-economic and philosophical viewpoints based on their innate understanding and conversion of these inherited energy patterns. All birth patterns follow this course of action as defined in their charts.

Sunset chart

Erect an *equal house* chart for sunset on the *previous* day or October 8, 1940, time 5: 26:31 P.M. The only interest we have in houses at this time is their cusp reference for timing at six year intervals. Place no other value or meaning on them.

To identify the focus of John Lennon's destiny, place the natal chart inside the sunset chart. Notice the importance of Mercury's placement near the Jupiter and Saturn conjunction, placing further emphasis on his 1940 natal energy pattern. These three planets are located in the second decanate and indicate the need for variety and change. Also, Mercury is indicative of the many decisions he made in his life. The natal Mercury/sunset Uranus configuration reflects his ability to think creatively, write insightfully and adapt easily to the needs of his team. On the negative side, the overall Mercury opposing Jupiter/Saturn/Uranus configuration could be shrewd and cunning with a one-sided view of life. It also speaks of interests in current religio/philosophical views.

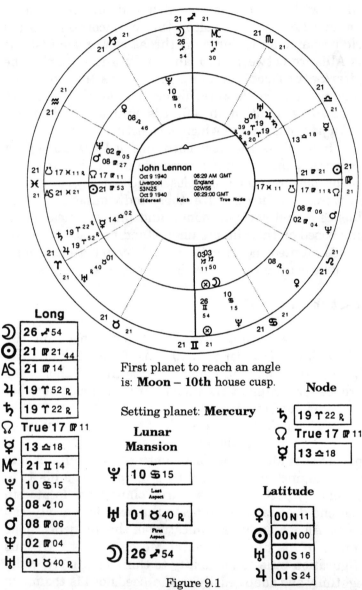

Long

☽	26 ♐ 54
☉	21 ♍ 21 44
AS	21 ♍ 14
♃	19 ♈ 52 ℞
♄	19 ♈ 22 ℞
☊	True 17 ♍ 11
☿	13 ♎ 18
MC	21 ♊ 14
♇	10 ♋ 15
♀	08 ♌ 10
♂	08 ♍ 06
♆	02 ♍ 04
♅	01 ♉ 40 ℞

First planet to reach an angle
is: **Moon – 10th** house cusp.

Setting planet: **Mercury**

**Lunar
Mansion**

♇	10 ♋ 15
	Last Aspect
♅	01 ♉ 40 ℞
	First Aspect
☽	26 ♐ 54

Node

♄	19 ♈ 22 ℞
☊	True 17 ♍ 11
☿	13 ♎ 18

Latitude

♀	00 N 11
☉	00 N 00
♅	00 S 16
♃	01 S 24

Figure 9.1

John Lennon's sunset (outer) and birth charts. The planetary
stack, the Node, the latitude and the lunar mansion. Note
the Moon in the tenth house with Mercury setting after the
Sun. Note also, that the 30 degree stack allows us to
instantly recognize his lunar mansion and Node position.

On the preceding page is John Lennon's sunset chart with his birth chart placed in the center. Note the "seeming conjunctions" between the two charts and other aspects. Sunset Jupiter and Saturn are located in the sunset first house of self-interest. It is important to note that these planets will rise five years later by rogression and exert their influence. Once activated by transit or progression, they become the indicators and timing of separations from loved ones.

This does not mean that Jupiter/Saturn conjunctions relate to separations in general. This conjunction is his *personal* reaction to their influence and remains so during his lifetime. Lennon's rogressed Jupiter/Saturn confirms this fact.

Lennon was personally (Ascendant) forced to decide which parent he wanted to live with after they were divorced. This all happened at approximately five and one-half years of age. He first chose his father, but he had second thoughts and ran to his mother's side. His parents' separation must have struck an emotional chord deep within his young psyche. Perhaps his song writing stems from wanting to say something to his parents to keep them together at the time of separation.

The Moon's strong influence and Saturn (the Moon's natural focus) conjoining the Ascendant indicate he would choose his mother. Important note: I cannot emphasize this fact enough: always watch the rogressed *motion* of planets to angles or aspects to other planets. Often we will see a rogressed planet make an aspect to an angle that has no immediate impact until a later aspect comes into play and galvanizes the original aspect. Sometimes this may take years. The first aspect sets up a situation and indicates *what* is to take place, the next aspect to the initial setup indicates the timing, *when* or with whom. In John Lennon's case, Mercury passed over the Descendant a full eleven months before he was forced to choose which parent would care for him. Once an aspect becomes activated, it redefines the initial incident and can be used to predict another incident that will take place at a later time! For instance, angular cycles are eighteen years apart.

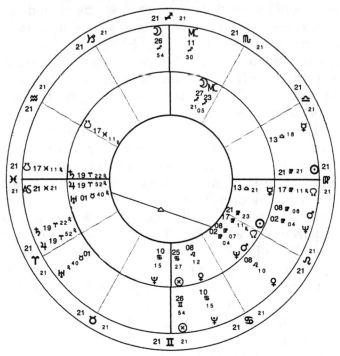

Figure 9.2
John Lennon's rogressed chart at age five.
At this time Lennon had to make a personal choice about which parent would care for him. Young John Lennon probably witnessed many disputes between his parents. Around the age of four and one half, Mercury passed the Descendant.

At twenty-two to twenty-three years of age John made another decision based on Mercury being activated by the fourth house cusp with the Jupiter/Saturn conjunction hitting the tenth house cusp eleven months later. By April 8, 1963, John and his wife Cynthia gave birth to their son Julian. At the same time the Beatles started to seriously record their songs. The rest is history.

The lunar mansion's rate of motion (ROM) is the distance the Moon travels in 24 hours. Lennon's personal ROM is 12°42' which initially aspects Uranus.

Therefore, to advance the Moon in the lunar mansion, one should add 12° 42', (ROM), to 26° Sagittarius 54' and we find the Moon moves forward to its last aspect sesquiquadrate Venus at 9° Capricorn 36', the approximate midpoint between Venus and Pluto in his sunset chart (irrespective of signs).

The Babylonian Moon was called the "Key to Heaven and Lord of Wisdom." We see this trebly reflected in John Lennon's chart. The Moon is in the tenth house, as well as being the highest degree planet, *and the first planet to reach an angle.* We can interpret this as being almost Cancerian in its strong emotional foundation and deep feelings for family, loved ones and causes. He longed for answers to solve his own inner conflicts and conveyed this seeking to others through his song writing. The Moon at the highest degree or near the Meridian indicates his search for a soul mate; no other union would do. This search would lead him to a number of different partners. His lunar position also indicates that he sincerely cared for those with whom he was close at the time although, like the Moon's influence, change was inevitable.

The near opposition to his sunset chart suggests a reversal of the energy fields into which he was born. Later in life he would be strongly opposed to bigotry and hatred, patterns so prevalent in the world at the time of his birth. However, there is a darker side to the Jupiter/Saturn conjunction. In his early teens he was said to have expressed himself in the very manner of his birth energies, ridiculing people whom he felt in some way were less fortunate or different than he, expressing his first decanate of Mars/Venus tendencies brought on by his parents at an earlier age.

The Moon is the first planet to reach an angle (defined by the Egyptians as coming forth), the tenth house or Meridian, indicating a strong emotional link and a sense of duty to his profession. He considered the other three in the group as his immediate family; they received first consideration. The Moon's *first aspect* completes a rather impressive grand trine to Uranus and Neptune. Normally, the trans-saturnian planets are enigmatic because they are indirectly influential in a chart, but they indicate the path to success if one decides to follow their influence (see chapter 5). Mercury and Mars become the stepping stones for Uranus with Venus acting as the stepping stone for Neptune. Both Mars and Venus are important because they are the same degree in the 30° stack (similar to a conjunction). If we were to discount the outer planets, Mars and Venus make the only planetary aspects to the Moon, further emphasizing his artistic endeavors.

Mercury, always seeking its chief attraction, Jupiter, is modified by the Moon and is the expressive planet setting after the Sun. This combination of Mercury and Moon indicates a search for spiritual guidance and wisdom. He expresses his ideal emotional values through communication, in his case, song writing. Further emphasis is placed on the Moon because it is the highest planet by degree of longitude and acts as a sub-dominant theme (tenth house). By definition, Mercury/Moon indicates mental activity initiated by emotional stimulus with a good perception of the world around him.

This additional lunar sub-signature is further modified by the sunset Mercury opposed to the natal Jupiter and Saturn conjunction. This expresses itself as a moody individual who constantly seeks comfort and acceptance from others. The double configuration of Mercury/Jupiter/Saturn suggests the philosophy that with each good event something bad will follow, or vice versa. It also suggests a reflective jumping jack wit, influenced (again) by his emotions. It further indicates that being helpless or out of control (either within himself or with others) is undesirable in any situation. Yet, he was swept into that very situation when the Beatles became famous. The Moon generally brings with it an awareness of what it from earlier experiences, but surely, his fame placed him in opposite circumstances which probably helped crystallize his awareness. The Sun represents a focus on attention-getting devices. It rests in a supportive position under the Moon in Lennon's stack. When placed in the third decanate, it takes on the form of self-idealization. According to Ebertin, the Sun, coupled with the Moon's influence suggests making contacts with partners and/or friends in the search for a soul union. These two planets would indicate an earnest and sincere drive to understand the significance of what he and his life were all about. He probably questioned why he was experiencing such an incredible rise to stardom and world-wide influence, further prompting his personal search for self-realization.

By placing his time of birth just before sunrise, his solar position is very close to the Earth point (Ascendant) opposing its sunset position. A birth at sunrise, coupled with the elevated Moon's position, suggests an expression of compassion and soul consciousness that will resist the social system with a disregard for the trendy influences or philosophies of his time.

The planet setting immediately after the sunset Sun is Mercury. Its influence suggests that the native will pursue recognition either by a vocal or mental expression. This is further emphasized by examining the biWheel of the birth chart with the sunset chart. We find that the natal Mercury rests between the Jupiter/Saturn and Uranus placement in the sunset chart. In John Lennon's chart, Mercury, with the Jupiter/Saturn configuration, can be expressed as a worldly outlook; Uranus with mental restlessness and the desire to cause changes. By rogression, these contacts always presaged a time of major changes and/or separation from loved ones.

In many charts Mercury will often set after the Sun and it is important to recognize its modifying sub-signature; specifically if it is near the MC or, as a secondary choice, the first planet to cross any angle. In this case it is the twice elevated Moon combined with Saturn conjunct Jupiter in opposition to natal Mercury. At times, there will be conjunctions or even a group of planets (a stellium) setting after sunset. The planet closest to the Sun is always the more influential, even if it's only by a few minutes of arc (combust). Additionally, the planet with the highest degree becomes the modifier if there is no planet coming forth or one near an angle (Ascendant, Descendant, Midheaven or Nadir).

In general, other than the lunar mansion, there are two indicators that will give us an idea of one's demeanor or the type of persona an individual expresses in public. They are planets located in the sixth house of the sunset chart and the two closest planets to the Sun by north and south *latitude*. Planets in the sixth house represent an objective experience–how people view an individual without really knowing them.

In John Lennon's chart, all planets located in the sunset sixth house reflected his appearance: by Venus semi-sextile Mars, Neptune and the North Node. What we *expect* is a rather good-looking, somewhat combative and self-assertive individual with an air of mystique and sense of other-worldliness, a larger than life expression, which was John Lennon's superstar stage persona. When meeting John Lennon, his stage persona evaporated quickly and the person we actually met was very different. During his lifetime, he had an air of being an outspoken, sharp-tongued wit coupled with a tough-guy attitude. This "bubble" was burst when people met John for the first time. Many were quite surprised by John Lennon's slight size and stature.

The Law of 72, Rogression

To reiterate, the rogressed timing of influences is determined by the Babylonian Law of 72, a universal mathematical formula often used for computational purposes. This law was based on the retrograde precessional motion which takes 72 years for the Vernal

Point to move one degree against the backdrop of the constellations. When applying it to a human lifetime, we divide the 360° circle by 72, its result of five degrees equates to one year of life. By rotating the chart clockwise, each planet, and the four angles, will aspect their own sunset position and the positions of the other angles within a 24-hour period. The 24-hour period is co-equal to the average human life-span of 72 years. This is the basis for the rogressed timing of the chart. For real sticklers who prefer *not* to work with the equal house system, divide each unequal house by six and the variable will equal one year of life.

By rotating John's equal house sunset chart clockwise 25 degrees (rogression), we find between the age of five to six the Jupiter/Saturn conjunction approaching his Ascendant. Continuing the process by rotating the *inner* chart's seventh house Sun/cusp to the fourth house (three houses of six years each equal eighteen years) brings us to the time of his mother's death. Later, when he was nineteen, his Moon rogressed to the Descendant. At that time he failed what he considered an important audition.

Space does not permit a year-by-year analysis of his chart, so we will jump ahead and highlight particularly important periods illustrating the process of rogressing the chart. At this time create your own sunset chart on John Lennon. This will allow you to follow along as we rogress and examine the wheel and the points of reference that indicate events in his life.

Let us fast forward to 1967 (see chart above). We see a time of more disappointments than accomplishments. The rogressed Moon is approaching the midpoint between his sunset Venus and Neptune. The rogressed North Node was also in contact with sunset Uranus while Uranus reached the Midheaven by rogression. The release of *Strawberry Fields Forever* and *Penny Lane* was the first time he and his comrades failed to reach the heights to which they were accustomed. However, by June 1967, they released a new album, *Sgt. Pepper's Lonely Hearts*

Club Band, their highlight of the year. It was a totally new approach which revitalized the group's popularity.

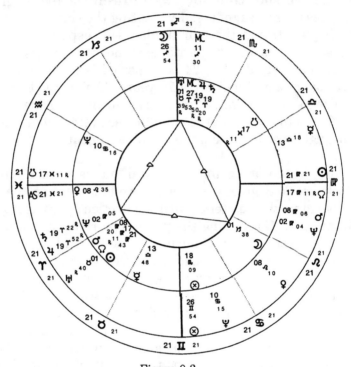

Figure 9.3
In 1967, Venus was rising on the sunset Ascendant of Lennon's chart.

During the rest of the year, upsets continued to plague the Beatles, Brian Epstein, their manager died; "All You Need is Love" was released; and the Beatles' first public disaster, the disastrous *Magical Mystery Tour* was filmed and released. The next years remained under the negative influence of Venus. Demonstrations for peace, Lennon's disappointment with the Maharishi, the Apple Boutique failure, his divorce from Cynthia—all took place while Venus was approaching the Ascendant.

By the time of Lennon's thirtieth birthday, his sunset Sun had rogressed to the second house *cusp,* forming an inconjunct aspect to the sunset Sun and approaching the position of Uranus. Mars was approaching his sunset Jupiter/Saturn conjunction (losses) by rogression. The band members became more and more discontent and by December 1970, Paul filed suit for financial purposes. By march, 1971, the court ruled in favor of Paul and they went their separate ways. The Moon conjoined sunset Venus by rogression while Venus was rising in the 12th house.

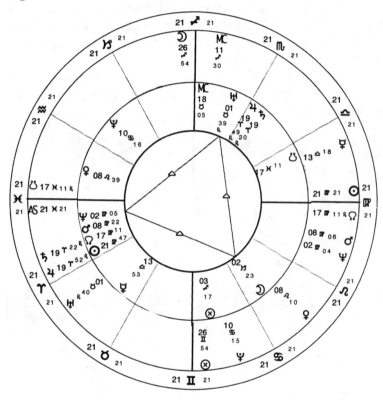

Figure 9.4
The official disbanding of the Beatles, March, 1971

The year 1973 was full of turmoil for John. Mercury began its approach, bringing with it many lawsuits, his deportation from the United States, his separation from Yoko and problems recording his next album, *Mind Games*.

By 1974 his rogressed Neptune and Mars made their presence felt while approaching his sunset Ascendant. Appeals to save Michael X, a man John felt was falsely accused of murder in Trinidad, failed (rogressed South Node to sunset Mercury while rogressed Mercury conjuncts sunset Uranus). By March that same year while producing Harry Nilsson's "Pussy Cats," he made headlines with his drunken presence and argumentative attitude at a famous night club in Los Angeles. By November 1974 he released the hit, "Whatever Gets You Through the Night" (rogressed Mercury to sunset Jupiter/Saturn). This can be readily seen in the previous chart by adding five degrees to the inner wheel's house cusps to equal each year's movement by rogression.

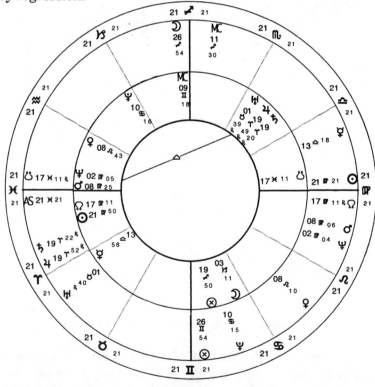

Figure 9.5
Chart rogressed to 1974, note the Mars/Neptune position.

The three divisions:

List the planets by longitude in a stack beginning with the highest planet and work your way down. Earlier we ignored the outer planets and the mathematical points but at this juncture we'll add them with notes.

Number the planets from one to twelve starting from the bottom of the stack. In your practice, you will notice that these numbers have a house correspondence. For instance, the seventh planet counting up from the bottom of the stack (not counting the MC) gives an insight into the type of partner the native looks for. Even though the ancients did not use this formula, research confirms the value of contemporary house meanings. Do this to Lennon's planets.

Note that the MC does not have an assigned number. The reason for this is the MC is considered the soul's memory with no tangible manifestation on the planet.

<u>ANU **20° 01'** and above. Planets located in this section indicate ideals sought.</u>

12 **MO. 26°** Also the **modifier** of the self-image planet and the highest planet; his personal ideal. Overall influence of the entire chart.

10-11 **SU/ASC 21°** The Sun and Ascendant are on the same axis and are a combined influence for the tenth and eleventh house (group activity leading to success). However, by using the birth Ascendant, we find that the Sun is conjoined the first house angle, with that, it is safe to say that Lennon was the unspoken leader of the group. This is one instance where knowing the time of birth comes in handy.

<u>ENLIL Planets in this section represent circumstances to adjust or overcome.</u>

9 **JU.** **19°** Overall influence of the middle decanate.

8 **SA.** **19°**

7 **NO.** **17°**

6 **ME.** **14° Setting** Self image, how he wants others to see or think of him.

M.C Soul's memory point (no number assigned).

5 Pluto **10°** (Activated by fame.)

EA Planets in this arena represent the physical appetites and attachments.

4 **VE.** **08°** Overall influence of the first decanate.

3 **MA.** **08°**

2 Neptune **02°** (Activated by fame).

1 Uranus **01°** (Activated by fame).

The planets in the first decanate indicate what the individual will learn from his parents as he grows. Mars and Venus are the indicators of his youthful personality traits and proclivities. As always, the *highest* planet by degree in *each* decanate has the most influence but is always under the overall influence of the highest planet by degree located in the Anu or third position. In the first decanate (Ea) it is Venus. This group of planets suggests that Lennon grew up learning to hide his feelings of helplessness (the Moon is the planet with the highest degree and is the overall modifying influence) with a tough, almost coarse (Mars) exterior (Venus/Mars by the same degree). Yet, he eventually recognized his unique artistic direction (Venus, ruler of this decanate section). The overview of Venus in the first decanate suggests an interest in the arts. Furthermore, he was probably very disappointed with his childhood circumstances. His Venus placement in the birth chart represents some form of disappointment. His artistic inclination turned from fine arts to music as a more acceptable expression of his gift.

The next decanate (Enlil) ranges between Pluto and Jupiter with Jupiter being the most influential in this decanate section. Through change, the planets located in this sector become life experiences. We know it as the "school of hard knocks." We learn either by resistance or we take an easy path through passive acceptance. These changes are influenced by transits and the rogression. In 1974 when Lennon broke up with Yoko, Mercury was approaching his Jupiter/Saturn conjunction in the sunset chart. As noted, throughout Lennon's life, the Jupiter/Saturn configurations (either by transits or rogression) presaged the separation in his relationships. This has been repeatedly demonstrated during the rogression by their conjunction in the sunset chart. With Lennon, the Jupiter/Saturn conjunction was the change that *reflected an influence of separation.*

Often recognized as a point of transformation, Pluto is located in the lower section of the second decanate between Mercury and Venus. This expression of Mercury/Venus has been found in numerous writers' charts. Lennon's Pluto was closer to Venus, indicating that his writing ability had a sense of mission. His Venus placement between Pluto and Mars showed a marked interest in the area of love, the unrequited kind, coupled with a passionate disposition.

Rogression and transits to Venus usually indicated disappointments and/or dissatisfaction, either in a social atmosphere or in the expected outcome of personal projects. John Lennon did not receive what he expected in the Venus arena of life, and he developed a cynical and sarcastic attitude. A typical expression of the tri-planet configuration of Venus between Pluto above and Mars below can be seen in the way he walked away from Cynthia and married Yoko Ono, in a way, replicating his father's activities many years earlier. This took place when his rogressed Neptune reached his sunset Jupiter/Saturn conjunction (1968). What ensued was their bed-in period (1969) which was expressed in a passionate (Pluto), protective (Mars) and, what they thought, an artistic expression (Venus) of their relationship (Jupiter/Saturn) between themselves and the world at large (Neptune).

Mercury between (MC) Pluto and the North Node indicates a writer or speaker who gains wide acclaim; a person who often speaks hastily or with a sharp tongue. The tri-planet configuration also suggests that there is an innate understanding that life is delicate and fragile and concerns chance and change. The Node in *this stack context* relates to meeting others with a mutual agreement (mental-Mercury) to organize goal-oriented objectives (Saturn), coupled with the tri-planet configuration (Pluto, MC, Mercury) and the North Node. His influence with the people he met would fuel his role as impromptu leader. Saturn located between the Node and Jupiter (Saturn is 30' earlier than Jupiter) relates to searching for meaning and purpose in a joyful and harmonious atmosphere with significant others. Additionally, this triad indicates a deeper sense that there is more to life than just being on the planet. This configuration is often seen as an influence that encourages others to follow in the footsteps of luminaries.

Mercury between Saturn and Pluto certainly indicates the attitude of *once said, never retracted* and Lennon was certainly never one to mince words. Often his sharp, outspoken criticisms were only partially quoted in the press, a problem that haunted him continuously. Additionally, Jupiter, the king maker, shows that his search for a higher spiritual purpose was truly serious, (conjunct Saturn) through songs like *Imagine* and *God*. However, he appeared to be quite light-hearted because of the overall Jupiterian influence. Where Jupiter is placed in a chart is generally reflected as a seemingly optimistic attitude with the appearance of taking life in stride. Regarding the breaking up of the group (Beatles), he was heard to say that, "It wasn't the end of the world," and that "People should get on with their lives."

Located in the idealistic third decanate, his Moon is the highest planet overall. This position recognizes ideals relating to the associations with the public, friendships and partners in joint ventures. The Moon placed in the highest position can be seen as a soulful search, a person who is looking for answers about life. Many people born with this Moon signature recognize how fragile life really is and seek ways to establish a stable and secure lifestyle. This lunar placement in the ideal decanate is enigmatic, as natives look for someone to "hold their hand" through unfamiliar territory or circumstances but, they are most prone to becoming teachers or leaders in group situations.

Beneath the Moon lies the Sun. The Sun has long been recognized as the conscious element of self expression. Solar types recognize what is needed for growth and development. The Sun in the third decanate supporting the Moon indicates an interest in becoming ideally involved with soul and spirit growth but not necessarily in a religious manner. This combination signifies the blending of the conscious and subconscious as well as the need to be creative. It also signifies tolerance for what others think and believe. Lennon *knew* he had a better answer, not only for himself but for the world as well. He saw the world at large as being hard and uncaring and, although the epiphany is much deeper than that, his song entitled "*All You Need Is Love*" was his message for the solution.

Planetary Latitude.

The next exercise concerns the latitude (not declination) of the planets. Place the Sun at the center and place each planet according to its degree of latitude north above the Sun and those planets in south latitude below.

Note: Uranus is closer by latitude to the Sun than Jupiter. Uranus is an outer planet that influences generations and in Lennon's chart that influence was generated by a unique and personable charm with the public. But it is the strength of the reflective Moon that enables us to see his boyish charm.

In the figure to the right we find Venus located above the Sun with Jupiter below. Venus is closer. This tells us about his artistic and sensitive side. Venus/Jupiter with a touch of Uranus is a combination that often produces lucky breaks and contributes to the wealth factor.

♀	00 N 11
☉	00 N 00
♅	00 S 16
♃	01 S 24

The outer planets beyond Saturn sway an individual according to the trend that is currently in vogue at the time of birth. In England, John's childhood planets of Venus and Mars were involved with the planetary energies of Pluto (the war), Uranus (the bombings), and later, as the war escalated, Neptune (uncertainty of the world's future).

It is important to remember that only the leading members of each country and its captains of industry are the trend setters. The potential for promotion to such positions of power can be linked to the energies of the trans-saturnian outer planets (page 128). The trans-saturnian planets indicate the power for directing large groups of people and for the most part, as mentioned earlier, do not exert a strong influence directly on the average citizen unless that person rises to a celebrated status. At that point, for good or evil, he becomes a trend setter. For the moment, the general population is made up of supporters and followers who are influenced only by the visible planets. For the average person, the trans-saturnian planets that make up the higher octaves act through the *visible* planetary influences. It is much like a canvas in a painting: Pluto relates to its size and intensity of the subject matter; Neptune relates to its inspiration and use of color; Uranus relates to its uniqueness of approach and design. Not everyone is an artist. The trans-saturnian planets offer intensity, inspiration and uniqueness. Unless an individual finds himself in a unique leadership position, he will probably never have a need of or the ability to work directly with these planetary energies.

In the thirties and forties, Pluto's influences drove an entire generation to war. Neptune's influence was responsible for concerns about the outcome of the war. In America, espionage, top-secret electronic projects, and movie star images captivated the public's interest. Unified war efforts were affected by the Uranian influence in all countries. A major concern was directed toward designing new weapons systems. From the end of World War II until sometime in the mid sixties, Pluto's energies had us concerned with the atomic bomb and restrictions imposed by conquering armies on the war's losers. Neptune's influence in the fiftie's put us in the ether of innocence through peace, the effect of television, teenage idols and the advent of the drug culture. The war effort stimulated American unity through standard industry procedures for improving commercial commodities until October 4, 1957, when the Russians launched Sputnik into outer space. What the Russians accomplished with Sputnik shocked (Uranus) the free world and inspired the development of the American space program and its resultant expansion of space technology.

The Node.

As the intersecting plane of the Sun and Moon, the Node was known to the ancients as the Hidden One. It represented the third position in the sacred trinity and was reflected in many world religions. The Node represents the animation process or meeting place of the soul/spirit with the material world.

The Node suggests the curiosity of inter-active experiences and represents the reason we incarnate. The sunset Ascendant is our innermost core being, what we associate with as our true inner hero; the Node is the link to its image and the appreciation expressed from our associates. Combined they are our physical/mental expression to the world and our response to the world's reaction regarding our deepest philosophy of who we believe we are and with whom we associate.

The North Node is a point which expresses itself by reaching out to the world for support, whereas, the South Node is more concerned with creating insurance's and reserves to offset its influence of attrition.

The Node placed with the most planets determines which one is the more influential. In Lennon's chart we can instantly see the North Node has more influence because of the planetary traffic surrounding it.

♄ | 19 ♈ 22 ℞

☊ True 17 ♍ 11

☿ | 13 ♎ 18

He seeks strong emotional support from those he meets and the world at large. In Lennon's case, we see Saturn above and Mercury below the North Node with Pisces on the sunset Ascendant.

The Pisces Ascendant (ruled by Neptune) gives focus to the triad of Venus, which rules his first decanate; the Moon, the highest planet by degree and Jupiter which is connected with Saturn by conjunction; all three of which comprise Neptune. It is very important that we use the true Node and not the mean Node. The true Node often travels in direct motion as can be seen in Lennon's chart. The Nodal point with the most traffic (planets) is considered the important part of the nodal axis in the chart.

The soulful North Node carries with it the influence of *accumulation* while the South Node is the influence of *attrition*.

The Node's direct or retrograde motion indicates inclination and yearning. Lennon's chart indicates that there is no immediate influence from the South Node (however, it is still active in transits or rogression). The Nodal position always tells us of the deepest interest of the incarnated personality. In this case the North Node is traveling away from Mercury and *toward* Saturn (Node direct). Such an involved combination of planetary configurations with the Node does imply his steely wit and, as Cynthia once said, "Whatever John sets his mind to, he usually gets."

Because the North Node is closer to Saturn than Mercury, we also find a witty, wisecracking personality with the psychological need to control the laughter of the people around him. In this manner he had them laugh *with* him rather than *at* him (an interesting aspect of Saturn in general). His witty, cynical remarks (Mercury) never failed to make a lasting impression (Saturn) on those whom he met(Node). The negative aspect of this Nodal triad is the need to express oneself in a coarse and vulgar manner when upset or when challenging an opinion other than one's own.

The Moon's position in a chart represents the influence of emotional vulnerability. As an individual matures, he seeks guidance and learns to fulfill his emotional needs represented by his lunar mansion. Just as he seeks to understand his emotional needs, so, too, do those who fall under his influence. John's Ascendant, above the Sun and below the Moon by degree, indicates his successful relationship with the other Beatles as well as his drive for recognition and fame. This triad also indicates a generous almost charitable nature, often dictated by his feelings.

On an esoteric level, John's North Node with Mercury and Saturn implies his love of reading, a sharp critical wit and the need to be with more serious minded people to reflect his own overactive mind. Lennon's sunset Ascendant in Pisces represents his need for understanding his inner person, soul development and recognition of a sense of deeper purpose i.e. his music. This Ascendant, with the symbolic chord between the two fishes as they swim in opposite directions, also represents the need to relieve stress and tension. As a youth, he could not stand the required studious regimen of schoolwork without disrupting classroom activities with silly antics or boisterous sarcastic remarks about his teachers.

Sagittarius Midheaven (desire), located between Mercury and Pluto in the stack, is the indicator of the soul's memory of past incarnations. As a young child he was quoted as saying that he wanted to be on the stage or become a prime Minister. As a young adult, he recognized his penchant for art, writing and music. Taking into account the combined effects of the sunset chart, stack, lunar mansion, node and latitude positions, we find a complex man whose purpose was to do exactly what he and his fellow Beatles did-herald changes in the world!

These highlights aptly signify the importance and accuracy of *timing* in the sunset chart. To cover John Lennon's life would take a complete volume. You are encouraged to continue this study on your own. John Lennon was shot and killed December 8, 1980, just two months after his fortieth birthday. His chart indicates certain movements which could only be kindly described as a crises: rogressed Mars in contact his twelfth house cusp; Mercury conjoined his sunset Ascendant; Jupiter/Saturn approaching his sunset Sun on the Descendant; and Pluto culminating and squaring the Ascendant.

ADOLF HITLER

Adolf Hitler was born on April 20, 1889, at 6:30 P.M., in Braunau Am Inn, Austria 48N15, 13E03.

First analyze the energies at birth and compare them to the activities the native will either conform to or rebel against. The year **1889** was a transitional year for Germany. Six months before Hitler's birth, William II became Germany's last demagogic emperor and ended years of internal feuding between the Social Democrats, Conservatives and the National Liberals. Bismarck's position and conservative views about taxes, expansion and colonization declined rapidly under the new emperor's rule. At the time of Hitler's birth, Germany was ruled by William II who controlled a powerful country which "*knew no moderation or limits to German power!*" When Hitler came into power this birth energy would replicate itself–placing Germany in the hands of a vengeful dictator.

Sunset Chart.

To begin, cast the horoscope for _April 19_, 1889, at 6:51:15 a day earlier than his birth. Hitler was actually born close to sunset on the following day, April 20.

Being born close to sunset, Hitler would reflect, absorb and follow the energy pattern of his generation. The lunar mansion indicates that the Moon's first aspect is to Mercury at about the age of six. The last aspect by the Moon is to Pluto. Thus, we see the possibility of him becoming a convincing speaker with power to influence the masses. A negative manifestation of this indicates fraudulence and misrepresentation in speaking or writing.

The first planet to come forth or conjunct an angle is Saturn in the tenth house which is also the chart's subdominant theme.

In analysis, a negative Saturn (in Square) is hypersensitive, discontent, as well as having a strong will with social aspirations all the while tending to be reserved and distrustful. Although Mars is in a negative square to Saturn and is closer to Venus, because it is after the setting Sun, Mars is more influential than Saturn.

The planet setting immediately after the Sun is the influence with which one _mentally associates_ and, combined with the Ascendant, presents the _ideal appearance or presentation_. The planet above the Sun combined with the attributes of the Sunset Ascendant is the planetary configuration the native associates with "the real me."

Mars, as the setting planet, will often reflect in the native as the willingness to champion a cause or take up someone else's fight as his own. His sunset Libra Ascendant is doubly expressed because its ruler Venus, conjoins Mars causing Venus to become a hard and bitter planet reflecting Mars' negative square to Saturn. Venus, has an enclitic nature and loves to reflect the energy of the conjunction.

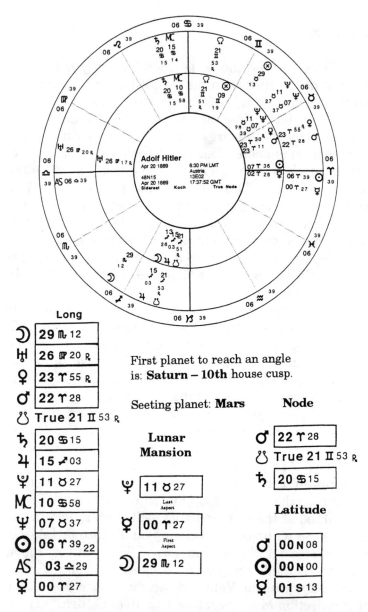

Figure 9.6
Adolf Hitler's sunset (outer) and birth charts. The planetary
stack, the Node, the latitude and the lunar mansion. Note
Saturn in the tenth house with Mars (and Venus) the setting
planet(s).

The overall configuration is an index of an unsatisfied and irascible being. Hitler's inner vision of himself (Ascendant) was that of a hero (Mars) championing a social cause (Libra) with acts of violence (square Saturn) against his enemies. Metaphorically speaking, during World War I his commanding officer was his mentor while the war itself became his inspiration.

In John Lennon's chart we saw Mercury setting. Lennon viewed himself as a messenger (Mercury) of peace and love (strong Moon). In Hitler's case we see him championing (Mars) the disappointment (Venus) of the German people stemming from the losses and destruction (square to Saturn) experienced during World War I. This configuration is one of the driving forces behind his rise to power and recognition. With Saturn as a sub-dominant theme (square sunset Mars), we have a view of Hitler as someone who exhibits vengeful, harmful, destructive energy. This is like a double whammy when we remember that he was born at a time when Germany knew no moderation or limits to its power! This configuration lends a dire note to this nativity suggesting a strong willful attitude combined with a lack of self-discipline.

Latitude.

As we can see, the Sun is flanked by heavily aspected Mars and lightly aspected Mercury. This configuration of planets show Hitler's ability to immerse himself in the created role of Germany's spokesman reflected by the placement of Mars in the northern position and Mercury in the southern position.

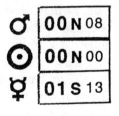

Having Mars closer indicates that we would see the passion of his oratory when he spoke to the German people.

His direct interest and role in the propaganda machine of the Nazi party on its inception all relate to the

301

Mars Mercury aspect of this latitude. Additionally, he also had a unique ability to exploit conditions favorable to his success and help foster the Hitler myth of his being a shrewd and calculating leader. This is further emphasized by the location of his Sun between Neptune and Mercury located in the stack. During Hitler's early years, we see his parental guidance. Additionally, he developed his deceitful abilities very well to protect himself from his abusive father.

The Node.

Hitler's choice of comrades is emphasized by his South Node position (self preservation) which is placed by degree between Mars square Saturn. This Nodal configuration works well to reflect his fascination with war, its trappings, and associations with military activity. After the war, many dissatisfied ex-servicemen who were unhappy with the armistice, began to settle in Munich and organize small partisan units to express their views and plot against the republican government in Berlin. Hitler joined a small, unorganized dissident group and began to surround himself with ardent followers. Both Hitler and the many subversive groups were determined to change government policies which Hitler saw as intolerable.

The South Node is always negative because of its attritional nature and is closer to Mars which is square to Saturn, instills even more of an 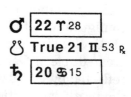 negative overall martial influence. Hitler never trusted anyone, he knew that it did not take much to turn an ally into an enemy–something he would do in an instant if he felt threatened.

♂ | 22 ♈ 28 |

☋ True 21 ♊ 53 ℞

♄ | 20 ♋ 15 |

We chose the South Node because it has planetary *traffic*. It is in the same sign and only six degrees away from a conjunction with Jupiter.

The Stack.

In viewing the stack we must recognize that 30° is the same as 0°. Hitler's Mercury, his lowest planet, is one degree fifteen minutes away from the Moon (Moon 29° Scorpio 12' and Mercury 00° Aries 27').

Hitler's Moon (and sunset Ascendant) suggests associations with the public, but his highest ideal is supported by a dark set of planets. His ideal was destructive as described by the South Node with the Venus/Mars conjunction in square to Saturn. This indicates an awareness of the public's vulnerability but ... was he aware of his own?

In response to the question, the answer would have to be "yes" because of the fact that he distanced himself from the people who had originally supported him. Hitler's profile discloses he was afraid his aides would try to usurp his power and have him removed from his position or killed. His actions reflected his chart very well as he had his rivals, both real and imaginary, expunged to keep them from actualizing any threat to his position.

In the arena of EA, the first decanate, there is Mercury, the Sun and an influence from Neptune. His ability as a public speaker verged on the psychic, as if he could sense the feeling and pulse of his audience. There is no question that his success was the product of sympathetic understanding of those he deceived and their reaction to Germany's losing in World War I.

The Sun has the most influence in the first decanate, but we do know that Neptune's influence was activated later in life. With the Sun in the more influential position, his ability to recognize what was needed for self protection was what kept him alive, sometimes against all odds. Neptune (Venus, Moon, Jupiter) in this case, became the ideal he wished to present to the world in the style of large banners with emblazoned symbols of the Nazi party placed throughout the country and the conscription of his massive army build-up.

Ancient Whispers from Chaldea

Additionally, in this case, Mercury plays a major role by being close by degree to the Moon's ideal placement as well as being the first aspect made by the Moon *and* by proximity to the Sun in his latitude placement.

The result was Hitler's convictions. Additionally, his ability as an orator induced him to become a politician after World War I.

The arena of Enlil, the second decanate, primarily contains Jupiter as the transition planet coupled with the mathematical point of the Midheaven and the yet-to-be-realized influence of Pluto. This Jupiter position may be the reason Hitler expected things to come his way rather easily.

Planets located in the place of Anu, the third decanate, are considered to be representatives of the ideal circumstance an individual desires. The entire range of planets placed in the higher degrees are all negative. This must have had an enormous effect on Hitler as a youth.

☽	29 ♏ 12
♅	26 ♍ 20 ℞
♀	23 ♈ 55 ℞
♂	22 ♈ 28
☋	True 21 ♊ 53
♄	20 ♋ 15
♃	15 ♐ 03
♆	11 ♉ 27
MC	10 ♋ 58
♆	07 ♉ 37
☉	06 ♈ 39 22
AS	03 ♎ 29
☿	00 ♈ 27

Venus describes artistic abilities, but his artistic ability was, at best, weakened by the conjunction of Mars, all the while square to Saturn culminating in the Midheaven. Sensitive Venus was smothered into the background by such harsh company. He never was accepted as an artist.

Hitler's poor scholastic performance was the result of his sitting back waiting for the world to come to him. He wasn't stupid. He just expected "his awards" to be handed to him without effort. By 16, Hitler left school with a very poor record and remained idle while he talked about grandiose schemes of becoming an artist.

However, with the first World War, Hitler found himself in his ideal element, indicated by his planets located in higher degrees. All the conflict, stress and misery that war creates fit right in with his concept of personal survival, a lesson well learned from his father's abusive behavior.

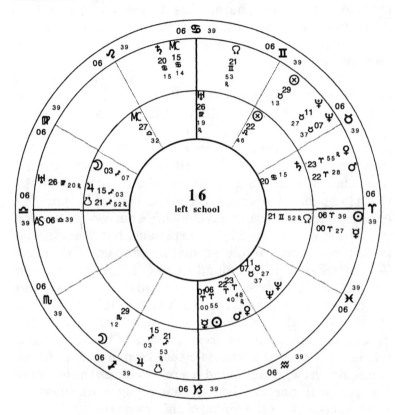

Figure 9.7
Hitler's inner chart rogressed to 16.

The Mars/Venus conjunction square to Saturn also indicates a mistrust of others and a promise of disappointments in his personal life. The energy of Mars is harsh and, when paired with languid Venus, the native finds it difficult to be trustful of close relationships, all the while desiring intimacy. The Venus side of the Mars conjunction is seen as being weak and socially inept. Hitler feared exploitation by others. His feeling of frustration, emptiness

305

and the need to express himself may have provided the impetus that prompted him to join the Nazi party. Even though he had close supporters, his upbringing taught him that he was either hated (his father's influence) or supported (his mother's influence), further compounding his frustration, jealousy, and mistrust. This must have eaten away at him.

This set the stage for the next level of his development. We have seen Hitler as an anti-social individual with little or no will to fulfill his youthful artistic ambition. However, when World War I broke out, that all changed. Hitler became fascinated by military life and the war effort. It was said that Hitler acted in an extreme manic behavior during combat and often would take risks that placed his life in danger. The war became his training ground and, in essence, created his life's purpose. After the war, Hitler was inspired by his experience but disappointed by the outcome. While promoting propaganda for the Worker's Party, Hitler found himself in the position to arouse small audiences into a state of hatred and vengeance by simply expressing his personal views about the Jews. Hitler had found a sympathetic ear in his colleagues with whom to decry the loss of the war, and a scapegoat to place the blame for the German defeat. As his popularity grew, Hitler found his role in life as the leader of his political party. The following pages discuss the rogression chart for the timing of Hitler's rise and fall.

Hitler was born the illegitimate son of a customs agent, and was constantly mistreated by his father, who was a strict disciplinarian. After school, when young Adolf came home late, his father would refuse to let him in the house. Thus, on cold nights, young Hitler had to sleep with the chickens to keep warm. During these episodes, his mother would sneak food out and try to comfort him. When he was fourteen, Hitler's father died: Jupiter/South Node rogressed to his Ascendant. His mother, who overindulged young Adolf's willful wishes, died in 1908 when he was nineteen years old. Saturn had rogressed to the

Descendant and the Sun rogressed to the fourth house cusp.

By the age of twenty-four he moved to Munich: Sun rogressed to third house cusp; Neptune/Pluto to fourth house; inner chart MC to Saturn.

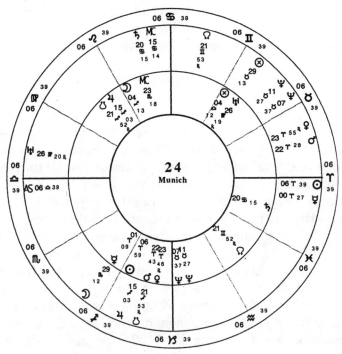

Figure 9.8
Hitler's chart rogressed to the age of 24.

At that time he was called up by the Bavarian Army but was declared unfit. Saturn had also rogressed to the Mercury position in his chart. He did, however, manage to enlist in the German army when World War I broke out as Mars/Venus rogressed to his South Node; rogressed Moon inconjunct Pluto.

In 1916 Hitler, at age twenty-seven, was wounded in the war: his Sun had rogressed to the sunset Moon's position, and Mars and Venus were very close by degree to his sunset Jupiter. The configuration of Venus/Mars near Jupiter was probably the reason he was only wounded and not killed. In 1918 he was gassed (Uranus approaching his Sunset Neptune) and hospitalized: Venus rogressed to his sunset Moon while Neptune had rogressed to his sunset Jupiter. On August 18, 1918, when the Moon rogressed to his sunset Saturn on the Midheaven, he received the Iron Cross First Class for bravery, an unusual occurrence for a corporal.

After the war, Hitler was released out of the hospital amidst the confusion of post-war recovery, he decided to take up political work to denounce the peace treaty. The following year, at the age of thirty, the Moon had rogressed to conjoin the Midheaven; Pluto had reached Jupiter; Jupiter was approaching sunset Saturn on the Midheaven. He joined a small, aimless political group, the German Workers' Party in Munich. It was this organization that was destined to become Hitler's means to political power.

In 1920, four months after his thirty-first birthday, rogressed Pluto crossed over the sunset third house cusp (the position of his Sun [at age twenty-four] when he first attempted to join the war effort through the Bavarian Army). Hitler left the Army when he was put in charge of the tiny Workers' Party propaganda and devoted his time to its reorganization. By August of 1920, the party underwent changes and was renamed the Nationalsozialistiche Deutsche Arbeiterpartei (abbreviated "Nazi").

By age thirty-two he became the president of the Nazi party (rogressed Jupiter conjunct sunset Saturn). He was arrested at age thirty-four (rogressed Pluto conjunct sunset Moon) and, while in jail, Mercury rogressed to conjunct with his Ascendant at the age of thirty-five (see Fig. 4.3 page 106). During this time he wrote his manifesto, *Mien Kamph*. When he was released from jail, he was forbidden to speak in public.

By the time his rogressed Sun had reached the Ascendant (age thirty-six), Hitler reasserted himself as a leader in the Nazi party. By the time he was forty he had gained considerable support and money; Saturn was approaching natal Jupiter by rogression.

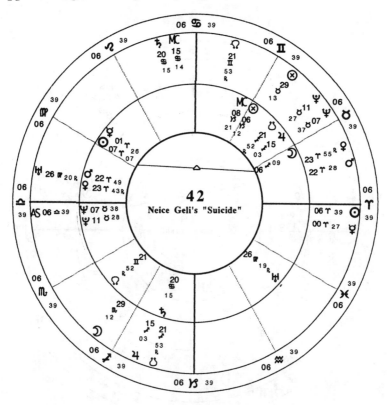

Figure 9.9 Geli's "suicide"
Hitler's chart rogressed at age 42

At forty-two (figure 9.9), he met his niece Geli to whom he became devoted. However, his jealousy and anger "drove her to suicide" in September 1931. Saturn rogressed to the placement of the sunset Node; Mars/Venus rogressed to Uranus; the Moon had rogressed to the sunset Venus of the Mars/Venus conjunction and the "phantom Moon had reached Neptune by the "age" factor (seven houses–add seven degrees to the Moon). Hitler was inconsolable for months. Shortly thereafter he met Eva Braun, a shop

assistant from Munich; the Moon rogressed to the sunset
Mars position.

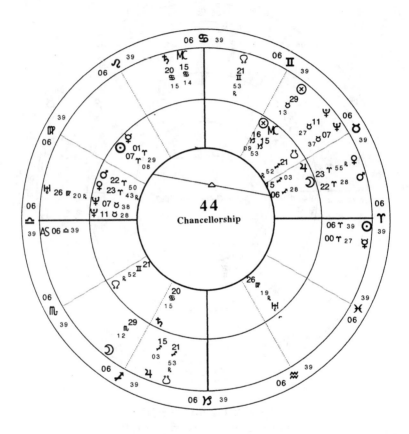

Figure 9.10
Hitler's rogressed chart to the age of 44.

The next fourteen years saw Hitler's rise to power
as Mercury, Sun, Venus, Mars, Neptune and Pluto steadily
rogressed to the Midheaven.

By January of 1933 at the age of forty-four, Hitler
was appointed chancellor to the Reichstag. One month
later the Reichstag building burned down which provided an

excuse for a decree overriding all guarantees of freedom in Germany. In March, Hitler was able to gather the combined votes of the Nazi, Nationalist and Center Party deputies thus giving him full power over those organizations. By August of 1934, President Hindenburg died and with that the office of chancellorship was merged with the office of the presidency. Hitler's power over the German people was complete.

The War Years

Hitler's army attacked Russia on June 22, 1941. He was so confident (rogressed Jupiter to sunset Mercury) that this would be a single campaign against the Russians that he refused to supply his troops with winter clothing and equipment. (Notice that the rogressed attritional South Node is conjoined his sunset Sun while the rogressed Sun is conjoined Saturn i.e., losses through attrition.) By December of 1941, the Russian counterattack made it clear that Russia was not the easy victory he had expected.

Up to this point, Hitler's power went unchecked but by the end of 1942 his first major defeat came at El Alamein and Stalingrad. The Russian Army had stopped the German war machine and then turned it back. This was the turning point in Hitler's war against humanity. With it his character and way of life began to change.

With his troops starting to retreat, the military campaign weakened and Hitler began to show the early stages of living in a fantasy world. He isolated himself more and more from reality; he ignored the recommendations by his generals and continually made bad decisions regarding different campaigns. As the war was drawing to a close and defeat eminent, his aid, Martin Bormann, made sure that the only information that Hitler received was pleasing. Ill and fatigued, Hitler became increasingly dependent on his doctor's care and relied heavily on injections he supplied to calm him. Still, Hitler remained in control and exercised an almost hypnotic power over his close subordinates and did not lose control over the Nazi party or the army.

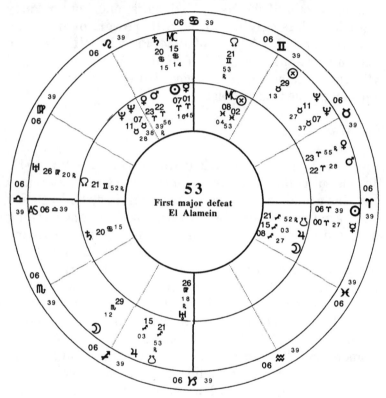

Figure 9.11
Hitler's turning point, his rogressed chart to the age of 53.

The German high command was aware of the inevitable defeat of Germany and wanted to negotiate a peace but Hitler would not cooperate and several failed attempts were made on his life–the most nearly successful on July 20, 1944. Hitler's fantasies or insanity grew worse as the war was drawing to a close. He made a last ditch effort at his headquarters in Ardennes by mobilizing the last reserves of manpower for its defense. His final defeat came at the age of fifty-six when he had himself shot rather than be taken captive (chart above). Rogressed Saturn reached Uranus and the Mars/Venus conjunction reached Saturn.

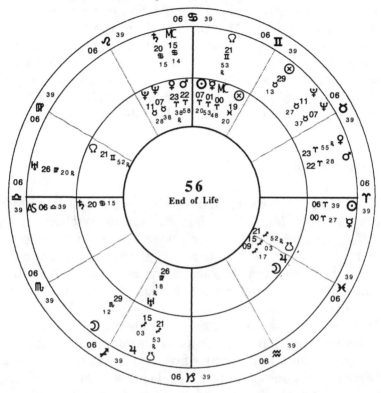

Figure 9.12
Hitler's rogressed chart at the time of death.

In John Lennon's chart, the Moon modified his setting Mercury and, with Hitler, it was a negative Saturn in square to Mars. The next chart we will survey is that of Mohandas Gandhi who has a Venus/Mars conjunction but with different planetary company that completely altered his life's course. With the former charts we noted planets modifying the setting planet from the tenth house but in Gandhi's chart it is Jupiter part of the triad that comprises Neptune. The reason for this is Neptune is the first planet to reach an angle and we do not use the outer planets early in the life, only their triads. The triad of Neptune is the Moon, Venus and Jupiter. Venus has one aspect, it is conjunct Mars. The Moon has two aspects, it is trine to Saturn in the sunset chart and trine to Jupiter from the Natal chart to sunset Jupiter. Jupiter has three aspects; sunset Mercury seemingly conjunct natal Jupiter; natal Saturn seemingly conjunct Jupiter and the natal Moon is in trine aspect to sunset Jupiter making Jupiter the focus.

MOHANDAS GANDHI

Our next chart characterizes a similar planetary conjunction of Mars/Venus but with modified influences by different aspects and associations. Gandhi's Moon is stabilized by a trine to Saturn, its natural attraction which gives the normally vulnerable Moon a sense of discipline. Neptune becomes the modifying planet to sunset Mercury because it is the first planet to reach the Ascendant. However, revolutionary Uranus is placed in the highest degree of the chart with Jupiter forming close support. Jupiter, Uranus and Neptune are all planets that work on a higher, more religious plane, indicating that the ideals Gandhi sought after would be more in keeping with a democratic, human rights view in mind. Gandhi's chart shows no planets located in the arena of the personal first decanate. This also suggests that our subject would seek or observe deeply religious views. In his chart, the Ascendant, Midheaven ,and Node are recognized as soul-inspired values that also pertain to religious values and the native's interpretation of God. This is also supported by Neptune and the Moon with Saturn located at 19°, a very significant number to the ancients as it was associated with completion and spirituality. Most importantly, only the decanates of change and ideals have planets located there. In such a chart the native takes on a completely different approach with regard to personal desires. The individual character is directed toward transformation and changes that fit an ideal.

Mohondas Gandhi was born on October 2, 1869, in Porbandar, India, 21°N38', 69°E36' at 7:11:48 A.M. L.M.T. We will start by analyzing the occurrence of different events during the year Gandhi was born. The **year 1869** in India was an intensely *transitional* one. Under British rule, the government was leaning toward establishing a taxation program and formulating committees to enact new laws and *social reform*. Remember, the energy being expressed through world events subtly flavors the charts of those born during such times. Additionally, the mother's mental and emotional outlook to these events has influence as well. The time of Gandhi's birth is opposite sunset and indicates that he would rebel against the energy patterns of his birth.

Sunset Chart

Calculate the chart for the *previous* day at sunset. In Gandhi's lunar mansion we find his Moon's rate of motion is 14° 24' in trine with Saturn by degree (only 23' separation). Saturn is the first aspect the Moon will make by trine about a week after birth. The last aspect the Moon makes is to Uranus supported by Jupiter indicating he had the potential to achieve social reform on a large scale.

The first planet to reach an angle is Neptune, the planet of inspiration and ideals. In childhood, the child reacts to trans-saturnian planets by their triadal counterparts therefore, the Moon, Venus and Jupiter are the reactive planets when natal Neptune is activated either in transit or by rogression. With Gandhi, Pluto and Jupiter are the first planet(s) to reach Neptune by rogression. Combined with Pluto, Jupiter becomes the active planet in both triads. Add all this to our earlier discussion on the previous page regarding Jupiter and it being the highest planet by longitude, all ties in with his early religious training from his mother.

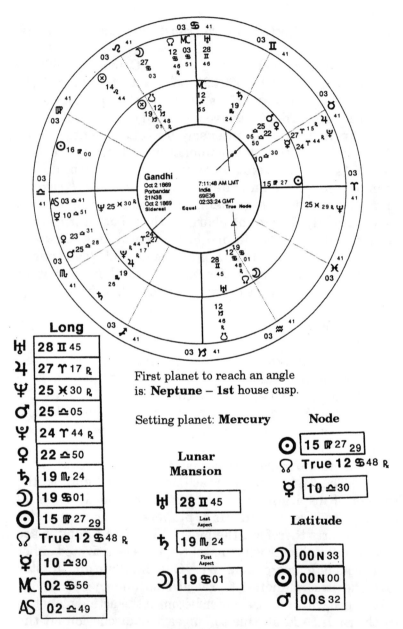

Long

♅	28 Ⅱ 45
4	27 ♈ 17 R
♆	25 ♓ 30 R
♂	25 ♎ 05
♇	24 ♈ 44 R
♀	22 ♎ 50
♄	19 ♏ 24
☽	19 ♋ 01
☉	15 ♍ 27 29
☊	True 12 ♋ 48 R
☿	10 ♎ 30
MC	02 ♋ 56
AS	02 ♎ 49

First planet to reach an angle
is: **Neptune – 1st** house cusp.

Setting planet: **Mercury**

**Lunar
Mansion**

| ♅ | 28 Ⅱ 45 |
Last Aspect

| ♄ | 19 ♏ 24 |
First Aspect

| ☽ | 19 ♋ 01 |

Node

| ☉ | 15 ♍ 27 29 |
☊ True 12 ♋ 48 R
| ☿ | 10 ♎ 30 |

Latitude

☽	00 N 33
☉	00 N 00
♂	00 S 32

Figure 9.13
Mohandas Gandhi's sunset chart (outer) and birth chart (inner).
* Pluto not discovered

However, Gandhi would not personally react to trans-saturnian planets until much later. In essence they are the circumstances of his generation by which he is influenced. So, we use Mercury as the first planet to reach an angle, as that planet will exert an influence in his earlier years, and remember, Mercury is part of the Uranus triad. Mercury, the setting planet, is the chief expression. Gandhi would orient himself toward the mental realm and the intellect. The Moon's influence is generally considered weak by nature and seemingly easy to manipulate, but its trine to Saturn alters this influence to one of emotional stability.

This changes the Moon's generally vulnerable influence into one of learning self-control and discipline. This is further emphasized with Gandhi's Moon leading the Sun in the three planet triad in the stack (30° wheel) as well the influence from his latitude triad.

The Moon located between the Sun and Saturn reflects Gandhi's somewhat deceptive, nondescript appearance. As an adversary, he was considered a slight nuisance who could be easily overlooked or defeated.

His Moon reveals quite a different story with its harmonious alliance (trine) and closer proximity to Saturn than the Sun (triad). We see a steadfast individual immersed in his principles who will do whatever is necessary, short of violence, to succeed.

Analyzing the ideals in the third decanate, we immediately see that Jupiter opposes the Mars/Venus conjunction in Venus ruled Libra. The conjunction in a Libra placement softens Mars' caustic expression and Venus/Mars expression becomes more benign and benevolent as a focus for Jupiter. In this chart we see a warrior with passion and an inclination toward his soul expression combined with tenderness and sentiment but nowhere do we see vengeance.

Gandhi was the gift of gentle representation. With this we also see early maturity and an awareness of sex. He was married when he was twelve years of age.

Latitude

The Sun is always zero as it describes the ecliptic. Above the Sun the Moon is supported by the Sun's proximity to Uranus by a mere 07' which is located between the Sun and Moon by degree.

☽	00 N 33
☉	00 N 00
♂	00 S 32

It is important to note that Gandhi did not directly use the expansive Uranian energy but the Mercury part of the triad until he became a public figure. At that time he then rebelled against the social injustice his people suffered under British control.

Combining the northern latitude Moon (0° N 33') and the southern latitude Mars (0° S 32'), we see only one minute of difference in their respective positions from the Sun. The planetary combination by latitude is one's sense of presence and with such a tight orb it can be expressed as discriminating judgment of one's actions and that of others. The Sun's latitude is positioned between the northern Moon and southern Mars, under other circumstances this Moon/Mars configuration would normally reflect an impulsive and intolerant behavior in a negative fashion. Fortunately, the lunar trine to Saturn gives persistence, balance and good judgment and Mars conjoined with Venus further relaxes Mars' normally irascible behavior–Mars is softened by its conjunction with Venus and opposition to Jupiter. This indicates an impulsive but more prudent approach in his dealings with both those in authority and his followers. Gandhi had a strong will energized by deep emotionally charged convictions. He was also inclined to be brutally honest and frank in expression, a trait normally associated with Jupiter and Sagittarius. This was expressed by his resistance to war-like activity and the ability to live under any condition and make the best of it, regardless of the level of discomfort.

The Node

His Node is retrograde and traveling away from the Sun to Mercury, placing the emphasis on Mercury. This placement realizes the power of thought, the spoken and written word, and the quest for knowledge.

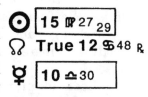

☉ | 15 ♍ 27 $_{29}$ |

☊ True 12 ♋ 48 R

☿ | 10 ♎ 30 |

Mercury/Sun also represents the common sense ability to recognize what is needed for growth and awareness of objectives. His associates and followers believed him to be a great one, a living persona of righteousness by whom their salvation was at hand from their oppressive rulers. Gandhi was a teacher of a great principle–his passive/aggressive soul force. We see very clearly in the combination of Sun/Node/Mercury that he and his word are one (Node) along with his communication (Mercury) with world leaders (Sun) as well as he himself (Sun) becoming one through his belief's.

The Stack

In the ideal section of the stack, note the good company in which Mars is placed, indicating that his actions were based on love and harmony. Pluto was not discovered until 1930, just before Gandhi was 61 years old, so we cannot really rely on its energy to be influential until then. However, by noting the triadal energies of Mars opposing Jupiter and natal Saturn with sunset Jupiter, the intensity we normally associate with Pluto is definately apparent. The disappointing nature of Venus was reflected in Gandhi's expectations regarding the behavior of India's reluctant rulers and his wish to change their policies. Note that Venus is closer to Mercury by degree than Mercury is to the Sun. This speaks to us as a person connected with writing and publishing: (Venus = artistic, Mercury = communication).

The stack draws immediate attention to the fact that there are no planets located within the first ten degrees! We find his planets in the arena of changes and ideals. To Gandhi his body was merely a tool to be used as needed.

Lack of planets in the first decanate meant personal freedom without the "ego problems" for him. With Saturn influencing the area of changes supported by the close lunar tie, we recognize his attitude of self control. With Mercury at the bottom of the stack (and thus part of his soul makeup), he felt he had a sense of duty to awaken his people to the fact that they were being exploited terribly.

	Long
♅	28 ♊ 45
♃	27 ♈ 17 ʀ
♆	25 ♓ 30 ʀ
♂	25 ♎ 05
♀	24 ♈ 44 ʀ
♀	22 ♎ 50
♄	19 ♏ 24
☽	19 ♋ 01
☉	15 ♍ 27 29
☊	True 12 ♋ 48 ʀ
☿	10 ♎ 30
MC	02 ♋ 56
AS	02 ♎ 49

With the reverse situation, where Venus comes before Mercury, we would find a person who is artistically expressive: painter, sculptor, etc. Venus is closer and is more influenced by Mars than Mercury. In this case Venus' lazy nature becomes energized by its alignment with Mars' energies. Remember, Mars likes to champion a cause. In this case we can see the application of effort (Mars) as rather passive as it is closer to Venus than Saturn. However, in the decanate of change, Saturn's energy is the overall influence and permeates the Moon, Mercury, Venus and Mars. Therefore, when conducting personnel or business affairs, this combination stabilizes his warrior nature with calculated action, prudence and cautious wisdom. The above signature epitomizes clarity of thought (Saturn-Mercury), a champion of human rights (Mars-Venus-Jupiter) and the use of passive/aggressive resistance (Saturn/Moon-Mars/Venus). Relating to the sunset chart, the rogressed rate of five degrees is equal to one year; six years to completely travel through each house.

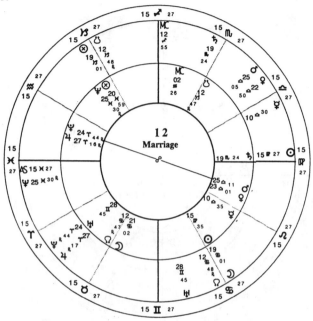

Figure 9.14
Chart rogressed to Gandhi's marriage at age twelve.

We find that Gandhi is married at the age of twelve when Saturn approached his Descendant and the rogressed Sun transited his Moon placement, an area where he had little or no control. Like all marriages in India at that time, his was pre-arranged and not of his choosing.

However, the marriage was propitious as Jupiter was coming forth or rising with positive Saturn rogressed to his sunset Sun. The marriage lasted more than sixty years. Gandhi graduated from school at the age of eighteen with honors. His rogressed Moon had reached his sunset Jupiter. At the same time his rogressed Venus (and Mars) had reached his sunset Moon and Mercury to North Node.

In 1893 at twenty-four, Gandhi personally experienced social prejudice. His rogressed Node and Moon were approaching his Ascendant with the South Node on his Descendant.

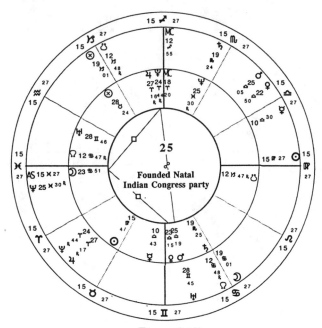

Figure 9.15
Gandhi's chart rogressed to age 25
when he founded Natal Indian Congress Party.

While traveling by train with a first class ticket, he was forced to give up his place to a white man while he was left cold and shivering in the waiting room.

A year later, at the age of twenty-five, Gandhi founded the Natal Indian Congress Party. He also joined the British army in the South African war and Zulu rebellion by organizing an ambulance corps. His rogressed Moon had reached his sunset Ascendant with Venus on the Nadir; Mars to Uranus; Neptune on Saturn; Saturn to North Node and Jupiter approaching his sunset Midheaven.

Eleven years later in 1904, Gandhi was ready to initiate the human rights movement in India. The rogressed Sun had reached the Ascendant. At the age of thirty-five, Gandhi took a vow of poverty.

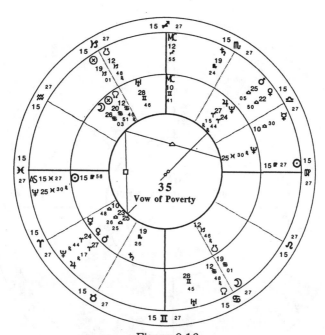

Figure 9.16
Chart regressed to age thirty-five
when Gandhi became "Mahatma," the great soul.

Later that same year, when rogressed Sun reached his sunset, Neptune was approaching his Descendant, he became known as *Mahatma* or "Great Soul." He also became the chief editor of the magazine, *India Opinion* (rogressed Venus/Mars to Sunset Jupiter).

Gandhi formulated plans for his march against fingerprinting Indian masses, (rogressed Jupiter to sunset Mars) and founded the *Satya Graha Asram* (rogressed Saturn trine sunset Sun). He did this along with twenty-five followers who had also taken vows of celibacy (Moon/Saturn) to observe truth (Saturn/Mercury), and nonviolence, fearlessness (Jupiter/Mars/Venus).

Five years later in 1909, at the age of forty, he wrote *Indian Home Rule* which was the quintessence of his ideas. *Mercury was approaching his Ascendant* by rogression, an important time in defining one's life.

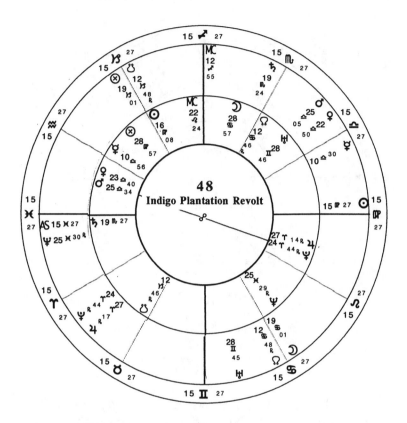

Figure 9.17
Chart rogressed to age 48, Gandhi's first case of "Satyagraha."

By April of 1917, Gandhi, at age forty-eight, assisted in fighting against the indigo plantations. He was ordered to leave the area but refused. He was arrested and pled guilty, but the government intervened and appointed him as a member of the inquiry committee. The committee ruled in his favor. This was the first case of "satyagraha" (soul force) in India: rogressed Saturn to his sunset Neptune; Sun rogressed to the South Node; rogressed midpoint of Moon and North Node to his sunset Saturn. In 1919 the government passed the Rowlatt bills, a law declaring that anyone who was suspected of sedition could be imprisoned without trial.

324

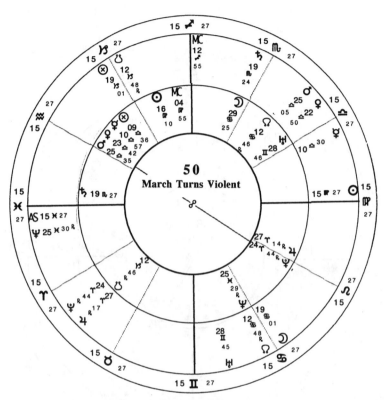

Figure 9.18
Gandhi's chart at age 50, violence in
Jallianwalla Bagh in Armritsar.

By April, 1919, Gandhi declared a "suspension of
business" in protest of the Rowlatt bills which resulted in
his arrest. During the same month, 10,000 of his followers
gathered in Jallianwalla Bagh in Armritsar where they were
machine-gunned: rogressed Moon to Saturn and rogressed
Saturn were coming forth or rising: North Node rogressed to
Mars with South Node to Jupiter and Uranus rogressed to
Venus.

By 1922, as rogressed Midheaven approached his
Ascendant, he led another non-violent revolt against
taxation. This time he was sentenced to six years in prison

for sedition. He spent two years in jail and was released
after an appendectomy.

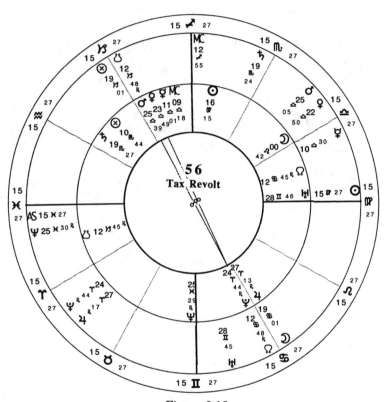

Figure 9.19
Gandhi at age fifty-six, tax revolt.

1930 saw yet another non-violent march against
the salt tax. At sixty-one we see Gandhi's rogressed South
Node approaching his Ascendant while the North Node and
Moon approached his Descendant. Pluto was discovered,
activating with Jupiter's influence, Gandhi was arrested
and interned but was soon released along with 100,000
other dissidents when the Irwin-Gandhi Treaty was signed.
At age sixty-four, Gandhi started his publication, *Harijan*,
which became his platform for peace. By 1942 it was

published in ten different dialects of the Indian language (rogressed Neptune had reached his Nadir).

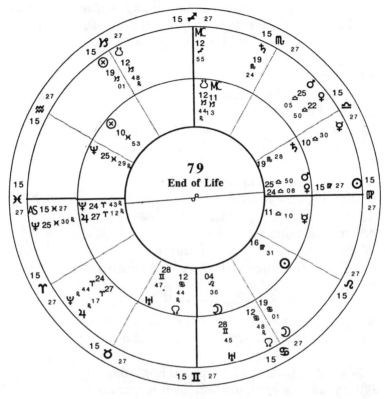

Figure 9.20
End of life.

On January 30, 1948, a young gunman took Gandhi's life, closing a chapter on one of the very few authentic humanitarians throughout history (rogressed Venus conjunct Mars was approaching his Descendant for the second time; Pluto approaching his Ascendant).

No physical planets located in the first ten degrees may indicate his unique understanding and awareness of the physical body's transitory nature and its use as a tool for spiritual purposes. Gandhi once said: "My life is an indivisible whole, and all my activities run into one another...." His life was a continuous search and process of evolution. For him, to know was to act.

The brief timeline of Gandhi's life that follows will enable the reader to further investigate his life by calculating the rogressions of his planetary points.

Age/Event
12-Married
18-Graduated from school
24-Social injustice
25-Founded National Indian Congress party
35-Chief editor for *India Opinion*, also wrote *India Home Rule*
37-March against fingerprinting
37-Founded Satya Graha
40-Wrote the quintessence of his ideas
46-Opened ashram
48-Fought against indigo plantations
50-March resulting in 10,000 being gunned down
53-Jailed for sedition
55-Released from prison after appendectomy
58-Appointed to council commission by Lord Irwin
61-Encouraged civil disobedience on taxation on salt and was arrested
62-Released from prison, went to England
63-Arrested, started his famous five-day fast

64-Started the paper Harrijan as his official mouth piece
73-Wife of sixty-plus years died. He was imprisoned
74-Famous fast of 1943
75-Released from prison
77-Nehru took office
79-Shot and killed January 30, 1948, about 5:00 P.M.

As an architect of India's freedom movement through nonviolent civil disobedience, Gandhi's chart continually emphasizes such a lifestyle. There is a lack of planets in the arena of self- interest. The Sun (point of focus of what is needed) is interactive with both his North Node (soul indicator) and latitude (lifestyle) and is coupled with the Moon-Saturn for self-discipline. He certainly exemplified these influences by founding his ashram along with twenty-five inmates who also vowed to observe his teachings. An indicator of his non-violent nature is the company Mars keeps between Jupiter and Venus in the ideal portion of the stack (Anu). Gandhi's planets of transition (Enlil) has Saturn in the higher degree reflecting self-control (Moon/Sun), his lack of intimidation by government officials (MC/Node) and serious mind (Mercury).

As a tribute to Gandhi's soul pattern, he was called Mahatma or great soul (Sun/Node/Mercury). With his North Node between the Sun/MC and Mercury, we find a man who clearly identified his life and its purpose as soul force, not only physically but mentally and spiritually. His reference to his movement as soul force is reflected as the latitude Moon/Sun/Mars. This signature was further underscored when Gandhi decided that the term "passive resistance" was inadequate and re-named his efforts "*Satyagraha,* the force of truth and love."

As we have seen, the sunset rogressed chart succinctly point to areas of life where major changes take place. Very often progressions or transits are not active when expected in an individual's life unless they are also indicated by the rogressed positions. In this respect the dual house system becomes very helpful as it indicates the ruler of a period and its activity in regard to the planetary positions and their house placement. The main focus in this chapter has been to help you develop an appreciation for the sunset system. One area we have not discussed is the use of the triWheel; placing the birth chart within the very center of the dual sunset biWheel. This method is very informative and fine tunes the delineation for the probability of future events. By practicing with the charts of Lennon, Hitler and Gandhi, you will be able to perfect your sunset chart skills.

CHAPTER 10

THE SOLAR RETURN

Astrologers as Occultist

Astrology is generally associated with being able to predict the future. The word *future* in this context swallows us in the dark veil of the mysterious, the sense that there is an ordained prescience. Many believe that astrologers have somehow cracked the cosmic egg and can view concealed secrets in some mystical fashion. Those who believe that astrologers can reveal these mysteries seek us out and, of course, ask us to act as their supreme cosmic lawyers to interpret whatever the great cosmos has in store for them.

This presents a major problem within the so-called *occult* field, a category into which astrology falls. Many who are involved in the ego-side of the trade perpetuate an attitude of superiority and require "reverence" from their clients and/or novice astrologers. To many, who claim to be occultists, this attitude goes unchecked. It fortifies their feeling of self-importance and, of course, pompous self-validation. In doing so, the general public views us as odd-ball fortune tellers who prance around in robes holding stick-like wands.

The fortune-telling myth could be partly eliminated by less ego and more serious research on projects that produce respectable results. Until such time, some astrologers will continue to perpetuate their holier-than-thou attitude while thinking that they have all the answers and must stubbornly rule over their clients lives. Hopefully, with the advent of the computer, a new generation of astrologers will emerge and destroy the myth of astrology as a fortune-telling device and produce proven valuable work.

Computers have also given the field of astrology increasingly complex methods, leading astrologers into the most exotic areas of specialization. Sticking with a few hard-and-fast rules that operate well will produce more insight and help the astrologer integrate technology with common sense. In this way astrologers do not have to convince themselves or their clients that the more exotic the method, the more accurate the reading. It is much more desirable to simply deduce the basic context of the chart, that in itself becomes the founding statement which produces correct and reliable answers regularly.

In every professional field, we find doctors, lawyers, lending institutions, even landlords requiring as much information as possible from their prospective clients to better serve them and prevent error. To maximize the astrologer's accuracy, the use of in-depth questionnaires would be a valuable tool. It is important for astrologers to compile an in-depth picture of their client's marital status, children, family size, parents, and health. It is essential that the astrologer demand the client to provide proof of an accurate birth time. The next essential step is to have a dialogue with the client and prepare a lifetime diary chronicling past milestones in his life. Be sure these steps are taken as part of the counseling session.

The rogressed chart provides an excellent tool for such an activity. As you rotate the inner part of the biWheel (or triWheel) chart, ask your client to explain past events as you reach each planetary position along the arc of the wheel. In this fashion you will determine valuable insight into the personal meaning that the planets have for him.

With correct information, these many experiences will offer a clear indication of the meanings of solar progressions, lunar progressions, rogressions and transits. Remember each of us is like a snowflake. We use planetary energies differently at different stages of our development. By tracing the soul's maturation in response to life's challenges, we are better able to predict which way our

331

client will respond to his next growth spurt. By observing planetary placements and conditions as well as the client's personal profile, you can accurately predict *when* and under what conditions the client will personally express his inner temperament, sensitivity and reaction to the outside world of events. All this will place you, the astrologer, in a more professional posture, and even more important, provide an accurate assessment of personal planetary response patterns.

When processing charts, there are countless ways to observe and predict all planetary movements. To augment your investigation, it is necessary to not only know the timing of outside events and experiences but the reflection of such events denoted in astrology charts. The aspects and directions of lunar tertiary or minor progressions, along with the rogression, have proven themselves to be accurate markers reflecting life events and its circumstances. Of all the progressed procedures, some are simple while others prove to be quite complex, the rogressed chart has proven itself time and again to be highly effective. It is difficult even for experienced astrologers to agree upon which method is best as we each develop our own program through personal interest. Noted author of *The Only Way to Learn Astrology* series, Marion March, has often wisely counseled, "Find the program that works for you and stick to it!" This sage advice eliminates much confusion.

The Solar Return, Hindu Method

The solar return chart is just one of the many techniques available to an inquiring mind. It proposes annual time periods based on the Sun's longitude which, when combined with natal and progressed factors, can determine periods of planetary heightened activity. This form of horoscopy is a most valuable predictive tool for many astrologers. The solar return should be viewed as a living, evolving entity. All charts, as well as the solar return; does not begin and stop on the anniversary of the birth but continues to move and unfold throughout the year by rogression. Other than the natal chart, the solar return chart demands more attention than any other chart and should be seen as the one area that clearly expresses an astrologer's expertise. Overall, this chapter will allow astrologers to draw confident conclusions in their final analyses of the solar return.

There are two methods discussed in this chapter. The first method will show you how to convert the difference of longitude between planetary positions into periods of time with the use of logarithms. This will be accomplished by translating the planetary longitudes into daily, weekly or monthly time periods. You will see that each time period is assigned a planetary rulership according to its placement by different degrees of longitude. For those of you who are drawn into this form of horoscopy, there are many books on the subject that can give you more information on the sub-periods as well.

It is important to recognize when the planetary ruler of each time period makes any aspect during the year. At the specified time periods, check the daily transits and compare them with the planetary birth stack *and* the solar return stack. Review the natal planets and signs, the solar return planets and signs and the transiting planets and signs. In all cases *note the motion* of the charts *and* especially the transiting planets.

Stacking the Planets

Calculate the solar return chart *based on the time of birth* (later, try using the time of the sunset chart) in the conventional manner. Once the solar return chart is cast, begin this exercise by stacking the planets based on the time of birth. This is identical to the first part of chart rearrangement in the sunset and interpretation chapters, only now we are working with one year as a time frame instead of a lifetime. Arrange them from left to right in ascending numerical order, beginning from the lowest degree to the highest degree.

To reference the following description, let the following chart serve as an example (Figure 10.1):

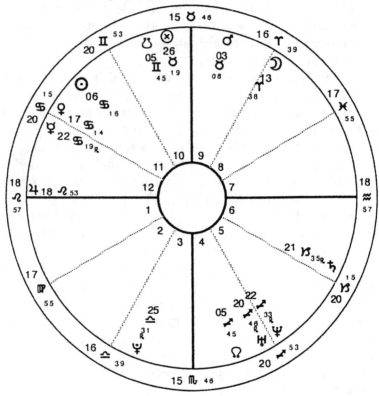

Example chart.   Figure 10.1
In this chart, we see that Mercury is the highest degree at 22°19'.

List all the planets in numerical ascending order and include the Ascendant and Node but *not* the Midheaven. Disregard the trans-saturnian planets and planetary signs for now, as our formula is based on the longitudinal degree and minutes only. Then, select the one planet or personal point that is the highest in degree or closest to 29° 59'. Note that in this case we only use the signs to determine aspects when comparing the transits to either the birth or solar return chart. If you can determine apects in your head, so much the better.

MA	NO	SU	MO	VE	AS	JU	SA	ME
03°	05°	06°	13°	17°	18°	18°	21°	22°
08'	45'	16'	38'	14'	43'	53'	35'	19'

Figure 10.2

One last note before we begin. The outer planets Uranus, Neptune and Pluto are *not used* in this method for the reasons explained earlier. However, pay attention to the triadal combinations that comprise these outer planets. Make a special note when the combinations are aspecting each other either in the birth, solar or transit charts. When all the triadal planets that compose a trans-saturnian planet are all involved by aspect, very often the trans-saturnian planet will act as a focus. When this is the case, look to the house that the trans-saturnian planet is placed for the foci of activity.

For those of you who enjoy the mathematical part of astrology, this will certainly prove to be quite an enjoyable exercise.

Section "A"

To Find the Logarithm.

When the planet of the highest degree is ascertained, convert only the minutes (not the degree) into its decimal equivalent. To do this, simply divide the minutes by 60. The next step is to divide both the degree and its decimal by 15 (the number of degrees the Earth rotates in one hour). The result is called Quotient "a." and will be noted as **Q.a.**. Later, we will convert all of the planetary and personal points to their decimal equivalents. For now, our first goal is to convert the highest degree of either a planet or personal point to its decimal equivalent.

This will establish the logarithm for all other pertinent calculations that follow.

Q.a. must then be divided into the sum total of hours in a year which is 8766. We find how many hours are in a year by multiplying 365 (days) by 24 (hours per day). Every year has an additional six hours that must be added. This is because of leap year which occurs every four years.

Section "B"

The result of dividing **Q.a.** into 8766 is called Quotient "b." From now on we will refer to this figure as **Q.b.**

Now divide **Q.b.** by 24 hours. The result is the logarithm which will determine the overall conversion of each planetary degree and minute of longitude into our daily time periods. The final number between the Q.a. and Q. b. figures is our *constant logarithm*.

Rule: Quick Review.

A.   Find quotient "Q.a.," referenced in section "A."

B.   Divide Q.a. by 8766 (it will always be this number), this is called Quotient "b" or Q.b.

C.   Divide Q.b. by 24; the answer is our constant log.

The constant log will be our constant multiplier of the different planets' longitudes by degree. This is found in the next step of planetary conversions.

We are now ready to convert the minutes into decimals of the remaining planets, (divide the minute by 60) including the Moon's North Node and the Ascendant. Omit the Midheaven or M.C. In the graph below, the bottom row is the minutes converted to their decimal equation.

D. Using the list of planets plus the Ascendant and Node, *subtract* each planet from the preceding one in the stack. Begin with the lowest planet and work your way up.

E. Convert the minutes (not the degree) to decimals.

F. Divide the answer to A and B by 15; the result is *its own* individual planetary log.

G. Last step is to *multiply* the answer by the *constant log*.

In the next step we must find the difference *between* the degrees of the planets and convert the difference into time. By knowing the difference between the planets, we can determine the timing *between* the planetary periods. Each resultant answer is the number of days which will be governed by that planet as its daily time period equivalent. Often, in cases where the planetary differences are very small, there will be no degrees, only minutes. We still divide by the constant log.

As you will see, these daily periods can occupy a very small space, as little as one day (very little difference by degree) or quite a long passage of time, sometimes months, depending of the variation of the degrees between the planets. Later in the chapter, we will also reduce the equivalent time periods into hours and even minutes so you will know exactly, to the minute, when each period will begin and end.

Rule. Note the difference by degree of longitude between each planet, Node and the Ascendant. To do this we subtract each planet in the stack from the preceding one. Convert all minutes of longitude to their decimal equivalent. Divide each planetary degree and its decimal by 15 and multiply that answer by the constant log derived from the highest planet by degree which is Q.b.

Summary of Steps

First step: Find Q.a. of 22° 19'. The minutes are converted to decimal 19' divided by 60 which equals .31666.
Second step: The complete figure (degree/decimal) 22°.31666 divided by 15 which equals 1.48777.
Third step: Find the number of hours in a year: 365 days x 24 hours + 6 = 8766 hours. This result is Q.b. Note that Q.b. will *always* be 8766 hours.
Fourth step: 8766 is divided by 1.48777 which equals 5892.0397
Fifth step: The sum of 5892.0397 divided by 24 which equals 245.50165. This is the constant *log*. If you use a calculator, use the total expression.
Next step: This is actually phase two. Refer to the list of planets and personal points in ascending numerical order (see graph 10.3 below).

We want to find the value between each planet. To do this subtract each degree and minute from the following degree and minute in sequential order. In other words, subtract Mars from the Node (the Node is 2°37' from Mars). Subtract the Node from the Sun (the Sun is 0°31' from the Node). Subtract the Sun from the Moon (the Moon is 7°22' from the Sun), and so on. We are only interested in the difference *between* each of these planetary points. Note that Mars has nothing subtracted from it because it is the first planet. The beginning planetary period will always be the entire degree and minute of the lowest planet. In this case it is Mars. The bottom row is the converted to decimal equivalent of the minutes

MA	NO	SU	MO	VE	AS	JU	SA	ME
03°	02°	00°	07°	03°	01°	00°	02°	00°
08'	37'	31'	22'	36'	29'	10'	42'	44'
.13	.61	.51	.36	.06	.48	.16	.07	.73

Figure 10.3

To ensure that the process is correct, the difference between the planets is added. When all the degrees and minutes are added together, the total sum must be equal to the position of the planet which has the highest degree.

We add the degrees 3°+2°+7°+3°+1°+2° = 18°.
We now add the minutes: 08'+37'+31'+22'+
36'+29'+10' +42' +44' which equal 259'.

Divide 259' by 60 (60 minutes in a degree) and the result is 4°.31666'. To obtain the minutes *from* the decimal, we *multiply* the decimal .31666' by 60, resulting in 18.9996'. Rounded off to the nearest whole number, we have 4°19'. Added to 18°, the total sum is 22°19' or the sum of the highest planet with which we began.

Now we are ready to convert the other planetary points to their decimal fractions: divide the minutes by 60 and then multiply that answer by our found *log*.

Mars = 03°08' = 3.1333 divided by 15 = .208 x 245.50165 (constant log)= 51 days. The decimal can be further utilized. If you want to know how many hours, multiply the remaining decimal by 24. Thus, you will find that Mars will be in effect after the solar return date a total time of 51 days and 7 hours. To find the minutes, multiply the remaining decimal by 60.
In order to know the exact timing of these planetary periods, use a calculator and utilize the entire numerical display in your calculations.

MA = Mars @ 3°08' converts to 3.1333, divided by 15 x 245.5016568 = 51.2820 days. Take the remaining decimal of .2820 x 24 = 6.768 hours and the decimal .768 x 60 = 46 minutes or 51 days, 6 hours and 46 minutes. The example below is worked out in detail for you to follow.

The calculations for all the positions follow:

MA @ 03°08' = 3°.1333
3°.1333 ÷ 15 = 0.2088 X 245.5016568 (log) =
51 days, 6 hours, 46 minutes

NO @ 02°37' = 2°.6166
2°.6166 ÷ 15 = 0.17444 X 245.5016568 (log) = 42
days, 19 hours, 48 minutes

SU @ 00°31' = 0°.5166
0°.5166 ÷ 15 = 0.3444 X 245.5016568 (log) =
8 days, 10 hours, 55 minutes

MO @ 07°22" = 7°.3666
7°.3666 ÷ 15 = 0.4911 X 245.5016568 (log) = 120
days, 13 hours, 36 minutes

VE @ 03°36" = 3°.6000
3°.6000 ÷ 15 = 0.24 X 245.5016568 (log) =
58 days, 22 hours, 04 minutes

ASC @ 01°29" = 1°.4833
1°.4833 ÷ 15 = 0.0988 X 245.5016568 (log) = 24
days, 06 hours, 37 minutes

JU @ 00°10" = 0°.1666
0°.1666 ÷ 15 = 0.0111 X 245.5016568 (log) = 02
days, 17 hours, 25 minutes

SA @ 02°42" = 2°.7000
2°.7000 ÷ 15 = 0.18 X = 245.5016568 (log) =
44 days, 04 hours, 33 minutes

ME @ 0044" = 0°.7333
0°.7333 ÷ 15 = 0.0488 X 245.5016568 (log) = 12
days, 00 hours, 02 minutes

To complete this exercise, now add the number of days, hours (remember to convert any excess of 24 hours into days) and minutes.

361 days, 97 hours, 286 minutes.

97 hours divided by 24 = 4 days, 2 hours.

286 minutes divided by 60 = 4 hours 46 minutes.

361 days + 4 = 365   2 hours + 4 hours = 6   hours. The 46 minute discrepancy is due to the calculator; strike that.

Your answer will be in very close approximation to 365 days and 6 hours.   Any slight discrepancy, and I do mean *very* slight, can be contributed to your calculator because of its decimal conversion limitations.

If there is a large discrepancy, then go back and recheck your figures.   Often the problem lies in the mathematical calculations.   You may have inadvertently hit the wrong key on your calculator or erred somehow in the conversion tables.   The most common error is to forget to include the first planet's degree and minutes or developing the constant log conversion.   Always double check your work.   The few extra minutes spent now corrects a lot more than simple mistakes—it saves time and frustration.

Once you have rechecked your calculations and are satisfied with all your work, refer to the table of days between two dates at the end of this chapter.   Be sure to remember to add a day to each leap year.   Find the number of the corresponding day on which the birth date falls (July 23 is day number 204) and simply add the number of days of each time period to the day number of that date.   As you list each period, you will note at a glance with which date each of the periods begins and ends.

The Mars' period is 51 days in length.   Add that period to day number 204.   The result is day number 255, which is September 12.

The Nodal period is 42 days long. Add that period to day number 255. The result is day number 297, or October 24. Simply continue the procedure until you have completed the entire year. There is a table of day numbers at the end of this chapter to help you work with the day factor.

Any planet in the *solar return* chart which is exactly the same *sign and degree* as it is in the *birth* chart indicates that the planetary period will be more intense for good or bad, and will be affected by the combined influence of both planets. If a planet is the same degree, but not the same sign or house, the period will be active but not as intense as the direct conjunction regardless of the aspect. The strength of the planets in the solar return chart is combined with the planets in the birth chart. The solar return positions must be evaluated just as you would the birth chart to find their planetary power as noted in the stack. The influence of the stronger planetary position in either chart will usually outweigh, assist or, in some cases, even cancel the influence of that planet in the other chart. To some degree each planet always influences the other planets by virtue of its position in the natal chart. Remember that the birth chart must always be considered the primary chart.

In using this method, all charts are secondary to the birth chart and are heavily influenced through its rising sign and also by the planets involved in the birth triads. A negative planet in the birth chart can, at best, be neutralized in a solar return. Again, use only one degree orb of approach to all planets.

Calculating the solar return in the above manner allows you to determine when and for how long, each planet will exert its influence. Coupled with the birth chart, it allows you to correctly predict positive, neutral and negative periods by comparing the overlay of house influences and their rulerships.

For example, suppose your client's birth chart reveals that he was born with the Sun in Leo in the fifth house with Aries rising. This placement suggests a person prone to speculative ventures through the house where Mars is placed. Let's say we calculate a solar return for the above chart and find Capricorn rising with the Sun in the eighth house. The *overlay* would be Capricorn (solar return Ascendant) over Aries (birth chart Ascendant), advising a curb (Capricorn) on the natural tendency to rush (Aries) into any speculative (birth Sun in Leo, fifth house) adventure. This is because the Sun in Leo in the solar return chart is *weakened by its eighth house position* during this solar return year. By rogressing the solar return chart you will notice that this advice is very succinct in about ninety days after his birthday when the Sun will have rogressed to the fifth house.

The rulers of Capricorn and Aries would also play a major role in the delineation and give us further insight as to which avenues to pursue by their placement in both the natal and solar return charts. The solar return chart indicates that the Saturn (Capricorn) and Mars (Aries) periods are the times to exercise the most prudence. The Sun placed in the weak eighth house during the solar return year advises prudence throughout the entire year but especially when the periods for Mars and Saturn occur or when the solar rogression mentioned above occurs.

The Sunset Solar Return

The sunset method, the sunset solar return, is basically a up-to-date chart which *times* any events throughout the forthcoming year by monthly rogression. Recognizing the fact that the ancient astrologers did not have the sophistication we have today, they more than likely used a different technique. It is doubtful they used a solar return chart at all, except for the return of the equinox or solstice. At any rate, the sunset theory works very well as a solar return chart.

First, prepare a chart for the sunset in accordance with the rules in the sunset section for the year of the solar return. *Do not* refer to the ephemeris and count days to correspond to the day equals a year method. Simply run a chart for sunset prior to the date of your birth for the upcoming year, nothing fancy. Next, place only the planets that have the same degree, regardless of sign, next to the stacked planet form based on your original birth chart. Note the aspects by adding the signs in which the planets are located. The planets that are the same degree will have an influential effect in the overall look and feel for the upcoming year.

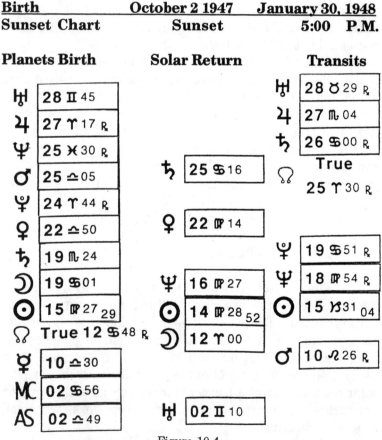

Birth	October 2 1947	January 30, 1948
Sunset Chart	**Sunset**	**5:00 P.M.**

Planets Birth   **Solar Return**   **Transits**

Figure 10.4
Gandhi's sunset solar return for 1947-48

Note the rate of motion of the Moon and its first and last aspects. Note the first planet to reach an angle. The Sun travels at the rate of one month for each house, 12 houses equals 12 months.

At first glance, in Gandhi's sunset solar return for 1947-48, we find Saturn, Venus, Moon and Neptune involved. Saturn is the same degree as natal Mars but in square aspect.

As an example, we will use Gandhi's chart for the year of his death.

There are quick indications that 1947-48 is an important year for Gandhi. The first is his age. He is entering his seventy-ninth year and any transits should be scrutinized with care. The solar return chart for this year has a distinctly Saturnine flavor, as Saturn exerts the most influence. Observe that it is the highest degree of active planets in his solar return and Saturn squares his natal Mars! Secondly, his soul (North Node) and physical expression (latitude) planets include the Sun, Moon, Mercury and Mars. Negative or harmful aspects to any of these points are potentially dangerous.

Venus is the same degree as natal Venus in semisextile. Moon is square North Node. Neptune is conjunct his natal Sun (Sun is always conjoined with the Sun in a solar return).

The Moon is in square aspect to natal North Node. Venus at 22° connects to his prenatal eclipse at 22° 51' Aquarius, a very important position at his age. Neptune, the first planet to reach an angle, is also an attritional planet and it conjuncts his solar return Sun, a negative aspect (we use Neptune because he is a world leader). On January 30, 1948, as the transiting Moon approached conjunction to his natal Sun, transiting Venus is conjunct his prenatal solar eclipse point and transiting Pluto is conjunct his natal Moon, while the North Node is activating a "T" square to transiting Saturn and natal Mars. Although Pluto was not discovered until 1930, it plays an important role in Gandhi's life from age sixty-one and, most certainly, at the end.

The rules for timing the solar return chart by rogression still apply. However, we are working within a year's framework; each degree equals one day. Therefore, each *house segment* equals a month, rather than six years. Should we rogress Gandhi's sunset solar return chart by four houses for the fourth month, we instantly see Mars is on the Ascendant at the time of his assassination.

While on his way to prayer, Gandhi was shot on January 30, 1948, at 5:00 P.M. by a young gunman. The transiting planets on January 30 heavily aspect both Gandhi's natal and solar return charts, indicating this date was extremely important.

At the beginning of this chapter, we studied a rather complicated approach for working out the solar return. This was done for chart comparison purposes. If you love the mathematical approach, then the Vedic method is definitely for you. However, when we view the solar return through the sunset method, we can still arrive at similar conclusions without all the fuss. This is good news for those who like Vedic astrology but not its mathematical component.

Those of you who are interested in pre-natal eclipses and their impact on death should read Richard Houck's excellent book, *The Astrology of Death*. It is well written and well documented.

A Table of Days Within a Year

The table of dates allows you to distinguish the number of days between calendar dates. To use this table, simply cross reference from the date (right) to the month (top). For example, to add 106 days to February 13 look at the number 13 of the day and under the month of February. The number for that date is 44. Now add 106 to 44 to arrive at 150: the number 150 corresponds to May 30.

Should the dates extend into the next year, either revert to the beginning of the table or add 365 to each calculated date.

Month

Day	Jan	Feb	Mar	Apr	May	Jun	Jul	Aug	Sep	Oct	Nov	Dec
1	1	32	60	91	121	152	182	213	244	274	305	335
2	2	33	61	92	122	153	183	214	245	275	306	336
3	3	34	62	93	123	154	184	215	246	276	307	337
4	4	35	63	94	124	155	185	216	247	277	308	338
5	5	36	64	95	125	156	186	217	248	278	309	339
6	6	37	65	96	126	157	187	218	249	279	310	340
7	7	38	66	97	127	158	188	219	250	280	311	341
8	8	39	67	98	128	159	189	220	251	281	312	342
9	9	40	68	99	129	160	190	221	252	282	313	343
10	10	41	69	100	130	161	191	222	253	283	314	344
11	11	42	70	101	131	162	192	223	254	284	315	345
12	12	43	71	102	132	163	193	224	255	285	316	346
13	13	44	72	103	133	164	194	225	256	286	317	347
14	14	45	73	104	134	165	195	226	257	287	318	348
15	15	46	74	105	135	166	196	227	258	288	319	349
16	16	47	75	106	136	167	197	228	259	289	320	350
17	17	48	76	107	137	168	198	229	260	290	321	351
18	18	49	77	108	138	169	199	230	261	291	322	352
19	19	50	78	109	139	170	200	231	262	292	323	353
20	20	51	79	110	140	171	201	232	263	293	324	354
21	21	52	80	111	141	172	202	233	264	294	325	355
22	22	53	81	112	142	173	203	234	265	295	326	356
23	23	54	82	113	143	174	204	235	266	296	327	357
24	24	55	83	114	144	175	205	236	267	297	328	358
25	25	56	84	115	145	176	206	237	268	298	329	359
26	26	57	85	116	146	177	207	238	269	299	330	360
27	27	58	86	117	147	178	208	239	270	300	331	361
28	28	59	87	118	148	179	209	240	271	301	332	362
29	29	**	88	119	149	180	210	241	272	302	333	363
30	30		89	120	150	181	211	242	273	303	334	364
31	31		90		151		212	243		304		365

** Remember to add a day when it's leap year.

CHAPTER 11

THE HOROSCOPOS

Astrology's Greatest Discovery

Ptolemy's ingenious system of using the Ascendant as a basis for determining planetary positions was a milestone in the history of astrology. Although created at a much later date, horary astrology represents one of Greece's finest contributions to this discipline. This tool, the horary chart, is designed to answer questions established for the particular moment a question is asked. The technique is so powerful that the name and style of the horoscope chart has lasted over 17 centuries and is *the basic format* astrologers still use today for genethliacal purposes.

References to the ascendant are found in ancient Babylon diaries. The Babylonians practiced daily observations in hourly periods (i.e., horary). Their basic premise was to determine omens from the heavens (astrology). At a much later period, celebrated astronomer Claudius Ptolemy developed his theories which became the astrological capstone emerging from Greece some 500 years after the conquest of Babylon and Egypt (B.C. 335 and 332).

Ptolemy, who was also an accomplished mathematician and geographer, had access to nearly 600 years of various historical Mesopotamian and Egyptian records from which he formulated his theories. What is known today is that the bulk of Hellenized astrological writing stems from the Alexandrian period.

Hesiod's poem, drawn from Mesopotamian wisdom literature, is the first record of stars being related to Earthly events. Two Greek scholars, Meton and Euctamon (fourth century B.C.), attempted to reform the Greek calendar which emerged from Babylonian methodology.

Aristotle, Plato, Eudoxus and a host of other Presocrats, all gleaned bits and pieces of information from both Egypt and Babylon although, frequently, the origin of many ancient writings and texts were difficult to determine.

Hipparchus, who compiled the first star catalog, is given some credit for popularizing astrology during the second century B.C.. Although the Babylonian influence in Greek astronomy is clearly visible, the extent of Hipparchus' knowledge of Babylonian techniques is unclear. What is very clear is that the Babylonians were not inclined to share their jealously guarded knowledge about the heavenly oracle. The foundation of the work done by Hipparchus and his predecessors was based on the style of mathematical calculations and constants used in the Babylonian ephemerides. Many discoveries later made by Greek Pre-Socratics were derived from clay tablets, these discoveries were not direct teachings handed down from ancient Egyptian or Babylonian mentors. Additionally, at the time of discovery, Babylonian procedures found on clay tablets were outdated. Nevertheless, such star-gazing procedures were still valuable in giving the Greek astronomer's insight into celestial mechanics.

Ptolemy's work is basically a comprehensive compilation of earlier works that possibly ranged from B.C. 700 to 150 A.D. His research came from early Babylonian and Greek astronomy texts that were partially available from many other astronomers and included practically all astrological achievements and mathematical methods of antiquity. However, there were many problems in these earlier methods and Ptolemy was able to recognize the technical drawbacks that Eudoxus, Hipparchus, and a handful of other astronomers and astrologers, had based their hypotheses. Undoubtedly, such drawbacks were the result of "imprecise" calculations noted in Babylonian tables and texts that were further misconstrued or only partially interpreted by the Greek scholars. Be that as it may, Ptolemy's theories based on his observations replaced those of his predecessors, moving them to the rank of mere historical figures.

Neugebauer states in *The Exact Sciences in Antiquity*:

> "When Ptolemy first developed his planetary theory, he had at his disposal geometrical methods by means of which solar and lunar anomalies were explained very satisfactorily, and similar models had been used also for an at least qualitative explanation of the apparent planetary orbits. Thus it had become an obvious goal of theoretical astronomy to offer a strictly geometrical theory of the planetary motions as a whole and the characteristic phenomena lost much of their specific interest, especially after the Greek astronomers had developed enough observational experience to realize that horizon phenomena were the worst possible choice to provide the necessary empirical data."
> (page 127 E.S.A.)

Apparently, Hipparchus either made clearer interpretations of the early Babylonian clay tablets or developed geometrical theories a little closer to the true mathematical values of celestial phenomena. At any rate, Hipparchus' knowledge of the theory of parallax, equation of time, fixed stars, precession and other astronomical theories is central in Ptolemy's refining process.

Ptolemy is best known for his mathematical work, *The Almagest*, which is the Arabicized name for *The Great Treatise*, an encyclopedic compilation totaling thirteen books in all. Book two addresses tables of mathematical chords for spherical trigonometry. Book three considers the Sun and Moon and their motion. Books four and five discuss the Moon's motions and the length of the month. Eclipses, planetary conjunctions and oppositions are dealt with in Book six. Books seven and eight concern fixed stars, precession and a catalog of fixed stars. The remaining five books primarily focus on the planets and are considered his most original work. *The Almagest* remained the ultimate authority on astronomy until the time of Copernicus (1543 A.D.).

Instead of using the sine and cosine to describe the heavenly arc, the use of mathematical chord principles presented anomalies on early theories. For fourteen centuries these erroneous misconceptions on astronomy were quietly ignored and not completely resolved until Kepler's work showed otherwise.

The Tetrabiblos, the bible of astrology, exhibits the mental climate and traffic of both the Greeks and the Romans of that period (200 A.D.). It is during this time that the first evidence of the *Ascendant* (intersecting the ecliptic) is used for casting a *horoscope* to determine heavenly positions for the *moment in question*. Trigonometric tables developed by Ptolemy defined the Ascendant and were crucial to the development of astrology. Ptolemy was the first to define the year as Tropical and was influential in naming the days of the week after the planets.

Scientific Astrology

Since the time of Ptolemy, astrology has become the study of the positions and angular aspects of heavenly bodies placed within a symbolic circular diagram based on the moment of birth (the Ascendant). The angular aspects are considered to have originated from the ecliptic or the Sun's path from the viewpoint of Earth. Most scientists treat astrology with disdain and declare it has no relationship to the geophysical sciences, such as geodesy, meteorology or oceanography.

Recently, however, astrology has become slightly more interesting to scientists who have accepted Michel and Francoise Gauquelin's indisputable research and work. Scientists are beginning to explore the laws of physics that may apply and support the principles of astrology. Dr. Percy Seymour in his studies on early man suggests that primitive man had the ability to navigate under bad weather conditions or at night with an internal geomagnetic sense or planispheric clock that works like instinct–similar to how birds and insects find their way. Today we can recognize this ability as the sense of direction that modern man innately uses to find his way about. Another theory is proposed by F. Gillian who postulates that the pineal gland is receptive to subtle planetary changes. A third luminary is David Bohm who theorized the idea of a holographic universe comprised of three basic manifestations: matter–energy–meaning whereby each enfolds the other two. Bohm further states that we recognize only a fraction of the flow of this holo-movement seen as an explicate and implicate order.

Quantum physics is intimidating to the average person but, with even a little understanding of the subject, we can recognize Bohm's ideas. More and more we find that the field of quantum physics relates closely to the idea of a holographic universe wherein each part replicates the whole; the smallest change effects everything. A butterfly landing on a flower in China can influence the rainfall in Brazil. Scientists who are beginning to reflect on the laws of physics as applied to astrology are finding more and more evidence in support of this discipline, thanks to the initial research by the Gauquelins.

Today's field of quantum physics is the best argument for the way astrology works. The idea that everything is interconnected allows astrologers to recognize not only the astrological model but the scientific one as well. Astrology, as a "primitive" interpretation of the laws of quantum physics, may have been something that early man was aware of some 6,000 years ago, but could not voice.

The Horary Chart

Horary astrology is best defined as the method for interpreting answers to questions based on the *time* a question is asked. To cast the horoscope, it is important to first formulate the question in a way that it is clearly understood. The astrologer must note the exact time he hears and understands the question. This form of astrology answers any question, however, for the novice, it is advisable to ask a question that requires a simple yes or no answer. This does not mean that complex questions cannot be asked but, for the beginner, the simpler the better.

To outline the rules for horary astrology would require more space than can be provided here. However, there are a number of excellent books on the subject which can turn an intermediate astrologer into a horary astrologer in no time. Early Greek astrologers had so many rules that by the time the answer was determined it was too late to do anything about it. Today we are fortunate as the books we have available succinctly set forth many of astrology's complex subjects in simple, easy to understand steps which work very well. *The Only Way to Learn About Horary and Electional Astrology* by March and McEvers is an excellent reference for those of you who wish to explore this area further.

There are key ingredients to becoming a good astrologer. One of which is, one must have a love affair with the clock. Time is the essential ingredient to all branches of astrology. An astrologer who does not make the effort to observe the clock as second nature is not an astrologer. Another ingredient is recognizing there may be gray areas and then taking the time to research them for clarity. And, most importantly, we must keep an open mind about each piece of information that could possibly be a key to important new discoveries.

The basics of horary astrology are similar to the principles of Genethliacal astrology prepared in the Tropical manner. Literally, there are three charts or wheels and each chart overlays the other like using three transparencies.

In the first basic chart, there are twelve fixed houses related to experience, each is numbered from one to twelve. This wheel never moves; it is the fixed matrix. Next, there are twelve signs of the zodiac related to time.

The three parts of the horoscope

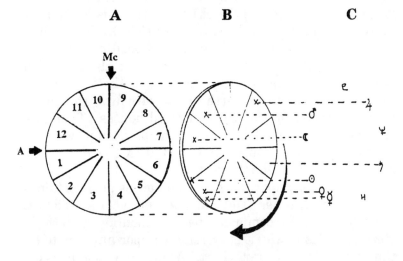

Figure 11.1

A is the background "Houses", the linchpin or matrix that acts as the foundation. B is the changing zodiac, each "sign" passes through each house approximately every two hours. C is the planets as they appear in relation to the "signs" located in the ephemeris.

This wheel moves over the fixed and numbered matrix completing one revolution in a 24-hour period. Thus, describing different influences for each fixed house at any given time by zodiacal sign. Lastly, there are ten planets and three mathematical points, namely the Ascendant, Midheaven and Node, any one of which can be any place within any zodiacal sign or house, depending upon the day, month, year and time the chart is erected. This interrelationship allows the astrologer to read the chart by weaving and unraveling the various relationships by the placement of each planet throughout the houses their signs and aspects to one another (figure 11.1above).

In the list below, the numbers refer to the house numbering system beginning with first house placed on the extreme left (9 o'clock position) of the astrological wheel and reading it *counter-clockwise* so that the *fourth house* is located on the bottom (6 o'clock), the seventh is to the right (3 o'clock) and the tenth on top (12 o'clock) as set forth below. The first chart with numbered positions of houses (A) is the background matrix which never changes. The zodiacal circle (B) is a different matter. As the sky appears to revolve around the Earth every 24-hours, the zodiac travels *over* the stationary numbered houses. Therefore, each numbered house changes one complete sign every two hours. Likewise, planets (C) located in the zodiac also appear to travel within the signs as well.

Another important note, the houses also pertain to time and distances. To really become acquainted with these concepts, I recommend the book mentioned above for starters. This is why it is extremely important to note the time when doing a horary chart. When a question is asked, the chart is erected at the time the astrologer hears the question! Now what has all this to do with the reading? When a question is asked, one must know in which department of life the querent is interested. The Sidereal chart below will serve as an excellent example.

When using the following list, it is important to recognize that each heading by number, sign and planet represents the same quality. Wherever any sign or planet is placed in the wheel it will always refer to its original description (listed below). The house description is further defined by the sign placed over it. Thus, if Gemini is placed on the first house cusp, the attitude, appearance, state of mind and health are all defined by the matters concerning the first house *with* Gemini—quick in speech, a nervous demeanor and nervousness. The querent will be interested in contracts, results from ads in magazines or papers, a new car, or short trip. To further your examination, with Gemini on the Ascendant, you would look to see in what sign Gemini's ruler, Mercury, is placed and also the location of the ruler for the sign placed on the third house cusp. Questions asked must pertain to the house involved, such as marriage pertaining to the seventh house, otherwise you are wasting your time and that of your clients.

The above example is best understood by first recognizing simple relationships:

1-Aries-Mars. Mars, Aries and 1, all mean the same thing. They relate to the first house, the person asking the question and his state of mind, health, attitude and appearance. Articles: tools, machinery, steel, pewter, iron or metal.

2-Taurus-Venus. Again, these all mean second house matters such as money, movable physical possessions, earning ability, as well as self-respect and prosperity. Articles: Art, jewelry, copper, bronze or polished metals. The second house itself and *the second house from any other house* represents *all* lost articles.

(For example if your brother lost his watch, your brother is represented by the third house [siblings]; his watch would be represented by the fourth house–the *second* house counting from the third as your initial starting point. Another example: your wife misplaced her expensive pair of glasses. Wife is the seventh house, her glasses are represented by the eighth house–the second house from the seventh.)

3-Gemini-Mercury. These mean communication, both verbal and written, contracts, texts, and tests. They also represent siblings, neighbors, cars and short journeys. Article: book, fancy bookmark, keys, and other useful artifacts in our daily lives.

4-Cancer-Moon. These represent domestic affairs, real estate, parents, food, kitchen, immovable objects and the outcome of a first house question. Article: items of subjective value, ordinary appearance, silver, opal, pearls.

5-Leo-Sun. Here we find children, courtship, forms of gambling, entertainment, and romance. Article: gifts, precious metals, gold, brass, shiny metals.

6-Virgo-Mercury. These can mean health, types of illness, coworkers, work and conditions, people you hire, agents, small pets, diets, stores and shops. Article: small pets, items that maintain a person's state of health, office supplies.

7-Libra-Venus. Here we find marriage, partnerships, lawsuits, and anyone you join or confront on a one-to-one basis. This also indicates the result of fifth house affairs. Articles: Important papers regarding agreements with partners, partner's possessions.

8-Scorpio-Mars and Pluto. These relate to banks, taxes, surgeries, legacies, insurance matters, other people's money or money expected from others. Article: plastics, items of little use or value.

9-Sagittarius-Jupiter. Here we find long-distance travel, publicity, advertising, dreams, affairs of the church, expression of opinions, the courtroom and the law, teachers, colleges and universities, and foreigners. Article: religious items, clothing, college books, souvenirs, good quality items.

10-Capricorn-Saturn. These relate to career, business, employer, status, prestige and honors, anything pertaining to notoriety, and the judge in court. Article: anything old or worn out but valuable to its owner, probably dark in color, made of stone, lead, pewter, rubber.

11-Aquarius-Uranus. These mean friends, hopes, wishes and desires, clubs and organizations, cooperation with others, social activities. Articles: computer, radio, TV, tape recorder, items that are electronic in nature, rare and unusual antiques, items made of various materials, checkerboard or hounds tooth designs.

12-Pisces-Neptune. These represent enemies, secrets, plots, disappointments, jails and other forms of confinement, large animals, drugs and drug dealers. Articles: trophies, photographs or photographic equipment or supplies, cheap items without real value except to the owner, glass, artificial materials, paint supplies.

This limited list is by no means final or complete and, for the serious astrologer interested in horary astrology, it is advisable to continue adding to this list as you become more familiar with this process. Additionally, extending the list encourages you to be more flexible and to see possibilities with greater ease.

Another point worth mentioning is turning the wheel. Often you will be asked to answer a horary question regarding someone other that the querent. These are questions generally asked about mothers, bosses, aunts, uncles, friends and so on. If you are asked a question about a friend's wife, for example, you would look to the natural fifth house. Why? Because the friend is the eleventh house and the wife of that friend would be represented by the seventh from the eleventh. Your brother's wife is represented by the ninth house for the same reason, brother third, seven from the third: ninth, his wife.

Test: Your auto mechanic knows you are an astrologer and asks you about his brother-in-law's health. What house would you use to answer his question? Answer: seventh.

The auto mechanic is represented by the sixth house, his wife is seven houses from the sixth house, i.e., the twelfth; her brother is the third house from the twelfth i.e., second; his health is six from the second i.e., seventh house. The sign, ruler and aspects would answer the mechanic's concerns.

A- The first thing to recognize is the *house* to which the question is related, *not the sign*. "Will I be married to my long-time friend?" is a question of marriage and relates to the seventh house only. The friend is represented by the eleventh house of the querent.

B- At this point we note the sign on the seventh house for marriage (Aries) along with its companion planet, its ruler (Mars).

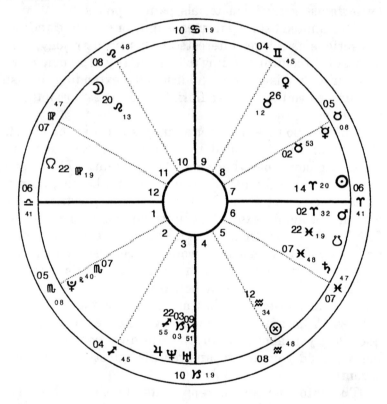

Figure 11.2
"Will I be married to my friend?"

C- The ruler of the seventh house sign will be located in one of the twelve houses (in this case the sixth). Locate the ruler and its relationship by the sign. In this case it is in its own sign. Now determine if it is in a *friendly* sign or house. The sign is friendly, yes, but the house is not because Mars is located in the weak sixth house in a twelfth house position (the house behind the seventh). Is it related to the other planets in a friendly way? No, Mars is square to Neptune. Is its house placement in good relation to the seventh? (No, counting from the seventh, Mars is in its twelfth.) Where is the Moon? In our case it is in the eleventh house in friendly trine of the long-time friend represented by the Sun. Does it relate to the seventh house (yes, it does, by trine) or its ruler? (No). Does the Moon answer the same questions we asked about Mars (ruler of the seventh) satisfactorily? (No).

Conclusion.

The Moon suggests that the long-time friend may not be as long as the querent states. Marriage is not likely as the friendly signs (Moon wide trine Sun) suggest that he is satisfied with just staying friends. The Mars square Neptune suggests that he may have indicated marriage but has other fish to fry and probably lied (Neptune) to the partner who wishes to get married. Mars in the sixth house suggests they met at work and our querent was quite taken by the slick conversation (Mercury trine Neptune)! The last aspect the Moon makes (not related to the lunar mansion) is the square to Venus indicating disappointment in the affair. They broke up a month after the call.

As you can see, the system is like weaving. You start from the initial house and sign represented by the question. You then locate the planetary ruler of the initial sign and look at the sign in which it is placed. Now look for its ruler's location by house and sign. Continue the process by locating *the next sign the last ruler was in* to the next house and sign. Repeat until you reach a house where the sign and ruler are the same or ends up where you started.

When all is said and done we have deduced how the other planets and their aspects support your answer.

Sometimes a house and sign are completely compatible, such as signs with the same quality like Jupiter in Leo or Sun in Sagittarius. At other times we find planets in signs that are not so compatible (Saturn in Leo or Cancer). Often the compatibility of planets and signs is enough for an answer. There are many more ground rules and terms that the student must learn but it is not as difficult as it sounds. As a matter of fact, when you read a birth chart, you are basically reading a horary chart based on the time when the person was born. For those of you who are interested in this branch of astrology, it is suggested that you find a good teacher. Once you learn to ask the question succinctly, the answer pops up almost like magic.

It is for this reason that astrology, in its present form as the horoscope, has lasted for so many centuries. A birth chart set up for the moment of birth has all the ingredients an astute astrologer needs for answering the right questions pertaining to the person or event. We just ask ourselves why was this person born? The planets and their positions are the themes that reflect our lives. For this reason, it is doubtful that we enjoy free will as such.

Free Will or Fate?

Babylonians and Egyptians felt that humanity was the result of a pre-determined archetypal form. Fate, not luck or choice, dominated. Philosophically, the whole concept of astrology quietly supports, and even suggests the idea that it is fate and *not* free will in operation. Otherwise, how could an astrologer predict coming trends?

The choices we do seem to have are limited within fixed circumstances and are described in the horoscope by the planetary positions and aspects. These circumstances are activated when different planets' motions form various configurations within the framework of one's life. The timing depends on their placement within the birth pattern. In this fashion we are locked into our destinies. Astrologically speaking, our charts reflect our "ground rules" here on the planet, and we must play the game of life according to those rules.

If there is indeed a human soul, then its journey is the process of creating its reality and individual selfhood. Planetary pictures in the horoscope are desires for this lifetime and describe challenges the soul has accepted at birth. Recognizing these fated patterns is one way we have of changing our reactive responses into proactive choices, and thus, changing ourselves.

Another way is to observe our mechanical responses to outside stimuli and then learn to turn them into calculated responses. By observing our actions and reactions in relationships with others, we are offered the unique opportunity to grow and change. This applies to both the "inner" soul experience and its "outer" physical manifestation. This practice becomes an awakening process where we create choices for our behavior and become caretakers for our own well being. This reasoning is the groundwork for examining new dimensions that will answer many heretofore unanswered questions about ourselves.

The Sunset Horary Method

The ancients had a simple but elegant view of the universe and how it worked. The same question we asked in the earlier horary method is reviewed here using the sunset method.

Using the preceding chart we will now answer the question asked about marriage with the sunset method. Placing the planets in a stack also shows that Venus indicates the querent and an overview of the question.

Venus is the highest planet by degree in the stack and is situated between Jupiter and Mars, clearly indicating her love and the hope of marriage (Jupiter represents marriage in a woman's chart). With Venus closer to Jupiter we find the hope and *ideal* of marriage (third decanate).

But Mars is located in the lower quadrant relating to childish fantasies and actions, the situation has negative nuances, possibly ending in separation. It also shows us that the lover (Mars) is unscrupulous and is motivated by selfish ends. His manner of conversation is slick and facile (Mercury located between Neptune and Mars). The Moon in the sunset lunar mansion starts at eight degrees of Leo and is leaving Saturn (lonely) in its own decanate (lower ten degrees) and then passing Uranus (instant attraction), then the Midheaven in Cancer (appreciation and caring), and then on to the Sun (the marriage proposal or suggestion).

	Long
♀	26 ♉ 12
♃	22 ♐ 55
	True
☋	22 ♍ 19
☽	20 ♌ 13
☉	14 ♈ 20 52
♅	09 ♑ 51
♄	07 ♓ 48
♆	03 ♑ 03
☿	02 ♉ 53
♂	02 ♈ 32

The Midheaven and Sun are located in the quadrant of *change* (ten to twenty degrees) so the marriage proposal probably was a ploy to build up her confidence but with no real foundation.

The Moon moves past the Sun toward the attritional South Node (meetings) and Jupiter by the same degree indicates that he might meet someone else and move on.

Furthermore, the attritional South Node is heavily aspected (not the North Node), thus indicating that the affair was waning and not meant to last.

The sunset chart can indicate a variety of circumstances and, while it is not intended to replace the current vogue in astrology, it certainly enhances the tools we already have.

On a diurnal or daily basis, one can set up a sunset chart and readily see what is in the stars for the next 24 hours. It is particularly important to recognize the periods we are entering by looking at the Ascendant and Meridian or Midheaven. The most prominent planet rising or setting at sunset marks the tone for what humanity will be experiencing as a whole during the next 24-hour period. Our personal experiences through the daily rising and setting planets is primarily indicated by where they are positioned in our charts.

The different planets indicate daily patterns and monthly trends. All one has to do is keep a short log of his daily experiences and watch the heavens and this idea will fall into place. If Mars is rising or approaching the Meridian, we can expect martial type experiences during that period based on where Mars is in our chart. People will generally be belligerent or boastful. Their driving habits will appear to be more rude than usual and so on. When Jupiter is rising or approaching the Meridian, we seem to find the world a better place in which to live. Everyone seems more open and optimistic; the economy improves and opportunities are more bountiful and so on.

Retrograde Planets

A major phenomena regarding all chart delineation is the retrograde movement of planets. It is probable the ancients considered such planets weakened and somewhat negative because they appeared to travel backward, retreating, and in the sunset case, "stepping down," or traveling toward the planet with the lesser degree in the triad.

A retrograde planet acts as if it has taken "time out" and withdrew its influence. Events seem more damaging when either triggered by transiting retrograde planets or direct transits aspecting retrograde natal planets. Additionally, any planet *not* retrograde in the birth chart is considered weakened by association when the same planet is transiting in retrograde motion, such as Mars in the example below.

Mundane Astrology

Mundane astrology is defined as charting local and national events or trends. Mundane charts for the birth dates of cities, their leaders or various countries and their leaders give us a glimpse of what to expect within those boundaries.

A perfect example of the efficiency of using sunset techniques for predicting events was the flooding at Grand Forks North Dakota on April 18, 1997 (Figure 11.3).

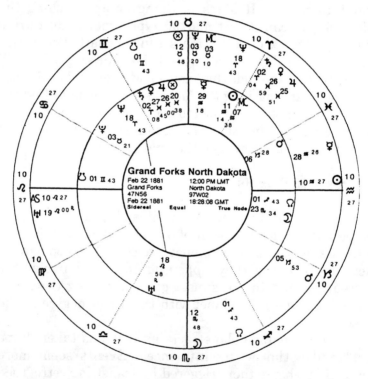

Figure 11.3
Center chart is the incorporation date and the outer is the sunset chart.

In *mundane affairs*, businesses, cities, states or countries, the rogression is calculated at **only** *one degree per year* and *not five* degrees per year–as in a natal chart for an individual. The first incorporation date for Grand Forks was February 22, 1881, at 12:00 P.M. C.S.T. 97° W 03, 47° N 55. The sidereal sunset chart is based on February 21, 1881, 5:55:26 P.M. C.S.T.. The incorporation date of birth chart is placed in the center of the biWheel chart with the outer chart cast for sunset a day earlier.

Rogression Grand Forks.

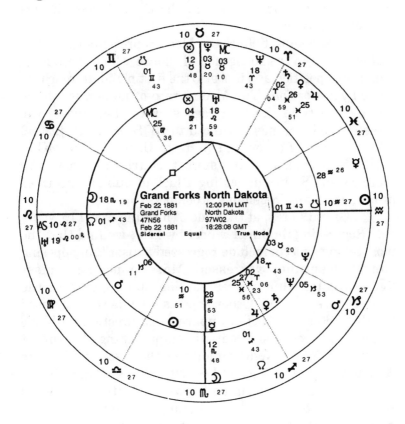

Figure 11.4
Rogression to the time of the Grand Forks flood disaster.

The initial sunset chart (inner wheel), compared with the incorporation time and date, immediately indicates eventual water problems; the corporate Sun is in alignment with sunset Neptune. The fact that the flood was unexpected is due to natal Uranus in trine to natal Neptune. Corporate Venus and Jupiter are conjunct the attritional sunset South Node.

In figure 11.3, note the position of corporate Uranus in relation to sunset Neptune, they are opposite one another. Now note the placement of rogressed Sun at the time of the disaster. Notice that the Sun has rogressed to the place where Uranus was at the time of incorporation opposite Neptune.

In the sunset chart the Moon represents the public and is placed in the sunset fourth house which is its most vulnerable position and it is also the first planet to reach an angle by rogression. The Moon's rate of motion is 13° 59' and by the time the Sun rogresses to the time of the disaster the Moon has advanced to 18° Scorpio 19'–just 40 minutes short of a perfect square to Uranus! The MC in both the corporate and sunset charts interact with Mercury and Saturn indicating a lack of public concern or awareness of any impending problems.

Grand Forks, at the time of flooding was 116 years old. Rogressing the inner wheel by 116°, we find that the most telling aspects include rogressed sunset Sun opposing sunset Neptune; rogressed Mars opposing sunset Venus/Jupiter while rogressed Neptune approaches the sunset Mars position! Other aspects include the rogressed South Node (attrition) in apparent conjunction with the sunset Sun; rogressed Mercury approaching the sunset Moon and North Node conjoining the Ascendant. The Ascendant has the signs of Leo with rogressed Sagittarius just entering the Ascendant's position with their rulers semi-square to each other. A unique situation arises in mundane charts when using the sunset method–that of relative aspects. Many times aspectsa in the birth chart develop into events when the rogressed chart reaches an identical aspect to itself–in this case the trine. The closest aspect in the Grand Forks incorporation chart is the trine from Uranus to Neptune. The event happened when the sunset chart rogressed to a trinal position to itself. This idea of replicating aspects is important to remember if you plan on predicting mundane (and often personal) events.

Transits

On April 18, 1997, natal Mars is weak because transiting Mars is retrograde while transiting Neptune is applying to corporate natal Mars by conjunction.

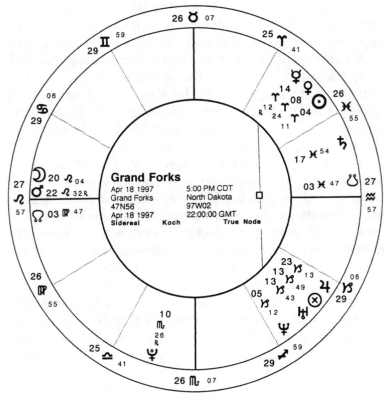

Figure 11.5
Sunset transits for April 18, 1997.

Transiting Mars is also inconjunct to natal Jupiter indicating many adjustments in any endeavor concerning those planets. With this under-standing we see that a weak Mars (both in the birth chart and by transit) indicates any amount of effort during a time of crises in Grand Forks would have been insufficient.

Additionally, while the city burned (Mars), the fire department could only watch helplessly as they were unable to reach the fires because of the flood waters, a reflection of transiting Neptune in conjunction with natal Mars. Furthermore, the influence of Uranus must also be considered. Remember it has a natal trine to Neptune and the transiting Moon *and* transiting Mars in Sidereal Leo was approaching a conjunction to natal Uranus while applying to an inconjunct aspect to transiting Saturn. The chief initiators of the event are easily seen in the rogression: Sun, Mars and Neptune. The secondary planets (either natal or transiting) include the Moon inconjunct Saturn while transiting Pluto nears a conjunction to natal Moon and squares attritional sunset South Node while conjoining the sunset Sun. If we had access to the many different occasions that the city fathers discussed the reinforcement or redesign of the Red River aqueduct, chances are Mars, Neptune and the Sun would show prominent at the time of such discussions. By knowing the past history of a person, place or thing and then isolating and relating events to match planets and their aspects, astrologers stand a better chance of prognosticating events more correctly.

A good astrologer becomes a better one by being an empiricist. You are encouraged to watch the diurnal motion and equating it with everyday experiences. In doing so you will soon understand how the planets are associated with their energies. With time you will notice how signs indicate a certain class of experience and how the houses help refine what the signs indicate. In astrology timing is everything and the sunset chart allows us to determine the timing of meaningful events. Knowing why, what, where and how is important. However, knowing *when* an event will take place is paramount. Armed with such knowledge you can take advantage of any situation.

As we have seen, the sunset chart combined with transits clearly express the timing of events and eliminates much of the guesswork. When coupled with progressions and transits, the astrologer becomes much more astute at interpreting events.

In Conclusion

In my opinion, the sunset chart can be used in every branch of astrology as it is the matrix for successfully predicting the timing of events. At any given time there are planets that are indicative (by decanate) of function, change or goals. These are always seen by their placement in the 30° stack. The timing of events cannot be ascertained unless indicated by the sunset chart and the sunset chart will align with any other chart system. That includes transits, secondary progressions, solar arc, Naibod, diurnal, both minor and tertiary lunar, and solar and lunar returns. It is recommended that every time you cast a chart, you compare the sunset chart with all your other astrological tools. Very shortly you will notice great improvement in your skills.

Just as the biological DNA precisely developed your physical being starting the moment you were conceived, your celestial DNA includes the development of your physical, emotional and mental growth on the day you were born. With a little study using the sunset chart, you will find that we are definitely involved in a master plan for self development. Just as the Egyptians envisioned, we are on the way to becoming stars ourselves.

CHAPTER 12

HARMONICS

Although the theory of harmonics is generally associated with music, its basic premise also works well for astrological application. A harmonic is basically a wave length whose frequency is a whole-number multiple of another number (like 5, 10, or 20 is related to 100). This is easily seen when we play stringed instruments such as the guitar. Each short small metal bar along the fingerboard (called a fret) is a harmonically placed division of the overall length of the strings. By pressing just behind the frets we, in effect, shorten the string length to produce a different tone. Each tone will respond concordant with the register of the string plucked. The resultant sound is what we hear as notes in the musical composition.

The theory of astrological harmonics works on the same principle; any division of the whole-number 360° by another whole number produces a harmonic related to the circle. Thus, 360° divided by 30° gives us the basic 12 house divisions of the horoscope or the twelfth harmonic.

For our discussion in this chapter we will cover three systems of harmonics. The current Western system which either *multiplies* the longitude of the planet by the number of desired harmonic or divides the 360° circle by the degree of the aspect. To find harmonic values, 180° or the opposition is the second harmonic, 120° or trine is the third, 90° or square is the fourth and so on.

Instead of using the 360° circle, the Vedic or Hindu method divides each whole *sign* of 30° for the harmonic desired: divide 30° by nine to establish the ninth harmonic or by six to establish the sixth harmonic. The sunset system uses the stack placed within each 30° house to establish sensitive points over a six year period. This format constitutes the personal resonance that is fixed in the chart at the time of birth rather than a rigid format that "shoe-boxes" the native into a pre-set standard. We will cover the Western idea of harmonics immediately following the Vedic section. The last section of this work will explore the simplified sunset version.

As we have found in the chapter, The Solar Return, using the Vedic method requires a little extra time as the calculations are somewhat laborious. However, if you *like* the mathematical part of astrology, and many astrologers do, you will not want to do a chart without incorporating these, and other forms of Vedic techniques. However, for those of you who like to work with an easier format, the sunset method at the end of this chapter works with the same results if not better. Before we begin, one last note: the intercepted house problem is solved by using the equal house system.

Over the past few years, Vedic astrology has become vogue with many astrologers and for this reason we will cover the Vedic system as our first exercise. Normally we would evaluate *each planet* in the chart, but doing so would require too much space so, for brevity, we will use only the Moon in Aquarius as an example. At first glance this amount of work looks very formidable but, if we slowly work out each planet and its segment location carefully, the amount of time spent will be well rewarded. Furthermore, we are interested in the visible planets only, therefore, Uranus, Neptune and Pluto are not used in this system, just the planetary range from the Sun to Saturn and the rulers of the Ascendant, Node and MC are used.

In all cases we divide only the houses that have planets in them. The subdivision will be called *segments* and we are required to use the ruling planet in *place* of the constellation. The rules to remember are: always divide by the number harmonic desired and, do not use the sign, use the planetary rulers of the signs instead.

For example, should we divide the sign by three, this is called the decanate but do not confuse the term with the the decanate in the sunset process. The decanate, *for this discussion only,* is the triplicity of a sign and is divided into three segments of 10° each. To explore our example, suppose we have the **Sun 15°** in the sign of Leo. In this case we are subdividing the fire triplicity, Aries, Leo and Sagittarius and we always start from the cardinal element for the first segment.

I might add here that many astrologers prefer to begin the initial segment with the sign the Sun is placed regardless of its quality. But, in consideration, this does not make any sense because a planet located 15° in a sign is in its apex position, being all that it can be, and should not be assigned in any other segment–only where indicated by degree. Furthermore, should the location of the Sun be in a cadent sign and on an angle, why would we want to declare it in a cardinal position by placing it in the first segment? Any planet so located already has a cardinal influence by virtue of its placement in the birth chart. The degree of any planet's placement is personal and its location pronounces the native's experiencial development. I think we would want to *understand* its influence rather than *declare it* as something we think it should be. In our use of mathematics, or when we read, we do not employ techniques removed from standard procedure–so why do it with astrology? Experience has shown that begining each segment from the cardinal element and assigning the following segments as fixed and cadent is the proper procedure because it maintains the integrity of the planet's location and the continuity of this work.

To further explore our example chart, the first decanate 0°– 9° 59', is ruled by the first or cardinal sign of the fire element which is Aries, in place of Aries Mars is placed in this segment. In the second segment, we place the Sun because it rules Leo, and 15° lies between the degrees of 10°– 19° 59'. The last sign of the same element is Sagittarius, that segment ranges from 20°– 29° 59'. Place its ruler, Jupiter, there (see Figure 12.1).

Sample graph

Aries = Mars	Leo = *Sun	Sagittarius = Jupiter
First segment (Decanate)	Second segment (Decanate)	Third segment (Decanate)

Figure 12.1

In this manner we have used the planets in place of their signs, which, in this case, rule the first, fifth and ninth houses from Aries.

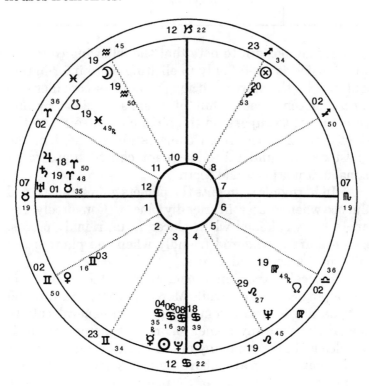

Figure 12.2

As a chart reference, the Moon 19° Aquarius 51' from the birth chart of July 23, 1940, 1:17 A.M. EDT York Beach, Maine, will be used unless otherwise cited.

Ancient Whispers from Chaldea

The Moon in our example chart (Figure 12.2) is in the constellation Aquarius, an Air element. In this graph place **Venus**, Libra's ruler, in the first 0°–10° segment. Next, the fifth house from Libra is Aquarius so place its ruler, **Saturn**, in the 10°–20° segment. Gemini is the ninth sign from Aquarius and represents the last 20°–30° segment. There we place the planet **Mercury**.

Libra = Venus	Aquarius = Saturn	Gemini = Mercury
0° - 9° 59'	10° - 19° 59'	20° - 29° 59'
	Moon is placed here	

It is important to note that the following course of chart division is useful only in eliciting more information about the birth chart. Although there is considerable information contained within this exercise, it is not by any means meant to supersede the birth chart itself. At the risk of repetition, the birth chart is always held in the highest regard, and all subsequent charts supplement original information to add depth.

In harmonic segments the planets gain strength and influence when located in friendly places. Conversely, the planets are weakened when placed in unfriendly places. Segments are considered friendly when the planets are similar in character and nature.

Basically, the Sun, Moon, Mars and Jupiter are in one grouping, a "clique," while Mercury, Venus, Saturn and the Node are in a different clique. The general rule to remember is that any planet (or more) from one group is not welcome in the company of the other "clique". In our sample chart, the graph above indicates that the Moon's placement under the rule of Saturn is unfavorable. The general meaning of unfavorable can rest on many circumstances. The possibilities vary such as, (1) he may not have his emotional needs satisfied; (2) the women in his life may have emotional problems; (3) he possibly has to deal with losses or (4) his associates have to deal with loses. This will be explained further when we get to the actual exercise below.

When delineating a chart it is a good habit to remember the "clique" of the planets. When we get used to the clique idea, we will find planets that are in or out of the signs ruled by these cliques work in the same fashion.

	Favorable	**Unfavorable**
Sun.	Moon, Mars, Jupiter	Mercury, Venus, Saturn, Node
Moon.	Sun, Mars, Jupiter	Mercury, Venus, Saturn, Node
Mercury.	Venus, Saturn, Node	Sun, Moon, Mars, Jupiter
Venus.	Mercury, Saturn, Node	Moon, Mars, Jupiter,
Mars.	Sun, Moon, Jupiter	Mercury, Venus, Saturn, Node
Jupiter.	Sun, Moon, Mars	Mercury, Venus, Saturn, Node
Saturn.	Mercury, Venus, Node	Sun, Moon, Mars, Jupiter

Getting Started

In this harmonic exercise, the twelve signs are subdivided into twelve different segments, some of which are in vogue right now (the decanates [division by three] and dwads [division by 12]). Each subdivision correlates

377

the harmonic number to the house number and its meaning in the chart i.e., the third harmonic relates to third house matters. The emphasis is placed on both the planet ruling the constellation within the segment and the birth planet's position noted by degree. (See example above, Moon in Aquarius). Notice that the chart is no longer used as a wheel, but carried out as a flat graph. This flat graph allows viewing the chart with all the divisions at a glance. The first harmonic is always the whole zodiacal sign.

Rule. Place each planet in its respective position by sign and degree found in the birth chart. Each sign is replaced and signified by its ruling planet and not its glyph. Throughout this exercise, as mentioned above, the Moon is placed 19° Aquarius 51' and shall be our point of reference. In all references, as we are dealing with the mathematics of the sidereal zodiac, the word sign is interchangeable with constellation. Yes, it is necessary to work out each planet to get the full benefit from this exercise.

We start with the first harmonic and the segment contains the entire 30° of the sign. Each harmonic will result in smaller segments as we further divide the sign signified by the house number.

First Division

The first harmonic is the entire house of 30°. It contains the planet from the birth data, its primary planetary position at the *time of birth*. Natal planets placed in segments ruled by friendly planets (see above) establish ease and power for the benefit of the native. Those placed in unfriendly positions are weakened and have a tendency to make life more of a challenge.

> In this segment we place the planet with the entire sign. Our example is the Moon in Aquarius ruled by Saturn.

The first harmonic corresponds to the first house affairs, and alludes to the personal and vital qualities. The Ascendant indicates our position of comfort. It is where we can operate as ourselves without any fear of consequences–as if we were comfortably living alone in a wooded area without having to please or react to anyone.

• The key reference by which all activity of the other houses and planets are reflected or experienced.
• The constitution of the native, the character-building process according to each planet's placement.
• The events in life that personally affect the individual as they unfold by direction or progression.
• The environment where we choose to be located.

In our sample chart, the Moon is placed in the first harmonic with the entire sign of Aquarius, symbolized by Saturn, an enemy of the Moon. The overall Moon's influence is in a weakened position and indicates that the native would exhibit an intense uneasiness when placed in helpless or frustrating situations. The segment placement of this lunar position suggests the native feels the need to be in some form of control in all situations with the tendency to take a dominate position with friends and acquaintances. He seeks permanent attachments but the Moon-Saturn configuration indicates a somewhat reserved form of friendliness based on the fear of being hurt by separation, while at the same time having a real need for emotional ties. The environment in which the native lives may somehow be depressed or the quarters may be small, untidy and messy. The events in life will be strongly influenced by the mother and mother surrogates. Further examination of aspects made by the Moon may modify and strengthen it, but this is the basic tendency upon which all other harmonic divisions based on the Moon will rest. Also, this exercise will concentrate only on the Moon's placement and not on any aspects acting as outlets.

Second Division

In the following subdivision the sign is simply *divided* in half. Generically, the first 15° represents *odd* signs (Aries, Gemini, Leo, etc.) and is always governed by the Sun. The second fifteen degrees, represents the even signs (Taurus, Cancer, Virgo, etc.) and is always governed by the Moon. In our case, the Sun governs the first half of the sign and the Moon governs the second half because our example chart has the Moon in the odd sign Aquarius (odd because it rules the natural eleventh house). This manner of division denotes wealth, speech, dependents, taste (both by tongue and in cultural values), stability, truth, temperament and the mouth and face as our outward expression. The first segment starts with the Sun. The Moon is placed with the segment governed by the Moon because it is higher than the 15° division point. All matters pertaining to the second house apply.

0° 00' to 15° 00'	15° 01' to 30° 00'
Sun	*Moon

This harmonic also represents the influence of feminine or masculine energy upon each planet. Masculine energy tends to be concerned with the quantity of objects, spontaneity of events, lack of consequences, carelessness and other childlike qualities. A predominance of solar energy would tend to squander money earned with a lack of concern about tomorrow. The feminine energy, on the other hand, is careful, planning, nurturing, has an eye to the future, the native is more interested in quality rather than quantity, and is concerned with the value of money.

The predominance of feminine energy in our sample reflects the ability to carefully plan monetary strategies and allow for future pitfalls. However, Moon in Aquarius is weakened because of its association with Saturn. With this combination the ability to provide for himself may not prove sufficient. The native may be attracted to types of work that does not pay well, or his ambition may be subdued because his sense of self-worth and esteem are low. One possibility is he may become impatient in his workplace because of the type of work, or its associates. Another possibility is he may not get promoted as fast as he likes and quits. The resultant lack of permanence could effect the native throughout his life, thereby keeping him from properly establishing himself in his field of interest. The mother or spouse may be required to be totally supportive until the native learns to trust his own basic abilities to provide for himself and his family. The attitude toward other people's money may be extravagant but on the basis of an ill-aspected Moon he may be retentive and penurious with his own. With this placement a good guess is that he would hide away "little stashes" of money to bring about a feeling of inner security.

Third Division

The third division is more commonly known as the decanates. It is actually the division of each triplicity. The sign is divided into three equal parts of 10°. Each ten-degree segment is governed by its *trinal sign* ruler or the fifth and ninth sign from itself. Always start with the cardinal sign ruler.

0° 00' to 9° 59' VENUS	10°00' to 19° 59' * SATURN MOON	20° 00' to 30° 00' MERCURY

This position represents the initial drive in life, what mentally excites and motivates the native, and his drive toward success. If a planet is located in the first decanate, personal concerns are tantamount with a "do it now," attitude. The second decanate works in the persistent "look how hard I can work at something" arena. The third decanate represents the inner principles of one's values and ideals ("my word is my bond") and represents the integrity and law of oneself. It also represents brothers, sisters, relatives as well as strength, courage and valor. The physical portions of the body involved are the ears, neck arms and legs.

The sample Moon is negatively placed here at the end of the second decanate (the fifth sign from Libra is Aquarius) ruled by Saturn. The Moon and Saturn are inimical towards one another but speech or writing is important. An interesting phenomena occurs in charts where two negative planets intersect: they tend to neutralize each other's negative influence! This position holds more of a Saturnine flavor reducing the Moon to a background influence. Moon/Saturn at birth with the second decanate ruler Saturn suggests the need for discipline in the learning process and the need to develop emotional stability by learning to trust and confide with significant others (partners).

With this placement the native would want to be seen as an authority in some field. This would supplement his need to associate with those "less knowledgeable" than he, as suggested by the initial negative Moon placement. In a positive way, the native could attract those in need of some guidance or leadership and he could possibly become their mentor in his chosen field. However, success may be stilted by trying to be too many things to too many people. But, as the native matures, his focus on singular interests will eventually emerge. Also, the emotional makeup of this planetary placement would suggest separation or minimal communication with the native's immediate siblings. The personalities of the siblings' may be too introverted or removed to nurture the native's mental or emotional needs.

Fourth Division

The method for the fourth division is to divide 30° by four which equals four segments of 7° 30' each. The ruler of each *angle* is placed in its proper segment according to the position of the angles by the rising sign in the *birth* chart. Thus, the sign of Aries rising, ruling the first quadrant, would be Mars as ruler for the first segment; the Moon for Cancer (fourth house); Venus for the third segment (7th house); Saturn for the fourth segment (10th house). It follows logically that for the Taurus rising in our sample chart, the cardinal points would be Venus, Sun, Mars, and Saturn (the rulers of Taurus, Leo, Scorpio and Aquarius respectively),

In our sample chart the first segment is ruled by the planet which rules the Ascendant, Venus. In the next segment we place the fourth house lord, the Sun; the third segment is the lord of the 7th, Mars, and the last segment is ruled by the 10th lord, Saturn. The Moon falls between 15° 01' and 22° 30' and so we place the Moon in the Mars segment (below).

7° 30'	15° 00'	*22° 30'	30° 00'
VENUS	SUN	*MARS MOON	SATURN

The Nadir or fourth "house" angle signifies the point where we feel we are most helpless. It is through this angle that we shore up our "lacks and deficiencies."

This harmonic division then is regarded as:
• The position one achieves in life from his education.
• It is also associated with the mother/child principle (a woman wanting to be a mother or a child wanting to be with its mother).
• The psychological feeling of being helpless in situations.
• It also indicates immovable property, changes of residences.
• Emotional ties that resist change in life.

In whatever segment the planet is placed, the fourth harmonic indicates an inner "understanding" indicated by the ruling planet of that segment. It indicates what one needs to achieve academically and shows either a strong focus or a narrow approach. A diverse selection of planets in the fourth harmonic indicates many interests. The native wants to learn a little from a variety of academia. It represents the idea of a "Renaissance Man" who is capable of many different activities. In viewing our example Moon, we see it is placed with Mars. The academic need is best served through physical (Mars) experiences such as acting, sports or acquiring a degree in some form of physical therapy. The negative side is very little schooling or dropping out before completion (Saturn).

Another reflection of Saturn-Moon/Mars is a strong need for discipline from a strong-willed partner to curb the high level of emotional intensity and impulsive nature which the Moon and Mars indicate. Yet, there is the impulse to act with impunity or a need to get away from the discipline of parents or any other authority. Home life would be unsettled in the early years with many moves (Mars), separations (Saturn) and relocations (Moon). With Saturn in the background, the absence of discipline or a male influence is suggested either by his not being home at all or his career keeping him away for long periods of time (background Saturn).

Fifth Division

Thirty degrees divided by five equals five segments of six degrees. When the planet is placed in odd numbered signs (Aries, Gemini, Leo, etc.), the first, second, third, fourth, and fifth segments are ruled in this particular order: Mars, Saturn, Jupiter, Mercury and Venus respectively, and in even numbered signs we reverse the above sequence. Our Moon is in an odd sign and we start with Mars.

6° 00	12° 00'	18° 00'	* 24° 00'	30° 00'
Mars	Saturn	Jupiter	Mercury Moon	Venus

This harmonic corresponds to fifth house matters such as:

• The act of new adventures and initiation.
• The native's skills and the dexterity of execution.
• The inner God or one's truest belief system.
• Intelligence, creative new ideas, the act of understanding or awakening.
• The individual's deepest true love, not necessarily the marriage partner but the ideal romance.
• The children's attributes.

The sample Moon in this division is again influenced by Saturn with Mercury removing the Moon into a background position. As noted earlier, a negative influence associated with another negative influence is like two magnets with the same polarity, they repel, *thereby lessening the negative influence.* The creative Moon here is associated with Mercury and the artistic capabilities would lean toward graphics and design. Moon/Mercury/Saturn indicates a deep interest in the creative aspects of life. The inner God would be sought through many aspects of religious thought and philosophies. Should the native become well versed in these subjects, he could display a seeming profundity in religious views and thought. The ideal romantic involvement would be in seeking those who would have a need to be rescued from their current emotional circumstances and, having been rescued, they in turn somehow rescue or reward the native. The Mercury/Saturn indicates children interested in scientific pursuits.

The Sixth Division

When 30° is divided by six, the result for each segment is five degrees. The classic planetary rulers are as follows: in *odd numbered* signs the rulers of the first six signs will be counted in order from Aries. In even signs the order will be reckoned from Libra. In addition, the sixth harmonic *also* uses the *personal house rulers* located in the *natal* chart. They are listed by counting from the Ascending sign of the birth chart. Combined with the rulers of the natural chart mentioned above, we now have *two rulers per segment* plus the planet. Our sample Moon will have three planets in the segment indicating health matters.

Start with the ruler of the *sixth house sign* in the birth chart. Count from the Ascendant if an odd sign, or count from the descendant if an even sign (the eleventh house ruler) and place them in their natural order into the corresponding six segments. Once they are inserted they can be judged as friendly or hostile. This evaluation allows us to reconcile the natural health situation (the standard horoscope as background) with the (conflicting or harmonizing) current health situation as seen in the overlay of the birth horoscope positions.

Top row: The Moon is in an odd numbered sign so we start with natural zodiac beginning with the ruler of Aries.

5°	10°	*15°	20°	25°	30°
MARS	VENUS	MERCURY	MOON	SUN	MERCURY
Mars	Venus	Mercury	Moon	Sun	Mercury
		MOON			

Bottom row: The sample chart has Taurus rising so we add our second row of personal planets starting with the eleventh house ruler (sixth from the descendant). The sixth house from Scorpio is Aries ruled by Mars. Here we place the planets in natural order.

The sample Moon is located in the segment governed by double Mercury which overrules the Moon, friendly to Saturn, i.e., unfavorable health through mental conditions such as nervous disorders from stress or depression. Other problems in health may be through an excess in lunar indulgences; certain types of food and alcohol. The Moon here is good for catering to public desire; working in an environment where food and/or communication is part of the service. Foreigners are "heady" types and the native will learn or benefit from their intelligence.

In sixth harmonic considerations we see:
- Health and what precautions are necessary to maintain it.
- Our working conditions and what we are willing to do to support the second house acquisitions.
- The ability to determine who our enemies are and our ability to vanquish them.
- Our association with relatives other than immediate familial ties.
- Foreigners we will meet and what their purpose in our life will be or vice versa.

Planets in the sixth harmonic will tend to be tainted just by their association with the sixth house influence. This normally produces strife and enmity (thereby health issues) by virtue of their placement unless the dual rulers indicate otherwise. In the chart above we see Mercury rules the third segment in both circumstances. The Moon falls in this segment by degree (less than 20°). The Saturn-influenced Moon is outnumbered by two Mercury placements that are friendly with Saturn. Result, good health through positive attitude and knowledge of health issues and exercise.

Strong planets, such as Sun, Saturn or Mars, will help defeat our enemies or place us in jobs which require inner strength. The resultant struggle will certainly be stressful and possibly show up later as health problems.

Soft planets, such as Venus, Jupiter, Moon or Mercury, ease the stress somewhat by diminishing the threat of enemies and placing us in a work arena which is more to our liking. However, overindulgence in the workplace as a workaholic or the need to work two jobs may become the health hazard.

The negative Moon in Aquarius is descriptive of a friendly, genteel and attentive attitude with a lack of sincerity or depth, even aloofness at times. Health problems may arise from trying to accommodate too many stressful female associations who are seeking the native's support and/or companionship.

The type of physical work suggests minimal abilities and endeavors. With double Mercury in this harmonic, becoming an artist, a sales representative or even a writer/lecturer has strong incentive. The Moon, doubly emphasized by Mercury, is associated with third and sixth house matters (both ruled by Mercury). Later, and with maturity, the means of financial self support may become focused. When that happens the native's interests will probably be supported by older females (Moon/Saturn) with similar interests (double Mercury) who will act as agents or patrons. Interest in historical influences, psychology or similar fields of analyzing problems of individuals (primarily female) may point to other types of work as well.

However, as Saturn is involved, finding direction in life may be delayed or meet with resistance or diversions. The early years may be filled with too much time spent on socializing, coupled with a lazy attitude and trying to find easy work loads. Additionally, the effect of a double Mercury suggests that the length of time it takes to be properly trained for credentials may seem too much of an effort. The native may also try to avoid hard work in life by looking for "quick buck" schemes or quick fixes to his monetary problems. In addition, the lack of education or dedication may have a negative impact in trying to overcome or achieve his goals. Health problems may arise when resistance or diversions to his goals do occur, resulting in frustration that can produce stressful reactions resulting in illness.

Seventh Division

Divide the sign by seven and the result will be 4°, 17', 8.6" for each segment. The seventh "house" or descending angle is a reactive angle and indicates awareness of situations that are not conducive to the native's interest. This is where, in a hostile environment, we seek out a friendly face or ally. This harmonic is more personalized because the seventh harmonic uses the rulers of the Ascendant or descendant in the natal horoscope. For *odd* signs use the *Ascendant* as sign ruler and enter each subsequent ruler in its ensuing order. For even signs, start with the seventh house ruler. Continue this pattern until the entire graph is completed.

4° 17'	8° 34'	12° 51	17° 18'	*21° 35'	25° 52	30°
Mars	Jupiter	Saturn	Saturn	Jupiter	Mars	Venus
				MOON		

- The seventh section traditionally refers to the marriage partner. It is the style of the individual the native is bound to attract.
- For partnering, this section evaluates long term relationships and the helpmate, not the same type of love relationship that we relate o the fifth house.
- It is also disposition of the native's children.
- This harmonic also allows us to see the finished product that materializes out of our creative visualizations, endeavors and projections (result of the mental force of the fifth house)
- The ruler of this angle along with the ruler of the second house also governs the native's death as it is the twelfth of the eighth.

Our sample chart has Taurus rising. It is an even numbered sign and we will start with the ruler of the seventh house, Scorpio. The Moon rests in the Jupiter segment (less than 21° 35'), endowing the native with a supportive marriage. Here the negative Moon/Saturn influence is placed in the Jupiter segment, thus making the native unwilling to change partners even though there may be many opportunities to do so. Again, there is a lazy feeling and a sense of avoidance concerning the Moon throughout all of the harmonic divisions, suggesting that the native will choose a partner who will happily carry most of the responsibility in the marriage.

This lunar placement shows a high degree of commitment in the partner (natal Moon/Saturn combined with harmonic Jupiter), and could be detrimental to the native because of the partner's excessiveness in her supportive role. The native's need to socialize may outweigh the need to achieve success because the partner is taking care of all the necessities. Most of these opportunities will undoubtedly become affairs, but the commitment to the marriage is solid (Jupiter is conjunct Saturn in the natal chart). The creative and artistic fifth house harmonic being resolved in the seventh harmonic is very promising, but because of Saturn's restrictions to the Moon in the birth chart, the talent may remain undisciplined and unschooled. Unless other factors in the chart prove differently, the negative Moon may be hard to overcome because of the partner's indulgence. However, if the native's mental pursuits are persistent and disciplined, success is imminent.

Eighth Division

Divide the sign into eight equal parts of 3° 45' each. This division is similar to the earlier personal divisions, as there is a fixed formula for obtaining the planetary rulers based on the birth chart data. *All* positions are considered by, and result from, the *fire triplicity only*. Should the planet at birth be in *any* cardinal sign, begin with *Aries* and count eight signs and then insert the planetary rulers in succession from the eighth sign ruler, i.e., Scorpio/Mars. For *all fixed* signs, count eight signs *from Leo* and insert their lords in a similar manner, i.e., Pisces/Jupiter. In similar fashion, *all* mutable signs will commence from the eighth sign *from Sagittarius,* i.e., Cancer/Moon.

As the houses are permanent positions in a horoscope chart and signs pass through them clockwise, note the significance of which sign is placed on which house.

Signs placed in their natural house positions determine secondary subtle values to the interpretation according to the rising sign in the birth chart.

The sample Moon for this harmonic is in Aquarius, a fixed sign. Following our formula we start with Leo, a fixed sign in the fiery triplicity. Our planetary segments start with the eighth sign from Leo which is Pisces, ruled by Jupiter. Placing Jupiter in the first segment and following in sequential order, the reference Moon is six segments from Pisces (more than 18°45' less than 22° 30') at 19° 51' placed with the Sun.

3° 45'	7° 30'	11° 15	15°	18° 45	* 22° 30	26° 15	30°
JU	MA	VE	ME	MO	SU	ME	VE
					MOON		

• The eighth house denotes regeneration, the ability to recover from an illness, etc.
• The life span; the cause of death as a result of the seventh house influence. Fighting and being defeated by one's enemies (the 6th is winning over an enemy).
• The underhanded nature of the native such as theft, violence, extortion, false pretenses, confidence games, and prostitution.
• Planets in this position destroy the inner virtues.
• Planets in this position relate to everything tainted or destroyed.
• Relates to our willingness or unwillingness to live up to other peoples' values and expectations, be they good or bad.

Our sample Moon is influenced by Leo's ruler, the Sun. Lasciviousness or depravity is absent as the Moon/Sun overrules the Saturn influence and places it into the background. This combination suggests protective, sensitive, positive and pleasing mannerisms and a willingness to please others. The native is protected while fighting for his defense: enemies are not considered fortunate and are weak in their position. The standards are high and the native expects others to operate along the same judgment values. Almost naive, the native will tend to think that other people are basically honest and are knowledgeable in their professions and willing to extend their help. The native may tend to be subservient, gentle and without enmity as the native does not like to disappoint another person's expectations.

Ninth Division

Perhaps the most unique and significant aspect of Vedic astrology is the harmonic ninth chart. Division of the sign by nine equals 9 segments in each sign of 3° 20'. To figure the placement of the planetary rulers, note the planet and sign from which you are delineating and start from the *cardinal* sign of its *element* and fill in each segment in the subsequent order of the zodiac.

You might want to construct a complete chart on this particular division. It will be an *entirely* new chart, *totally different* from your birth chart but full of information as it relates to the ideal person you would like to be and the ideal partner for you. In India, no marriage is considered before the ninth harmonic is reviewed for the prospective spouses.

To establish such a chart simply begin with the cardinal *element* of your Ascendant. We now want to determine how many multiples of 3° 20' can be divided into the degree and minutes of the Ascendant (such as 3°20' into 14° equals 4 [or four signs]). The answer is the number of signs away from the cardinal sign from which you began. Once determined, you place each house by sign in succession. In our example chart (Fig. 12.2), 7° Taurus 19' is the rising sign so we would begin with and count from the sign of Capricorn. Our *new* Ascendant is Pisces (3° 20' divided into 7° 19' is only two [with a remainder of less than 3° 20'], and Pisces is two signs away from Capricorn). For the second house place Aries, for the third Taurus and so on. Do the same with each planet and place it accordingly.

Another example for the luminaries and planets: the Moon at 19° Aquarius 51' is an air sign. Begin with Libra and its ruler Venus, the cardinal air sign. We divide 19° 51' by 3°20' for the answer of five. Five signs from Libra is Aquarius. We place the Moon in the fifth segment under Saturn, the ruler of Aquarius (5 x 3° 20' = 16° 40' and 6 x 3° 20' = 20°). The Ninth harmonic has a double Saturn placing the Moon into the background. In this case, the ninth harmonic Moon remains in the same sign as the natal chart.

Rule. With this harmonic we are preparing a new and different chart. To erect a ninth harmonic horoscope chart, observe the Ascendant of the birth chart by sign and degree. Note the element of the rising sign and start counting from the *cardinal* sign of the *same element*. Each segment of 3° 20' represents the *next* sign in succession, place the sign that is dictated by degree on the new horoscope wheel as the new Ascendant. Place each successive sign on the appropriate house cusp.

3° 20'	6° 40'	10°00	13°20'	16° 40'	20°00	23°20	26° 40'	30°00
1	2	3	4	5	6	7	8	9

The ninth harmonic horoscope chart is read just like the birth chart. This chart *assists* the birth chart by its support and agreement to the basic natal chart. The inner nature is revealed by way of the spiritual drive as well as the perfect mate to help employ spiritual balance.

Sometimes Vedic astrologers substitute the planet with the highest degree in the birth chart for the Ascendant. In this case they convert the planet into the sign it rules and proceed from that point. The general atmosphere of ninth house matters are blended throughout its composition with all the planets. The ninth harmonic is said to reveal our greatest planetary influence because it represents our deepest innermost values, our spiritual motivation and drive towards spiritual unfoldment. In essence, it is who we really are without any ego involved.

The ninth house in Vedic astrology is the same as its western counterpart with a few minor differences.

- The ninth represents the father.
- The inner values and philosophy taught by the father are most sincerely regarded, evaluated and revered.
- Shows our deepest values associated with the fifth house idea of our inner belief of God.
- It indicates our most respected teachers.
- A deep inner search to find the values and truths about religious teachings and its philosophies to attain inner peace.
- It is in the ninth harmonic that we can develop a non-attached Moon by finding its true balance with the Ascending sign personality. There is a special inner feeling concerning the purpose of being born, it is as if the native has recognized some secret code to life understood only by him. A woman with her Sun placed in the sign and degree where a man's Moon or Venus is located makes a good wife. For a woman, a man's Sun placed where her Moon or Jupiter is placed makes a good husband. This holds true for the birth chart as well.

The attitude is one of "the joy of living," happiness and playfulness. The father is looked upon as the vehicle to allow the birth process, not to love or hate, but to simply observe, perhaps as a mentor. In our example chart, the ninth harmonic is closely related to the seventh harmonic because the Moon/Saturn is with a Saturn contact. This is reflected in the old adage, "When the student is ready the teacher will appear." This Moon placement has the ability to recognize fortune, good or bad, as a synchronous spiritual lesson with whom the experience is shared.

Tenth Division

Each sign has ten segments of 3° each. Should the sign which *governs the tenth house* in the natal chart (not the house of the planet we are working with) be an odd numbered sign (Aries, Gemini, Leo, Libra, Sagittarius or Aquarius), start with the ruler of the tenth house sign and place the ruler in each segment of the subsequent signs in its natural order. In even numbered signs, place the lord of the ninth house sign (the one preceding the tenth house in the horoscope; do *not* count nine houses away from it) in the first segment and, counting backwards, place the planetary rulers *in reverse order* of their natural succession.

3°00	6°00	9°00	12°00	15°00	18°00	21°00	24°00	27°00	30°00
JU	MA	VE	ME	SU	MO	*ME	VE	MA	JU

The tenth house in a chart is best described as reaching the highest point in one's chosen profession. It is the angle of control. Planets placed therein are looked upon as very active and represent power by the nature of the planet. The native wants to be visible and desires to be titled by the nature of the planet. As a vocational house it is the ideal of the second house and represents the skill, achievements, honors and prestige the native can hope to attain in this life. So too, the harmonic subtlety reflects the above description.

Our sample Moon is placed in the 21° segment, i.e., seventh segment, as each segment is three degrees. Starting from the ninth house Sagittarius, (Capricorn on the tenth is an even numbered sign), the Moon is placed in the Gemini segment which has Mercury ruling this segment. In this case the tenth house signifies prestige and the seeking of honor through any form of communication.

The need to be recognized as a leader in the native's professional field is paramount. Planets in this position do not want to work for someone else as an employee.

However, with the Moon falling in the Mercury segment, should the position be titled as partner or independent contractor, the native would work hard and for less money. The Moon in the Mercury segment signifies importance in communications. Coupled with Saturn, the latter part of life may find the native becoming an authority in his chosen field. That will happen if the native has decided to overcome the sixth house obstacles previously mentioned. Additionally, the Moon in the tenth is naive and business-like experiences would be based on trust rather than knowledgeable business procedures. The Mercury segment suggests the native should learn more about business and management programs.

Eleventh Division

The sign is divided by 11 segments each measuring 2° 43'. To acquire the 11 segmented lords, start with the twelfth house from the Ascendant of the chart and count *backwards* in a clockwise direction.

In our example, the Ascendant is Taurus. The first segment is ruled by Mars, the ruler of Aries, the ruler of the 12th. Next would follow Jupiter, the ruler of Pisces, the 11th house and so on.

2°.7	5°.4	8°.1	10°.8	13°.4	16°.3	19°	21°.7	24°.4	27°.1	30°
MA	JU	SA	SA	JU	MA	VE	*ME	SU	MO	ME

This division isn't popular because of the odd numbered segments, but its value is unquestionable as the eleventh harmonic is related to gains and increases. Whatever planet is located here will bestow its qualities upon us in abundance. This harmonic also represents the 11th house qualities normally found in the horoscope: our idea of position and power or egoism, luck, credit, resources, aspirations, hopes, wishes, and desires. Our sample Moon is placed in the Mercury segment (more than 19° 01' and less than 21° 44') giving an abundance of friends with mental acuity. Their resourcefulness would augment the native's resources well, and would be at the native's disposal. Support, material gains and power come through friends and lovers. Because of the Saturn influence the native associates with only those who help make the path easier in the fulfillment of desired goals.

Twelfth Division

The twelfth harmonic has become somewhat trendy in the last few years and, even though it has been indiscriminately used, will probably be recognized by many astrologers as the dwad. The sign is divided into twelve segments of 2° 30' and the ruler of each segment commences from the house sign in which you are working.

2°.5	5°	7°.5	10°	12°.5	15°	17°.5	20°	22°.5	25°	27°.5	30°
SA	JU	MA	VE	ME	MO	SU	ME	VE	MA	JU	SA

*

For example, our Moon sign is Aquarius. Start with Saturn in the first segment and continue throughout the signs, placing the rulers of such in their natural order. Had we started from Taurus, the first planet, Venus, would be placed in the first segment of 2° 30'. In our example chart the Moon will be placed in the dwad for the Sun (more than 17° 30' but less than 20° 00').

- The twelfth harmonic has been acclaimed as one of decrease, losses, decay and erosion.
- This is the harmonic of entropy and wasting away providing the chart is susceptible to escapism.
- Planets placed here tend to lose their ability to perform well, usually in a slipshod or less than desired manner. However, a person with a strong chart can overcome this influence and become excellent in his chosen field.

Situations that are unacceptable and incorrect should simply be avoided. Fear is what drives us away from influence and there is very little that is considered positive under this placement (house or harmonic). But persistent work and faith in ourselves allows the use of fear as an impetus to move us into action either through the eleventh, as avoidance, or the first house of escape.

A planet located in the 12th represents the one place we would rather not be, or the things we would change if we had our lives to live over again. Understanding consequences can lead to positive influences by avoiding negative acts. Our example Moon is located in the Sun segment of this harmonic, signifying an underlying fear of being falsely accused of wrongdoing, being imprisoned or caught in the act of infidelity. The native is constantly aware of avoiding incorrect behavior which could have negative consequences. Involvement in activities that might be potentially harmful, cause physical impairments or limitation of freedom, is corrected by safety precautions, proper diet, and good judgment in any given situation. The native's regrets may be from lack of achieving the status he has sought throughout his life, by not finishing projects he set out to do or by just giving up on life in general.

The above descriptions are brief but they give you a good idea of the house meaning and how they reflect as ability with the native. Throughout the chart we find a predominance of Mercury giving the native an overall Gemini and/or Virgo quality. With such a strong Mercury the native should be advised to follow up on mental activities indicated by houses three (communication), five (creativity), six (work habits), ten (career) and eleven (social organizations) and further refined as indicated by the type and quality of the signs and rulers. Also the combination of those harmonic positions provide a major clue to the type of work or profession to which the native is attracted and in what field he is most likely to become successful. Harmonic ten, eleven and five in any combination suggests working with successfully creative people or celebrity types.

The Western Harmonic Divisions

We have all heard of bio-rhythms–the study of the cyclic or rhythmic behavior patterns displayed by mankind. These cycles range from Cerebral Neurons, the information transferred through the nerve cells at the rate of 1000 cycles per second, to the Bone Calcium Cycle of about 200 days. To many scientists the fact that these cycles exist, both in single organisms and the social order of mankind, is demonstrated through the ups and downs of agricultural and industrial production and even the stock market.

John Addey, an English astrologer, and at one time president of the Astrological Association, was dissatisfied with standard astrological procedures. He studied the effects of different rhythms and wave patterns of people who lived to an older than average age. He found no evidence that the standard Sun sign for age, i.e., Capricorn or its ruler Saturn, played any significant part in their charts or in the fact that they lived longer. Addey further studied young victims of poliomyelitis and again, found no astrological accountability as evidence that traditional astrology would predict their plight either through signs or aspects. However, Addey's research of statistically arranged material uncovered that planetary and nodal wave-like fluctuations played an integral part in the numeric harmonic relationships of the planetary positions in birth charts.

To date, many astrologers are studying this fascinating branch of astrology. As covered in the beginning of this chapter, to find any harmonic, simply divide 360° by any aspect (as an example divide 360° by 90° and we get the fourth harmonic, the signature for the famous "square" aspect). Similarly, should we divide by the trine (120°), we come up with the third harmonic, likewise, divide by the opposition (180°) for the second harmonic. This form of harmonic division holds true for any harmonic. This form of harmonic division holds true for any whole number. Addey did not directly support the higher numbers (non-aspects) and questioned their validity.

For the most part, Addy's work (probably) shows to be most promising in the field of subsistence which is related numbers that add up to a desired number in the harmonic. The *subsistence* of 9 (for example) is 9°, 18°, 27°, 36°, 45°, 54°, 63°, 72° and 81°, each number adds up to the number nine. Another example is the number six: in this case 6, 15, 24, 33, 42, 51 and 60, each number adds up to six. Any subsistent number relates to its basic harmonic in delineation.

It is fair to say that this type of astrology does *not* diminish the standard astrological practice in any way. It's just another approach that has yielded very positive results in the field. The study of harmonics is rooted in the statistical approach and those interested in this branch of astrology extend themselves into the field of wave patterns, planetary bio-rhythms and their relation of human reaction to these influences.

To further investigate this form of astrology would require more space than is available. For those of you who may be interested in this field there are many books on the subject to help you. Many practitioners of harmonics claim that this study is similar to, and enfolds, the earlier Vedic forms of the harmonic divisions you have read about in the first section of this chapter.

The Sunset Harmonic Divisions

The sunset astrologer is more interested in what the client has to say about his personal planetary reactions rather than follow "set and standard" meanings that the client must believe or respond to.

Each client reflects the different planets in different ways than any other client. With transiting planets or a rogression approaching Mars, one person may get sick while another finds energy and vigor and yet a third may have children during those Martian periods. In this fashion we see how each planet in the client's life relates to his own vibratory harmonic and can then recognize recurring patterns at different times and levels in his lifetime.

This is readily seen when we look at the 30° house cusps that designate each time period. Should we place the stacked planetary positions on the rim of the wheel relating the same degrees of the planets between each 30° house segment, we get results that can be considered harmonic. In addition, we know the time when they will recur in each department and at what age.

This is simple yet very effective. We know that every five degrees is equal to one year of life. Any planets so placed by degree within that period will influence the client in some manner. Every 25 minutes of arc in the chart is equal to one month of real time; one degree fifteen minutes of arc is the equivalent to three months, etc. Starting with the descendant, use the equal house system and place the 30° stack on the rim *within* each house cusp regardless of the actual degree of the houses (Fig. 12.3).

Rule. *All* houses will repeat the same structure in reference to the stack. Remember that each house begins with the lowest degree to the highest and *advances* by degree *counter*clockwise while the rogression moves in a clockwise manner. As you can see, the rogression reaches the planet with the highest degree in the stack first and moves toward the planets' with the lesser degrees, a form of entropy. This explains why we get a brilliant idea at times but when we work out the mechanics the idea devolves into more work than expected. We can further designate the timing of our client's harmonic responses because the complete 30° stack on the rim in each house is the harmonic.

In the example chart below we will use John Lennon's 30° stack and see how it fits into a house. We will look at the age from 36 years to 42, the location of the 12th house. Keep in mind that every five degrees is equal to one year and each "six-year house segment" will have the same planets repeated in the exact same position throughout the wheel. The Moon (for example) is almost four degrees away from the beginning house position for each of the next six-year periods. This remains fixed and applies to each house. Thus, John's *lunar harmonic* related in years is (approximately): 1, 7, 13, 19, 25, 31, and 37. His *Martian harmonic* occurs every fourth year after the beginning of each six-year period indicated by the house cusps. These are (approximately): 4, 10, 16, 22, 28, 34, and 40.

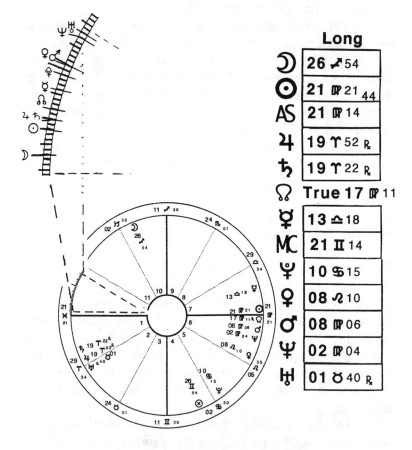

	Long
☽	26 ♐ 54
☉	21 ♍ 21 44
AS	21 ♍ 14
♃	19 ♈ 52 ℞
♄	19 ♈ 22 ℞
☊	True 17 ♍ 11
☿	13 ♎ 18
MC	21 ♊ 14
♇	10 ♋ 15
♀	08 ♌ 10
♂	08 ♍ 06
♆	02 ♍ 04
♅	01 ♉ 40 ℞

Figure 12.3
Lennon's harmonic chart–ages thirty-six to forty-two.

On December 8, 1980, John Lennon was taken away from us by being shot down in front of his New York apartment. His rogressed Sun at the age of forty is on the harmonic point of Pluto and approaching the Mars/Venus point. His phantom Moon had advanced by seven degrees and reached his Jupiter/Saturn harmonic. Coincidence? I'll let you decide for yourself whether or not this was a dangerous period.

Note. In the chapter on the Moon we learned that the Moon advances one degree every six years. This is known as the phantom Moon and this rule still applies. However, using the stack for harmonic purposes, we keep the Moon the same degree as in the sunset position because it remains a very powerful point in the chart.

Following the same procedure in Gandhi's chart, we recognize that the Pluto Mars point equates to one year after he initially begins each six year period. Gandhi was shot at the age of seventy-nine—one year after he started his next six-year period! His rogressed Sun had reached the point which is just past his Mars harmonic approaching his Pluto harmonic. Coincidence? Again, I'll let you, the reader, decide for yourself.

Hitler's death by suicide also coincides with the sunset Mars harmonic point. These three example charts have many points of interest in common but their diverse paths ended with similar results. That is why they were chosen. In doing your own chart this formula can be very enlightening for future trends. Harmonics is the one aspect of astrology that answers the age old question: "How does astrology work?" We, as professional astrologers, can answer that question with a resounding cry: "the planetary cycles are in synch with our own cyclic, bio-rhythmic patterns!"

Part Two

We are presumptuous and venture ideas of our own; turning more
modest, we merely form concepts that might be analogous to those
primordial beginnings.

Goethe

Defining the Indefinable

All of nature is reflective. Every natural object
throughout the universe, from the mineral to the animal, is
the reflection of its own innate intelligence. When we look
into nature we see cosmic functions incorporated into life
forms. This reflective action is Unity extending itself into
duality. Its resultant form is its own living hieroglyph which
the Egyptians called medu-Neter. We cannot imagine
something that does not exist outside the laws of nature.

The Egyptians believed that the divine aspect of
man and true knowledge was understood and interpreted
not through the mind but through the heart. Noted in *The
Egyptian Book of the Dead,* we often see the pictograph of
the deceased being judged by a scale with his heart counter-
balanced by a feather to portray his guilt-free life. As with
all Egyptian scripture, the hieroglyphs or medu-Neter,
contain deeper meaning than just their conventional
organized *ex*oteric interpretation. Make no mistake, when
reading the Egyptian medu-Neter, each line, each color,
every detail, was significant and intentional. Each letter
recognizes natural, *es*oteric laws inherent in the glyph itself
and what it represented.

The meaning of the *term* esoteric can be described
but its true understanding can never be clearly expressed in
a cerebral manner. The esoteric values of nature are
inherent and innate. The student who seeks higher
consciousness must be prepared to grasp it by seeing and
hearing it reflected in all of nature. The path is not one of
knowing but one of ability. Those who claim to reveal

esoteric knowledge use allegory, metaphor or parables–the play of words that simply replaces one word with another in an inefficient attempt to reveal spiritual "secrets." These devices actually hinder the true seeker because of their lack of openness or clarity. As with the Medu-neter, it would be easier to communicate the esoteric using only nouns without connections. That way the listener or reader could make sense by way of what he understands (boy - store - candy - home - appreciation). Sacred science can only be discovered and understood by the initiate who, in turn, teaches his pupil how to "hear" the Word with his heart rather than his intellect. He does this by observing and listening to the nature of the world around him, the macrocosm, and his own inner nature, the microcosm.

Natural Laws

The teachings of Pythagorus reveal that within all ancient myths lie two fundamental laws: the law of the triad and the law of the octave. The triad or Law of Three comes into play as a *neutralizing unity* between an active force and an inactive medium (a match, when ignited in a darkened room, will reactively reflect from the inactive objects thereby revealing their form and location). With Unity, One instantly equals three. The sages throughout history have never taught otherwise. The activity between One–Unity, and Two–Duality, produces a third reactive state *between* them. This sacred trinity has produced and formed all of nature with its epitome being man. The Law of Three implies the act of creation.

The *Law of Three* is fundamental. From the very beginning of mankind, the Trinity underlines all aspects of creation. Basically, there are three principles which represent the creative force in all aspects and diversity of phenomena. All of existence, from the molecular to the cosmic, is the result of the combination of these three principles.

The contemporary view, that we live within a dualistic world, falls short of the Law of Three. The ancients saw that One could exist as a singularity, containing all things within it. But the moment *two* is placed beside one, the result is automatically three, as shown in the tectractys (∴). One dot when coupled with two instantly becomes three. The result is a *relationship between* two opposing forces: active against passive, which is a reactive neutralization of the two immutable forces resulting in the immaterial becoming form.

The resultant third force is this process of *transition*, the moment in time of *"becoming"* that is so sacred–the process of living from one moment to the next! Consider a sculptor and a piece marble, as separate entities, he and the stone are only what they are. When the sculptor adds inspiration and begins to work on the block of marble, it is at that moment that his activity becomes the third force: sculptor + block of marble + inspiration (the very act of creation) the result of which becomes the work of art.

The teaching of three forces was rudimentary to all ancient systems. The pyramid in ancient cultures replicates this very thought. The very tip of the pyramid can only represent the infinitesimal in non-dimensional form while the base of the pyramid represents the opposite–physical volume in dimensional form. With this line of thinking the absence of the capstone on pyramids would make more sense: separately they are "the act of intention" and "result of the intended." The distance *between* the point of the pyramid and its base describes the size of the structure. The first force (or potential) is the top of the pyramid and is recognized as active or positive; the second force (or potential) is the bottom of the pyramid and recognized as passive, negative or reflective. When combined with the third potential, distance, we see both top and bottom *neutralized* into its definitive shape (the entire form of a three dimensional pyramid). All three aspects (point, plane and distance) interact simultaneously while their juxtaposition is the place in which they exist physically as volume. Thrust into a three dimensional world, the topmost point can only remain a point while the base plane can extend into a square flat surface or field. Similarly, the tetrahedron has *three* sloping faces on a *triangular* base, and is associated with fire or light representing the first emanation of creation.

The second fundamental expression in nature is known as the octave or *Law of Seven* corresponding to the octave in music. The Law of Seven is the *genesis* or continuing process of the Law of Three. The Law of Seven simply stated is: No *process* in the physical world continues without modification or interruption. This modification or interruption can be at any level but is usually seen in the third and/or seventh level.

An object or vibration passing through any medium such as air or water meets with resistance which tends to slow the object or vibration down. Some source of power must be continually exerted to overcome the resistance of these mediums. When the source of power is expended, our object will slow down and eventually stop. The same principle works from boiling water to celestial mechanics, and if we look for it, we can see this principle in every aspect of life.

A bell, for example, cannot be heard until the active clapper strikes the inactive side resulting in the creation of its sound. This first act replicates the very act of creation. The law of three in this case is (1) the clapper (2) bell and (3) the act of striking (the side of the Bell with the clapper). The reactive result is the sound and its vibration pattern is only heard through some medium, in our case, air.

To have initially produced this sound an effort had to be made. If we strike the bell only once, the sound will eventually decay into silence. However, as long as we repeatedly strike the side of the bell with the clapper, the sound overpowers the passive medium (air) and we hear its continuous ring. As soon as the continuous effort to ring the bell has ceased, the passive medium overpowers the active vibration. It is *at that point* the vibration starts to decay. As we listen, its sound becomes fainter and fainter until there is no sound at all. Inertia rules the whole of physical nature and in the absence of a new impulse, energy decays and goes the way of least resistance or entropy. These laws are expressed by the symbolic striking of large cymbals or gongs in Buddhist temples.

The Law of Seven not only describes the genesis or *process* of events, it also describes how these events lose their force or change direction. When we divide one by seven, the result is 0.142857. The first two doublets to this sequence are 14, then 28. The number 28 exactly doubles the former number of 14. The third doublet is the oddity. Instead of doubling 28 for 56 we find 57, doubling the former number but with a remainder of "one," depicting a new form of *seed*. With this remainder or "universal seed," nature is able to repeat the process thus insuring future universal growth. This resultant "universal seed" is the reason why there are no straight lines in nature. Notice that it is the *third* doublet that is different.

These two laws also operate within the parameters of the seven planets. In this model, we pair the planets according to their opposite natures. The triad of the emotional axis of (1) the Moon's fearful reaction to (2) Saturn's authority (3) follows guidelines. Thus, we continue: (1) Mars, as action, for (2) Venus' appeasement (3) becomes satisfied; Mercury's (1) need to understand (2) Jupiter's expansive nature (3) is perception. In reverse order, (1) Jupiter's need to (2) express its wisdom (3) through Mercury's understanding; Venus' (1) languid nature in (2) need for sensation and (3) activity through Mars; Saturn's (1) expression of self-control is (2) to overcome the (3) the fear of the Moon's emotions. The balance of each extreme becomes the solution when we shed light on the matter represented by the Sun. Who has not heard the phrase "to see the light?"

Below are three triads based on the nature of the planets with the Sun displayed as the fulcrum point. Any excess influence from any one planet imediately disturbs the balance. Thus, when we see an excess influence in a person's chart, it reflects the same disturbance in his make-up or life-style.

Sun

Fear - Moon <– LAW –> Saturn - Authority
Aggression - Mars <– HARMONY–> Venus - Protection
Curiosity - Mercury <– PERCEPTION –> Jupiter - Wisdom

Embodied within the Law of Seven is the octave of the musical scale. By association with the Western musical scale, the Law of Seven is readily seen as it relates to the seven whole-tones through its 13 *half-step intervals,* the eighth tone being the repetitive point of the first. In this fashion the Law of Seven formulates recognizable harmony called a scale.

Below, we start with "A" and note the thirteen half steps, in succession. By applying the diatonic formula of two full steps and then a half step followed by three full steps followed again by the last half step, we have the basis for the Western major diatonic scale beginning with the note of "A." Notice that there are no sharps between the notes "B" and "C" or "E" and "F." They are half-step anomalies that are their own half-tone indicators. This plays an important role to the Western musical ear.

When the formula is complete we find: Do-1- (A); re-2- (B); mi- 3- (C#); fa-4- (D); sol-5- (E); la-6-(F#); ti-7- (G#) and finally Do-1/8 is its octave (A) the point of repetition. By lowering the *third* note one-half step, the major scale becomes the minor scale. When adding the *minor* seventh note (lowering 1/2 step) to the dominant chord, the ear expects to hear its resolution to the tonic or first chord in the registered key (adding G natural instead of G# to the chord E). The law of the triad comes into play when we simultaneously play the first, third and fifth tones or A with C# and E: three notes out of the scale to create the sound of an harmonious chordal tone.

The musical scale as the Law of Seven formula follows:

A			
A#			
B	one step	A to B	A
C			
C#	one step	B to C#	B
D	**half**-step	C# to D	C#
D#			
E	one step	D to E	D
F			E
F#	one step	E to F#	F#
G			
G#	one step	F# to G#	G#
A	**half**-step	G# to A	A

We can start this formula at any point in the thirteen-tone scale and the result will describe any key with the necessary sharps (#) to indicate its "key." However, the formula also plays an important role in the formulation of the foundation to life itself. The Law of Seven not only applies to the musical scale but can also be found in relation to the atomic scale used by scientists.

The Law of Seven can be seen in all of nature as a process. Metaphorically speaking, the third and seventh step are only half-steps and may be interpreted as having half the "energy" of the other tones. This idea works well with the angles in an astrological chart.

The Laws in Astrology

The aforementioned laws are expressed in the *mystical* astrological wheel as well. The wheel represents the Law of Seven from the ninth *house* to the fourth *house cusp*. The seventh house angle is reflected as the half step, as is the angle of the fourth house. In the astrological model a half step indicates needed energy or *assistance*. This is repeated and *reflected* from the third to the tenth house cusp on the opposite side of the wheel with both the Ascendant and the Meridian as a half steps. The seventh and first houses, along with the Meridian and Nadir, are representative of the principle of the acceleration and decay intervals.

The ninth house is the initial vibratory configuration that starts the whole process. The ninth house is the note "A;" the ninth-house *cusp* is "A#;" the eighth house is "B;" the eighth house cusp "C;" the seventh house is "C#;" the seventh house cusp is "D;" the sixth house is "D#;" the sixth house cusp is "E;" the fifth house is "F;" the fifth house cusp is "F#;" the fourth house is "G;" and the fourth house cusp is "G#." Starting with "A" for the third house we mirror the scale to the tenth house cusp.

The Law of Three is represented by joining together the eastern and western halves to create the entire astrological wheel as a whole. Had the Egyptians developed a horoscopic wheel, the above description would have probably been its symbolic representation.

The ancient astrologers honored the Law of Seven with the association of the seven *visible* planets in the solar system. Counting the planets starting from Mercury, Earth is the third planet from the Sun with Saturn the seventh. The positions of Earth and Saturn represent the interval half steps. Earth with its life and Saturn with its rings make them the most distinctive planets in the solar system. Should we incorporate the trans-saturnian planets of Uranus, Neptune and Pluto we find that the Earth is the *third* planet from the Sun and the *seventh* planet from Pluto.

The philosophy of the Law of Seven, with its weak half-steps of acceleration or decay, can be applied to working with projects as well. Remember, each major angle in the chart represents these decay or acceleration points. The seventh house angle symbolizes additional energy as assistance from others. The tenth house angle symbolizes additional energy and impetus that comes from receiving awards or rewards. The first house symbolizes self motivation and the will to achieve. The fourth house symbolizes a gray area where we lack understanding and where we need to seek guidance or clarification as its cusp represents the weakened or confused area in our charts.

Once a project has begun, the individual will take it as far as his knowledge and skill will allow. At this point the individual may find himself in a position where he can no longer proceed and seeks further assistance. Different resources must be acquired to continue the work depending on the stage of the project. The decay or acceleration point where the project either stops or continues is denoted by a square position to the initial starting point. If new resources are unavailable, the project will eventually peter out and stop. On the other hand, if new resources are acquired at the desired level represented by the angle of decay, the project will continue, like picking up a seed lying on the sidewalk and placing it in soil.

The Ages of Man

It is interesting to note how the positions of the planets and houses correspond to our life issues. More interesting is the Egyptian division of the wheel and the underlying influence of each segment. Using the pentade format (five degrees equals one year), each 30° segment corresponds to six years of life. With this we can easily recognize the periodic development throughout our lifetime (page 73). As we incarnate, our inner light represented by the Sun descends into the darkness of the sixth house. Mars represents the first six years as a toddler and is generally descriptive of the first years of discovery on the planet. Next we encounter Saturn who slowly teaches us the responsibilities of life between the ages of seven and eighteen.

By eighteen or the fourth house cusp, society teaches us new forms of direction and we experience our first real love during the lunar stage represented by the

Moon. By the age of thirty-six (Ascendant), Mercury helps us develop the idea of self-recognition. At this time full realization of our potential flourishes as we decide to state our views and aim our individual efforts toward a goal. By the age of forty-two (12th house), we expand our ideas and contacts throughout the world. It is during this time that our broadest views of service to mankind become important as well as developing more spiritual values.

The age of fifty-four brings us to the tenth house. It has great promise as we reach a culmination with our own standards of life. The Egyptians equated this period with taking a bride, both figuratively and metaphorically. By now the individual is in full realization of his/her life. Perhaps the idea of one more great and final achievement can be fulfilled. Relative to actual time of day (the interval of twelve to two o'clock in the afternoon), the Sun is in its hottest period equating to age fifty-eight to sixty-six years. These are the golden years when we can look back at our moments of glory or the disappointment of unfulfilled promises. As the Sun's light diminishes on the horizon, so too does our own light as we prepare for our own sunset.

Early Views

For nearly 3000 years the Egyptians flourished and developed their own science, art and architecture without any outside influence. But one of the most remarkable features about this culture is, aside from calendrical achievement, is its apparent lack of interest in celestial phenomena related to astrology. All other cultures had some form of superstition or belief system that somehow related their lifestyle to the stars and planets. What the Egyptians did do, however, was develop their own unique form of prediction based on yearly, monthly, daily and hourly periods. With a little stretch of the imagination this form of "fortune telling" can be seen in an astrological light (see 50–Egyptian Cosmos).

If we read "between the lines," the following chapters on Chaldean Astrology and Egyptian Cosmology set the course for us to grasp the philosophy that is behind the basis of this book. As we will see by these chapters, numbers have always been the basic organizing principle that gave structure to the universe. The ancients considered numbers as proof of the gods' intercourse with the universe and the secret behind its construction.

The Law of Three becomes the concept behind the tri-planet configurations in the 30° wheel. It was this third force that mostly intrigued ancient thinkers. They realized that the neutralizing effect of the first two laws cannot be directly observed except at the point of application. An artist and a canvas do not create a picture until the artist *applies his inspiration* to that canvas. Similarly, a mathematician and a set of numbers do not produce results until the mathematician manipulates the numbers by addition, subtraction, etc., to form his answer.

The *Rule of Three* has long been held in astrological esteem and generally believed to mean either sign triplicity or three different planetary *configurations* to support the proposal of an event. In light of the above, it is conceivable that ancient astrologers were not only interested in the positive or negative aspect of the planets, but their manifestations as well, i.e., what did the planetary configurations produce and in what medium? How else could they have surmised an omen? The tri-planet configurations or planetary pictures clearly demonstrate this line of thought.

Each planet has two planetary companions, one above and one below. The middle planet is modified by the other two and becomes the medium of their combined expression. Meditate and reflect on this concept for each planet sandwiched between the two other planets in the stack. Allow for dimensional vitality, definition and structure. The other Rule of Three aspect is the birth chart in relation to the sunset chart. The two charts create a response pattern innately inherent to the individual thereby revealing his nature and purpose.

The Law of Seven is shown by the process by which we rotate the chart to determine the evolution of events. As each rogressed planet passes over the sunset planets that are "fixed in position" in the sunset chart, we see the planets-as-experience process of growth as well. As any rogressed planet passes over a fixed-in-place sunset planet, the fixed-in-place planet absorbs the rogressed planet's nature *as experience*. For example, should the rogressed Sun be the first planet to aspect sunset Venus, this first experience develops the native's basic love interest and social aims, the native's style and grace is outlined by the Sun's nature. The types of people the native will be attracted to are seen in a positive light and will tend to be extravagant, fun-loving social types who are interested in being in the limelight through the arts. As each additional planet aspects Venus, the native becomes more complex because each new aspect is *added* to the basic nature of Venus.. Thus, we see the experiential and psychological growth of the native in relationship to his Venus.

CHAPTER 13

CHALDEAN ASTROLOGY

Where It All Began

1.   On any clear night, look up at the sky. The first star which attracts your eye is probably one of the brightest. Over many centuries the dark skies with their brilliant stars have sparked the imagination of mankind. Poets mused over the wondrous points of light against the velvet blackness and philosophers expounded on their familiar and easily recognizable patterns.

During the early neolithic stages of man, however, such patterns were probably not more than luminous spots in the night skies. One important item was surely recognized–daylight was associated with the Sun and nightime was associated with the Moon. The changes from being a nomadic food collector to a settled food producer marks the significant stage of social changes for mankind. This important period is called the neolithic and ends about the time men discovered the use of metal. One of many changes was the need for a calendar, a way by which they could determine important schedules in their life other than periods of daylight and nightime. While learning to rely on the seasons and star patterns, the development of agriculture by the once nomadic tribes was probably a hit-and-miss affair at first.

The Sun was difficult to observe directly and so the Moon was looked upon as the basis for timing important events and for establishing agricultural practices. But the lunar calendar presented a large problem. Agriculture depends on planting crops in the early spring months. The Moon's cycle of 29 1/2 days is only 354 days, 11 days short of the solar year of 365.25 days. By following the Moon, within a few years time planting and harvesting would fall behind schedule because, eventually it would still be in the middle of winter when the lunar calendar declared it was spring.

For this reason the people of Mesopotamia needed a more sophisticated calendar to suit their ever-growing need to forecast these vital agricultural events. The early Mesopotamians eventually accomplished their goal by observing the many different constellations and associating their perennial rising and setting with seasonal changes.

Discovering seasonal alignments with fixed stars marked a turning point in post-neolithic communities. It gave them a sense of religious evidence that the Earth and heaven were complementary. This is the probable basis for their cosmological-religious beliefs.

The usefulness of the fixed star markers must have been discovered early as they are mentioned in the fifth tablet of the creation myth the *Enuma elish*. It states that the Babylonian god, Marduk, determined the seasonal boundaries and defined the divisions by setting up three constellations for each month for the twelve month year. The sets of three constellations were set up into four groupings. The four cardinal points came about by using the summer solstice as a mooring peg. Once established, the Babylonians followed the Sun along the ecliptic, referred to as *the Way of Anu*. The year was divided into approximate 90-day periods, depending on the length of the Moon's lunations. These are recorded on tablets known as "astrolabes", the earliest of these tablets dating around B.C. 1100. Astrology had not yet found its way into the culture, but recognition of star patterns was certainly a way of life.

2   Over the last 150 years or so, various wedge-like cuneiform records and texts have been discovered and have given us a glimpse of ancient knowledge and imagination. The small clay packages of cuneiform tablets are about the size of a hand and were found in the sites of ancient Babylon and Urek.

These tablets reveal that over 5,000 years ago in Mesopotamia, the area known today as southern Iraq, an astounding phenomenon occurred. In lower Mesopotamia, there emerged a powerful, advanced civilization, a highly complex and sophisticated culture with a powerful army, formal religion, animal husbandry, hunting, fishing and a sustained agricultural system. These peoples established themselves along the Tigris-Euphrates Rivers and its tributaries with various small city-like compounds called "tells." These settlements were collectively known as Sumer. What makes this event so remarkable is that it was not a slow or gradual development. It happened rather suddenly.

3.   Among the many and diverse creations of Sumer was one especially remarkable feat. A form of writing called cuneiform was developed and, it seems, with a great deal of enthusiasm. To date, over a quarter of a million tablets have been found, impressive for a people with only about a .04 per cent literacy factor. Cuneiform writing involved the use of a stylus shaped in the form of a wedge and pressed into soft clay and formed monosyllabic words. These tablets later translated as praise of their folk heroes, religious canons, temple ceremonies, omens, ephemerides for astronomy and refined social accomplishments; none of which spoke of astrology. Yet, their tablets describe a tremendous interest in gods relating to the heavens and planets. Many archeologists and Assyriologists agree that very few tablets concerning early Sumerian chronology give us any *direct* information about ongoing celestial observations.

4   Regardless of the lack of direct celestial information, Sumerian texts reveal that the heavenly vault was an important part of their civilization. One such Sumerian text, known as the *Enuma Elish* or *Epic of Creation,* is written on seven clay tablets and outlines their idea regarding the creation of the solar system.

5.   Another amazing tool Sumer developed was mathematics to record daily mundane affairs such as

accounting, cattle, grain inventories and other business transactions. The Sumerian use of mathematics also extended to celestial observations that outlined a yearly calendar for their New Year's festivals, religious holidays, planting, harvesting and other important annual events. The Sumerian ephemeris of the Sun, Moon and other celestial motion shows amazing methodology in their mathematical abilities. A full discourse on the many multi-level mathematical tablets is not within the scope of this discourse. However, a sample on the various Sumerian concepts and elements of space and time may serve to shed some light on the thousands of tablets recovered.

The Sumerians used both the sexagesimal and decimal as an interactive mathematical system and many tablets refer to extended multiples of cycles based on 6 and 10. One such numbering system enumerates the years as $6 \times 10 = 60 \times 6 = 360 \times 10 = 3,600$ total years, called a *sar* (the root for the term saros cycle). The number 3,600 had great significance to the Sumerians; it was referred to as the *lord* and was the basis of many mathematical tables. It was also the basis for, or connection with, divine order. It is interesting to note that the span of 3,600-year cycles relates to man's cultural peaks in history. These large numerical tables and listings were prolific throughout Sumeria and have influenced many cultures down through the ages.

Another example which merits comment is the number 432,000. From the beginning of Sumer the widespread belief in the number of 432,000 Earth years is an underlying thread throughout many ancient religions. It is said to be of great importance as a divine cycle. According to Sumerian texts, the number 432,000 was a result of $3,600 \times 120$ years, the number of years of the great flood. (The number 120 is presumably used because Sumerian texts indicate this number to be the age of man in reference to God as well as Biblical references [Genesis, chapter 6 verse 3]). Geologists' studies show sea level changes and deep sea climatic records show a 430,000-year quasi-periodic cyclicity. We find this number in the Norse tales and in the Hindu *mahayugas* (ages). It is also the basis of the total number of syllables in the verses found in the sacred Sanskrit book, *Rigveda*.

Some incredible tablets describe mathematical tables of division that begin with the number 12,960,000 and end with the number 60. These extraordinary tables were developed in Sumer as early as B.C. 3200 and matched celestial order so concisely that it baffles many modern researchers. Most perplexing is the fact that the Sumerians did all this without the use of "scientific" data or without the ability to recognize definition from generalization. What is gathered from their texts is that they were unable to understand or distinguish the law of cause and effect even though there are numerable examples of its operation. Ancient men of letters accepted current logical notions and practices without worrying about their origin or developement. Theirs was a kind of existential experience to life without much thought of the proofs and arguments directed to the intellect. Much of what has been learned from the cuneiform texts has had to be extracted from Sumerian myths and poems which lacked any systematic approach in regard to their treatises.

When we review the clever, creative abilities and vast knowledge the Sumerians possessed, a great mystery looms. The absence of texts about astrology or any other form of omina in such a star-religious culture, as shown in their planetary and celestial ephemerides, is startling. Was their understanding "of the heart?"

6.   In general, the people of Sumer and its rulers maintained peace through a powerful army, but over a period of time the civilized Sumerians became sedentary. The many captive slaves, along with mercenaries in the Mesopotamian army, eventually learned the military techniques of their conquerors. Sumer's rulers and kings never recognized their vulnerable position until it was too late.

The more ambitious captives, who became well versed in the techniques of Mesopotamian warfare, in all likelihood escaped and joined with marauding nomadic tribes and amassed large armies. These culturally immature tribes, led by unstable rulers of preditory dispositions, admired Sumer's abilities but no longer feared their knowledge and power. With jealous and envious eyes they beheld Sumer as the final jewel in their war crown. The marauding armies poured through the buffer territories and invaded lower Mesopotamia. With Sumer isolated and without allies to help them, the barbaric armies attacked the Sumerian cities with impunity.

7.   By B.C. 2331 the Semitic chieftain, Sargon, had completely conquered the entire region of Sumer. What was once a civilized and peaceful community became little more than a dusty regional center. Their writings, originally full of praise about its leaders' social order, architecture and the arts, were replaced by boastful tales of the conquering Semitic tribes. The newly appointed scribes wrote of glorious wars and praise for the conquering hero-kings. The death toll through raids of plunder and destruction was the sole character trait the king displayed in his quest for the ascension to power; he could kill better than any other chieftain. Conversely, once in power, Sargon became lazy and "citified" and eventually ruled the entire area of Babylon with his subjects' interest at heart.

7-b   Sargon, who began the first dynasty of Akkad, also marked the beginning of the end of Sumer. In the beginning of Sargon's rule, many elite Sumerians undoubtedly fled to India and China in the east, Europe in the north, and Africa to the southwest. As the Sumerians migrated into new territories, they taught their grantors of refuge writing, mathematics and religious ideas through their myths and stories.

But the conquerors themselves were not all that secure in their new environment. They, too, were besieged by nomadic tribes, and through all the skirmishes, wars and changes of kings throughout the following centuries very little information about the earlier civilization of Sumer survived.

As for astronomy, the Akkadians listed only the brightest 36 stars in their heaven as "counting stars" now more accepted as *normal stars*. These normal stars were called the *chiefs* of their respective *assigned positions*. The Sun was known as the son of the Moon. The Moon and Venus were assigned to male gender. Later, the planets were named after mythological deities or personifications of the rivers, storms and other natural forces or occurrences. Marduk (Jupiter) became the chief god of each city, replacing the earlier Sumerian gods, thereby further discounting the celestial heritage left by Sumer.

Above all, the Moon, with its observable and regular periodicity, remained the basis for the proto-calendar. The Moon reigned as the supreme influence and designated the assigned times for crop planting, harvesting, festivals, and religious ceremonies of everyday life. However, its effectiveness, like the nature of the Moon, waned because the lunar year kept slipping back and falling out of synch with the actual occurrence of spring; all holidays kept slipping back at the rate of about one month every three years.

With the lunar cycle of just under 30 days, the priests/scribes overcame this slippage problem with the idea of calendar intercalation or the act of inserting an extra lunar month to correspond with the solar year of 365.25 days. The result was either a 12 or 13 month year depending upon either the precise day and moment of the summer solstice or by crop evaluation. With this new calendar in place, agriculture became somewhat stable and ensured the Babylonians bountiful winters. They felt that they had finally succeeded in creating the perfect calendar. The periodicity of Venus, always an observable phenomena, did not contribute much to their calendar but was watched and occasionally noted.

8.   Another form of calendar "slippage" is caused by the precession of the equinox. The precession can be easily

recognized by selecting a prominent star in a constellation as it rises from the horizon. This is called its heliacal rising. Remember the shape of the constellation and the star's position. Each year, about the same time on the same day, the chosen star and constellation will appear on the horizon almost at the same place but gradually the star will appear a little later on the horizon. At first it will not be noticeable but *in 72 years our chosen star will arrive a whole day* later. In 360 years our chosen star will arrive about five days later. In Babylon, this concept eventually became known as *5 times 72*. It was the fundamental link between heaven and the solar calendar.

9   In the centuries that followed, Babylon gradually formed its vast empire and its observation of the heavenly vault never wavered. The idea of astrology as we know it did not yet exist. There are suggestions that astrology was not necessary because many of the kings could hear their gods speaking to them directly. Some of the best known archeologists in their field suggest that these gods, with whom the kings spoke, may have been living beings possibly known as the Nibiru, the unexplained angels noted in the Old Testament. Rival provincial kings, eager to please these gods as well as fulfill the need for expansion, engaged in many destructive wars between the Semitic tribes throughout Mesopotamia.

10   However, there may be another possibility. A leading psychologist from Princeton University suggested that the early inhabitants of the world had emerged with a bi-cameral mind. That is, the brain's dual cerebral hemispheres could interact independently and speak with each other. With this ability, the early elite could hear voices inside their heads and they would talk to themselves as two individuals, in a form of schizophrenia. He cites his evidence through epic writings such as the *Iliad* and *Odyssey*. Each narrative in both texts is curiously devoid of any reference to subjective consciousness. Supporting evidence of the bi-cameral mind is also found in earlier forms of biblical text also lacking in subjective thought.

In the Old Testament, oracles known as the Nabiim or Khabiru would be "speaking the voices they hear within themselves but believe to come from outside them." This theory suggests that, apparently, in the early stages of mankind's development, the hemispheric differences in cognitive function would echo different voices heard as God and man. Indeed, there are many references describing religious leaders hearing such heavenly commands throughout contemporary Bibles as well. Early cuneiform texts and later writings that form the basis of the Bible state that the king and his followers actually heard the voices of their gods speaking to them. Pictorial versions that support both theories and which can be seen in temples throughout the world. All of these pictorial versions have sculptures and/or reliefs depicting the king in direct eye-to-eye contact either in conversation with or embracing his steward-god.

11   This practice however, seems to have come to an abrupt end by B.C. 1230. Tukulti-Ninurta I, the tyrant of Assyria, became ruler and conqueror of Mesopotamia and built in the city of Ashur a stone altar that completely differed from every other altar in the known world. Until then, every city built its stone effigy with the ruler or king standing side by side or face to face in the posture of directly communicating with the god of that city. Tukulti had the stone altar built with Tukulti himself kneeling before an empty throne! The kings and rulers *before* Tukulti *could hallucinate and hear their gods directing them* and they followed those directions unfailingly.

By building the altar in such a way, Tukulti suggested that, while earlier kings hallucinated contact with their gods, he could not. A king without contact or direction by his god was impotent and ineffectual. In the years that followed, central and local governmental control began to erode. The kings and their subjects started looking elsewhere for some kind of guidance to establish ground rules for their decisions. Clay tablets indicate that prayer *by supplication* and petition was unheard of before the second millennia B.C.!

With hallucinated guidance lost, decisions made by those in power became mere guesswork rather than the proposed previous guidance. The kings needed something or someone to guide and direct them as surely as before. In their desperation they searched for seers who claimed that they continued to converse with the gods of yore. Divination began to replace the function of hallucinated guidance. Omens, as they were known, considered everything under the Sun: wind direction, rain, abundance of crops and cattle, fog, mist and even the coloration of clouds at sunset. Most omens were associated with natural mundane events along with meteorological and celestial phenomena. Omens upheld ancestorial beliefs that heaven and Earth were complimentary without one having more influence over the other. Crop failures, pestilence, wars or even the death of a nobleman were thought to depend upon natural events, the Moon and planetary synodic cycles. Records of daily lunar activity and periodic solar eclipses were developed and kept for each and every day of the year along with each omen that accompanied the event. Through their empiricism the Chaldeans developed theories that the same phenomena would recur in cycles.

O. Neugebauer in *The Exact Sciences in Antiquity* writes:

"It is difficult to say when and how the celestial omens developed. The existing texts are part of large series of texts, the most important one called *Enu Anu Enlil* from its initial sentence, similar to papal bullae in the Middle Ages. This series contained at least 70 numbered tablets with a total of 7000 omens. The canonization of this enormous mass of omens must have extended over several centuries and reached its final form perhaps around 1000 BCE."

11.-a   Today there are more than 80 forms of divination but only four distinctive categories: omens, augury, sortilege and spontaneous divination.

Omens are viewed as an expected sequence of events that might recur—much like the training of animals who learn to respond by reinforcement of natural habits. If A occurs and B follows, then B will be anticipated anytime A happens again. For example, an ancient observer on night watch wrote, "The Moon rises with the horn (pointing) to the West, heavy rains." This omen suggests they expected rain every time the Moon rose in such a manner. This form of omen became increasingly popular, as early clay tablets depict.

11-b **Augury** goes back a long time. The Bible speaks of it often as extispicy or animal sacrifice followed by examining its entrails for divine signs and indications. The earliest mention of augury by pouring oil on water is found in cuneiform texts. Placing a small bowl of water in his lap, the diviner would pour a little oil on top and watch its course. Each movement meant different signs known only to the diviner. Another popular form of augury was to drip hot wax into cold water; divine answers came from the different shapes.

11-c **Sortilege** is the casting of lots such as dice, bones, yarrow sticks or stones. The fallen arrays of the cast objects were to "talk" to those who could understand.

11-d **Spontaneous divination** works well with the notion of astrology because of its nature. Both the idea and method are relatively easy. Imagine an individual with a problem who needs a viable solution. The puzzled individual will explain the situation to the diviner who looks about for a natural sign. The sign can be almost anything visible to the naked eye—a dog chasing a cat, a halo around the Moon or a rising planet. Thus, the diviner would interpret the visual phenomena as an omen or sign. The petitioner, now directed by the omen and instructed to meditate upon its relationship, would reach a solution. There would be no correlation of a time-frame between omen, event and solution. In this fashion, events related to the omen at the diviner's discretion.

It is notable that divination and omens were a matter of synchronistic signs and not considered as causes. At the time, the ancient scholars did not attach any philosophical or religious causative influences to such omens.

Astronomy with omens probably developed because various forms of divination required special tools and a great deal of preparation. The procedure and clean-up process of augury were difficult to perform in a ceremonious manner suitable to the position of the diviner. One just did not casually wipe the blood off of oneself or indulge in a wrestling match with a reluctant sacrificee without despoiling the diviner's dignified position. The advent of omens with astronomy probably came with a sigh of relief. Star divination provided the prestige much more appropriate to the office or title of Priestly Diviner.

The earliest astronomical influences are written by the Babylonians on cuneiform tablets that date from a very early period. These texts are known as the *"Enuma Anu Enlil."* However, it seems that direct omens relating to astronomical observations date about B.C. 786, these texts were called *"mul apin."* These crude texts refer to monthly planetary observations based only on visibility and invisibility of the planets. Initially, star gazing techniques in all ancient cultures were instrumental for timing calendar and other mundane events associated with the star patterns and planetary motion against the background constellations. The word "astrology" or "horoscope" or the "zodiac" per se are not mentioned in any earlier cultures especially that of Babylonia or Egypt. However, some later texts are definately the expression of astrological interpretation while other texts can be construed as vague and insinuating divinatiory events caused by the stars as gods. Therefore, much has to be adduced or deduced in compiling views of each culture's cosmology.

12. The previously adopted lunar phases with 30-day "counting star" patterns along the ecliptic were well in place and by B.C. 1600 the prototype of astrology began.

Observations of Venus were commonplace as an evening or morning star, and in the same century King Ammi-Saduqa ordered the appearances and disappearances of Venus to be stringently recorded. The Babylonians gave not only the Moon and brightest stars prominence but now included the planets of Venus, Jupiter, Mercury, Saturn and Mars. However, these observations were deficient to later astronomers as these observations were at best very poor. Much of this difficult observation served no real purpose until such observations were later used for the determination of empirical material for Babylonian omina. Several hundred years later, Claudius Ptolemy would comment on the *lack of reliable Babylonian planetary data* because, and unfortunately for the Greek scholars, Babylonian observations turned out to be primarily concerned with only synodic cycles and periods of appearances and disappearances.

Even today, direct translation of Babylonian horoscopes are of no real astrological importance as the information has very little to do with astrology as we know and understand it. For the most part there is more to be learned from the overall astronomical diaries than the too few resources found to date on astrology per se.

13 What the ancients needed to conduct their "pure science" of celestial sightings was a clear view of the horizon as the essential primary point of observation. The Greeks ascribe that the origins (B.C. 1600) of astronomy from Babylonia were due to the level nature of the land and its clarity of atmosphere. Clear visibility was the chief requirement for sighting the first initial phase of the new Moon as early as possible after sunset on the western horizon. This was also true of the last sight of the old Moon. However, when this was not possible due to clouds or dust storms, the Babylonians relied on their ephemerides and "calculated" these events. Modern day science can be thankful for clouds because poor visability was the major reason the science of mathematical tables was born.

Other important observable phenomena were the various timing sequences between the rising Sun to the setting Moon or the setting Moon to the rising Sun, the planetary stations and their synodic periods, the position of the stars, and the opposition of two planets simultaneously rising and setting. Every celestial periodicity was timed, noted and later assigned a name for reference. As the king needed omens as guidance, these observations were of paramount importance. Thus, each and every appearance and disappearance in the sky was noted when possible.

13-a   Still, many of the early cuneiform omina state that the horizon was often obscured by dust storms, clouds or rain. To insure better visibility the Babylonians decided to overcome the obstacle of low-level observation by building large stone temples known as ziggurats. These incredible structures served as both temples of the gods and celestial observatories. Colors were associated with the planets and the seven-story ziggurats were color keyed to represent the seven planets. The bottom tier was colored black to represent Saturn. The next tier was brownish-red for Jupiter, rose-red for the Martian tier, gold for the Sun, white-gold for Venus, dark blue for Mercury and, on the top tier, silver for the Moon. There were many such structures built for observational purposes throughout Mesopotamia.

13.   The Moon known as Sin, the Lord of Wisdom, was depicted as the numeral **30** ⟨⟨⟨ (30th day) to coincide with the number of approximate days in the lunar calendar. Each new lunar month began with the first visible sighting of the lunar crescent after the new Moon. Regardless of which day the new crescent fell, the first day of the new month was called the day of the Moon, much like our Monday (Moon-day). If the lunation came on a short month of less than 30 days, the other days throughout the year were simply discarded — adding to the problems of their calendar as mentioned above.

The Moon remained supreme and was considered the father of time. The number six has always been associated with time as noted in the Babylonian sexagesimal system. The Moon was also associated with the number six because the lunar progression during the month can be divided into four six-day periods when describing the number of "working days by law" in the week. The Babylonians held the day after each six-day interval was as sacred as the quadrature of the Moon which happened every 7, 14, 21, and 28 "correct" days. Later, two additional days were added, the 19th and 29th.

The idea that 19 was an ill-omened day becomes curious because 19 was considered the holiest of holy by many cultures. The number 19 is replete with celestial phenomena and cycles. The symbolic relationship between 7 and 19 are considered hexagonal numbers because six six-sided hexagonal figures, forming a circular figure, *creates* one in the center, for a total of seven. Similarly, if we continue to surround the seven hexagonal figures with more tangential hexagons, the total is 19. The 19-hexagonal figure has a series of three hexagons to each side, the four three-sided figure represents the 12 zodiacal locations in the sky.

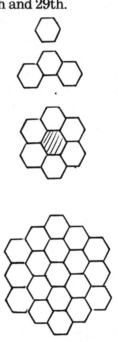

The first day of the new Moon and the fifteenth day of the full Moon were considered days of rest and festivity. However, every seventh day the Moon enters its next quarter and every seventh day was considered *ill-omened* and unlucky for the performance of any task or business and not for any Sabbath or festivity. During the reign of Hammurapi all work was forbidden on the 7th, 14th, 19th, 21st, 28th and 29th days of the month. The *29th day was considered the unluckiest day* of all. It was the day of darkness as the Babylonians eagerly awaited the arrival of the new Moon. It must be remembered that the

Babylonians seemed to live in the "now" as suggested by their writing style. Although not the case, they *seemed* to lack the understanding that the Moon would return. It's like the mentality of a baby when something is gone from sight. To the child, it is gone forever and when it returns it is totally new.

14.   About every six months a natural phenomena, with which we are all familiar, takes place in the sky. This phenomena is known as an eclipse and was keenly observed and recorded by the Babylonians. Each beginning eclipse was interpreted as *the Lord Who Opens the Gate into Heaven.* Once the gate was opened, the Moon god Sin was said to descend into the nether world to visit the realm of the dead. Before B.C. 2200 the year was only six 30-day periods long or approximately six months, dividing the solar year in half from eclipse to eclipse. The Moon god's resurrection from the dead manifested itself in the appearance of the next crescent and Sin, the *Lamp of Heaven and Earth,* began the New Year's festival. Here we can see how the Babylonian mind worked in accordance with naming the various activities and positions of the Moon with the Sun. This model was also used for the planets as they entered each new constellation.

15.   The earlier form of constellations held a natural frame of planetary reference and was divided into three broad bands. The name of these bands was known as (1) the Way of *Enlil,* Lord of Command, as North (an Earth sign or Earth-god); (2) *Anu,* He of the Heavens, the ecliptic (an air sign or air-god); and (3) *Ea,* He Whose House is Water, as South (a water sign or water-god).

These bands were called *kaskel, harranu* or "roads," "paths" or "ways" and were parallel with the equator. They were each 30° wide in latitude called *beru.* The northern sector **Enlil** began at 45° north latitude and descended to 15° north latitude. The central sector **Anu** began at 15° northern latitude and descended to 15° below the equator. The southern sector **Ea** began at 15° south latitude and extended to 45° south latitude.

16.   The constellations were called *the twelve times three*, the 12 lunar divisions consisting each of 30° *beru*, (zodiacal constellations) that made up the the solar year. There were three constellations Enlil, Anu and Ea each denoting the three "paths"–the Northern, central and Southern "road" respectively, in the Babylonian sky. The 12 lunar divisions in the central section *Anu* were where the lesser gods were said to be *standing in the path* (of the Moon) *whose sector Sin passes.* Each constellation "stayed in its assigned place" and was said to hold dominion within the framework of the 30 day period.

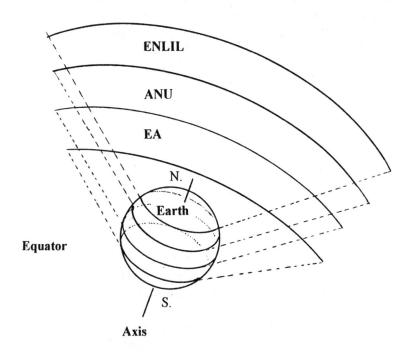

"The way of Anu to Enlil, back through the way Anu on its Southerly journey to Ea." The Sumerians and Babylonians projected the three bands of heaven onto the celestial sphere. These three divisions enabled the astronomers to place the planets in Enlil, the North latitude, Anu the ecliptic circle within the zodiac and the Southern latutude, Ea.

16   The Moon, Sun and five planets (Jupiter, Venus, Mercury, Mars and Saturn) were called interpreters. As they traveled through the different star patterns, the names of the planets were changed by their observers to designate their whereabouts in the zodiac. The form of the name "*interpreter*" was to be taken literally. Each planet was said to *interpret a message for mankind* in the framework of an omen from the chief god of each zodiacal sign. Comets were observed, noted, and were considered harbingers of coming events which needed cleansing or aversion rituals (*namburbi*). The concept of planets interpreting stars was indeed the first prototype for astrology but the terms zodiacal belt, zodiac sign Ascendant or astrology were not used.

17.   To reference the location of the Moon and planets, they were written as *sag* "approaching" for the East, *panu* (sometimes *igi sa*) "in front" for the West, *saqu* "above" for the North or *sutu* or *ar sa* "below" for the South of a normal star or constellation. Thus, it was said that the Moon traveled *in the way of Enlil* (the northern most sector), *below the constellation of the Pleiades* (in lieu of longitude) on its way to the Anu stars. In essence, and without actually doing so, the Babylonians were describing the Moon's longitude and latitude as it traveled toward the equator from north to south. The planet's movement by latitude included a much wider path, 10° to the northern latitude or above the ecliptic, and 7.5° to the south latitude as below the ecliptic.

18.   About B.C. 884, Ashurnasirpal II conquered the southernmost part of Mesopotamia and referred to the land as Kaldu or Chaldea. By this time the southern Babylonians or Chaldeans, as they became known, were well versed in omens and signs and had been for several centuries. Furthermore, Middle Eastern cultures of the then known world became interactive through war and trade routes. The Libyan dynasty, inaugurated by Sheshonq I, now ruled in Egypt. Many kings from distant empires started to look to Egypt as their next war prize.

The incredible form and beauty of Egyptian temples, as well as their intricate social organization, inspired and filled all visitors with awe. Egyptian art and knowledge were highly refined and were prized by the kings and nobles of many lands. Tales of Egyptian wonder and stories of strange powers reached Chaldea. Tempted, scholars began making pilgrimages to Egypt to learn the secrets of the mysterious Egyptians.

19   It is through selective observation, in accordance with their needs, that cultures develop their own idiosyncrasies. When two different cultures merge, each will acquire ideas and properties of the other. This meeting and mating of two different peoples mingled old ideas with new.   The Egyptian empirical methods were rooted principally in the observation of nature and the natural process of spirit becoming form through matter. The Chaldeans wholeheartedly embraced the idea that omens represented divine guidance.   The conflation between Chaldean omens and Egyptian teachings devolved over time, and as the centuries passed the Chaldeans became increasingly dependent upon the practice of divination for decision-making. Referred to in the Bible as the Magi, the Chaldeans developed a reputation as masters of the correspondences between heaven and Earth.

20.   By B.C. 747 King Nebonassar declared that a more rigorous, systematic form of observation was necessary. From this time on, the Babylonians kept better records of their astronomical observations of the Sun, Moon, planets and their interactions within their normal star system of 18 constellations, 12 of which related to the 30-day lunar phases. Undoubtedly based on earlier material, these observations were capsulated in two texts called the *Mul Apin* which contained the summary of knowledge of the elementary astronomical concepts of the time. The main basis of this was for the identification of the Babylonian constellations. The *Mul Apin* lists the simultaneous rising and setting of different stars, helical rising and dates of the

Anu, Enlil and Ea stars, their culminations and the stars and constellations in the Moon's path.

21.   Before B.C. 480 Babylonian intercalations of the lunar calendar lacked regularity although their diaries and tables indicate knowledge of synodic periods between the Sun and planets. There were times when scheduled eclipses did not occur. The reason for these inaccuracies lie, as previously mentioned, in the fact that the Chaldean 30-day civil calendar did not match the actual Sidereal lunar month or lunation of 29-1/2 days. Consequently, 12 lunar months amount to 354 days, 11 days less than the solar year, plus the fact that they just dropped days from their calendar when the new Moon arrived earlier than expected. Additionally, 33 days are missing at the end of three years making it necessary to add an extra month to align the lunar year to correspond with the beginning of the solar year. Tablets dated from B.C. 763 indicate the Chaldeans were well aware of both the overall 223-lunar month or Saros cycle of 70 eclipses, probably from early Sumerian tablets and the solar Metonic cycle of 19 years (235 months). The name "Metonic cycle" was not known as such by the Babylonians but was later acclaimed through its rediscovery by Meton of Athens as the Metonic cycle.

Until the solar-lunar intercalation rule, monthly intervals that made up the year were sporadic, sometimes using a 12-month period and at other times using 13 months to make up the year, which usually depended upon the condition of the harvest. Once the proper calendrical intercalations were in place, the Babylonians could predict the timing of eclipses within a few minutes. Over all, the rule consisted of 12 months containing a standard of 30 days each. This was equal to one year: seven intercalary years consisting of 13 months combined with 12 years of 12 months, completed the 19 solar year or the Metonic cycle. This was accomplished at some point around B.C. 500 and the zodiac was well known by now and used primarily as a computative embodiment for mathematical purposes, and as a almanac and ephemeris.

22.   As to the age of astronomy, it is said by Epigenes to date back as far as 720,000 years. On the other hand, Hipparchus dates the Sidereal science only 270,000 years. Why the incredible difference in time spans? This may be explained in two ways: first, by the odd use of the cuneiform style of numbering; second, the Greeks had access to the Babylonian cuneiform texts which refer to the large volume of numbers used in the early Sumerian texts. The Babylonian system of enumeration was sexagesimal, that is, *based on 60* (clock-time, 60 seconds = one minute, etc.). It used only two basic figures, a   wedge ⟩   for the number one and a chevron ⟨ for the number 10.   Different combinations were made for numbers up to fifty-nine; sixty began the system all over again with one large wedge mark.

For example, the number one, written with a small single wedge-like mark, meant simply one. However, a slightly larger single wedge mark meant 60 and an even larger single wedge mark meant 600. On the other hand, a single wedge mark *with a space* was also 60. Confusion began with the number 61, using ⟩⟩ which confusingly resembles the number two. Also 61 could be written with a slightly larger single wedge mark next to a small one, the spacing optional.

This system, like the Egyptian system, was merely additive. Unlike the Egyptians, however, the Babylonians developed the notion of place value, which is probably one of the single most profound developments next to the invention of the alphabet. The early development of the system did, however, have its problems. The concept of vacant or zero was not recognized as a number and the placement for zero was simply a space. The zero spacing was carefully placed so as to not confuse the numerical value. Still, it was not until the development of a symbol to represent zero did the Babylonians remove the ambiguity of such notations.

23.   Because the concept of zero or vacant was indicated by a blank space (or by B.C. 300, a small triangular mark), the number 61 was confused with several different

436

interpretations: from 61 or 361 or as much as 3,601 or just two. Whereas, the Greeks would write 140 degrees 17 minutes 20 seconds of arc in a circle, the Babylonians would write the same notation as 2 (space) 2 (space) 17 2 (space) or, 2 (0) 2 (0) 17 2 (0) which is 2 times 60 plus 20 = 140 with 17 minutes 20 seconds (spaces substituted for the numeral zero). To the untrained eye, notation as such could be confusing and, if read as a decimal, the above notation looks like 22,172 or as much as 20,201,720. As one can see, it is easy to recognize why the Greeks assigned such large numbers referring to the antiquity of the Babylonian astronomy. However, it is difficult to explain why Plato, in his book of cabalistic rules, interpreted 1,10 (=70) to mean 195,955,200,000,000!

Whichever date of antiquity the Greeks and Romans assign to astronomy or to whom, present day science dates the earliest accurate clay tablets to B.C. 763. The Greco-Roman classic writers and their belief in astronomy's antiquity written on the Chaldean cuneiform tablets stems from the fact they could *not* read them all correctly.

23-c   For the most part, Greek interpretation of the cuneiform tablets was difficult since not only were the terms obscure and removed from those of ordinary Greek life, but a large portion of the tablets were found to be written ideographically. Accordingly, while the grammar was Semitic, the words were often Accadian and sometimes Assyrian. This admixture of the three vocabularies increased the difficulty of decipherment and transliteration. In this fashion cuneiform tablets containing astrological information was unintentionally concealed from the uninitiated. Moreover, the same ideograph was often used in totally different senses. The combination of Babylonian, Assyrian and Accadian inscriptions were unintelligible to the Greek scholars. Consequently, not only were astrological omens concealed, but so was most of the text.

Greek scholars could only guess as to what the Babylonian scribes had written on the clay tablets.

Although personal knowledge was jealously guarded, the tri-lingual cuneiform tablets were not intended to hide their true meaning from colleagues (which has been disputed by different Assyriologists) but would certainly contribute to the Greco-Roman mis-conceptions of Chaldean astrology. Additionally, the Egyptians did the same thing with their "enigmatic" hieroglyphics. To date, the enigmatic hieroglyphs still defy trans-literation.

24. The genesis of Hellenistic astrology, as we know it, seems to have developed about 62 A.D. when Greece attached its own cultural attributes and meanings to the stars, planetary positions and their rising and setting. However, the cuneiform tablets to which Greek scholars refer primarily relate to only solar and lunar eclipses. Other tablets contain minimal planetary phenomena of appearances and disappearances and more often than not referred to the planets only by their phases.

25. The visible outer planets, Jupiter and Saturn, were constant and easy to observe. Mars was more erratic but Mercury and Venus did something altogether different. They did not seem to follow a course in the heavens as did the Moon, Sun or other planets. Mercury and Venus seemed to appear and disappear in different constellations during various times of the year, thus creating the need for a new and different style of ephemeris.

Venus moves through the heavens in an eight-year cycle. In an approximate 1.61 years, one periodic synodic cycle of 583.92 days, everything about Venus will precisely repeat in eight years or multiples of eight (on which the Mayan calendar was based and fine-tuned). Intrestingly, some astro-archeologists have recognized that reign of some kings lasted the length of multiples of so called "Venus periods." Of primary importance were the theories and visibility procedures referred to as seven phases. The synodic period is 263 days (evening star); then 8 days of concealment by the Sun (its disappearance); then 263 days (morning star) with 50 days disappearance.

Directly observing Venus we find:

End of retrograde 50 days
Greatest western elongation 220 days
Superior conjunction 50 days
Greatest eastern elongation 220 days
Start of retrograde 22 days
Inferior conjunction 22 days
End of retrograde (repeat)

The Babylonian reference and identification method is as follows:

Reappearance after invisibility
Duration
First station
Opposition
Second station
Disappearance
Duration

The outer planets (beyond the asteroids) are not as precise as Venus. Their cycles appear to behave differently. Even so, all planets were listed in somewhat the same fashion.

25.   As noted earlier, each month consisted of 28 to 30 days resulting in roughly a 354-day year. Within the seven-to-12-year cycle, sometimes intercalary days would be included. There is mention of the twelfth month with the prefix *"Ve"* added to it (*Ve*-Adar) the *"Ve"* indicating an additional or *incidental* monthly period. Many names of the months speak for themselves. For example, month nine, Chisleu, must have been the start of the winter. Others, such as month six, Elul, *the errand of Istar or Allat,* are not readily identifiable. However, with a little stretch of Greek imagination, we can associate month six with young slave girls going into orchards and gardens each morning to select only the finest fruits and vegetables for the nobles and

priests of the temples while the tillers and merchants awaited their turn. If these were indeed the customs in Greece at the time of their scholarly emergence, it is not difficult to imagine how the current sixth sign of Virgo and its attributes of scrutiny, selectivity and service came about.

26.   The names of the Babylonian months were as follows:

	MONTH	MEANING
1	NISSAN	Altar - **Bara** - Sacrifice - first new Moon of the spring equinox
2	AJARU	Prosperous Bull
3	SIMANU	Laying of Bricks - dedicated to the Moon
4	DU-UZU	Sun of Life - Seizer of Seed (tammuz)
5	ABU	Fire of the Fire
6	ULULU	The errand of Ishtar or Allat
7	TASRITU	The Holy Altar-the claw of Scorpio
8	ARAHSAMNA	The Prosperous Foundation - first month of 30 day calendar
9	KISLIMU	Many Clouds - Rain - The Giant
10	TEBETU	Month of Light - winter solstice
11	SABADU	Want and Rain
12	ADDARU	The Sowing of Seed
13	ADDARU ARKU	(intercalary)

In Babylonian tablets, the position of the Moon inferred the Sun's position:

Sun in <u>Anu</u> from month   12 to 2   =   Winds blow.

Sun in <u>Enli</u> from month   3 to 5   =   Heat and harvest.

Sun in <u>Anu</u> from month   6 to 8   =   Winds blow.

Sun in <u>Ea</u> from month   9 to 11   =   Weather cold.

27.   The days of the week were seven in honor of the Moon and Sun with the five planets. Although modern day thought assigns the names of the days of the week to the Chaldeans, that is not accurate. The Greeks, in honor of the seven planets, gave us our modern weekday names. The Chaldeans had their own special code as to the names assigned to each of the days.

The Chaldeans named their weekdays as follows:

1st day	SUGI - Of the Helm
2nd day	UTUCA-GABBA - Light of the White Face
3rd day	SIBZIANNA - Shepherd of the Heavenly Flock
4th day	KAKSIDI - Creator of Prosperity
5th day	ENTEMASMUR - Tip of the Tail
6th day	DKHU - The Eagle
7th day	PAPILSAK - The Goddess-Bahu

The 24-hour day was divided into two portions of twelve hours starting at sunset. The term for hour was the Akkadian, *simanu*, which referenced the seasonal hours. Other references to the hour depicting a particular point in time is seen as *us* (4 minutes), *beru* (2 hours) or half-*beru* (1 hour). The watch periods also had specific terms for telling time such as:

Sag Ge – the beginning of the evening watch
Usan – the evening warch
Murab – the middle watch or the middle of the night
    (Murab = middle, Ge)
Zalag – the last part of the night (dawn)

Often, there are different references to various timeframes depending on the observers context relating to different times of the month. At other times there seems to be direct quotes from other texts that correspond with the observers needs at the moment.

28.   Each planet had many names depending on its elongated position in the zodiac in reference to the Sun. The

Babylonians gave different names to each planet to relate its position to the zodiacal chiefs or constellations. This is similar to the name John in English, Ivan in Russia or Johann in German.

The order and generic names of the planets are as follows:

MOON   Star of Istar (probably refers to the Euphrates)
SUN   Star doubly great or star doubly little, (East or West of Regulus). Probably relates to the seasons: summer doubly great, winter doubly little.
JUPITER   Star of the King
MERCURY   Star of Nebo (a spirit or maybe a sprite)
VENUS   Star of Brilliance. (its magnitude)
SATURN   Star of Black Sparks- Seed of the Sun
MARS   Star of Nergal

The Moon and Sun were often referred as "the big ones who walk about like wild oxen."

29.   **MOON – SIN 《《《 (30) or DINGIR**

NANNA (Sumerian)

In a nation where astrology was the chief science, it is not difficult to understand why the night skies were precedent and the Moon its chief underpinning. Considered the chief male deity, the Moon was the father of both time and the divine twins, the Sun and Venus. As the head of the astral hierarchy, all other gods had to confer with Sin for advice and direction. Astronomy and astrology were an evening-to-dawn experience that followed the concept that day emerged from night, or that light emerged from darkness. The Moon, often referred to by its quarters, had different names during its aging: 1-15 days from new to full and 15-28 days from full to new. In addition, each period was further divided into five days each. The five-day periods probably related to the latitude of the Sun as the

Moon's movement (combined with the declination) intersects the ecliptic within five-day periods. In general, lunar eclipses were considered destructive and calamitous, except those on correct days. Most of the negative cuneiform attributes have survived into contemporary astrological literature.

30.   **SUN – SAMAS 《 (20) or UTU**

SAM-SU (Sumerian)

Listed as son of the Moon god, Samas was considered a lesser god in a supportive role of the Moon. This is difficult to understand as the symbol of the Sun is an equal armed cross and represented the king. The Sun was portrayed as the deliverer of justice during adverse times and chief administrator of rituals to help avert disaster. Samas was often referred to in ancient terminology as the planet Saturn, one of many confusing and ambiguous double statements concerning Chaldean planetary observations. The reason for this is unknown, and seemed to be a peculiarity of the ancient Babylonian astronomers. However, any planet that rose before the Sun would assume the name *bringer of light* and was referred to as such. Thus, if Mercury or Venus were in an invisible phase when Jupiter was rising before the Sun, Gu Ud (Mercury) or Dilbat (Venus) might be written off and Jupiter would become the bringer of light. For some reason, the Babylonians did not seem to have any problems with planetary interpolation, but Greek and later translators did have a difficult time with this concept. Additionally, the day of the week may have had an influence on determining the name of a planet said to be rising. The Sun, difficult to observe directly, was usually observed by the movement of its shadow with sundials, temple steps and ziggurats. Solar seasonal alignments or solstices combined with the Moon

Ancient Whispers from Chaldea

marked the turning point in the history of mankind for calendrical purposes.

31. JUPITER - MUL BABBAR

Lubat Guttav, ⟨☰⟨ᴬ⟩ **MARDUK** ⟨ (10)

Jupiter, the *King star*, was a steady, majestic light that strayed no more than one and one-half degrees from the ecliptic. Its motional majesty and unhurried movement was neither as fast as Mars nor as slow as Saturn. Jupiter, as Marduk was always considered the planet of victory and power. Associated with the spring equinox, the first sighting of the new Moon began the festival of Marduk. This was the first day of *Nisannu,* a great religious festival which would last for 11 days, symbolic of Jupiter's 11-year cycle. Jupiter was associated with the star Regulus, the *Star of the Reigning King.* Further omina relate Jupiter as: *of the King,* the *Furrow of Heaven,* the *Light of the Hero*, the *Creator of Prosperity,* the *Star of the West.* In other translations the term "Guttav" means *luck and good fortune.* However, in contradiction with today's astrological tenets, any planet conjunct Jupiter was considered ill-omened and associated with gloom. Jupiter was also associated with the rainy season, the ninth month of Chisleu, perhaps because of too much rain or to rekindle hope for the spring.

32 VENUS - DILBAT, ⊢ ⊁ ⟨ ⟳⟳

Nin-si-anna, Ishtar or **Inanna** (Sumerian)

Venus or Ishtar could often be seen as a crescent with the naked eye and was described as the first born of the Moon god, Sin. Venus was the queen of heaven and goddess of love, sexuality and childbirth. Ishtar was also the goddess of the temple whores. She was often referred as *Horns of Ishtar,* the goddess of lust. Temple prostitutes were held in reverence without the stigma attached to prostitutes today. Venus held many names and attributes as goddess throughout the Mesopotamian era. Many names ascribed to Venus are due partly to the fact that various Semitic tribes throughout the Middle East regarded Venus in a wide variety of forms. Additionally, the early Babylonians seemed to be unaware that Venus, as the morning and evening star, was one and the same planet. Even so, it is interesting that the Akkadian word used to describe Venus translates as "male-ess," an androgynous term. As the evening star at sunset, she was described as Ishtar, *the Lady of Defenses of Heaven,* and associated with love and sexuality. At sunrise Venus, as the morning star, became Attar, *the Lord of Defenses of Heaven,* a male entity who often developed a beard while transiting the Pleiades and was pictured carrying an ax as the god of war. During month nine, Chisleu, Venus was regarded as *Spark of Gulf,* while during the month of Abba Uddi (10), *the Spark of the Double.* In the month of Sabadhu (11), Venus became the *Dilgan of Babylon* (Dilgan means representative) and in the last month Venus acquired the name of *Spark of the Fish.* Often, Venus was simply *the Brilliant.* Dilbat means phosphorus and was referred to as the *light bringer.*

33. **MERCURY - GU UD**

Nabu,   Sihtu

Mercury's closeness to the Sun made it difficult to observe: Gud-Ud *means person that jumps* indicating that Mercury looked as if it were jumping around the Sun. Mercury, known as Nabu, son of Marduk (Jupiter), also earned the title of *the Crown Prince* "whose light is well known in the kingdom" and, for the most part, translates as *the rising planet before the Sun* or *the rising planet who heralds the Sun.* The name "Nabu" was assigned to any

445

planet rising before the Sun and thuis created problems for later transliteration. This is especially true on the first day of the new Moon of the spring equinox, Nisan (Nisannu). Nabu, the divine scribe, would arrive during the spring festival to rescue the missing god, Marduk. Nabu was also the chief scribe of the gods and each spring equinox he would record the assemblage of the gods as they decided the fates for the next year. Nabu as a god is believed to have rivaled Marduk as early as the reign of Hammurapi. The primary names for Mercury are: *messenger of the rising Sun and the burning of fire of the rising Sun*. Another name for Mercury during month 2 was the *Light of the Heavenly Spark*. In month eight it was known as *the Mighty* and *the Shadow Image;* month nine, the *King of Woodwork*; month 10, the *King of Light*. In month 11, Mercury became *the Great* and during the last month, the *Sower of Seed* or the *Fish of Earth*. Mercury was also termed *the Blue Star, the Burning of Fire,* the *Prince of Men, King of Light,* and *Chief of Beginning*. The term *Proclaimer* was associated with *Tu*, the god of death, similar to the Egyptian god Anubis, who guided the dead into the afterlife. As with all the planets, Mercury's description depended on when and with which constellation the planet was positioned in the firmament.

34 SATURN - GENNA

Ninurte or Lubat sakis

This enigmatic planet was often signified as Shamash, *the Night Sun* and the *Star of the Sun*. Saturn was often associated in some fashion with the Sun but, as mentioned, it is believed that there is no logic behind this name. The early Babylonian astronomers associated the Sun with justice, which may be the reason for the interpolation. In earliest legends, Saturn battled with the ancient powers of chaos and emerged as the conquering hero who recovered the tablets of law and order, thus giving structure to the chaotic abyss in the primal womb of creation. For his act of bravery, Ninurta, seen both as king and stag, was given custody of the *tablets of fate,* and thus control over fate and destiny. One of Saturn's many names was Sakkut associated as the *god of sunrise*; an associated term "Sakis" translates to *man, head* and *top of the head.* The periods over which Saturn reigns usually were written as peace, prosperity and harmony, *chief* and *first born, eldest born of the Sun god, righteousness* and *justice.* The Saturnalia festivals were full of great joy and merriment (Christmas). Yet other terms were used to translate the omens of Saturn: the *black, darkness* and often referred to as the *Black Spark.* Saturn was associated with the month of Abba Uddi or the month of light (10th month) as the *attendant of Ishtar, Lord of Bliss, Lord of the Earth, the Strong* and *the Hero of Setting.* Saturn was considered most sinister when in conjunction with Nergal (Mars) who was associated as Saturn's evil brother.

35. **MARS - AN, ►►⌐ SAL BAT ANU**

NIB A,   NERGAL, ⵉⵉⵉ   ⟨⊨⫟⫟

The celestial motion of Mars is inconsistent and his legends were associated with rudeness and cleverness to bring about his own ends. Its retrograde motion varies and can be as long as 354 days. On an average it can cross a constellation in about 45 days, but spend as long as seven months in the same constellation. Mars was watched closely and because of its irregular motion was reviled as the god of plague, fevers, war, death and the underworld. As *Nergal, Lord of the Dead,* Mars was considered most dangerous when it made is nearest approach to the Earth. The name Nibatanu translates as *the Lord of the House of Death* and the *Star Which is Not.* Seven different names for Mars came under the different "phases." They are the

447

Hyena, the Hostile, the Enemy, the Sultry, the Wolf, the Plunderer and *Agent of Deaths*. Other times there is mention of Mars being *of the Chariot* and *Sanctuary of Anu* and finally *Wanting*.

36. **STARS - CA CAB** 𒆠𒅆 **or KAKKABU**

Thirty-one stars, called the *counselor gods*, were divided as fifteen above and fifteen below the Earth, often referred to as "the little ones who are scattered about like grain." During a ten-day period, one star would appear to travel from the upper region to the lower. Under the 31 gods, there were 12 chiefs, one for each month. Many texts mention either whole or partial asterisms or only a single star. Alderbaran and Antares were fiduciary. Regulus was associated with the enthroned king; any planets conjunct this star were regarded as an omen of war. Other war omens were in the constellations of Taurus, Libra, Scorpio and Sagittarius. The constellations of prosperity were Cancer and Virgo. Within the Babylonian zodiac were 18 stars and asterisms. These were named *judges*, nine of whom resided North of the equator and nine to the South. Originally, the constellations featuring the Assyrian or Chaldean references are as follows:

Babylonian/Assyrian	Name	Translation
LU.**HUN**-GA	hireling	Aries
Sag **Hun**		
MUL-MUL	possible reference to the	Pleiades
GU-AN-NA	bull of heaven	Taurus
Gigur, Mul-Mul		
SIPA-ZI-AN-NA	true shepherd of Anu	Orion
sitaddaru		
SU-GI	old man	Perseus
sibu		
ZUBI	hooked staff	Auriga

MAS-TAB-BA-GAL-GAL	great twins	Gemini
Mas Mas		
ALLA-LUL	crab	Cancer
UR-A-GU- A	lion	Leo
nesu, sag.A		
AB-SIN	barley-stalk	Virgo
ser-u		
ZI-BA-NI-TUM	balance	Libra
Rin		
GIR-TAB	scorpion	Scorpius
zu qu qipu		
PA-	Sag = beginning	**Sag**ittarius
pabilsag		
SUHUR-**MAS**.KU	goat-fish	Capricornus
GU-LA	giant	Aquarius
KUN.MES	tails	Pisces
nu nu (nun = same)		
SIM-MAH		
Zib Me	swallow tails	SW Pisces
sin un utu		
A-NU-NI-TUM		
Mul Kur	ribbon	NE Pisces

Compare the earlier Sumerian twelve-fold zodiac called UL.
HE "Shiney Herd"

1. **GU.AN.NA** ("Heavenly Bull"), <u>Taurus</u>
2. **MASH.TA.BA.** ("Heavenly Twins") <u>Gemini</u>
3. DUB ("Pincers", "Tongs") <u>Cancer</u>
4. **UR**.GULA ("Lion") <u>Leo</u>
5. **AB.SIN** ("Her Father was Sin") <u>Virgo</u>
6. ZI.BI.AN.NA. ("Heavenly Fate") <u>Libra</u>
7. **GIR.TAB** ("Which claws and cuts") <u>Scorpio</u>
8. **PA**.BIL ("Defender") <u>Sagittarius</u>
9. SUHUR.**MAS** ("Goat fish") <u>Capricorn</u>
10. **GU** ("Lord of the Waters") <u>Aquarius</u>
11. SIM.MAH ("Fishes") <u>Pisces</u>
12. KU.MAL ("Field Dweller") <u>Aries</u>

Planetary Associations

37.   The early Chaldeans were said to have planetary
order associated with the speed (periodic cycles) of the
mean daily motion: Moon, Mercury, Venus, Sun, Mars,
Jupiter and Saturn in that order. Knowledge of periodic
diurnal cycles, the mean daily motion, cannot be
substantiated as this motion was not discovered until the
advent of Greek spherical trigonometry. However, it should
be noted that the Chaldeans did have an order system of
the planets that began as early as the first ziggurat. The
order of the Ziggurat stages started with Saturn (black) on
the bottom and topped by the Moon (silver).

37-A   Ziggurats were built as temples and each step was
encoded with a color. The seven steps represented the
seven planets. The order in which the planets are
mentioned in cuneiform texts varied; the Moon and Sun
always ranked as upper-most by entitlement.

Many early tablets list the planets: Mercury, Venus,
Saturn, Jupiter and Mars. By B.C. 700-500 this order was
changed to Jupiter, Venus, Saturn, Mercury, Mars. And
later, they were changed again about B.C. 400 to Jupiter,
Venus, Mercury, Saturn, Mars. The Seleucidian rank was
probably Venus, Jupiter, Mercury, Mars and Saturn. This
last ordering may refer to the order of magnitude or
brightness as seen with the naked eye.

In view of the changes in the planetary ranking,
however, apparently their rank related to cultural
idiosyncrasies and biases. The Moon took the lead because
the night watch was deemed more important than the day
watch.   Chaldean astrologers referred to the planets as
seeing and talking to each other from their respective
locations. The description of seeing and talking is most
likely the Chaldean poetic voicing for aspects.

An interesting note is that the Babylonian
horoscopes listed the planets differently than in the *Mul
Apin* or the *Enuma Anu Enlil*. With the exception of Venus,
the use of abbreviations were often used to describe the

planets. Another exception is the use of the numerical value of the Sun and Moon referred to as 20 and 30 respectively. This may have been done to distinguish the difference between astrological descriptions and astronomical or mathematical ephemerides.

38.   Starting from B.C. 475, an accurate record of eclipses by sign position in the zodiac was noted. It was at this time that the long-established civil lunar calendar of 30 days and 12-fold division of the year became interrelated with the zodiacal belt. The first well touted Babylonian (cuneiform) horoscope of a birth dates to B.C. 410 of a young boy in Assyria. There are about thirty-two such horoscopes or texts referring to birthdates of individuals found to date, most of which say very little about astrology as we know it. With few exceptions, there are little or no planetary degrees in longitude given, NO Ascendant or house sign, only the planets are mentioned with an occasional mention of the solstice or equinox. In fact, many tablets, except for the mention of a birth, is like any other tablet describing celestial phenomena with meteorological conditions concerning the omina of the period. The remaining few horoscopes do give a loose form of prediction concerning the life of the individual.

It appears that the Babylonians had information of the Sumerian zodiac but preferred to develop their own form of astronomy and later a loose form of astro-divination. By the fifth century B.C. the zodiac was in place and by the fourth century B.C., the Babylonian lunar eclipse ephemerides were accurate within minutes, but according to modern-day computation, the horoscopes were in error by as much as five days! Because of their methodology the Babylonians were obviously content with approximations of their astrological observations with the exception of lunar activity.

39.   In summary, the Babylonians had knowledge of the solar position in the ecliptic as indicated in various texts; the dates of the solstice or the equinox is often mentioned; the lunar Node (*murab*) and its procedure for finding the

"negative" or "positive" degree of latitude was known; the planetary synodic cycles and degrees of latitude and longitude (although the mention of degree of longitude was infrequent). As we can see, a knowledgeable formula for celestial observations was established and the ancient mythological attributes of gods and their eventual tie to the planets have produced an astrological nucleus that has survived intact for over 4,000 + years.

A.   The interpolation of Saturn and the Sun is indicated by the fact they both symbolized the law as well as justice, i.e., they work well together.

B.   Planets rising before or setting after the Sun were announcing the inevitable, similar to medieval trumpeters whose names were not important so long as they heralded the king's arrival. All planets rising or setting 15° (one-half *beru*) before or after the Sun were in exaltation.

C.   Saturn and Mars may have been linked because the ancients determined that their combined characteristic movements best symbolized warfare through merciless, deterministic self-willed obstinacy and destruction (i.e., for good or bad Saturn and Mars work well together).

D.   The planetary synodic periods based on the distance of arc from the Sun related to long-termed timing of omens. Relative to, but in a shorter time-frame, the timing of planets setting after or rising before the Sun, also determined Babylonian omina. The timing of actual synodic events, in relation to our contemporary astrological rank and file charts, could take more years than we are alive. Therefore, I have utilized the concept of these periods and placed them in the sunset chart scaled to a 24-hour period.

E.   Jupiter and Saturn have always been notorious as good and bad respectively in today's cookbook write-ups. In ancient texts, their contemporary meanings were often reversed depending on their heliacal position at sunset. Study these two in relation to your own birth chart and you will observe that Jupiter is often of malefic nature or an indice of a negative event.

F   Before B.C. 500, the idea of any influence from the zodiac signs and houses did not exist. The influence of omens depended on planets that were observed in succession from dusk until dawn, month to year and synodically. Planets that rose and set simultaneously were considered very important, especially at the moment of sunset or sunrise. Otherwise planetary placements, their position in the sky in association to other planets, star clusters and/or full asterisms were all of secondary import to the Moon. However there is mention of "secret places" or "secret houses" (*bit nisirti*) where a planet may reside by which the native is (apparently) positively empowered– often, but not always, this has shown to be the planet with the highest degree of longitude!

G.   Much of what has been presented here indicates many ideas that Greek scholars probably incorporated to develop their concept of an astrological treatise. It is also obvious that Greek scholars did not receive direct tutelage from the Babylonians and failed to read between the lines, thereby missing the essence of Chaldean wisdom.

It would serve us well to revise our thinking and research our own charts according to the ancient techniques. I do not know how many times I have heard an astrologer say that he cannot read his own chart. That is absurd. How or why do the rules change? It is like being unable to count your own money!

Conclusion

In conclusion, this chapter has been an overview on both the Sumerian and Babylonian culture with emphasis on Babylon's process of developing stargazing techniques for the purpose of developing a calendar to time natural events through celestial observation. Astrological evidence derived from early horoscopic texts are not befitting with the contemporary context of astrology at all. From the information available, daily planetary positions, so important to todays horoscopes, were not the main objective. Although there are daily computations for Jupiter and Mercury the purpose of these computations is not really known or as important as the dates of synodic phenomena. The positions for Venus, Saturn or Mars are mentioned by sign in horoscopes but are not found in Selucid ephemerides (their positions however, could have been formulated by computation from such ephemerides). By "reading between the lines" we can be certain that knowledge of daily planetary positions were desired as the horoscopes attest.

Many may argue that the Babylonians were mentally incapable of thinking logically or intelligently on cosmic realms. To others, the ancients are thought to have had an intellectually unspoiled mind that allowed the scribes to naturally penetrate cosmic truths more perceptively. In either case, the Sumerian and Babylonian thinkers believed that their preception on creation was absolutely correct. The Sumerian precepts were adherently followed by the Babylonians and initiated a dogmatic following throughout the entire Middle-East that was observed for centuries. It can be safely stated that the Sumerian and Babylonian scholars were every bit as intelligent as our scientists of today, skilled in the wisdom of their time even though they lacked the scientific data or definition that we have at our fingertips. Still, they developed marvelous myths, a sophisticated mathematica, and a scientific method that influenced their contempory world with some principles that have extended into our world of today. Overall, Sumer and Babylon had woven together, although very ancient, a highly sophisticated culture. We cannot overestimate nor underestimate the philosophical or theological mind of the ancients.

The early religious practices of Babylon were based on Sumerian concepts of celestial beings who were worshiped as kings and queens. The Chaldeans later refined and developed these myths with observations on natural phenomena into the remarkable forms of divination we now know as omens. This was all accomplished with scientific veracity.

One such notion was the function of the Sumerian pantheon. These gods were believed to be the guiding force controlling the entire cosmos. Different gods were said be in charge of heaven, Earth, the Sun or Moon, storms and clouds, the rivers, the mountains, the plains or even their cultural entities such as the cities, the dikes and ditches. The gods influence extended right down to the agricultural implements, like the plow or pick-ax. The gods were assigned rank and file and varied in power. Taking a cue from their own human state of affairs, they knew that one god's rulership over a herd of cattle was not as important as one who was in charge of the course of stars. The Babylonian idea of the heavens and Earth were equal and complimentary–neither held more significance.

The Babylonians assumed that the gods recognized one of their own as ruler and the other gods would function as an assembly under the god-king. When relating to the "seven gods of fate" and the 50 great gods, they were always written and related in a numerical sequence, the number 60 represented their chief god, An.

The basic components for creation consisted of a primal sea that was later followed by heaven (An) and Earth (Ki). When An-Ki separated, it was done by their offspring, An and Enlil. The god An carried off heaven and Enlil carried off Ki. Thus, there were four gods who controlled heaven, Earth, air and the sea. These four gods were the creative ones and everything created thereafter, including other entities, was fashioned by the plans, rules and regulations of one or the other primal gods and the eventual creation of humankind. These mythological deities remained as the pantheon for many centuries with relatively few changes.

After Sargon united Babylon, the Akkadian (northern Babylon) and Sumerian (southern Babylon) people basically lived side by side without any antagonism toward each other. Sumerian language remained in use beside Akkadian: there are royal inscriptions that are bilingual. In this manner the succession of kings was accepted by the peoples of Babylon. The function of the king, besides having his name glorified, was to keep in touch with the gods and act as their spokeperson while keeping the peace and nourishing his subjects both spiritually and physically.

Although we take a calandar for granted, it was the primary mainstay to perpetuate the myth of the king. The king gained rulership by power but held sway over the people through their belief that he could communicate directly with god. This belief was confirmed by maintaining a calendar that correctly aligned seasonal changes with agriculture. To make a mistake with the calendar was tantamount to jeopardizing the king's position. When the crops were good the gods were considered favorable to the king; when bad, the king was being punished and the people suffered with him.

The lunar calendar remained in use for religious purposes but a civil calendar was needed for civil and agricultural purposes. For this they used the tropical solar calendar. But in the beginning the larger problem was the incompatibility of the lunar and solar calendars. Over time the need to consolidate these calendars pressured the priesthood to make viable changes. Through the accumulated knowledge and experience of many previous generations, the Babylonian scribes had amassed considerable information about both calendar and stargazing procedures, all of which were jealously guarded.

Eventually, the ruling class decided that the priests, who were required to advise on religious and agricultural conditions, should also address the king's personal state of affairs. To accomplish this feat it was required of the priests to come to some sort of better understanding of the capriciousness of the gods whims through nature. Their search developed into the use of omens–learning to recognize physical events that would presage upcoming trends. These physical events and trends were said to be indicated by the stars and planets. The proto-type for astrology had begun.

CHAPTER 14

EGYPTIAN COSMOS

The conquest of Egypt in B.C. 332 by Alexander the Great gave Grecian scholars total access to one of the greatest libraries of this period. There are constant references relating Egyptian thought processes in the corpora of Greek literature. Yet, it was not Egyptian but Babylonian mathematics and astronomical techniques that influenced Grecian advances in those fields.

41.   Today, the ancient Egyptian culture is instantly recognized by its magnificent architecture and picturesque hieroglyphics. It presents images so beautifully expressed that one cannot help but sense the mystical experiences its visitors must have felt in Egypt's early pristine stages. With such an aura of otherworldly grandeur, it is no wonder that Egypt has become the symbol and "magnetic" center for those interested in metaphysical or occult phenomena.

As we enter the new millennium with our advancements in technology, the doors to understanding past history are becoming ever more widening. More and more researchers will undoubtedly start looking to Egypt for answers about astrological origins. Many astrologers today believe that the early Egyptians recognized corresponding events between heaven and mundane events here on Earth. And that astrology, in any form, would have been of natural interest to the ancient Egyptians. Knowledge of natural events was always part of the power structure for rulership in all ancient cultures. And, of course, empirical study of the star patterns would have been just as important to the Egyptians as it was in every other culture. But Egypt was indifferent to astrological premises, and this lack of interest is what makes the early Egyptians enigmatic. Cyril Fagen, well known astronomer,

Egyptologist and astrologer, was convinced that the Egyptians were well versed in astrological lore. His conclusions are based on his study of hieroglyphics concerning celestial renditions on the walls of tombs and allotment of monthly, weekly, daily and hourly deities.

Other than that of Mr. Fagan, research to date has not uncovered much in the way of any Egyptian beliefs or its use of astrology in any form, at least not in any accepted "scholarly" findings. There may *not* be a lack of information, however. We may have to readjust our thinking to the magnitude the ancient Egyptians seemed to possess. The entire expression of ancient Egypt might well be the history book they left behind in the form of the temples they built as its pages. Similar to the discoveries found by Schwaller de Lubicz at the Temple of Man with its relation to the human body. By contrast we would be like ants walking on a page of a book looking at each letter and marveling at each shape, its size, and amount of ink without ever knowing the entire context of its printed matter.

Early Egypt

42. The Egyptians were protected by the vast desert to the west, mountains and the Red Sea to the east, the Mediterranean Sea to the North and a mountainous region to the extreme south. With all this natural protection, invasions onto Egyptian soil proved difficult. Egyptians rarely had the need to defend their homeland as often as other developing cultures of the time. Their agricultural needs were taken care of by the annual flooding of the Nile River which somewhat corresponded with their solar calendar of 365.6 days a year. The result was a relaxed environment which allowed the Egyptian mind to delve into completely different philosophies concerning life and its creative process of harmony and design. This freer state of mind set the stage for the development of a society directed

toward the arts and sciences reflected in their architecture, fine arts and hieroglyphics. The Egyptian religion was based on "living with the heart" as a preparation for death and the afterlife.

Egyptian Mysteries

43.   Egypt, is often referred to as the enigmatic land of mysteries and not without good reason. The largest ancient structure ever erected with stone blocks is the great pyramid located at Giza. Its size and dimensions are incredible even by today's standards. The great pyramid measures 755 feet along each side of the base which covers an area of 12.5 acres in its entirety. The entire foundation (equal to 144 city blocks) does not exceed the plumb level of plus or minus one inch. Its height of 480 feet is achieved by 201 layers of huge granite blocks some of which measure, at the base of the pyramid, five feet in height. It is estimated that it is constructed of 2.6 million blocks weighing a total of seven million tons. The four sides of this dynamic structure align to true North, South, East and West respectively. The Giza pyramid is one of many awe-inspiring structures in all of Egypt. Yet, there is hardly any mention of this monument anywhere in ancient Egyptian writings. Above all, its imposing size and engineering precision were seemingly built from crude mathematical procedures.

There are suggestions that the pyramids were built long before the Egyptian culture came about and that the age of the pyramid is over 10,000 years old. The same goes for their interpretation of the religious integration of the planets and stars which obviously held great importance. With this view we can only surmise that the Egyptians inherited something from the culture that preceded them about which they knew nothing. One problem with such a declaration: where is the rest of the archeological evidence usually left behind by extinct cultures? If the Egyptian Pharaoh Khufu (B.C. 2589-2566) had the great pyramid built, as suggested by "accepted" archeologists, the lack of hieroglyphic information about the great pyramid or any other of the pyramids becomes the most incredible understatement of the obvious ever devised by any civilization.

44. Likewise, the reconstruction of the history of Egypt is at best a difficult task because there are so few records or artifacts of early man's settlement on the Nile. With so little evidence there is a lot more room for dispute among archeologists than agreement. During the last 150 years, however, archeologists have made tremendous progress in unraveling the wealth of information accumulated by this 5,000+ year-old culture. Even so, scholars hold many differing opinions. The German scholar, Kurt Sethe, believed that Egypt, during the late pre-dynastic period of B.C. 3000, was ruled as one land. However, research indicates that the religious cults always followed two different deities—that of Horus to the north which is decidedly of Asian influence, and Seth to the south which is essentially African (the concept of two lands also supports their religious belief of duality within Unity).

The war between Horus and Seth is fundamental in Egyptian lore. Hieroglyphic texts persistently use the term, *the two lands,* to reflect the contrast between them. For this reason many scholars dispute Kurt Sethe's work, and so the story goes. Although there is a certain amount of disagreement between different scholars regarding the origins of Egypt, most agree that the Egyptian civilization probably sprang from the gradual migrations and eventual conflation of the African peoples of the south and the Asians from the north.

At any rate, the fact remains that at one time there were two different rulers of Egypt. One in upper Egypt (south, in the Nile Valley) held residence in the city of Nekheb, the capital of that region, whose symbol was the vulture, Nekhbet. The other kingdom of the northern Delta region or lower Egypt held its capital in Buto whose symbol was that of the cobra, Wadjyt. Kings and pharaohs of later dynasties wore the two symbols joined together on the royal diadem to symbolize the unification of the *two* lands under *one* pharaoh's rule.

The thousands of years of Egyptian history are broken into segments and referred to as dynastic periods. The term *dynasty* means the succession of rulership over a period of time by one family. The dynastic periods are also in dispute by certain scholars. One such dispute regarding the time frame of Egyptian rulership as related to biblical chronicles is believed to be incorrect. This theory shortens the contemporary time line by 300 years less than is currently accepted.

Even with all the ideas that are currently in flux, much of what we know about Egyptian history still rings true but, with the advent of computers, much of that truth may change. The new breed of investigators is forging ahead with exciting, new, bolder concepts about Egypt and its past.

Development of Writing Style

45.   The ancient Egyptians expressed their ideas in picture signs called hieroglyphics believed to have developed about B.C. 3200. Very early pre-dynastic pictographs were simple pictures representing a natural object. These pictures were homomorphic symbolic analogs that depicted, as accurately as possible, their exoteric and esoteric sentence structure. The Egyptian term for this type and style of writing was *medu-neter (metut-neter)*, "words from the god (Thoth)," and held the same reverence as the Christian "Word" in the Book of Genesis. As the culture developed and the early dynasties emerged, the need for a more sophisticated form of expression arose. Pictures alone were no longer enough to express complex ideas. To indicate more concise meanings, homophonic ideographs and signs (same sound different meaning) commingled into

polyphones and syllabic values (distinct symbols for distinct sounds), and so, the Egyptian alphabet developed.

For further enhancement of phonetic values with hieroglyphics, determinatives were added to indicate a singular genus, class or group with no enforced predication. We can better understand the nature of hieroglyphics if we associate them with the idea of today's commercial *logos.* The word logo is short for the term logo gram, a symbol or letter that stands for an entire word, such as $ for money or value. Many logos represent different companies and, over the years, develop into an inseparable relationship representing the entire product line: The most popular names for products such as "Vaseline" for petroleum jelly or Kleenex for facial tissue—are good examples. Another example is today's want ads. They give us a glimpse as to how Egyptologists add vowels to the consonantal form of writing—Apt fr rnt gd cndn w/a grt vu— (Apartment for rent, good condition, with a great view).

The early writings were for the elite only (it is believed that only 0.4 percent of the Pharaonic Egyptian culture was literate), and the special training required was orally transmitted. In this manner, the nuances for the different symbols were passed on as well. For those who could read them, hieroglyphics may have prompted a picturesque heart-symbol=mind relationship that allowed the reader to experience the glyphs and form his own possibilities between their relationships while still getting the basic message. All Egyptian symbolism had a precise purpose. Hieroglyphics lose a lot of meaning by simply assigning a syllable or word to them. The result is exoteric continuity but the intrinsic values and nuances by color and placement are lost.

45-a   Today, as more and more scholars search for a much deeper understanding of hieroglyphics, it is still basically recognized as an unknown language. Having been construed as consonantal in nature, we cannot interpret our sources completely. Even with their determinative and phonetic compliments, hieroglyphics are read denoting only the subject matter which then loses any connotative implications. For example, the word for brother outside immediate family is confusing because kinship terms, such as *my uncle's brother, your sister's brother or brother-in-law*, etc., do not exist. This distinction to the brother is lost. The obvious setback to this position is that interpreters of hieroglyphics *can construe proof relevant to their personal hypothesis* and no one can really dispute them. The Grecian term, Hieroglyphs, are read with the intellect. The Egyptian term, medu-Neter, is read with the heart. Interpreters need to fuse both the intellect and intuition if any wisdom is to be gleaned from our ancient teachers.

To complicate matters, until very recently, reference to daily Egyptian life on a mundane level did not exist. Texts found in the tombs and caskets are confined to only the ruling classes and the official aspects of the state religion. Apparently, the commoners only contributed a life of service not worth mentioning by the elite class and, therefore, was excluded from Egyptian historical writings. Further complications set in when we read texts about the pantheon of gods worshipped. There are three versions which subtly changed through the ages. This one-sided view, along with the apparent overall simplistic approach to life in Egypt, reveals very little of their everyday world. We have to read between the lines. Yet, with all these restrictions and limitations, we are able to piece together and explore, with some certainty, the most beautiful and enigmatically mystifying culture of the ages.

Egyptian Mathematics

46. The encrypted silent secrets of Egypt continually rekindle a sense of fascination for many. These secrets beckon us to the ancient monuments, the pyramids and colossal temples as we continually attempt to understand the "how and why" of how they came to be. Speculation on how these monuments were built is basically vacuous as today's engineers cannot duplicate the process. These

massive monuments require an engineering ability completely foreign, not only to us, but which (considering their mathematical mindset as we understand it) may have been foreign to the ancient Egyptians as well.

Obviously, their skill and knowledge of geometry and linear measurement are clearly expressed in many of their monumental structures, but written theoretical principles are yet to be discovered. There are many possible explanations such as the monuments are themselves the text of ancient knowledge, or written records were lost during the burning of the great library in Alexandria. We have found information about Egypt hidden in the form of temples and hieroglyphic *puns* revealing holistic views and philosophies. Another simpler explanation might be that the Egyptians kept their knowledge to themselves. After all, they were isolated from the rest of the world during their early history and besides, who could they talk or write to except other priests, engineers and those in training?

If the pyramid's incredible structure is one of implicit and spatial mathematical relationships, as has been suggested, this must be true of all the other structures in Egypt as well. R.A. Schwaller de Lubicz spent years studying the Temple of Man in Luxor and his conclusions are startling. He believed that the temple represented and depicted the entire human organism and that each room or chamber revealed and explained the functions of organs and nerve centers by their spatial relationships.

There is yet to be found any mention of principles dealing with higher mathematics in the Egyptian culture. The Rhind papyrus seems to be nothing more than a child's primer for arithmetic. It is remarkable that all of the building in ancient Egypt was accomplished without using the place value system of tens, hundredths, thousandths, etc. Without such a system, the mathematical requirements of such engineering feats are as monumental as the structures themselves. Yet, we have not found any records about the early construction of these monuments (note: we do have some records about later structures). All that has been recovered are early documents revealing a crude methodology for mathematics, which only adds to the mystery.

To illustrate this point, let us look at the early Egyptian mathematical procedures. The range and procedure of Egyptian mathematics are essentially additive. Computing addition and subtraction is the same simple principle we learned in school. Multiplication and division are extended into the basic idea of addition.

To determine a sum by multiplication, continue to double the multiplier and the multiplicand. When partial duplications equal the multiplier, add each desired partial unit and subsequent doublet indicated by an asterisk.

46-a Examples of multiplication (using addition) follow in examples:

	Example A 12 times 14		Example B 9 times 23		Example C 26 times 33	
	1	14	* 1	23	* 2	66
	2	28	2	46	4	132
	* 4	56	4	92	* 8	264
	* 8	112	* 8	184	* 16	528
ans.	*12 total	168	* 9 total	207	* 26 total	856

In example A, the addition of units 4 and 8 equal 12 and are the result of multiplying 12 X 14. In example B, the addition of units 1 and 8 are the result of multiplying 9 X 23. In example C the multiplicand is larger and we continue to double the units until two or more additives result in the proper answer. By using Arabic numerals with a place system the process looks simple but remember the Egyptians used hieroglyphic symbols for enumeration which demanded much more space.

Division is computed by the same process as in the following examples D and E.

	Example D			Example E	
	60 divided by 5			60 divided by 6	
	1	5		1	6
	2	10	*	2	12
*	4	20		4	24
*	8	40	*	8	48
Answer	12		Answer	10	

Although fractions were not an everyday affair, they were basically derived by the same computation using a table of duplications of the fraction involved. As we can see by the preceding examples, Egyptian mathematics were simple. Egyptian written mathematical procedure did not have *numeral equivalents* as we do. Instead they used the pictorial ideographs from the alphabet as reference to numbers.

Thus, a picture of an upside down horseshoe ∩ *met* is 10, ∩∩/∩∩ = 40. The picture of a coiled rope ℮ *u* or *saa* is 100, ℮℮ = 200, or the picture of a small frog ⌇ *hefen* is 100,000. The number of months in the year ∩∩ ‖ or 365 ℮℮℮ ∩∩∩/∩∩∩ ‖‖‖ days in a year. The largest numbers were written from the left working down to the smallest to the right, .

This form of mathematics presents a real problem. Writing large numbers becomes quite burdensome. The figure 9,805,465 would require dozens of pictures. However, using the place value system only requires the limited amount of space we see in the figure itself—even if we used hieroglyphics. On the surface, their simple mathematical system worked as the necessary tool required to develop their complex civilization for over 3,000 years. Yet, Greek scholars traveling in Egypt were said to have been astounded beyond their imaginations by the principles of geometry and astronomy found there: what principles found where? Modern scholars have not seen any such findings.

Perhaps we should pay homage to Pythagoras and his Egyptian mentors. His teachings may provide an important clue to the inherent structure of Egyptian wisdom. Pythagorus is said to have spent twenty-two years studying in their country to acquire the wisdom he later taught the Greeks.

Calendars and Time

47 Egyptian math was not required to produce the most intelligent calendar of the entire early civilized world. It was based on a fixed time scale, without any intercalations, as they waited for the constellation Orion and the Sun to herald seasonal changes. The annual inundation of the Nile river was announced by the sight of Sirius (*spd-t*) rising just before the Sun every year on a Sidereal (measured yearly from star to star), not on a Tropical (measured from season to season) basis.

The difference between Tropical and Sidereal observation is based on the time it takes the Sun to return to a given fixed point in the sky. Using the equinox as an example, Tropically, the Sun requires 11 minutes less than 365.25 days to return to a fixed point (equinox). It arrives earlier. With the Sidereal relationship to the fixed stars, the Sun requires nine minutes more to reach the equinox. Thus, it arrives later. Therefore, Tropical observations need to be adjusted to accommodate the apparent backward motion of one degree every 72 years to equate the Sidereal observations.

This practice eventually waned because of the precession. However, the star Sirius also had another special meaning to the Egyptians: the apparent motion of Sirius is a little less than the apparent motion of all the other stars. When measured by the rising Sun, star patterns rise about 20 minutes later each year on any given day. Sirius rises only 11 minutes later. This difference in rising time *suggests* that they might have believed that our Sun (along with the entire solar system) may revolve around the incredibly large star of Sirius, much like the planets revolve around our Sun (or vice-versa), while the entire configuration of stars revolves around the Milky Way.

48. Over the years Egypt developed a wide variety of calendars because of precessional circumstances, some for civil use and some for temple use, and each served a different purpose. The Sothic calendar was based upon the heliacal rising of the fixed star, Sirius, or Sothis at Heliopolis. The ideal heliacal rising would be exactly sunrise on the first day of the first month of the season *Akhet*. For Sirius to rise *exactly* in the same place at the same time is referred to as the *Sothic Cycle* and was revered as the cosmic alignment of the calendar. This happens every four years or 365 days 6 hours 9 minutes 9.54 seconds X 4 = 1,461 days. This was the equivalent of our leap year. The Sothic Cycle was considered divine and the Egyptians converted the cycle from days to years as the Great Year or the *Cycle of Eternity*. Thus, a mean cycle of 1,456 years equaled one divine year. There are indications that the Egyptian *eternal day* of 1,461 years may have commenced in the pre-dynastic period of B.C. 4228. Additionally, the Egyptian concept of *one day equals a year* or *one year equals a day* may have eventually found its way into Greek astrological circles as the *form of secondary progression* astrologers use today.

Another calendar, based on a 25-year cycle, equaled 309 lunar months or 9,125 civil calendrical days. The 25-year cycle was divided into 16 years of 12 months and nine *Great* Years of 13 months. Every fifth year the last two months were 60 days long to equal the 9,125 days required for completion. The 25-year calendar supplied simple rules to determine accurately the dates of all future lunar festivals for as many as five centuries to come. It was the custom in Egypt to give calendar dates for every second month. The intermediate months were probably used to adjust a hollow lunar month (less than 30 days) to a full month (30 days) as necessary.

Heavenly Observations and Seasonal Changes

49.   Many variants of the lunar calendar were observed along with the civil calendar, but the lunar calendar was used primarily to regulate festivals. The common or *true* calendar changed very little from the first pre-dynastic period: the yearly watch of Sirius; the monthly lunar return; the 36 ten-day periods called decans; and the 24-hour day which was divided into two 12-hour segments of two-hour watches. The civil or common calendar was used for purely practical reasons with no relation to astronomy, other than to observe Sirius on the new year. The new year began on the first day of Thoth (between the 16 to the 19 of July) and was grouped into three seasons of four months each, based upon agriculture and the conditions of the Nile River.

The three seasons were:

Akhet Winter	**Proyet** Spring	**Shemu** Summer
(inundation)	(receding waters/sowing)	(harvest)
1 Thoth	5 Tybi	9 Pachon
2 Paophi	6 Mesheir	10 Payni
3 Athyr	7 Phamenot	11 Ephipi
4 Chiak	8 Pharmouti	12 Mesori

The four winds were probably the solsticial or equinoctial points:

QEBUI	The north icy wind	God is Qeb.
SHEHEB	The hot south wind	God is Shehbi.
HENKESES	The east wind	God is Isis.
HERATCHA	The West wind	God is Hatcha.

The four elements of life were:

GEB - EARTH   **USHEB** - FIRE

SHU - AIR   **ASUR** - WATER

49-a.   The standard year *(renpit)* ⌈ ☉ was composed of the Egyptian *decan* system of observation. They divided the skies into ten-day intervals for a 360-day year with 12 months of 30 days. Five epagomenal festival days were added at the end of the last month to finish off the year. The day was divided into "the two times ": 12 for the daylight hours and 12 for the nightly hours. The term *hour* is referred to as a general description of time. It could be as short as 40 minutes during summer months and as long as 75 minutes during the winter. Each watch consisted of two such hours or 36 decans during any 24-hour period. As the asterisms can only be seen at night, the ideal would be to observe 18 decans (180°) per night, but in the summer months only a third or 12 decans could be observed.

The ratio derived from 36 decans becomes 12:24 or 1:2. This ratio reveals a deeper understanding of advanced mathematics or geometry that connects the square to the Golden Number Phi to Pi, the mathematical function of all circles, spheres and rotational motion. This same ratio can be attributed to the pyramids and other classical Egyptian sculptures and temples. An interesting note to the living function of Phi relates to the growth of plant life as it reaches toward the light. The average angle of branches separating from their trunk to allow for maximum exposure to the Sun is 137 degrees 30 minutes 28 seconds. Subtract that figure from 360, The result is the Golden Division of a circle or Phi, 222 degrees 29 minutes 32 seconds! Yet we have found no direct evidence of this knowledge.

As summer commences, dusk and dawn present a problem by depleting the nightly hour count, as each decan will rise approximately every 40 minutes. This depletion was overcome by using a decimal daylight system. This system allowed one hour for twilight and one hour for dawn with a duodecimal system for night-time observation. In this fashion the ten-day periods worked with the hourly observation periods.

The day was further subdivided into three periods as *young, middle* and *dying*. The Egyptians associated the morning horizon as symbolic rebirth of each new day. When the Sun, planets, stars, and Moon were first noticed upon the horizon, they were referenced by the gender *boy*. As the Sun ascended to the Midheaven, the gender of boy took on the personification of a *man*. Finally as the diurnal motion progressed to the Descendant, the Sun became *old man*. When the Moon could be seen during daylight hours, it underwent the same transformation by name.

Egyptian Magical Beliefs

50.   Egyptians did believe that lucky and unlucky days were controlled by auspicious and evil deities. Various deities prompted the course of action for certain periods, such as starting out journeys, marriages, business transactions, etc. Not only did the deities govern the hour, day, week, month or year, but the pantheon of gods covered most aspects of life itself including meteorological elements.

These periods were observed carefully for good and bad influences. A different deity was assigned to each new day and to each new two-hour segment of the 12-hour divisions. These segments were watched as the approaching hourly deity would either struggle or conform with the daily deity for good or evil. Deities at odds with each other were considered at war and various tasks were either put aside or *magically alleviated* by a priest who was an expert in such matters. Herodotus reminds us that the Egyptians "assign each day and each month to a god and they tell what fortune, to what end and disposition a man shall have according to his birth." Much of what is determined about Egyptian astrological precepts is based on these last passages. It has been suggested by many scholars, both early and contemporary, that these lucky and unlucky days were probably seen as a form of early or primitive "horary astrology" although the terms "horary" or "astrology" were not used at the time of their rediscovery.

The Decanate Star System

51. The process of determining the decan star system falls neatly into place as a star clock. The ten-day star observation periods were also calculated into the nightly watches as each star would heliacally rise in approximately 40 to 70-minute intervals depending on the time of year they were observed. During the watch each star interval would be listed. At the end of the tenth day, a newly assigned star was noted about the last hour before sunrise. Assigning *new stars* is a misnomer as the Egyptians were able to localize each star by a system inscribed on tablets known today as diagonal or stepped calendars. The tables and design of the step calendars probably commenced with Sirius or Orion and were formed by 36 columns dissected by 12 lines *representing* the 12 hours of night. The name of each decan is located on the top of each column and each consecutive column is one line higher than the former. By knowing the rising time, listed on the step calendar of the monthly decan, the priest would know the hour of night.

52. To illustrate, let us assume that the first star of the cycle is star "A" and is poetically termed, "*the last hour or the end of night*" star. Each day the eastward motion of the Sun will be a little earlier (about one degree) and likewise "A" will appear to rise earlier. Consequently, "A" will be seen for a longer period of time each consecutive day before sunrise. Therefore, at the end of a ten-day period, star "A" will rise approximately an hour earlier before the Sun. Obviously, since "A" is rising an hour before dawn, it can be no longer be noted as the *star of the last hour*. At such a

time, the step calendar indicates a move forward to the next column. Star "A" is now relegated to the second column. The next column, denoting the decan and indicator as star "B", will represent the last hour of the night taking the place of "A". Star "B" will indicate the last hour of night for the next ten days until star "B" is rising a full hour earlier than the Sun. At that point in time star "C" in the next column is designated the last hour of the night star and so forth. At that time,, having been replaced by "B" and "C," star "A" is rising two hours before the Sun and has receded to the third decan position. One year and 36 decans later, star "A" starts the procedure all over again.

This necessary replacement procedure would be repeated year after year. These ten-day periods were called *Bku* or *working stars*. The 36 stars neatly correspond to the 360-day year; the required extra five-day festival was dealt with in a different manner. The first day was called the "birth" of *Osiris,* the second for *Horus*. *Set* was born on the third day, *Isis* the fourth and *Nephthys* on the fifth.

Decanates or Pentades?

53. Star patterns were often placed on the ceiling or walls of tombs of the departed spirit. These star patterns often depicted the "ideal heaven" for the home of the dead. On the walls of the cenotaph of Seti I at Abydos, one such star pattern shows the goddess of the sky, Nut, symbolically arched as the heavens with a form of step calendar design which archeologists refer to as ten-day periods or decanates. The word decan comes from the Greek *decem,* meaning ten: pentade from the Greek *pentas*, meaning five.

An interesting controversy developed when Egyptologist and astrologer, Cyril Fagan, who made insightful investigations into the cenotaph, indicated a possibility that the so-called *decans* only covered 180 degrees of the sky. Based on his findings, he declared that the Egyptian decan system was actually a *pentade* system or based on five-day star groupings (36 divided into 180 = 5). He furthered his nine-point argument by comparing measurements of zodiacal asterisms in increments of five and ten degrees. His findings show that the ten-degree measurements were awkward and related to very little or *meaningless constellations* within the diagram. However, he found that measurements by five-degree increments within the 180-degree celestial diagram correctly synchronized with the names and locations of many of the constellations.

Most Egyptologists did not agree with Mr. Fagan. They declared that the artist's intentions of the celestial diagram is a composite of dawn to sunset. They point out that there are many references that support this theory, such as four Suns at different positions: rising, midday, setting, midnight. However, there is only one Moon which is placed in a *new Moon* position but put in the old Moon's place (indicating a different date altogether). The decans themselves are thirty-six in number within a 180-degree of arc, and in other tombs they are sometimes placed in different step columns or arrangements. The Sun, located in the asterism Leo, is in such a position that association to other constellations on the ecliptic is impossible using the decan system.

Fagan was rebuked by Egyptologists saying that the artist had placed the diagrams to display an event with several meanings as they contain the elements of both dawn and sunset. This is possible because each day in the temple, as opposed to the civil calendar, began at sunset. To express a double meaning of the Sun in such a manner suggests that the star pattern at the cenotaph of Seti I could have had a double meaning as well. If this explanation of the Abydos diagram is true, then it cannot be used as evidence that the decans were in reality only five degrees of arc although all thirty-six of them do appear between the two horizons. Another oddity is that there are no planets indicated in the rendition unless planetary influence is considered null or void in the Egyptian afterlife. But if this were the case, why would the planets be listed on other cenotaphs and especially why would the planet Mars be relegated to a "harmless" position?

Egyptologists have long based their ideas on the idea that Egyptian art is loose, with little consideration to actual design or reality. They felt that many Egyptian artists placed the hieroglyphs, diagrams and other artwork where it suited them or as space allowed. This looseness seems especially so where the constellations are concerned with the *Nut* diagram in question. However, "looseness" seems highly irregular for Egyptian artists whose exacting rules for artistic relationships were formed through mathematical calculations—looseness is remotely possible, but *very* unusual.

53-a   The Fagan/Egyptologist controversy places us right back at the point that incomplete understanding of our sources allows any interpreter to construe his case with little or no opposition. However, as we have seen in earlier chapters, these five-degree segments in the astrological chart play an important role in the life of individuals for "aging the chart." As a working program, the pentade stands out as the most viable procedure.

Egypt as a Metaphysical Culture

54.   Reason functions by affirmation or application to reactive circumstances, by counterweight or countervalue. Metaphysics is non-polar, non-physical, independent of duality and nature. It is a state of fusion, and because of this it cannot be associated with the function of reason.

The Seth–Horus myth is the allegorical story of Unity (Set) and the assorted "not I" fragments of nature (Horus). The Egyptians' philosophical world lies in their awareness of holistic, metaphysical perspectives with an intrinsically divine overview of nature as a whole. The ancient Egyptian may have seen the material world as the end result of the spiritual–its *form* of existence. The mind of Ptah and matter *interacted* in the form of *heka* thus creating different *conscious* characteristics and levels of life from his higher form of thought. Heka can be best described as a form of magic that made any user of it superior in power to anyone who did not possess it. The Egyptian creation myth suggests that heka was the *Word* uttered for creation to begin. In other words, the application of Heka enabled Temu, or Ra to assume a material form. It is also clear that Ra employed *heka* in constructing heaven, Earth and the underworld and after that heka is referred to as divine magic or conjuration.

Should we take the whole of Egyptian civilization as a symbol of characteristic development for these abstract states, it is easy to recognize that the Egyptians perceived the universe as the experience of consciousness taking on embodiment through heka. With this view, the Egyptian philosophy and mode of expression are purely geometric in nature. It is my opinion that heka may have symbolically described the rhythmic currents of various vibratory levels. Vibrations create nodal patterns and, at the intersecting lines of force, the interference with those lines of force at different frequencies created a new level of organization or geometric form. Imagine covering a powerful magnet with a piece of paper. Sprinkle iron filings on the paper covering the magnet. In this manner the pattern of magnetic force can be visibly seen. Place an additional magnet on top of the first magnet. The filings will arrange themselves into a new pattern.

I am of the opinion that the Egyptians recognized such changes and believed everything in the universe was basically in geometric form, its volume created by the result of intersecting lines of force. By this act of nature, no one thing in itself is random or accidental; everything is interconnected and thus harmonious. Perhaps, this is the connotative implication that is overlooked when we view Egypt, its temples or hieroglyphics. This is similar to higher mathematical formulas such as algebra or quantum mechanics which leave out the lower forms of arithmetic because they are already understood and simply accepted.

If this is indeed the case, our current form of analysis of hieroglyphics may be way off base.

55.   Death was the centralized theme of Egyptian art, religious thought and philosophy.   The idea of the bi-cameral mind (Paragraph 9) could be applied to Egypt as well as all other early civilizations. This is depicted on the walls of tombs showing the pharaohs in direct contact with their gods (Paragraph 12). Might it not be suggested that through bi-camerality the voices of the deceased pharaohs could still be heard by their survivors? If such mental contact were still possible after death, it would make sense to bury the entire treasure trove along with plenty of sustenance and supplies with the deceased. This is not as farfetched as it initially sounds. For when we look at Egypt as a whole, we notice that nothing is left to chance. Everything had a design and purpose. Every chore was executed according to precedent and within the conventional constraints of the period, from the alignment and placement of tombs, to the strict art form with its underlying square-shouldered, left-foot forward stereotypical poses and pre-ordained proportions.

Sir Norman Lockyer was the first to notice that ancient *temple architects* intentionally built their complexes to conform with the cosmic alliance of the equinox and solstices. This discovery started a new branch of astro-archeologists: the study of design, arrangement and cosmic alignment of temples for the purpose of discovering the time frame in which these structures were built.

As for mathematics and astronomy, the Egyptian mind may well have relegated such matters to the mundane world of existence. However, if the world of material existence were nothing more than the residue of vibrational activity, then just as easily, mathematics could have been viewed as a residue of higher forms of thought. Egyptian processes of such matters might have been similar to the idiot-savant who *just knows* the answers to mathematical problems without having to take the intermediate steps for solution.   Like mathematics, perhaps their astronomy also fit into this pattern of thought.

What we call the magic of the past might well be what we wish to learn through our present day technology. We obviously do not understand why the ancient Egyptians failed to mention such prominent structures or their principles of construction. Did they simply decline to state the obvious such as the color green as "a *green* tree" or *blue* sky? If the myths and stories are principles in pun form, then the stars were not simply clocks, but the embodiment of a much broader understanding and interpretation of the cosmos. Was the process of heka their understanding of the entire cosmos? After all, the deceased god-kings passed on to continue their lives in the vast, star studded, heavenly home of the gods.

Metaphysical Religious Beliefs

56.   To illustrate transformative changes, the following is the story of how the Sun God Ra changes from Khephri, to Horus then Tem and back again to Khephri in the course of a 24-hour period.

As the Sun *Horus* travels through the heavens, his finest hour is one hour past noon, the hottest part of the day. As he ages toward sunset, he becomes *Tem*, the ram-headed god, preparing to meet with *Hor-Tesher* (Mars) who will destroy (de-form) Tem to make way for the new (cycle). By sunset, Tem is swallowed up by *Nut*. During the next hour Tem is transformed from a single source of light into the scattered form of many stars and is dispersed into the night's heavenly vault. Later, the now destroyed Tem once again becomes the spirit of *Ra* and meets with *Hor-Ka-Pet* (Saturn). It is here that the spirit of Ra decides to begin the re-pre-form process (the very beginning of *becoming a concept* as in a seed i.e., heka) and once again proceeds to re-emerge into the next cyclic pattern of existence. For four more hours the spirit of Ra condenses from the ethers and becomes the generic seed of the Sun. It is here that a generic seed can take on any form, but his "inner blueprint" is already developing to bring him back into *that which he already is,* the Sun God *Ra.*

His "inner blueprint/seed form" is now guided by the light of *Khen-su* (Moon) through the depths of the underworld to re-form (come into being) by his own will and change into the natural structure that Ra, the Sun, has conceived (of himself) when he was with Saturn. Just as the dawn is scarcely beginning, the now burgeoning seed of Ra conjoins with *Sebgu* (Mercury) to become in-form (birth of consciousness) by two steps: (1) to again be born to the material form of the solar disc by reclaiming the light from the "flowers of the night" (stars) to re-assemble his divine being, and (2) by becoming conscious of his new mission as solar deity for the new day.

At the point of sunrise, the world joyously sings the praise of Ra as he rises in his new form of the winged beetle *Khepri,* pushing the solar disc, triumphant in the realization of his newly acquired rebirth. For the next two-hour period, Ra as Khephri prepares to meet with *Upesh-pet* (Jupiter) and begin his transformative rites from the young early morning Sun Khepri into *Horus,* the noonday Sun. As Khephri becomes the noonday Sun he is transformed into the form of a Man. Ra, now Horus, prepares to meet with *Isis,* the goddess of fertility, with whom he will wed when he reaches his zenith (noon). He begins the journey into his finest moment when he meets with *Seb-Uati* (Venus) to perform the ritual of conjoining opposites, the taking of a wife. Horus symbolizes the moment when the real touches the ideal, the meridian or noon. This is also symbolized by Venus simultaneously rising every eight years with Sirius, a moment revered as the Sacred Marriage of Isis and Osiris.

57.   The next deductive step is to present these beliefs into a more holistic viewpoint that abound throughout Egyptian texts. From the above we can conceive that the energy forms for the planets are as follows:

SUN	Pre-form	The potential seed-idea, the spirit of creativity that is the thought process for the inception of an object. Unity.
MERCURY	In-form	The recognition of becoming form, the spirit developing from seed-idea into a form. Duality.
MOON	Re-form	That which already has form must by nature change its form. The aging process.
MARS	De-form	The process of dismantling or destroying to make way for the new. Death and dissolution.
JUPITER	Trans-form	The old form changed into the new, brought about by Mars' dismantling. Self-realization.
SATURN	Re-Pre-form	Final dissolution and decay. As the world lives on its own waste material, the biodegradable process creates the necessary "food/heat" for the growth of other life-forms.

From the story above we can surmise the implication of different levels of energy that are seeking to become form at their nodal points and, once they have material form, are forever changing.

The Egyptian Cosmos

58.   This next section is designed to allow us to look through the eyes of the Egyptian scribes and priests and see how they might have viewed the planets and stars. Ra (pronounced Ray) was considered the chief god in the Egyptian pantheon, the Sun was Ra's right eye and the Moon his left. Ra held various positions of rank depending upon which pharaoh of the different dynasties supported him as the chief god. The Sun as Ra became the supreme deity during the reign of Akhenaten (B.C. 1352-1336) and the Moon became a lesser god. During Akhenaten's reign

the universality of the sun cult Ra was demonstrated by adding Ra to the deities' names; thus, Amun became Amun-Ra and Montu became Montu-Ra and so forth. Eventually, all the deities were replaced into this comprehensive category of Ra, the disc of perfection.

An important point to remember is that the Egyptian's views were based on what happens after death. Life was the preparation for this final act. These philosophies were different in each settlement along the Nile and mundane names for the planets were derived from the many different legends and philosophies from each Nome or settlement.

59 **The Sun   RA -** ☉ **KHEPHRI-** 🪲 **HORUS-
TEM-** ₀ 𓏏

The Sun was seen in three different forms: (1) *Khepri* (beetle), the morning Sun; (2) *Horus* (Ra), the noon day Sun; (3) the pre-dynastic name *Tem or Atem* (ram-headed man) for the Sun in the evening or "He who comes to an end." He was first noted in B.C. 2865 and reached his peak as Ra in B.C. 2566 by Djedefra. Usually depicted as a hawk-headed figure of a man wearing a Sun disc headdress during the day, he sailed on the barque as Tem, the sheep-headed figure, during his travels through the underworld at night. Ra reached his universal deity status under the reign of Akhenaten (B.C. 1352-1336) where all other gods were absorbed under the rule of Ra. Many names were used for the Sun god. Depending on its position in the sky or poetic value, some of the Sun's references are as follows:

Aak Hu	Light god
Aak Hu-T	Fiery light, Eye of Ra
Art-Ra	Midday Sun
Art-Ua	"One eye"
Ar-T-Unem-T	Right eye of Ra
Hai-T	Brilliance, light, radiance
Hai-Ti	Two light givers

Shu	Light, Sun, Daylight
Utcha-T	Right eye of the sky god

The barque of Ra was guided by four rudders. The hieroglyph for rudder translates into *justified* and is often written as the last part of an eulogy as *true of voice*, to designate the honor of a deceased person.

The four rudders of the solar barque were written as:

Sekem Nefer	Beautiful Power, the North Rudder
Teben Semu Taui	Guide of the Two Lands. Revolver, the West Rudder
Her-AB Et Ashemu	Dweller in the Temple. Light God, the East Rudder
Khenti -her-Ab-Het-Tesheru	Governor Dweller in the Temple of the Red Gods, the South Rudder

60. **The Moon IAH- AAH- KHONS (Khen-su)**

With many different names in each Nome or Egyptian *Sepat*, Khons was regarded as *the Provider* and associated with healing powers. *Osiris* was also known as *Min* or *Asar-Aah*, as the god "whose annual death and resurrection personifies the self-renewing vitality and fertility of nature." The god who raised Egypt *up through the waters and mud* by damming the Nile at the site of today's Aswan was also known as *Ptah* (associated with the Moon). The Moon marked a time of cyclical creation in matters of life and death by appearance and disappearance. Khons stands on a *plinth* ⟺ for law and truth and wears the symbol of the *new Moon in the old Moon's arms* on his head. In his hands he holds the *Ankh* ♀ of life, the *Djed*, 𝍖 for stability, the *Shepherd's Crook* ? to show guidance rather than despotic rule; he carries the *Flail*, 𝄃\ for power and the *Was* ⌐ for dominion.

A youthful figure with the *Menat* 𝄢 behind his neck symbolizes the goddess power and its transmission. He sails over the sky in a boat called *boat of millions of years*. He assists *Thoth* in the judgment at death. The predynastic month started on the morning when the old Moon became invisible. True to Egyptian tradition, the Moon, had many references.

Aabi	The left eye of heaven
Aab-T	Left eye
Aah-Tehuti - (Tchehuti)	Thoth the Moon god
Art-Aabt	Left eye of horus
Khensu	Traveler, Moon god
Meh Utcha-T	Full Moon on the last day of the month (6th month of our year)
S-Baq	Shining eye of the Moon
Sbeq-T	Left eye of Horus
Tena Tep	First quarter
Uhem Qai	Renewer of form
Utchait	Goddess of the Moon
Ucha-T	Left eye

61.   **The Earth GEB-**

Geb appears as a white-breasted goose or goose-headed man. Geb was the god of vegetation and fertility. In funerary context Geb was regarded as a malevolent force as he *held the dead captive in his body*. He is often depicted as a man lying with an erect penis in a supine position under the arched figure of Nut, his sister and wife. In his association with Osiris and Horus, he was considered a protector and often pharaohs were referred to as the *heir of Geb* in their title and protective role.

Other names for Geb are as follows:

Aker	Earth god with a lion's body with a head at each end
Akeru	The gods who guarded the great tunnel

	through the Earth
Heri Ka	Son of Shu and Tefnut
Ta	The primal Earth
Tannen	Very early Earth god
Tenn	Primitive Earth god, Tennit female counterpart.
Tha	The male name for Geb
Urek	Earth god
Usekh-T Geb	Another name for the Earth god

62   The Sky NUT- ☼ ▭

Nut is the female goddess and a counterpart of Geb. The vault of heaven was personified by the goddess as an arched figure leaning over with her hands and feet on the ground in the pose resembling the glyph for the sky (depicted as a flat plate, *pet* ▭) representing a physical ceiling with pointed projections or drops at each end. The Sun and Moon traveled beneath this plate while the stars or lamps were attached to the plate-like sky similar to lamps hanging from a ceiling. ⯎ The sky had four pillars that supported the sky that looked like an elongated letter "Y." Geb and Nut were said to embrace at night and were both considered bi-sexual. Nut was said to eat the Sun in the evening, dispersing the light of the Sun into the light of the stars and later to focus the light of the stars back into the Sun each morning. The legend of Nut created a suitable funerary figure and, consequently, she was held in high esteem as one who would help guide the dead to their homes among the imperishable stars. She is spoken of as enfolding *the body of the deceased kings.* Many coffin lids have her image engraved thereon, depicting the dead as being back inside the body of his mother awaiting rebirth. Other names for Nut are as follows:

Usekh-T Shu	The space between Earth and sky
Uthesit	The name of the sky and sky goddess
Utcha-T	A name for heaven or sky
Baa	The material of which the sky and

	heaven are made
Beg-T	Sky
Pet-Pet	The two halves of the sky, day and night
Men	That which endureth (pyramid), the sky
He-T Uab	"Pure house" the name of the sky
Khi and Khi-T	The sky, heaven

63. **Jupiter UPESH-PET,**
     Sba shema - Heru-up-shet

Jupiter was often called *the Light Scatterer of the Sky* and was referred to as *the Star of the South*.   Jupiter was also called *the Abundant Provider* when rising in the East. Other names are as follows:

Heru-sba-res	Horus, Star of the South
Sba Shema	Traveling star
Sba Tua	Jupiter as morning star
Smet Res-T	Jupiter

64. **Saturn HOR-KA-PET,**
     Neter-tchai-pet, Sba amenti tcha pet

Saturn was called *the Old Man* and *Star of the West Traversing Heaven*. Saturn was often depicted as a bull-headed hawk and referred to as *Sba Amenti Cha Pet*, *Horus, the Bull of Heaven*.   Later this was shortened to *Horus the Bull*. Other names are as follows:

Heru -P-Ka	Horus the Bull
Neter-Chai-Pet	Saturn

65 **Mars HOR-TESHER, Harakhte**
    Sba åabti tcha pet

The *Red Horus* or *the Star of the East Heaven* was also known as *Har-Akhti* or the *Horus of Two Horizons*. In many instances, this planet was referred to the god *Ra* as a hawk with a star above his head. This association with *Ra* is peculiar unless we associate it with the scorching heat of the mid-summer Sun, because Mars was thought to have had a vile nature. Many times in funerary registration, he was *magically reduced* or simply removed from celestial diagrams altogether. Always a harbinger, Mars was said to *journey backwards in traveling**.

> *Sba Aabi Tcha Pet "The planet that moved onwards and retreated."

It is interesting to note that many Egyptologists feel the term *journey backwards* means retrograde, relating to planetary motion opposed to that of the Earth's rotation. But how can that be? The Egyptians *observed* Mars with full knowledge that Mars is not in constant retrograde motion. As a matter of fact, Mars is not retrograde all that often. The intrinsic reference may be that Mars was recognized as a planet of dire consequences. And, as a magical rule, it was always to be written as weakened, inverted or reversed, as is the case of many funerary texts. These texts show Mars relegated to the bottom of the list or, in some cases, simply omitted.

66.   **Venus-BENU**

Seb - Uati, Sba tcha

Venus was known as *the One Who Crosses* the goddess Isis, or the evening star. She was often depicted as the *Benu Bird*, a large venerated water fowl. Venus was referred to as the *Ferryman of Osiris* (the Soul of Osiris). As the morning star, Venus was called the *Neter Tuau, God of Dawn*, or Horus of the Duat (underworld). The morning star was masculine and was said to give birth to Orion as the Death King. In later periods she/he is depicted as *Pi Neter Tuau* as a double-headed man/hawk, with each head wearing the crown of upper and lower Egypt. This double reference to Venus sheds light on the question whether or not Venus was known as the same planet rising in the evening and/or morning. She is also referred to as the bride

of Sirius as she rises with that star every eighth year.
Other names are as follows:

Sba Tcha	Venus
Siu Uati	Venus as the morning star
Tcha Benu Asar	Traveling Benu (bird) of Osiris
Tuai	God of early morning
Tuat	Venus as the morning star
Tua Ur	The great star of the morning

67. **Mercury** ⌣◖ 𝔹 ✶
SEBGU or SBEG (Sbek) ⌠ 𓄿 ⌣✶

Mercury or Sebeg held dominion and charge of the
stepped staircase which represented the mound of Earth
that rose from the primeval ocean at the beginning of
creation. It is said in Egyptian mythology that Ptah
mentally performed this action. Sbeg as the staircase is
often considered the interface between life and the afterlife
(*Book of the Dead*). Even with this important mythical
position, Mercury is rarely mentioned. Perhaps it is
because its proximity to the Sun made it difficult to
observe. Sbeg is depicted as a man with a star above his
head. The god of this planet is the evil Set (Seth), which is
another curious association of the Egyptian mind set.
Other names are as follows:

Seb	Mercury
Sbak Sebakau	Mercury
Sbeg	Bull-headed hawk
Set	The star of Set
Smet Meh-T	Mercury
Sbek	Mercury

68. **Stars**
SBA (Seba) ⌠ ⌡ ✶   plural ⌠ ⌡ ✶✶✶

The stars are considered eternal. They played an
important role in the cosmology of Egyptian religious
beliefs. Yet, there is very little mention of the
constellational star patterns or their relation to religion.

Astronomy in some form always existed by virtue of the rising of the Nile star Sirius. The names of the 36 prominent stars defined some constellations and divided the heavens for the year as well as the hourly watch during the evening. Other names for stars are as follows:

Akhakh	Flowers of the sky
Tchet-T	The time of culmination of a star, star
Genkha	Star or luminary
Siusiti	Shooting star
Sba - Siu -Khebs -	Khabs - Khakha
Netru -Ankh -Ab = all mean or refer to "Star'	

There were only two major divisions of the sky, north and south:

AKHEMU SEKU   "The imperishable ones" indicated
the northern or circumpolar stars
which never set or "fail."

AKHEMU URTU,   The southern stars were known as
"the stars that never rest," confusing,
as it is the same term for planets.
The most important star was Septet
or Sirius known as the Dog star that
began the new year as well asannouncing
the inundation of the Nile.

The major constellations were:

a   **SAH**

Sah was Orion, *the Fleet-Footed, Long-Strided God, Pre-eminent in the Land of the South.* SAH was the *Father of the Gods* who was identified with Horus and Osiris. He is often depicted with a great star over his shoulder or sometimes with a star in his left hand. His feminine counterpart was called SAH-T, *Souls of Heliopolis.* SAH was the celestial ferryman and is often confused with Septet and Canopus.

b   **PLEIADES**

It is often called *the thousands* and was often depicted as seven cows and a bull.

c   **SHESHMU**

This was an important point in the Egyptian zodiac denoting the sixteenth (pentade?) decan. It was the beginning of the harvest. Sheshmu was also identified as a lion god and the executioner of the dead souls for Osiris.

d   **MESSHET**

Messhet was known as *the Slaughterer, the Great Bear, Leg of an Ox*. These were names which often referred to Mesekhti who was identified with the evil god Set. Today it is recognized as our constellation Ursa Major. She is depicted as a hippopotamus with a crocodile on her back and her foot or left leg near a *mooring peg*. She is also called Ment Uret, the *Great Mooring Post*.

e   **SOPDET**

The Dog star or Sirius marked the beginning of the Egyptian new year and has a long and varied tradition.

f   **SERQET**

Serquet was known as *She Who Relieves the Windpipe* or a morning star goddess.

g   **NEKHEKH, (UA TI)**

The constellation of the sickle or lion or the Sphinx.
    The heavenly vault represented a balanced unity between the sky and Earth. It was believed that *one*

reflected the other; as above so below, an edict that rings eternal in the annals of astrology.

Egyptian Philosophies

69. Unfortunately, for the most part, the study of the ancient Egyptian culture leaves us with more questions than answers. But be that as it may, we still can deduce a general but limited overview of that culture. To the non-materialistic Egyptian culture, the universe was the experience of consciousness taking on physical embodiment and its eventual return to its source. The effects of forces were far more important than their shape or value. By this we can see the Egyptians developed a heightened mental capacity by training their minds to perceive the worlds of reason, cerebral identity or thought, emotion directed by the heart, along with recognizing spirit as energy in all things. All of nature possessed energy and evolved at different levels while growth patterns formed all existence as visible reflective forms of its own energy field (as depicted in the medu-Neter [hieroglyphic]).

To the Egyptians, man's body symbolized the imagery of the three distinguishable yet inseparable processes of sky-air-Earth, that is, consciousness, mind and body, the combined result being the embodiment of man. It seems that they believed everything in the universe was created through three different sets of vibrations: active, passive and the process of the two. The faster energy patterns crossed slower ones and, at critical nodal points, neutralized the other two and created a third vibration—the process of interaction. The residue of the process of interaction formed physical matter and its volume. This is much the same way as light is invisible to the naked eye until it is reflected as color from an object or as heat and cold combine to form clouds. The medu-Neter (hieroglyphs) were written to portray the idea that energy consciously transforms itself into its own image. Religions and philosophies throughout the world contain traces of this idea in their teachings. But they are well disguised within seemingly unimportant passages such as the original idea that man is created in the *image* of God.

Throughout all of Egypt, constant recognition of duality as a reflection is well attested in such books as *The Book of Going Forth by Day* or, as referred by scholars, *The Book of the Dead.* Many ideographs were often inscribed as doubles. Mars was often referred as *Horus of Two Horizons.* The phrase, *time of the head of the goose in two horizons,* is the observation of stars heliacally rising and setting simultaneously. Any astrologer will attest that when the Ascendant is known, the Descendant is known without having to mention it.

This idea of simultaneous interaction between active an inactive energy patterns, combined with the nodal point of energy, may also be the significance of the Greek term *Zoidion*–the idea of planetary energy reflecting the principle of life and transforming itself into a material, archetypal image. This concept also corresponds to the Egyptian principles of the Ka and he*ka*.

In many instances, hieroglyphs were engraved as symmetrical inscriptions, written in identical terms facing each other on opposite walls or door jambs. This symbolized the reflection of the triune nature of man and the universe. Images written in this fashion represented self-perception. The third part of this symbolic trinity is the viewer looking at the reflection of duality. Picture yourself as being one of three men walking. To each person there are only two.

Egyptian Contributions to the West

70.   For many scientists, there have been no contributions from Egypt to the exact sciences because, in their view, Egypt oriented itself exclusively toward religious matters and art forms. Many "scientific" observations by the Egyptian are seen as "silly" to today's scientists. For example, Egyptian observation of the heavens and

planetary transits used an outline of a seated man for the purpose of reference. An assistant would position himself on the edge of a platform in such a manner as to appear to be sitting on the horizon from the viewpoint of the observer. As the night progressed the changing positions of the stars and planets were noted by their relative positions to the assistant's head, ears and shoulders. Planets were never thought to be *in* a constellation and they were said to be located in the south, east or west with respect to our seated man. "It is clear," scientists state, "that from the mass of Egyptian papyri that astronomical observations as a science were non-existent, for there are no direct references to eclipses or any other astronomical phenomena." Yet, these scientists ignore that there are many indirect, poetic verses such as the songs of *Isis* and *Nephthys* which do verify the observation of eclipses and stellar events indicating a deeper insight into the celestial sphere than previously supposed. Today's scientific minds demand recognizable contributions as the term "exact sciences" is defined. Yet, we continuously read about the vast knowledge ancient Egypt imparted to its Grecian visitors that later influenced the entirety of Western thought.

71.   From the onset, Egypt's culture and philosophy were based purely on the observation of emanations of heat and light, resonance and sound frequencies and time, "the process from seed to fruit," with which they developed laws that evolved into geometric form to describe the material world as volume. The result of energy flux and fields was thought to generate a form of residue. Such interplay through time and space created the material world. The Egyptians primarily regarded these three energies as the basis from which all forms of life came to be on Earth.

The hieroglyph *ahet* ⌂, displays the interconnection of opposites within a cycle. Today we use symbols, as did the Egyptians, to express substitute images for objects we can see as well as objects we do not. Just look at any automobile logo or cartoon figure that large corporations use to express the idea of their product or service. As we impart no dimensional reality to such symbols, neither did the Egyptians thousands of years ago.

72.   Archeological research shows that Egypt was a flourishing culture, complete with writing, agriculture and hunting, along with religious values and laws. This very advanced culture simply appeared in the Nile valley around B.C. 3100. These conditions are similar to the Sumerians who appeared just 300 years earlier. To date there is little archeological support that Egypt and Sumer were aware of each other even though they were approximately only seven hundred miles apart. The cosmogony of the Egyptians, as we can see, was entirely different from the omina of Chaldea indicating a lack of intercourse between the two cultures. However, the time reference between the rise of Sumer and the similar emergence of Egyptian culture, together with similar religious traditions and creation myths, suggest that there may have been a slight Sumerian influence or, at least, interaction. Long protected by mountain ranges to the east and vast desert expanses to the west, Egypt controlled and ruled the Nile Valley for most of the twenty-five dynastic periods spanning over 3,000 years. However, by B.C. 656, Egypt's strength began to decline through many short intervals of wars with the Libyans and the pirating sea peoples. Recognizing Egypt's weakness, Assyria conquered Egypt and brought an end to the longest ruling class in history.

Summary

73.   The Egyptians focused their reasoning on the dynamics of causal relationships. Their mythological ideas of creation and its resultant gods bear a similarity to many of our own contemporary religious concepts. Within the Chaldean chapter and this one, we can certainly find many references to the Greek origins of Sun sign astrology. However, it is unlikely that the Egyptians taught the Greeks their art of stargazing directly. Early Greek references are desultory and their fragments reflect, at

best, remote similarities to what the Egyptians or Babylonians probably had in mind, even as Ptolemy himself suggested (see **page 428**).

74.   Below is a diagram depicting the Egyptian concept of the Sun's diurnal journey, its destruction by sunset and eventual resurrection by sunrise [see page 479]. The position of the planets below are placed in the form of fixed positions to best illustrate this idea. The planets represent the following energy patterns: Mars, the destroyer of life; Saturn, the awakening of the deepest inner spark of life, recognition and reorganization; Moon, guidance and understanding; Mercury, self-awareness, intellectualism; Jupiter, growth and expansion; Venus, self-integration and unification; and finally the Sun, perfection of the self.

The example wheel shows the ancient planetary positions as they relate to the background influence of the area in which they are placed. This is somewhat similar to our present day house system rulers. The approximate planetary placements are the point where they exert the most influence. Should we relate them to the modern 12-house system, we would notice Jupiter's influence would be approximately on the cusp of Pisces in the area where Pisces would normally be. With a Pisces influence in the lower half of the quadrant, one could blend a Sagittarian influence to the upper half, ending where the eleventh house cusp is normally located.

The area in which Jupiter is stationed would represent the approximate degree of Jupiter's most influential position which is 24° to 28° above the horizon. Venus occupies the tenth house position and the first 20° would have a Taurean nature while the last ten degrees closest to the tenth house cusp or Meridian would have a Libran quality or tendency.

The Sun occupies the whole upper Western quadrant and has the influence of Leo with its position of about 30° (where the ninth house cusp should be) as its most influential position. Mars in the sixth has the Scorpio influence in the first ten degrees with Aries for the last 20°.

Planets placed in the tenth house set the "tone" of the overall chart. The planet also modifies the planet setting immediately after the Sun by its nature and aspect.

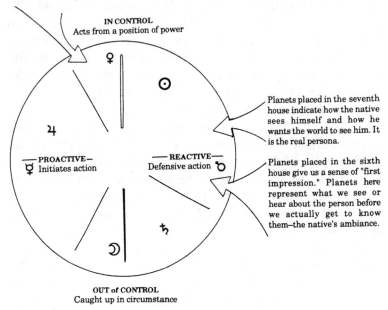

IN CONTROL
Acts from a position of power

Planets placed in the seventh house indicate how the native sees himself and how he wants the world to see him. It is the real persona.

Planets placed in the sixth house give us a sense of "first impression." Planets here represent what we see or hear about the person before we actually get to know them—the native's ambiance.

——PROACTIVE——
☿ Initiates action

——REACTIVE——
Defensive action ♂

OUT of CONTROL
Caught up in circumstance

Figure 14.1

The planets so placed in the chart above are the principal ruling energy for each section. Their placement, position and the section they occupy is the point of their most intense influence. (As an exercise) It is suggested that the reader use this house system as an underlying theme for modern birth charts. For example, those of you born with planets in the contemporary first and second houses would feel a Mercury influence more intense at the Ascendant, less intense on the third house cusp. Planets in the twelfth and eleventh houses would be under the influence of Jupiter and so on.

Saturn influences the position where the fifth and fourth houses would be with the Capricorn influence governing the first 30° and Aquarius governing the last 30° to the Nadir. The Moon holds sway over the third house and is positioned about five degrees from the Nadir. Mercury holds sway over the area where the first and second houses would be with Gemini for the second house and Virgo as the first. Mercury is at its most powerful on the Ascendant as it places emphasis on cognizance.

Conclusion

Primarily based on the Babylonians, this method of sunset chart construction is an abstraction of both the Chaldean and Egyptian cultures. Many of the ideas set forth in this book are not of astrological origin but from related works concerning the Babylonian and Egyptian way of life. Often, understanding may be gained by examining a subject or theory in a peripheral and/or obverse manner rather than directly. Much of this research was taken at "face value," rather than a direct translation of each idiomatic syntax. Mars, for instance, was associated with everything hated or feared by both the Egyptians and Babylonians, it was predictably an "unpredictable" and erratic planet. Thus, when Mars was related to a "Hyena" or "Wolf" my impression was to consider the energies and activities of a hyena or wolf in the manner suggested by the text. I did not care *why* the hyena or wolf were hated, that is rather obvious, but why both civilizations, who were unaware and independent of each other, engendered the same reference for Mars.

Another principle was the notation of the Ascendant and planets *visible above the horizon* during a solar or lunar eclipse. It was only the visible planets that determined the intensity and nature of any omen. Today, this can be said of any chart using the first and last visibility of the Moon on a daily basis. Those of you who do full Moon meditations may want to make a special note of visible planetary activity associated with Moon's influence during that time. This especially holds true for the first and last aspect the Moon makes following sunset.

The principles set forth in the sunset chart method can be used in every branch of astrology as it is the matrix for successfully predicting the timing of events. At any given time, there are planets that are indicative, by their placement in the decanate, of function change or goals. The timing of events cannot be fully ascertained unless indicated by the sunset chart. It is recommended that every time you cast a chart, that you compare it with the sunset chart and very shortly you will notice an improvement in your skills.

Just as the *biological* DNA precisely developed your physical being starting the moment you were *conceived*, your *celestial* DNA includes the development of your physical, emotional and mental growth on the day you were *born*. With a little study using the sunset chart system, you will find that we are all definitely involved in a master plan for self-development. As the Egyptians envisioned, we are on the way to becoming stars ourselves.

When asking the purpose of creation, astrology becomes a powerful guide. The philosophy of astrology allows us to ponder and search our own psyche deeply. Astrology is also a science that easily merges with religion. We find relative circumstances that provide clues to our connection with the whole of life. Astrology is an art through which we can participate in the reciprocal dance of the universe. Acting and reacting with the cosmos, we then find ourselves able to go with the current, allowing its rhythm to take us on the crest of its waves. In this manner, our lives will reflect what is happening in the universe: as above so below. All this can be accomplished without the interference of false *black cat* viewpoints, which are *no more valid than our own.*

Good fortune to you who are about to go forth on this new vision quest. If you feel only a portion of the intense excitement that I have experienced while discovering and studying this work, then my astrological purpose is complete.

Bibliography

Baines J. and Malek J., *Atlas of Ancient Egypt*, Facts on File, 1989

Barton, Tamsyn, *Ancient Astrology*, Routledge London 1994

Bauval, R. &Gilbert, A., *The Orion mystery*, Heinemann London 1994

Bradley Donald A. *Solar and Lunar Returns*, Llewellyn Publications 1968

Bramley, W., *The Gods of Eden*, Avon 1989

Braha, James T. *Ancient Hindu Astrology for the Modern Western Astrologer*, Hermetic Press 1990

Budge, E.A.W. *From Fetish to God in Ancient Egypt*, Dover, 1934 (reprint) 1988

_____*Egyptian language*. Dover 1857 (reprint) 1966

_____*An Egyptian Hieroglyphic Dictionary*, Dover 1978

_____*Egyptian Religion*, Gramercy Books 1959

Busteed, M., & Wergin,D., *Phases of the Moon*, A.C.S. Publications 1981

Butler, Hiram E., *Solar Biology*, Esoteric Publishing 1923

Campbell, Joseph, *The Hero with a thousand Faces*, Paladin Books London 1988

_____ *Oriental Mythology, The Masks of God*, Penguin Books Ltd. 1962

Christensen, Larry B. *Experimental Methodology*, Allyn and Bacon Inc. 1977

Clark, Graham, *World Prehistory an Outline*, Cambridge University Press 1965

Coleman, Ray, *Lennon*, McGraw Hill 1984

Collin, Rodney, *The Theory of Celestial Influence*, Arkana-Penguin 1954

Dalley, Stephanie (translation &edited) *Myths From Mesopotamia*, Oxford University press 1990

Dobyns, Zipporah P. Ph.D. *The Node Book*, TIA Publications 1973

Ebertin, Reinhold, *The Combination of Stellar influences*, Ebertin-Verlag Germany 1969

Encyclopedia Britannica 1992 –96 Edition

Fagan, *Astrological Origins*, Llewellyn, 1971

Faulkner, DR.R., (translation) *Egyptian Book of the Dead,*
        Chronicle Books 1994
Frawley, David *Astrology of the Seers,* Morson publications

Gauquelin, Michel, *Written in the Stars,* Aquarian press, 1988
_____*The Cosmic Clocks* Astro Computing Services, 1982
Gettings, Paul *Dictionary of Astrology,* Rutledge &Kegan 1985
Gleadow, Rupert *The Origin of the Zodiac,* Atheneum, 1969
Green,H.S. *Directions and Directing,* A.F.A. 1972
Goldstein-Jacobson, Ivy M., *The Way of Astrology,* Pasadena
        lithographers 1967
Grendahl, Spencer *Astrology & the games people play,*
        Llewellyn publications 1994

Hall, Manly P., *Astrological Keywords,* The Philosophical
        Research Society Inc. 1966
Hancock, Graham, *Fingerprints of the Gods,* Heinemann Ltd.
        Great Britain 1995
Heindel,Max, *Simplified Scientific Astrology,* L.N. Fowler & Co.
        1928
_____ *The Message of the Stars,* L.N.Fowler & Co. 1972
        (eighteenth printing)
Homage to Pythagorus Rediscovering the Sacred Science , (colected works)
        Bamford, C., Critchlow, K., Lawlor, R.,Macaulay,   A., Raine,
        K., Zajonc, A.G. Lindisfarne press 1994
Houck, Richard *The Astrology of Death,* Groundswell Press
        1994

Jaines, J., *The Origin of Consciousness in the Breakdown of the
        Bicameral Mind,* Houghton Mifflin Company Boston 1976

Kerenyi, C., *The Gods of the Greeks,* Thames & Hudson London
        1974

Lau Theodora, *The Handbook of Chinese Horoscopes,* Harper &
        Row 1979
Logan, Daniel, *Your Eastern Star,* William Morrow & company
        New York 1972
Lorenz, Donna M. *tools of astrology-Houses* Eomega Grove
        Press 1973

Marion D. March & Joan McEvers *The only way to Learn Astrology* , ^6 Vol Series ACS Publications 1994
--------------*The Only Way to learn About Horary and Electional Astrology* ACS Publication 1994

Neugebauer, O. *The Exact Sciences in Antiquity,* Dover, 1957 (reprint) 1969

Ozaniec Naomi *The Egyptian Wisdom,* Element Books Great Britain 1994

Palmer, Helen, *The Enneagram,* Harper & Row 1988

Peat F. D., *Synchronicity The Bridge Between Matter and Mind,* Bantam 1987

Pestka R., *The Planetary Pyramid,* Aries Press, 1986

Pingree, David *The Yavanajataka of Sphujidhvaja,* Harvard University Press 1978

Powell, R. & Treadgold, P. *The Sidereal zodiac,* AFA, 1979

Raman B. V., *Ashtakavarga, System of prediction,* IHB Prakashana 1981
_____ *A Catechism of Astrology* (vol I & II) IBH Prakashana 1984
_____ *Three Hundred Important Combinations,* IBH Prakashana 1983

Rasajo *Horary Numerology of the Turf,* D.B. Taraporevala sons & Co. 1990

Rele, DR. V.G., *Directional Astrology of the Hindus,* D.B. Taraporevala & Sons 1983

Sayce, A.H. *Astronomy and Astrology of the Babylonians,* reprinted from Transactions of the Society of Biblival Archeology (1874) Wizards Bookshelf, 1981

Schmidt, R., *Project Hindsight,* The Golden Hind Press 1995

Schwaller de Lubicz, R.A., *Sacred Science: The King of Pharaonic Theocracy,* Inner Traditions International, Vermont 1988

Seligman, Martin PHD. *Helplessness: On Depression Death and Development.* Simon and Schuster

Sellers, J.B.,*The Death of Gods in Ancient Egypt,* Penguin, london 1992

Seymour, Dr. Percy, *The Scientific Basis of Astrology,* St. Martin's Press 1992

Shaw I. & Nicholson P. *The dictionary of Ancient Egypt*, The
        British Museum Press, London 1995
Sherrill, W. A., (editor) *The Astrology of the I Ching*, Weiser
        1976

Sitchin, Zecharia *The 12TH Planet*, Avon, 1976
_____*Genesis Revisited*, Avon 1990
_____*When Time Began*, Avon, 1993
_____ *Divine Encounters*, Avon 1999
Talbot Michael, *The Holographic Universe*, Harper Perennial
        1991
Thurston, Hugh. *Early Astronomy*, Springer Verlag, 1994
Watters Barbara H., *Whats Wrong With Your Sign?* Valhalla
        Paperbacks ltd. 1970
West, John Anthony, *Serpent in the Sky*, Harper & Row New
        York 1979
Wilhelm, H., Baynes, C.F., *The I Ching*, Princeton University
        Press 1950
Wilkinson, Richard *Reading Egyptian Art*, Thames and
        Hudson 1992

Zauzich, Karl-Theodor *Hieroglyphs Without Mystery*,
                University of Texas 1992 (Translation-Roth,A.M.)
Zukav, Gary, *The Dancing of The Wu Li Masters*, Morrow 1979

Video- Pharaohs and Kings, David Rohl, Produced by The
        Discovery Channel VHS-24878

Order Form

Inquiries: Telephone (562) 598-0034

Web: http//www.bookmasters.com/marktplc/00337.htm

Postal orders: INTELIGENESIS,
P.O. BOX 545, SEAL BEACH CA. 90740

Please send me_____**copy(s) of:**

Ancient Whispers from Chaldea

Order direct! Call ...1 800 247-6553
for *immediate*, same day shipping!

Name:_____

Address:_____

City:_____State:_____Zip:_____

Telephone (_____)_____

Sales tax:

California residents please add $1.70 tax.

Shipping:

$5.00 for the first book and $2.00 for each additional book.

Payment: Cash_____Check_____Money order_____

(sorry no C.O.D.'S)

For credit card purchase call 1 800 247-6553

Order Form

Inquiries: (562) 598-0034

Web: http//www.bookmasters.com/marktplc/00337.htm

Postal orders: INTELI*GENESIS,*
P.O. BOX 545, SEAL BEACH CA. 90740

Please send me_____**copy(s) of:**

Ancient Whispers from Chaldea

Order direct! Call ...1 800 247-6553
for *immediate*, same day shipping!

Name:_____

Address:_____

City:_____State:_____Zip:_____

Telephone (_____)_____

Sales tax:

California residents please add $1.70 tax.

Shipping:

$5.00 for the first book and $2.00 for each additional book.

Payment: Cash_____Check_____Money order_____

(sorry no C.O.D.'S)

For credit card purchase call 1 800 247-6553

Order Form

Inquiries: Telephone (562) 598-0034

Web: http//www.bookmasters.com/marktplc/00337.htm

Postal orders: INTELIGENESIS,
P.O. BOX 545, SEAL BEACH CA. 90740

Please send me_____copy(s) of:

Ancient Whispers from Chaldea

Order direct! Call ...1 800 247-6553
for *immediate*, same day shipping!

Name:_____

Address:_____

City:_____State:_____Zip:_____

Telephone (_____)_____

Sales tax:

California residents please add $1.70 tax.

Shipping:

$5.00 for the first book and $2.00 for each additional book.

Payment: Cash_____Check_____Money order_____

(sorry no C.O.D.'S)

For credit card purchase call 1 800 247-6553